Re-Constructing Archaeology

NEW STUDIES IN ARCHAEOLOGY

Series editors
Colin Renfrew, *University of Cambridge*
Jeremy Sabloff, *University of Pittsburgh*

Other titles in the series include
Graham Connah, *Three Thousand Years in Africa*
Richard E. Blanton, Stephen A. Kowalewski, Gary Feinman and Jill Appel, *Ancient Mesoamerica*
Ian Hodder and Clive Orton, *Spatial Analysis in Archaeology*
Keith Muckelroy, *Maritime Archaeology*
Stephen Plog, *Stylistic Variation in Prehistoric Ceramics*
Peter Wells, *Culture Contact and Culture Change*
Ian Hodder, *Symbols in Action*
Geoffrey Conrad and Arthur Demarest, *Religion and Empire*
Patrick Kirch, *Evolution of the Polynesian Chiefdoms*
Dean Arnold, *Ceramic Theory and Cultural Process*
Graeme Barker, *Prehistoric Farming in Europe*
Daniel Miller, *Artefacts as Categories*
Robin Torrence, *Production and Exchange of Stone Tools*
Rosalind Hunter-Anderson, *Prehistoric Adaptation in the American Southwest*

MICHAEL SHANKS and CHRISTOPHER TILLEY

Re-Constructing Archaeology

Theory and Practice

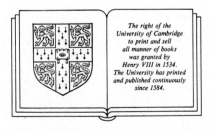

The right of the
University of Cambridge
to print and sell
all manner of books
was granted by
Henry VIII in 1534.
The University has printed
and published continuously
since 1584.

CAMBRIDGE UNIVERSITY PRESS

CAMBRIDGE

LONDON   NEW YORK   NEW ROCHELLE

MELBOURNE   SYDNEY

Published by the Press Syndicate of the University of Cambridge
The Pitt Building, Trumpington Street, Cambridge CB2 1RP
32 East 57th Street, New York, NY 10022, USA
10 Stamford Road, Oakleigh, Melbourne 3166, Australia

First published 1987

Printed in Great Britain at the University Press, Cambridge

British Library cataloguing in publication data
Shanks, Michael
Re-Constructing archaeology. –
(New studies in archaeology)
1. Archaeology
I. Title
II. Tilley, Christopher
III. Series
930.1'01   CC72

Library of Congress cataloguing in publication data
Shanks, Michael
Re-Constructing archaeology.
Bibliography.
Includes index.
1. Archaeology – Philosophy. 2. Social archaeology.
3. Material culture. 4. Archaeological museums and collections – Great Britain.
5. Archaeological museums and collections.
I. Tilley, Christopher Y. II. Title.
CC72.S5 1987   930.1'01   86–18400

ISBN 0 521 30141 6

For ELIZABETH and KARIN

CONTENTS

ILLUSTRATIONS

Tables

ACKNOWLEDGEMENTS

Thanks to Ian Hodder for contributing the Foreword, and to Tony Giddens and Jonathan Steinberg for comments on an earlier version of Chapter 3. To K. W. Osborne, Honorary Secretary of the Labologists Society, U.K.; Lars-Eric Gustavsson, Stockholm; M. L. Willers and M. Berriman of Vaux Breweries; Pripps Brewery, Stockholm; The Campaign for Real Ale; The Brewers Society; Centralförbundet för alkohol – och narkotikaupplysning; Svenska Bryggareföreningen; Thomas Kolk, Socialstyrelsen; Erik Malmberg and Göte Nylin, PLM Pac, Malmö, thanks for help regarding Chapter 8.

All the computer analyses were performed on the old Cambridge IBM 370/165 and the new IBM 3081 computers. Thanks to Paul Callow and members of the Cambridge University Computing Service for their help.

The drawings were prepared in final form by Michael Shanks. Thanks to Ann Hartshorne for Figure 4.2, John Duncan for Figure 8.20 and to Stefan Rousseau for help with the photos of beer cans in Chapter 8.

Christopher Tilley would like to thank the British Academy and the Swedish Institute for funding for some of the basic research for Chapters 7 and 8; the Master and the fellows of of Trinity Hall for providing such a stimulating environment in which to live and work, and colleagues at Lunds Universitets Historiska Museum.

Warmest thanks also to Jenny Vaughan, Alan Campbell, Kate Swearman, John Goodenough, Nancy Tilley, Jonas Lindh, Mats Ericsson, Ewa Rosén, John Duncan, Suzanne Cederfeldt, Anne Nilsson, Ole Heggen, Jan Fredén, Kenneth Winsborg and above all Elizabeth Shanks and Karin Tilley – they will know why.

This book breaks ground in a number of ways. It is therefore not surprising that the text introduces concepts to which the archaeological ear is unaccustomed. This difficulty should not dissuade us from grappling with the challenge. For this is also an extremely important book which issues in a new generation of archaeology – a new age of a philosophically informed and critically aware discipline.

It is easy to gain the impression that archaeology lags behind related disciplines. Archaeologists hung on to, and even embraced, positivism long after serious scepticism had been established elsewhere. Functionalism and systems theory were adopted as if the critique of functionalism and the notion of structure did not exist. At a more detailed scale, spatial archaeology owed much to the New Geography, David Clarke's (1972) *Models in Archaeology* was modelled on Chorley and Haggett's (1967) *Models in Geography* as earlier Glyn Daniel's (1962) *Idea of Prehistory* borrowed from Collingwood's (1946) *Idea of History*. Undoubtedly some counter-influences could be cited, but the general pattern of a retarded borrowing is well established.

One reason why this book is demanding to read is that it suddenly asks archaeologists to catch up. Having for so long been content with a limited theoretical field and having only recently begun to grapple with structuralism and limited aspects of contemporary Marxism, the archaeologist is now asked to jump beyond structuralism to post-structuralism, and to consider also critical theory, hermeneutics, phenomenology, and realist and post-positivist philosophy. I am not sure that archaeology as a whole will be able quickly and effectively to enter the debate, and in a sense the book may be before, or out of, its time. Archaeological teaching and literature have much to absorb before the full implications of the ideas discussed here will be adequately criticized and assessed in relation to different bodies of archaeological data. But what the book does do, courageously, is to set us a target. Shanks and Tilley offer an integration of a variety of contemporary social theories in relation to archaeological data. In trying to understand what they have done, our own level of debate is raised. That this is a demanding book should not dismay us. Our task over the next decade is to educate ourselves so that we can read this book.

Perhaps the most distinctive aspect of archaeology since its inception has been its predominantly empiricist and positivist orientations. The break with this tradition is a particular way in which Shanks and Tilley prepare new ground. The debate has always been couched in terms of the confrontation and interaction between subjective and objective views. The fear of a cynical relativism has always lurked around the corner for those attempting to walk towards the subjective components of human experience. The empiricist and positivist emphases remained dominant, even if at times they seemed to take insufficient account of the role of the analyst, situated in his or her time.

Shanks and Tilley seek to transcend the tired divide between subjective and objective approaches. They place emphasis on the social practice of the interdependence between the real and the theoretical. Many will want to argue as to whether it is adequate to claim that archaeology is ideological practice which sustains and justifies a capitalist present. At times in this volume the reader will be faced with the issue as to whether the past is any more than politics and manipulation in the present. But whatever the individual viewpoint, Shanks and Tilley have pitched the archaeological analyst more fully into the scene. The presentation of the past is no longer simply the concern of the government official, but of all archaeologists, since all archaeological texts re-present the world of today in the past. It is hardly surprising then, that a portion of this book is devoted to the role of the museum. Theory and practice are integrally linked.

As part of the alternative viewpoint offered in this volume, the past is seen as a forum for debate. There is not one meaning in the past to be discovered. The process of archaeology involves polysemy and debate. This spirit of discussion and the rejection of a unified agreed methodology contrast significantly with the strictures of the New Archaeology. And it is in this spirit that this book should be read. The question to be asked is not 'is the view of the world described by Shanks and Tilley correct?' but 'do we agree with it, and if not, why not?'.

It has been argued by many in archaeology that the New Archaeology was more a methodological than a theoretical breakthrough. A final way in which this volume is novel, both in relation to recent and traditional archaeology, is that it can legitimately claim to propose a radical theoretical proposition. Basic philosophical and theoretical proposals stretching from the nature of archaeology, to the relationship between individual and society, structure and action are discussed. The nature of material culture is questioned and the meaning of style.

Few who read this book will remain unabsorbed by some new angle on their taken-for-granteds, their assumed dogmas. Shanks and Tilley challenge us to think – to think harder, deeper, more critically. In so far as they encourage argument about silent issues, the authors will have achieved their purpose, and ours.

IAN HODDER

INTRODUCTION

The doctrines and values of the 'new' archaeology are in the process of being broken down; for many they were never acceptable. Books such as Hodder's *Symbols in Action* (1982b), *The Evolution of Social Systems* (Friedman and Rowlands (eds.) 1978), *Symbolic and Structural Archaeology* (Hodder (ed.) 1982), and *Ideology, Power and Prehistory* (Miller and Tilley (eds.) 1984) have demonstrated the value and importance of fresh research orientations for the analysis of the relationship between social practices and material culture patterning. Many archaeologists may very well be persuaded that the kinds of studies undertaken in these works do represent a significant and important departure from the kinds of research characterizing the new archaeology while still remaining unclear as to the kinds of knowledge claims being advanced. It is the case that no systematic evaluation has been made of the epistemological and methodological basis underlying a non-positivist and non-functionalist archaeology. Similarly, criticisms of the new archaeology have been largely confined to demonstrating the inadequacy of specific approaches such as systems theory or ecological frameworks for the understanding of the past. Metatheoretical issues of fundamental importance, for example the relationship of theory to data and the idea of value-freedom, have hardly been touched upon.

This book is designed, in part, to try and fill that gap. The purpose of the book is to attempt to clarify some of the goals, the conceptual structure, explanatory content and procedure of a social archaeology concerned with material culture as not merely an object of analysis but forming part of a social reality charged with meaning. It is intended both as a challenge and as a radical alternative to the disciplinary practices of both traditional and 'new' archaeology.

The book ranges widely across a number of schools of thought that have remained largely unconnected within archaeology or have not been discussed at all. Reference is made to positions in the philosophies of science, of history and of action, Marxism in a number of variants, most especially critical theory, hermeneutics and structuralism. However, the book is not simply a theoretical work but argues strongly for the need to dismantle current barriers between theoretical argument and the business of practical research – be it excavation or analysis, or the relationship between professional archaeologists and the public. This concern with linking theory and practice is a fundamental feature of the book. The linkage developed involves a transformation of such perspectives as the problem orientated hypothetico-deductive approach. It is maintained that theory mediates data and vice versa, and that any adequate consideration of the connection must involve setting archaeology in its historical context – contemporary society. Through a systematic critique of the pathological antimonies (e.g., subject/object; fact/value) of established positions, archaeology is revealed as truly being what it can only aspire to be, an active relationship between past and present.

In this, the book is intended to be a contribution towards a reflexive archaeology, an archaeology which is critically self-conscious. It is argued that any adequate conceptual and theoretical framework developed in studying the past must incorporate reflection upon archaeology as a professional discipline in the present. The process of gaining knowledge of the past depends on exploring the meaning, form and context of that process in the present.

This book is not a discussion or exposition of the arguments and positions of others, be they archaeologists, philosophers or sociologists. It is a critical encounter rather than an attempt at exegesis. We refer to works and ideas as a means of developing and elucidating our own concern – an archaeology which respects the *humanity* of past and present, which can make a meaningful contribution to the present. We are not concerned with establishing allegiance to one or a group of established philosophical or sociological positions. Naturally, we share certain approaches with other authors, but we are not concerned to provide a label for our own work, to claim that it is part of a 'school' or 'paradigm'. Others will be only too ready and willing to do that.

The chapters in the book have been written and arranged as separate essays, complete in themselves, and each tackling a number of issues. This means that they can be read in any order. The chapters are thoroughly cross-linked throughout the book; issues only briefly referred to in one chapter are taken up and discussed in detail in others. To say that the chapters are more or less complete in themselves does not imply that their ordering in relation to each other is arbitrary. The reader who wishes to get the most out of the book will follow it through as it is presented, from the beginning to the end. In organizing the book in this manner we hope that it can be studied on a number of different levels in terms of the individual chapters and their relationship to the whole. The material relationships of the parts to the whole make it what it is.

We have adopted a four-part structure. Part I begins with general questions of ontology and historiography, and an evaluation is made of how archaeologists and historians conceive of the past. Questions of time, authorship, conservation of the past, and the justification of archaeology are considered. Chapters 2 and 3 consider in detail the manner in which the past has been approached in the new archaeology. We set out a rigorous critique of its epistemology – positivism – and confront a major issue – that of objectivity and value-freedom. In Chapters 1 and 3 we counter those approaches we criticize with a radically different conception of the relation between past and present; we argue for a critical and reflexive archaeology. Ultimately, the issues of the first three chapters are inseparable from the ideological and political implications of archaeological research and archaeologists as participants in contemporary capitalism. Accordingly, Chapter 4 looks at the relation between academic archaeology and presentation to the public; we present a series of interpretative studies of museums, focussing on the aesthetics of display, and identify possibilities for a creative and non-ideological relation between past and present in the museum.

Part II presents a philosophical and conceptual basis for a truly social archaeology, following up criticisms and alternatives outlined in Part I. Chapter 5 suggests archae-ology should be interpretative practice, and considers the link between theory and data. Chapter 6 poses the question of the object of a social archaeology and presents a series of concepts to deal with material culture and the social.

Part III consists of two substantial analyses of material culture: change in ceramic design of neolithic pottery from southern Sweden; and the design of beer cans in con-temporary Britain and Sweden. Both analyses draw on and elucidate some of the dis-cussions of previous chapters. It is, however, important to remark that it is not possible to judge this book simply by reference to these chapters which work with data. They are not an empirical 'test' by means of which the value or otherwise of the rest of the book may be assessed. They are simply aspects of a critical encounter with the archaeological past and present, as are the other chapters in the book.

Part IV contains some final remarks.

Our framework is provisional, frail and flawed, a product of a personal encounter with the past and its present. No work can be anything more; there are no final answers. We offer our feelings and ideas in the hope that they will stimulate others to think and render what we say inadequate and so move on. The past opens up possibility. We must live this possibility. It is to this end that we write.

Issues in archaeological theory and practice: critique and development

1

The present past

Introduction

The past (which others may call the museum, the archive, the library) recedes in an indefinite, perhaps infinite series of galleries. Archaeologists wander the winding and seemingly endless corridors, forever unlocking doors which appear new, armed with different analytical keys, picking over the skeletal remnants of past societies, scrutinizing shelves of death or gathering 'truths' from self-referencing site reports. The archaeologist is devoted to the embalmed relics deafeningly silent yet sacred in their meaninglessness, devoted to the preserved past. The past is a mystery and theories abound as to its meaning, its construction, its constructors. In their antiquarian amnesia and isolation (isolation in the midst of all the human debris), some frantically unlock door after door, compiling an infinite inventory of facts, self-evident truths. Others seek to map the labyrinthine floor plan, illuminating the corridors with the lengthening shadows of the present. But are there new doors? new facts? new truths? Is there a way through the maze of the past? Or has the archaeologist been condemned to eternal mythical repetition of the present, to forgetfulness? The solution is to demolish the museum, but *destruktion*, not *zerstörung*; the task is to dismantle the great metaphysical and rhetorical structure, the architecture of discourse erected in the name of a conserved past, not in order to smash and discard the contents, but in order to rescue them, reinscribe their meaning.

Time is central to archaeology. It constitutes the major problem of interpretation and yet is the reason for the discipline's existence. By definition the past cannot be present and yet the traces of the past surround us. The past is both completed and still living. But in concentrating on the time of the past the time of archaeology tends to be forgotten, i.e. archaeology as social practice and personal experience which takes up people's time in the present.

In this chapter we consider the nature of time as an abstract concept. Time is not just something manifested in C-14 chronology or publication dates. We argue that it is not simply a neutral device with which to analyse the past and discuss the nature of archaeology as an active relation with the past. Archaeologists spend their time (the metaphor is not incidental to what we have to say) producing a past in the present. They survey and excavate and eventually write for an audience. We examine the nature of what archaeologists do and produce and how they justify their activities. We attempt to emphasize archaeology as event and experience in the present, as social practice which cannot escape the present.

The intention is not to sacrifice objectivity and replace it with an extreme and disabling relativism with archaeologists locked into the present. In the works that archae-ologists write there can be no simple choice between fictional creations and objective copies of the past. We confront the conventional opposition between subjectivity and objectivity and argue that there is a need to move beyond it. Our aim is to investigate the nature of current fissures in archaeological theory and practice and relate them to their origin in a problematic present.

The problematic past

The present's relation with the past is no longer self-evident. Past and present are separated by a chasm of misunderstanding. A need has been perceived for a special field of activity, for a class of experts or professionals, to deal with the problems the traces of the past pose to the present. The basic problems are:

(1) how to observe the traces of the past objectively;
(2) how to bridge the distance between the traces in the present and their social origin in the past;
(3) what to do about the destruction and disappearance of the traces of the past;
(4) why these problems are worth posing and considering anyway.

There is a consensus in archaeology as to how to observe the traces the past has left behind – by means of survey and excavation, detailed 'scientific' examination. This aspect of the practice of archaeology aims at producing high-quality information (the sceptical and practical empiricist would forbid us to term it 'objective'). It aims at filter-ing out the 'noise' of subjective experience – the rainy days and the wandering cows. The problems involved at this level are the practical problems of obtaining and managing a 'skilled' workforce, of producing an intelligible site report. The result is the 'objectivity' of the C-14 date (Binford 1982, pp. 134–5), of the accurately observed and drawn site plan or section.

There is much less agreement about the route from present to past and what is there at the end of the journey, about the interpretation or explanation of the archaeological record. Argument has raged for at least the past twenty years as to what archaeology should be – an historical discipline producing a description of what happened in the past, a science of human behaviour, a science of 'culture process' or a science of the traces of the past themselves in the archaeological record. Concern has also been focussed on ideological distortion of the past for present purposes.

The traces of the past are disappearing in the present, excavated away in one way or another at an alarmingly rapid rate. What is to be done? Under a consensus in academia and among others enlightened by a 'conservation ethic' there is a belief that it is right to preserve the past. The problem is largely seen as an administrative one involving plan-ning procedures, legislation and funding. It is also to a certain extent an educational problem of inculcating and marketing the conservation ethic, respect for the past.

There has been little concern with justifications for archaeology, little serious ques-tioning of the basic reasons for doing archaeology. With notable exceptions the concern has mainly expressed itself as rhetorical gesture, justification after the act, after-thought.

We shall consider each of these problems, beginning first with that of bridging the distance between the past and present.

Time travel: getting from the present back to the past
Topological thinking

> Topological thinking, which knows the place of every phenomenon and the essence of none, is secretly related to the paranoic system of delusions which is cut off from experience of the object. With the aid of mechanically functioning categories, the world is divided into black and white and thus made ready for the very domination against which concepts were once conceived.
>
> (Adorno 1967, p. 33)

The past is over, completed, and so much of it is lost in the distance. There are still traces with us; the problem is how to use these to enable us to see the past, to visit the distant past. The traces of the past which we find in the present 'belong' to time other than the present. The problem is how to relate to this otherness. The traces belong to a time in the distance which we cannot see clearly. In this way time is conceived spatially, as distance. Spatial time is at the centre of the problematic past. We shall consider its characteristics and its relation to problems of interpreting the past.

The past is conceived as completed. It is in grammatical terms 'perfect', a present state resulting from an action or event in the past which is over and done. This 'perfected' past is opposed to the flow of the ongoing, incompleted, 'imperfect' present. Although the past is completed and gone, it is nevertheless physically present with us in its material traces. But the attribution of the traces to a 'perfect' past, distant from the present, brings ambiguity, the problem.

A 'perfect' past does not imply a mode of presence with an investigating archaeologist, but one of absence. The past is temporally absent, belonging to another time. A 'perfect' past is an 'allochronic' past (Fabian 1983). In such a conception the past is absent not as the contrary of physical presence – the objects of the past are here with us now – but as the contrary of the continuous 'imperfect' present, which is a process, a continuing, incomplete state.

The spatial temporality of objects locked in a 'perfect' past, an evanescent moment of time, implies a mode of possession. The object belongs to the past; time possesses the object locked into its present, its moment in the ceaseless flow. 'The object *has* been, it *has* happened': the perfect tense itself hints at this mode of possession. Time reduced to spatial distance is simply a system of spatial coordinates – literally a fourth dimension – according to which a potentially infinite number of uneventful data may be recorded. The time of an object becomes a property possessed, equivalent to mass and dimension. The object is conceived as an empty container. Its coordinate in time, location in empty spatial time, is one of its possessed properties, contingent, accidental. In Latin it is *subiectum* possessing *accidentes* (see the discussion in Heidegger 1978, pp. 153ff., and in Rose 1984, pp. 62–3).

So the past becomes contingent; our relation to the past becomes accidental and mysterious. The past is gone, distant, and so a mystery, a problem presenting a challenge to penetrate through the dust and debris to find the way back, to see what is hidden in the distance. But the distance, the other-ness, the absence of the past is postulated as a condition of the challenge. It is this which obscures. Inquiry becomes topological thinking, setting the traces of the past in their place, in the distance. The material traces of the past are ordered, classified, presented with identification papers and locked up. The past becomes a vast labyrinthine edifice to be inhabited. The archaeologist wanders the corridors weighed down with keys, administrating, surveilling, dominating.

Commodified time

> The quickest runner can never overtake the slowest, since the pursuer must
> first reach the point from where the pursued started, so that the slowest must
> always hold a lead.   (Zeno in Aristotle, Physics Z9 239b15)

Zeno's paradox of Achilles and the tortoise depends on an infinitely divisible time; it is a time composed of an infinity of durationless moments. But the point is not that Achilles can never overtake the tortoise, but that this is inscribed into the nature of the race itself and who organized and fixed it – ancestors of the anonymous factory time-keeper.

Spatial time is uniform, abstract and commodified time, the time of capitalist pro-duction, the time of Zeno's race. It is in essence the abstraction of irreversible time, all of whose segments must prove on the chronometer their merely quantitative equality. In reality the nature of this time is simply its exchangeable character: measured empty duration, separate from the content(s) of existence that fill it up, freely exchangeable with all other time.

Such abstract clock-time allows the exchange of labour and its product; commodified time is the link between the commodity form of goods and commodified labour. 'The calculation and coordination of exchange values by labour time is a specific feature of the commodification of economic relations introduced by the convergence of money capital and the formation of wage labour characteristic of capitalism' (Giddens 1981, p. 119). Capitalism depends on spatial, commodified time.

Empty commodified time applies to all events. All events are comparable according to such time which maintains that a pot and the spread of farming belong to the same calculus, a calculus which is indifferent to them both (*cf.* Berger 1984, pp. 9–10). The past disintegrates when the meaning of an object or event lies in its assignation to a point in time. Such assignation occurs at the cost of the integrity of our experience of the past. It amounts to a loss of memory, a betrayal of the past which is forgotten. As a sequence of 'nows' history exists separately from people. It loses its specificity, its coherence and it becomes a problem; hence the paradox of Zeno's race.

Yet such a history or conception of the past also forms a continuum, a seemingly organic whole:

> The exchange of commodities is at once smoothly continuous and an infinity
> of interruption: since each gesture of exchange is an exact repetition of the
> previous one, there can be no connection between them. It is for this reason

> that the time of the commodity is at once empty and homogeneous: its
> homogeneity is, precisely, the infinite self-identity of a pure recurrence
> which, since it has no power to modify, has no more body than a mirror image.
> What binds history into plenitude is the exact symmetry of its repeated
> absences. It is because its non-happenings always happen in exactly the same
> way that it forms such an organic whole   (Eagleton 1981, p. 29)

This continuous whole forms the basis of some populist work which claims that archaeology is in the process of discovering 'our' history, 'our' past or the past of the whole of
humanity. Such a viewpoint does not take into account the qualitative historical
moment of conflict, rupture or discontinuity. It is unable to comprehend the notion of
qualitatively different archaeologies, archaeologies other than those written by middle-
class white western males (*cf.* Hodder 1984, pp. 30–1). Individuals, interest groups, and
societies all have different perspectives on the past. There is and can be no monolithic
undifferentiated PAST. Rather, there are multiple and competing pasts made in
accordance with ethnic, cultural and gender political orientations (see Hall 1984; Ucko
1983; Conkey and Spector 1984).

Commodified time entails that our consciousness is itself set in time like any other
phenomenon. It cannot deal with subjective experience. Objective time is separated
from the subjective individual, analogously work is separated from leisure. The work of
the archaeologist cannot be related to his or her subjective experience of doing archaeology. Commodified time implies the abolition of that time created by the event of
consciousness – human practice, the flow of actions in and on the world in indi-
vidualized time.

The archaeologist is an Achilles chasing a past which seems so easy to reach and yet
they never quite get there. Commodified time is the unexamined premise of so much
archaeological work. It lies behind the allochronism of archaeology – the assignation of
the objects and the traces of the past to another and always distant time. This breaks the
relation between past and present, destroying the integrity of experience of the past.
Questions of investigation and preservation of the past become apparently unanswer-
able. Problem orientation or general recovery? What should be recovered and why?
There can be no coherent consideration of these questions, only rhetorical appeals to
accepted values, to pluralism or expert consensus, or a resignation to scepticism.
Commodification of time denies the historicity of archaeological work itself, its place in
contemporary society, the present's production of the past.

Commodified time forms a premise of traditional typological work involving the
assumption that the temporal classification of an artifact somehow provides a clue to its
meaning, that empty time itself explains (see Chapter 7, pp. 138–9). It also produces an
homogeneous history, permitting the equal treatment of culture at all times and places
– comparative method. It allows general classificatory stages to be developed in which
different societies are shunted into evolutionary sequences. Qualitative substantial time
which recognizes difference is replaced by quantitative classificatory time. All 'tribes'
are considered to be equivalent and hierarchically placed in relation to 'chiefdoms' or
'bands' or 'states'.

The role of the archaeologist

What is the relation between the archaeologist and the artifact? What is the role of the archaeologist in reconstituting the past by means of the artifact and other traces of the past? What is the role of the archaeologist in the time travel, in overcoming the distance between past and present? The answers to these questions, answers implicit in the theoretical affiliations of archaeologists, are conditioned by the distance, the gap between subject and object, past and present being always-already a problem.

Science may be asserted as the means of getting back to the past. The archaeologist is to construct a vehicle which is to get to the past on its own. The vehicle is science. Subjectivity is to be eliminated; it is to adapt itself to the objective.

On the other hand the implications of subjectivity may be recognized. Scepticism and its doctrinal embodiment relativism maintain that subjectivity just has to be accepted; there can be no completely objective account of the past. The 'truth' of the past can never be known for certain; objects are locked into their time, archaeologists into theirs. Archaeologists can draw increasingly close, but never quite get there because of subjectivity, belonging to the present. (See for example Daniel 1962, p. 165 and Fowler 1977, p. 138. See also the discussion below on archaeology as ideology.)

Wheeler (1954, pp. 17–18 and chapter 17), Hawkes (1968) and others have asserted the positive value of subjectivity, the humanities-trained archaeologist, the imaginative individual breaking with the ties of the present to feel the way back to the past. So the role of the archaeologist is one of empathy, breathing life into the dusty relics, inspiration, imaginative reconstruction, affective affinity. Archaeology becomes a personal confrontation with the past; ultimately it is based on a longing for a dialogue with the past, getting beyond the objects to their human creators, being in their presence.

These two features of the confrontation with subjectivity are frequently found together. Wheeler (1954) also stresses the limitations of the archaeological record. For Coles 'archaeology seeks the evidence and *experience* of life' (1979, p. 1, our emphasis) and this aim provides a rationale for experimental archaeology, using empathy and imitating as closely as possible the ways of the past to find out what it was like, 'to glimpse some of the constraints and encouragements that influenced the patterns of life of ancient man (*sic*)' (1979, pp. 209–10). Yet clearly 'it is not possible to "live in the past"' (ibid., p. 210). It is impossible to repeat the past exactly, in the same way that it is impossible to truly know the past, lost as it is in the distance. That experimental archaeology 'lacks the clear ring of truth, of absolute certainty, only aligns it with all other aspects of prehistoric or early historic studies, that archaeologists can do nothing but deal with opinions, with the possibilities and probabilities of past unrecorded events' (Coles 1973, p. 168).

The truth in scientific archaeology's denial of subjectivity is its reflection of the fetishized position of people in contemporary capitalism: fragmented, isolated consciousness separated from overwhelming objective process.

Correspondingly, the imaginative and autonomous individual is a myth, an ideological mystification of contemporary alienation. Yet such a notion makes implicit criticism of the dominating exchange principle and division of labour whose root in commodified time we have argued is also the source of the always-already problematical relation with the past. The myth is an assertion that society is intrinsically meaningful, produced by autonomous, creative actors. Society and the past are supposedly open to understanding by those with the necessary hermeneutic energy or empathy, imagination or feeling.

The contradiction is a familiar one. The individual situated in the capitalist market, supposedly free, confronts an objective reality of truths existing independently of volition. We are all bound intimately to the capitalist labour process by our participation in it, and by a chain of consumer goods and values. Yet its objective necessity is shut off from our knowledge and reflection. In the same way the past is at the same time so near and so far; it is an intimate part of ourselves and still estranged. There is experienced a passive conformism before the object world, reverence for hard science, and a simultaneous fascination with the mystery, the magic of the past, its aura and wonder: C-14 dates and, ultimately, ley-lines. This contradiction results from a mistaken notion of historical experience. That the past is produced in concrete practice, is reworked and reinscribed in the present, has been neglected.

The destination

What is at the end of the trip in time? A Hollywood epic? A television arts programme? A sociology lecture? It is quite clear that archaeology does not reveal everything that happened in the past. Traditional 'humanist' archaeology wants a living narrative history: key events and aspects of the past articulated into human narrative by the professional archaeologist (who else can perform this service to the present?). (See Daniel 1962, pp. 164–5, for example.) Key facts are selected and given meaning by the archaeologist.

We wish to build on two critiques of traditional 'humanist' archaeology: first, that the relation between the archaeological record and 'history' is not at all a simple one; second, that the implications of the present, of subjectivity, need to be taken more seriously, are more subtle and complex, than the idea of the creative expert.

A fundamental advance of 'new' over 'traditional' archaeology was its recognition that there is no direct correlation between objects and their relationships and a story of the past. Clarke argued for a body of theory to deal with archaeological data, an archaeological systematics which had only an incidental relation to historical or social reconstruction. 'Archaeological data is not historical data and consequently archaeology is not history . . . we fully appreciate that these (archaeological) entities and processes were once historical and social entities but the nature of the archaeological record is such that there is no simple way of equating our archaeological percepta with these lost events' (1968, pp. 12–13). The serious archaeologist should no longer be writing 'counterfeit' history books (ibid. p. 12).

For Binford, the archaeological record is a static record which needs translating into the dynamics of past cultural systems. What he thinks is needed is a body of middle-range theory, a rigorous observation language, a system of scientific inference allowing past cultural systems to be read off the archaeological record (Binford 1982; 1983b; 1983a, chapters 17, 27, 28). Such a concern with the relation of material culture to 'the past' and to socio-cultural factors in general (see also Schiffer 1976) has provided a rationale for ethno-archaeology, for modern material culture studies, and for experimental archaeology. Some have even given up the trip to the past, at least for the time being.

What comes at the end? For some (e.g., Fritz and Plog 1970; Schiffer 1976; Watson, LeBlanc and Redman 1971) laws of culture process or formational process in the archaeological record, beyond the particulars of historical event, laws by definition applying to all times and places. In *Analytical Archaeology* Clarke is more concerned with making archaeology a respectable social science than with the past and he asserts the autonomy of the traces of the past. The past as event is over and gone. In general it is the case that most work is ultimately concerned with linking objects and their relationships to the social conditions of their creation in the past (e.g., Renfrew 1972; Flannery (ed.) 1976; Renfrew and Wagstaff (eds.) 1982). Discussion continues as to what these social conditions are (see Chapter 6).

We agree with the general premise of such work, that there is no simple direct route from objects and their relationships to conventional narrative history. We also firmly agree that this means that archaeologists should expand their concern to include material culture in contemporary societies. However we would strongly criticize the view that there is a mechanical, albeit indirect, relation between material culture and the contexts of its production. The aim of a science of material culture, a science of the archaeological record, is a mistaken one, a futile search for scientific objectivity. As we hope to show, there can be no *objective* link between patterning perceived in material culture and processes which produced that patterning.

It has been argued that the work done by archaeologists is not neutral, self-contained or objective. Interpretation of the past is affected by present 'ideology' – a point of view related to present interests (Leone 1973; Trigger 1980, 1981; Meltzer 1981; Kohl 1981). This work represents a valuable elaboration of the common sense realization that there is a subjective element to archaeological research.

However, such work has tended to lapse into relativism (Trigger 1984, p. 293). The present's use of the past has been viewed as just another source of bias with consciousness-raising or self-reflection allowing the archaeologist to control for this (Leone 1973). It is essential that the concept of 'ideology' is not reduced to a universal relativism or considered as just another source of bias. Both these reductions neutralize the critical value of the concept.

Referring to the work of Trigger and Meltzer, Leone has remarked that such 'self-reflection offers no real link to the past and, even though it may impose constraints upon the archaeologist, it has not offered a different interpretation of prehistory, nor is it likely to' (1982, p. 753). Such work is mere consciousness-raising which doesn't affect the way archaeologists go about doing archaeology. Leone argued instead for 'critical self-reflection or critical-theory' (ibid.). Building on the work of Leone (1978, 1980, 1981a, 1981b, 1982, 1984) and with Hodder (1984) and Rowlands (1984), we wish to draw out the full critical implications of the realization that archaeology is a practice in contemporary capitalism.

So, there is no direct route to the past and we must remember that archaeology is something done in the present. We will now consider the nature of the relationship between past and present established in the practice of archaeology. We shall find that the past 'as it was' is not what comes at the end of the trip; we are on a return ticket.

Recreating the past

It is a revelation to compare Menard's *Don Quixote* with Cervantes's. The latter for example, wrote (part one, chapter nine):

. . . truth whose mother is history, rival of time, depository of deeds, witness of the past, exemplar and adviser to the present, and the future's counsellor.

Written in the seventeenth century, written by the 'lay genius' Cervantes, this enumeration is a mere rhetorical praise of history. Menard, on the other hand, writes:

. . . truth whose mother is history, rival of time, depository of deeds, witness of the past, exemplar and adviser to the present, and the future's counsellor.

History, the *mother* of truth: the idea is astounding. Menard, a contemporary of William James, does not define history as an inquiry into reality but as its origin. Historical truth, for him, is not what has happened; it is what we judge to have happened. The final phrases – exemplar and adviser to the present, and the future's counsellor – are brazenly pragmatic.

(Jorge Luis Borges: 'Pierre Menard, Author of the Quixote', 1970, p. 69)

Menard produced a recurrence of the exact words of the seventeenth-century Cervantes (a few pages of the Quixote) in the twentieth century. Not a copy but a recreation. Several points relating to our argument can be taken from this mythical achievement.

Nothing can be said twice because it has already been said before. This is to deny empty time. Eventful moments cannot be exchanged. Every cultural artifact is inseparable from the context and conditions of its production and appropriation. Every cultural artifact is always more than itself.

The supreme achievement and *impossible* novelty is to recreate the past without copying it. Menard 'never contemplated a mechanical transcription of the original; he did not propose to copy it' (Borges 1970, pp. 65–6). Nor did Menard arrive at his Quixote through a supreme effort of empathy – reliving Cervantes's life – but via his own route in his present. 'To be, in the twentieth century, a popular novelist of the seventeenth seemed to him a diminution. To be, in some way Cervantes and reach the Quixote seemed less arduous to him – and, consequently, less interesting – than to go on being Pierre Menard and reach the Quixote through the experiences of Pierre Menard' (Borges 1970, p. 66). Empathy denies the historical character of present practice, forgets, despairs of the present, in the longing for a genuine past. Empathy cannot achieve truly historical creation which relates past and present, holding them together in their difference, in the instant of the historic present.

Reliving the past without copying would be an entirely different experience. History doesn't repeat itself because it has already happened before. Recreating the past necessarily involves the present – the conditions and context of the act of creation. Recreating the past is a practice which reveals the author, the subject in the present. To copy the past 'as it was', as exactly as possible, is to reflect the past; it is an illusion, a tautology. To reproduce the past 'as it was', to relive the past as a reflection is to produce an image which hides the observing present.

But archaeologists are not often attempting to relive the past 'as it was', to understand the past through empathy and copying the ways of the past (but note experimental archaeology, Coles 1979, chapter 6). Archaeologists survey, excavate, examine finds with the aim of producing texts.

Archaeology – history
Text and rhetoric
Archaeologists observe the traces of the past then record and write about them. Archaeologists produce texts. Archaeology depends on texts. The importance of publication has long been stressed. Long ago Pitt-Rivers argued that a discovery only dates from the time of its being recorded, that the archaeologist is obliged to publish, and this is still widely held as a basic principle (e.g., Frere 1975; Renfrew 1983). However publication is seen as a technical matter; it is a technical means to an end – the means of recording, storing and communicating the past to an audience. Its function is archival. So attention has focussed on the efficiency of the practice of writing and publishing: how much should be published or circulated, what form publication should take (see in addition Grinsell, Rahtz and Williams 1974; Webster 1974; Barker 1982). But the implications of treating publication as a practice of translation of the material traces of the past, of the transformation of the object past into a linguistic medium – implications which go beyond the concern with how efficiently the past is preserved – have not been considered.

Gardin (1980) has explicitly concerned himself with the intellectual processes 'by which we move from the apprehension of a set of archaeological materials . . . to the formulation of verbal statements' (p. 7) which he terms 'constructions' – 'any written text presented as a distinct unit in the archaeological literature' (p. 13). However Gardin is aiming at efficiently harmonizing means with ends; with the explosion of archaeological information he wants a more efficient form of storage of basic data than site reports and suchlike, suggesting 'data-networks' (pp. 148–50); he wants efficient definition of subject matter and aims in explanatory texts (p. 151).

We wish to concentrate not on these technical matters but on the nature of archaeology as the production of texts, conventional literary and data network included.

The word 'history' covers this practice. History is both the events of history and the history of events, what has happened and its apprehension. The word contains both a subjective and an objective genitive. (See Ricoeur 1981c, p. 288; Rose 1984, p. 61.) The discourse of history, textual production, is part of the process of history. Apprehension is internally related to the process of the past. So history does not take place primarily as happening, as event, past and gone, that which has happened, evanescent, ephemeral, locked into a moment of time. There is no abstract concept of 'event' which exists separately from the practice of apprehending and comprehending the past.

It is worth contrasting the word 'memory'. The noun 'memory' presumes the active practice of remembering, incorporating past into present; it is a suspension of the subject-object distinction. There is however no verb which corresponds to the noun 'history' – a word to express the practice of rendering the past comprehensible (Frisch 1981, p. 17). We wish to explore this absence. Before doing so we will point out another dimension of archaeology's dependence on texts.

In its dependence on texts archaeology reveals its rhetorical nature which the ideals of objective method would deny. 'In philosophy, rhetoric represents that which cannot be thought except in language' (Adorno 1973a, p. 55). Text as language, language as expression: archaeology is fundamentally expressive; it depends on a relation with an audience. Without a persuasive, expressive purpose, archaeology as textual production would have no practical dimension.

To realize archaeology as textual discourse is to 'attempt a critical rescue of the rhetorical element, a mutual approximation of thing and expression, to the point where the difference fades'. It is to 'appropriate for the power of thought what historically seemed to be a flaw in thinking: its link with language . . . It is in the rhetorical quality that culture, society and tradition animate the thought; a stern hostility to it is leagued with barbarism, in which bourgeois thinking ends' (Adorno 1973a, p. 56). Rhetorical does not mean subjective, self-referring; it means, quite simply, written. We shall now elaborate on archaeology as text, archaeology as rhetoric.

Distance
The materialist notion of archaeology as production of text means there *is* radical discontinuity or distance at the root of archaeology-history. But this is not the alienating distance of the problematic, distant past. There is difference between the objects of the past and their representation in the archaeological text. This is a realization that archaeology is the object or product of a practice. Similarly, the artifact is a product of someone in the past; it is not identical with, it goes beyond the subjective intentions of its maker and the meanings invested in it.

Such difference, non-identity or distance is emphasized in Ricoeur's use of the concept 'distanciation'. In order to avoid an 'alienating distanciation' (for archaeology the past being considered to be locked into its own time as an object confronting the archaeologist) and 'participatory belonging' (attempts at bridging distance through empathy, affective affinity or imagination) Ricoeur takes the standpoint of 'the text which reintroduces a positive and . . . productive notion of distanciation . . . The text is much more than a particular case of intersubjective communication. As such, it displays a fundamental characteristic of the very historicity of human experience, namely that it is communication in and through distance' (Ricoeur 1981a, p. 131). This notion of distance implies that:

(1) the event or act of production does not coincide with the object produced;
(2) the meaning of what is produced goes beyond what was meant or intended by the author;
(3) the meaning of what is produced goes beyond the meaning communicated to the original audience;
(4) the work produced does not just refer to the social conditions of its creation, but in its articulation in the present through the process of interpretation the work points beyond.

So to conceive of the past as a problem because it is distant, to attempt to recover the past, bring it to the present and preserve it, in fact means that the archaeologist is incapable of realizing the object of study as a product of someone in the past, is incapable of maintaining sufficient distance to experience the past dialectically as non-identical with its objects and with its representation in a text. It is to treat the past as its objects and not to realize that archaeology is a practice producing its own objects – *texts*.

The archaeologist as 'storyteller'
Objective reason dispassionately viewing the march of history emphasizes objective process, an objective past of data and event, an informational past dependent on empty chronometric time. Such a past either lacks an integrating basis, threatening to dis-integrate into a meaningless series of events and facts, or the practice which draws the past together is forgotten. Such an objective past, abstract happening, abstract event existing separately from its apprehension, is a quantification of experience. It represents a proliferation of information or an administrative inventory of 'facts' which becomes the primary medium for recording experience. For such an inventory meaning is a very real problem.

In contrast to such *erlebnis* (experience as event isolated from meaningful context: disconnected information) is *erfahrung* (experience as event integrated into memory: conceptual mediation of the event). For Benjamin, *erfahrung* is the experience of the storyteller (1973c). Storytelling is the reflection and creation of a world where experi-ence exists as continuity and flow, where meaning and time are organically related, where history or archaeology is an organic series of events saturated with meaning.

Memory: the noun assumes the practice of calling to mind, of remembering. Story-telling is a mnemonic practice, a bringing to mind, an incorporation of past into present. It also addresses an audience and so is performance or rhetoric. Mnemosyne was, after all, the mother of the Muses.

The storyteller does not aim to convey a pure abstract essence of the past, in the sense that those creating a great inventory of facts or information might try to do. In a story, the past is incorporated into the life or the social praxis of the storyteller in order to bring it out again. 'Thus traces of the storyteller cling to the story the way the handprints of the potter cling to the clay vessel' (Benjamin 1973c, p. 92). The story is the product of an individual but is authorless; like a pot it has a collective dimension. Its truth lies in its use, the intention behind the creative act. Stories invite retelling or elaborating. The audience is invited to make a productive response.

Benjamin's lament for the disintegration of *erfahrung*, nostalgia for a mythical past of an integrated fabric of experience, for community, is regressive; the choice is not a simple one between community and story, and capitalism and fact (Wolin 1982, pp. 225–6). However, his analysis of the storyteller is a fertile one. Events *are* meaningful only in relation to being incorporated into texts which make sense to an audience, being incorporated into 'stories'.

Meaning is established by constructing configurations out of successions of events, by producing constellations of concepts, which cannot avoid an act of narration, of 'storytelling'. This of necessity involves a narrator. We experience archaeology-history as 'storytellers', as a series of texts, texts which are simultaneously analytical and expressive.

Archaeology – narrative

We are not defending traditional historical narrative. The narrative we propose is analytical and retrospective, it views the past from the present. But this does not mean that opening the book at the end solves anything: history has no end.

The aim is not to construct a coherent continuity, a complete story of the past. The past is forever reinterpreted, recycled, ruptured.

> There is no set of maxims more important for an historian than this: that the actual causes of a thing's origins and its eventual uses, the manner of its incorporation into a system of purposes, are worlds apart; that everything that exists, no matter what its origin, is periodically reinterpreted by those in power in terms of fresh intentions; that all processes in the organic world are processes of outstripping and overcoming, and that, in turn, all outstripping and overcoming means reinterpretation, rearrangement, in the course of which the earlier meaning and purpose are necessarily either obscured or lost.
>
> (Nietzsche 1956, p. 20)

The aim is to break ideological coherence – historical continuity which denies difference and ambiguity, fills an empty time of the past with coherent, consoling narrative, ties the past to an immediate coherence. This is not to deny that real historical continuities or traditions exist but it is to recognize that archaeology as production of text or narrative is not identical with the past. The production of history through the practice of archaeology is included in the reality expressed. Narrative is not restricted (and cannot be) to the perspective within which the people of the past viewed themselves. It necessarily includes the narrator's or the archaeologist's point of view. So all textual production has the character of a judgement. It follows that the past cannot be tied down to a traditional form of narrative with a beginning flowing through inexorably to an end. The past is always already begun and has an infinitely deferred end. It is always being reinscribed and reinstated in texts but all texts begin and end. In this most basic way all archaeological narrative is ironic.

Archaeology attempts to forge a linguistic expression of the past congealed in objects and their relationships. The words used in the texts remain concepts substituted for the objects. There is always a gap or difference (a distance) between the words and that to which they refer. This flaw in every concept, its non-identity to what it refers, makes it necessary to cite others, to construct structures, constellations, narratives or 'stories' in order to make sense or produce a meaningful representation of the past. However, material culture in itself has no fixed meaning which can be pinned down forever or stabilized in the use of words or concepts. The objects and their relationships only possess meanings under determinate conditions. In other words meanings are always temporally constituted (*cf*. Adorno 1973a, pp. 52–7).

The main problem is one of trying to deconstruct our textual representations of the past. This book is, in a sense, a protest against the mythology of a fixed and unchanging past. The archaeologist may textually cement one piece of the past together but almost before the cement has dried it begins to crack and rot. We suggest that archaeology should be conceived as the process of the production of a textual heterogeneity which denies finality and closure; it is a suggestion that archaeologists live a new discursive and practical relation with the past. This relation is one of ceaseless experiment, dislocation, refusal and subversion of the notion that the past can ever be 'fixed' or 'tied down' by archaeologists in the present. It involves an emphasis on the polyvalent qualities of the past always reinscribed in the here and now.

Truth and archaeology as narrative
The previous discussion might have given the erroneous impression that because archaeology is a practice in the present involved in constructing texts about the past objectivity is necessarily sacrificed to subjective whim. In this section we attempt an initial resolution of this opposition which we have already noted is an artificial one. This involves considering the nature of what passes for truth:

> What then is truth? A mobile army of metaphors, metonyms and anthropo-morphisms – in short a sum of human relations which have been enhanced, transposed, and embellished poetically and rhetorically, and which after long use seem firm, canonical and obligatory to a people: truths are illusions about which one has forgotten that this is what they are; metaphors which are worn out and without sensuous power; coins which have lost their images and now matter only as metals, no longer as coins. (Nietzsche 1981, pp. 46–7)

Truth is in a sense metaphor. Metaphor is figurative practice which establishes an identity between dissimilar things or objects. It is a production of new meanings through the discovery of similarity in difference. The truth of the past is metaphorical. It is to be found in the traces of the past, it is present in-itself in the past, present with us. At the same time the traces of the past point towards an absent truth, a truth outside the past found in the reception of the traces by the interpreting archaeologist. This metaphorical truth unites the perfected and imperfected aspects of the past. So we do not begin with the truth of the past, produced by the people in the past, and end with that truth revealed by the archaeologist in the archaeological text. We find our affinity with the past through our difference to it, through practice which links past and present. Truth is delivered by the interpreting archaeologist on a detour away from the past, a detour to truth.

The interpreting archaeologist fills gaps in the past, but these gaps are always already there. They are not simply a feature of preservation or inadequate amounts of survey or excavation. Like a metaphor the past *requires* interpretation. There can be no coherent justification for an archaeology which fails to take this into account.

Truth is a mobile army of metaphors, an 'entire thematics of active interpretations' (Spivak 1974, p. xxiii), an incessant deciphering. It is a practice which reveals no primary truth of the past, no primary signified beneath the incrustations of interpretation, metaphor, metonym. Truth does not reside in a presentation of the past in-itself. The traces of the past need to be articulated through speech or language expressing meaning in their translation or transformation, in their presentation to an audience. The interpretation and presentation of the past via textual conversion does not transport *a* truth, a *property* of the past acquired in the present. Instead it transforms, translates or reveals.

Truths are 'coins which have lost their images and now matter only as base metals'. Coins depend on being stamped, on inscription, to be more than pieces of metal. All objects depend on being written before they have meaning. But this is more than a surface inscription. Objects depend on being incorporated in texts; they are internally constituted by the changing script of social relations into which they fit (Eagleton 1981, p. 32). It is vital to remember the same of truth and knowledge.

This relationship with the past is one of *mimēsis*. This concept as used by Aristotle refers to a relation between reality and the production of a text. The mimetic text does not copy or duplicate reality but imitates creatively. It is neither an objective duplicate nor a subjective fantasy. Theory and the facts are not separate but combined to make a productive and potentially expansive unity which ties observer and observed together into a whole which cannot be reduced to either. It involves an active rearrangement of the elements of observed empirical reality, not taking them as they are immediately given, but rearranging them until their new relationships reveal their truth. Mimesis is an *ars inveniendi*, an art of coming upon something, a practice combining invention and discovery (Adorno 1973b, pp. 341ff.; Ricoeur 1981b, esp. pp. 179–81, 1981c, pp. 291–3). This knowledge is never certain, it is always provisional and ready to be re-presented or reinscribed in a fresh framework. It is an act of translation of the empirical past, simultaneous reception and spontaneous elaboration of an original (Benjamin 1973a). It is empirical while at the same time denying the validity of empiricism (see Chapter 5).

Such a conception emphasizes archaeology as historically situated practice. The production of the past is itself time bound. What is implied here is not the quantitative time of the capitalist labour process, of the factory clock: 'prior to all calculation of time and independent of such calculation, what is germane to the time-space of true time consists in the mutual reaching out and opening up of future, past and present' (Heidegger 1972, p. 14). Archaeology as practice is a mode of presencing, a practice which unites and yet holds apart past, present and future. Presencing involves qualitative historical time (Heidegger's fourth dimension). It is an historic present including everything absent (perfect) and everything present (imperfect) (Rose 1984, p. 76). Presencing accepts the presence of the past as imperfect, incomplete, opened up to human agency, creativity and development. Such a past is open and not fixed and 'given' in its own realm of empirical data. The past is imperfect, incomplete, requiring interpretation; it exists as a project in the present, a concern, the object of theory and practice.

As we have argued, interpreting the object cannot be reduced to grasping the meanings invested in the object by people in the past. Knowledge is not the agreement of consciousness with an objective past, however this might be achieved, e.g., procedures modelled on natural science or empathy. Events always become historical posthumously. The truth of the past is located in the present in the sense that 'the true histories of the past uncover the hidden potentialities of the present' (Ricoeur 1981c, p. 295). So the culmination of interpretation is not an image of the past in-itself but self-understanding of the present. Interpretation is an act of appropriation of the past which renders the past contemporary and yet confronts the difference, the otherness. Interpretation is not a search for a hidden past to be possessed through empirical information and description, nor is it a dialogue with the king behind the gold funeral mask. The confrontation with difference brings self-understanding in the articulation of past and present which opens up or discloses possibility. It is encapsulated in the Greek ἀλήθεια – *alētheia*: a truth, a denial of the condition of forgetting, of latency, of obscurity, of that which has escaped notice. It is a resurrection of the forgotten, a remembering. The conventional attitude to the object past is of selecting what seems important, what seems memorable, and this problem of selection is central to contemporary policies of conservation (see below); we are to remember the past. But this is a passive preservation, not an active calling to mind. It is a selection according to the values of the present which preserves not the past, but the present. So often it is not a confrontation with difference. Resurrecting the forgotten requires us to suspend our values, treat them not as universals but as contingent, historical, open to change. The authority of archaeology, the knowledge it produces is not to be found in the past but in the direction of its transformative practice. The truth is not to be found in history; history is to be found in the truth.

The practice of archaeology
Spectacular archaeology
The production of 'facts' about the past still dominates archaeological work. Despite the relatively recent concern with theory, most archaeological writing consists of factual description. A survey of the books and journals in any university library would confirm this and is well worth undertaking, although the results would inevitably be depressing. Flannery (1982) has expressed a wish to get back to the certainties of fieldwork and without doubt others are similarly disenchanted with theorizing and speculation. Yet the split between data acquisition and explanation remains, and fieldwork is by no means a technical and neutral practice.

Archaeological fieldwork is based on a visual metaphor of knowledge; the traces of the past are observed and recorded. But an observed past is a problematic past. It is based on commodified spatial time; archaeology is conceived as observation of objects of the past separate from the viewer, a past locked into its own time. Hence the objectivity of fieldwork – the objectivity of conceptual detachment, non-involvement. However there is an obvious paradox: excavation does involve 'the past'; it destroys it. This link between destruction and observation is just accepted, sometimes mitigated through planning and sampling, but often it is forgotten.

Observing the past imports illusions of simultaneity, first into the elements of the observed past – for example, the idea of 'heritage', a palimpsest of unspecific 'history' all around us – but especially it introduces simultaneity between the object and the act of contemplation. No account is taken of the time of the act of 'observation'. This again involves a disregard for the active and productive (or destructive) nature of fieldwork and excavation, for its roots in contemporary historical contexts. What is historic in thought – the practice of archaeology, our experience of digging – is equated with irrelevance.

Despite the fact that it involves physically interfering with the past fieldwork as observation and recording remains essentially passive. It is a spectacular archaeology. In the society of the spectacle (Debord 1983) that which is lived directly (the past itself and the practice of archaeology) is shunted off into the realm of the spectacular. The past becomes a series of objects and events, a parade before the archaeologist who merely reviews. The practice of archaeology becomes the observation of a separate past and its representation as 'image'. Scientistic 'objectivity' requires this to be a mirror image. In effect archaeology becomes a voyeurism. The realm of the spectacular escapes the involvement of individuals.

Archaeological method and theory have no way of dealing with the subjective experience of doing archaeology – Flannery's fun (1982, p. 278). Yet this is a major feature which attracts people to archaeology: the moment of personal discovery, personal contact with the past; it dominates the popular image of the archaeologist – romantic adventure and discovery. Flannery's (1976 and 1982) and Binford's (1972) excursions into their personal experiences are entertaining and diverting; they have no *necessary* relation to archaeological method and theory. The same applies to the personal reminiscences in *Antiquity* – the 'Archaeological Retrospectives', and indeed the editorials.

The importance of individual experience is devalued, becoming meaningful only when reduced to the status of entertaining anecdote or as the spectacular excesses of an Indiana Jones. However, the archaeological object *is* constituted in practice: sites are excavated and pots scrutinized. Objects come to possess meaning in the work of the archaeologist. Such practice requires time. Time is an aspect of archaeological work, but not as an independent variable, a device for applying to the past, to classify and supposedly understand. That which is analysed becomes part of the archaeologist's life, his or her experiences of doing archaeology. In the aridity of the informational report all this is forgotten. The past experiences of the archaeologist, such as working out the sequence of deposits in a section of trench, are claimed not to be subjective but objective, facts and not fictions. So the presence of the past as objects and their relationships in the present is based on the archaeologist's experiences, its origin is autobiographic. This autobiographic origin ties the archaeological object to the present because it is always produced. So the archaeologist is not leading knowledge from the present gropingly towards the firm ground of the past but rather the reverse, from the archaeologist's past into the object's present. Flannery (1982) asserts the primacy of the experience of doing good archaeological work. In a very different sense we would agree. The experience of archaeology is not irrelevant and it is essential to consider those who experience the production of the past. Archaeology is not a neutral instrument for exploring the past but its theatre. What is required is a critical sociology of archaeology.

Conservation and heritage
The past, its preservation, and the work of archaeology are in the hands of professional archaeologists, academics, state employees and local government workers. In this work the conservation issue is paramount: planning, managing and rescuing the past is a vital concern.

In the literature of cultural resource management (see Schiffer and Gummerman (eds.) 1977; Green (ed.) 1984 and articles in *American Antiquity*) the traces of the past are defined as of value to the present (Lipe 1984). Their utilization and disappearance requires management; they are, after all, a non-renewable resource. Central to the management of the past is the assessment of individual items in the resource base and this is seen as a problem of significance: is this site or burial mound worth digging or preserving rather than another? In effect this is a pricing of a past turned into a commodity. Decisions are taken by 'accountable' professionals, knowledgeable, autonomous, trusted, acting for the clientele. The professional body has self-written rules (Society of Professional Archaeologists Code of Ethics; Davis 1982; Green (ed.) 1984), is concerned with integrity and its responsibilities (King 1983) and business efficiency (Cunningham 1979; Walka 1979). Justification for the profession is seen as being essential: 'if people aren't educated they won't want to adopt a conservationist stance towards the past as a whole' (Cleere 1984, p. 61; *cf.* Lipe 1977, p. 21). The past and its study are thus marketed.

In Britain the problem of significance has been solved by recourse to inventory – listed buildings and scheduled monuments – although there are problems with the system. Although the body of archaeologists and other workers concerned with the past is different from that in the United States (employed almost entirely by the state, local government and educational institutions), they are considered no less 'professionals' – 'professional guardians of the cultural heritage' (Cleere 1984, p. 129), with credentials authenticated by government and professional bodies (academic qualifications, Museums Association, Institute of Field Archaeologists) – looking after and presenting the past to the public.

The language of cultural resource management might be termed the language of cultural capitalism. It is a practice in which a series of individuals assert a hegemonic claim to the past and organize the temporal passage of this cultural capital from its historical context to the present of spectacular preservation, display, study and interpretation. The professional body decides on the basis of *its* claimed knowledge what is worth either preserving or excavating. After subsequent interpretation or conservation the public, or non-professionals, are informed that this is *their* past, their heritage, and that it should be meaningful to them.

The language used and the strident advocacy of professionalism does not make the past produced any less alien from the public (or the 'client') but only more so. All that is required of the non-professional is to consume the past presented at a distance and in leisure-time. The past, history or archaeology becomes an other, an alien factor passing before people. For the public the commodified past has the contradictory relation to the buyer of any commodity: available to purchase while mysterious in its origin, in the technology of its production. The production of the past remains a mystery isolated from the present in the hands of the professional elite or the authoritative planner. Reaction against the sense of alienation created may take the form of pot hunting, metal detecting or unauthorized excavation.

What is needed is not the promotion and protection of a commodified past but its active reworking in the present by archaeologists who do not assert themselves as managers of some unspecified general heritage, a mythical landscape worn with time. What is at stake is not the preservation or non-preservation of the past but the practice of archaeology. This practice has come to lie increasingly in the power of a professional self-appointed minority and it tends to have the effect of denying people their *active* participation in history, in the practice of making history and coming to an understanding of the present past. Instead what is all too often presented by the 'managers' is a petrified past which is constantly in need of preservation, a decaying corpse in need of embalming before the smell becomes too strong.

Justifications

A concern with the justification of the work of the profession has expressed itself recently primarily in the literature of cultural resource management. Indeed the question of justifications for what archaeologists do has become critical: the treasure hunting public are plundering the past, financial stringency requires archaeology to specify its value and relevance and scientific archaeology seems so irrelevant. Of course, there have always been archaeologists who expressed a concern with the purpose of the discipline but the literature dealing with justifications for archaeology is comparatively sparse. The main aspects are summarized in Fig. 1.1. The justifications focus on:

(1)   the actual practice of archaeology and related fields (e.g., fieldwork, planning or conservation);
(2)   the objects and monuments produced and preserved;
(3)   the images associated with the objects and monuments (scientific explanation, descriptive narrative, etc.).

The question of justifications itself implies a contemporary society born *free* of a connection with a slowly unfolding and never-changing past. What may lie behind these justifications and the perceived need to supply them is a critical contradiction in the historical consciousness upon which they are based. It resides in the disconnection between past and present which does not fully take into account the active production of the past and that the archaeologist and the past are inextricably linked. The justifications also have their basis in a disjunction created between professionals producing the past and a public passively consuming: isolated professionals lonely in the crowd of contemporary society and unable to cope with the subjective, experiential, practical and transformative aspects of their historical work.

Why do archaeology? Because it entertains or educates 'us' with the achievements of humanity, 'our' common roots, 'our' symbolic unity, 'our' heritage. It is 'our' past and 'we' need it. Why archaeology? Because it's natural, everybody wants to know about 'their' past. Why? Because we know and we're telling you.

Whose past is it? Who are the 'we' of 'our' past? Who is speaking and writing? The justifications, of course, come from those involved in producing the past and supplying it to others. It involves a persuasion to accept the past being supplied and the practice of those who supply it, a persuasion to accept the authority of those who pass judgement on the past. In fact the question of justifications is posed and answered by those with a guilty conscience. Most, if not all, archaeologists realize this. Many of the justifications given at present reveal real need for history, for the past. They do not embody the realization that people, everyone, not just professionals, make history, produce it *now* in the present, actively tying together past, present and future: the realization that history is not the consumption of a supplied image.

There have been encouraging and positive responses to the problem of justifications,

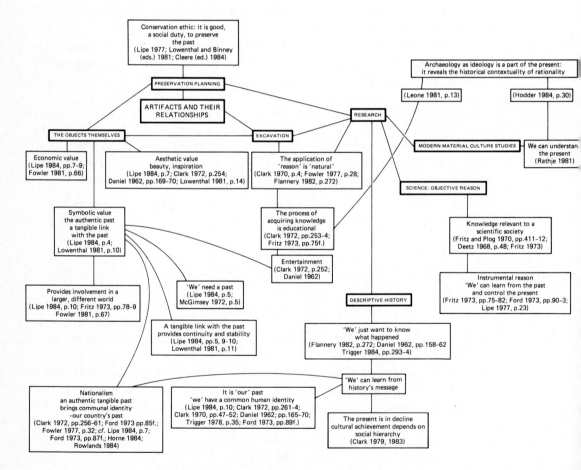

Fig. 1.1 Some justifications for archaeology.

reactions to self-contained scientific objectivity, and suggestions that we understand the present's use of the past which go beyond expression of a simple sceptical doubt about objectivity (see above, pp. 14–15). In particular, Hodder has argued (1984) that archaeology is not neutral knowledge but plays an active social role in the culture in which it is produced. It is an active product of the present and its relationship to non-archaeologists must be considered. This provides a rationale for much-needed surveys to find out what the non-professional thinks and feels about the past and its study. For Hodder, archaeology can show the historical contextuality of rationality while excavation becomes interpretative experience rather than a technique. This argument clearly accords with ours.

Conclusions

The word history finds one of its deepest roots in the Greek ἴστωρ (*istōr* or *histōr*) – one who knows law and right, a judge. The features of the court of contemporary archaeological reason and the archaeological judgement are familiar. The past has been arrested and presents a problem, a mystery brought before the archaeologist who sits as judge. He or she observes and questions the accused and witnesses, extracting information through instruments of torture, confessions of what happened and why (though he or she is often, if not always, over-enthusiastic and kills the witness). The archaeologist employs accusations, κατηγορίαι, 'categories', to partition and dominate, to reveal order in the mystery, in the chaos of evidence. The accusations are made according to the Law, the law of timeless reason. The archaeologist as judge reflects on the mystery, separating, distancing reality from its representation by accused and witness. Eventually they pass sentence – *sententia* – the act of penal speech which defines and dominates. The verdict is made public, published. The accused is never found innocent; sentence is always passed; the archaeologist is a hanging judge. What right has the judge to sit in judgement? What claim, what justification, what legitimation? It is the judge's institutional relationship with the accused, the possession of power, power justified by the Law, abstract and impersonal. Such a Law is mythical; it has no history and knows no history.

An alternative: the judgement of the Homeric *istōr* – arbitrators to whom a dispute is brought. Giving opinions for disputants to accept or disregard, they judge and are in turn judged. There is no exclusive judge, no exclusive accused, no separate consciousness and object, subject and object, no pure subjectivity or pure objectivity. The event of the dispute maintains the ambiguity, clarifying and connecting. Both judge and disputants are subjects of the law and act according to its prescriptions while recreating, reaffirming the law in the act of arbitration (they are the true subjects of the law). The law is not formal abstracted law, timeless and remote, possessed by an independent subjectivity distant from the dispute, the object of concern. The law is the pre-Olympian Δίκη (*Dikē*) – justice, one of the *Horai*, the seasons. *Dikē* is the stream and current of lived duration, the way of life, of living, of doing, of practice: the law of substantial not empty time, eventful, communal, mortal time, lived time, *history* (Rose 1984). It is *Dikē* who in Parmenides holds the bolts to the gates of time through which is found truth – *alētheia*.

The truth or practical knowledge of the present-past, borne and transmitted through the actions of individuals is suspended and frail; it flits by to be snatched at the instant when it can be recognized and is never seen again. Knowledge of the past is precarious, destroyed by the archaeologist's trowel. There is another aspect to this most basic feature of archaeology, that it destroys the very past it investigates: it is that we must do without the consolation that the truth of the past cannot be lost. But there is no eternal image of the past to be rescued in its material traces. Knowledge of the past does not consist in some eternal heritage or in empiricist/positivist science. The past is never safe, never divorced from the present. Even the dead aren't safe, stacked on the shelves in the archive, or displayed in the hermetically sealed museum case. The past is colonized and appropriated by a narcissistic present. Breaking down the barriers, moving beyond subjectivity and objectivity, realizing that theory is critical practice, allows us to reinscribe and transform the void of past/present to a productive present-past and create an archaeology which has social and political relevance to the society in which it operates.

The shadows of the present crisis loom over us – educational cut-backs, the philistine assaults of the new right, populist imagery of a conflict-free heritage, visions of solidarity cloaked in mythical images (or of conflict defused by 'scientific' understanding – subsystem disequilibrium?). It is necessary to forge a practice in keeping with this, facing the contradictions of our contemporary relation with the past, unravelling but not resolving. Such archaeological theory and practice must express itself as an undercutting of authoritarian impulses to pin down the past and will entail a radical pluralism, an unceasing reworking of the past. This archaeology is not a calm and isolated act according to a vision of timeless reason, merely a glimpse of bygone times. The archaeologist stands vulnerable and exposed, strategist in the conceptual struggle for a meaningful past.

2

Positivism and the 'new archaeology'

'Recipes for the Good Society used to run, in caricature, something like this –
(1) Take about 2,000 hom. sap., dissect each into essence and accidents and discard the accidents.
(2) Place essences in a large casserole, add socialising syrup and stew until conflict disappears.
(3) Serve with a pinch of salt.'   (Hollis 1977, p. 1)

'The wish to establish a natural science of society . . . probably remains, in the English speaking world at least, the dominant standpoint today . . . But those who still wait for a Newton are not only waiting for a train that won't arrive, they're in the wrong station altogether.'   (Giddens 1976, p. 13)

Introduction

How should archaeologists come to have knowledge of the past? What does this knowledge involve? What constitutes an explanation of what archaeologists find? This chapter considers the answer to these questions accepted by the 'new' archaeology; it considers epistemological issues raised by a study of the past in the archaeological literature post-dating 1960. New archaeology has embraced explicitly and implicitly a positivist model of how to explain the past and we examine the treatment of the social world as an extension of the natural, the reduction of practice to behaviour, the separation of 'reality', the facts, from concepts and theories. We criticize testing, validation and the refutation of theory as a way of connecting theory and the facts, emphasizing all observation as theory-laden. The new archaeology polemically opposed itself to traditional 'normative' archaeology as a social *science* and we begin the chapter with a consideration of this change and why it took place. The tone of this chapter is again critical. We argue that existing positions in the archaeological literature are inadequate at an epistemological level and fail to offer much insight for a study of either past or present social processes and their relationship to material culture.

The new paradigm – or traditional archaeology resurrected?

In the early 1960s what subsequently became known as the 'new archaeology' was born. Initially this was an American development originating with the work of Binford and a famous paper 'Archaeology as anthropology' (Binford 1962) and followed by a series of influential articles (Binford 1972). The British expression of the new framework was soon articulated in the works of Clarke (1968) and Renfrew (1972). It is difficult to assign any precise dates but by around 1972 a new hegemony had been established in archaeology and new archaeology which had once been unorthodox became accepted by many. Naturally there were some who dissented (Bayard 1969; Hawkes 1968; Trigger 1968, 1970) but these failed to offer any clearly articulated or acceptable alternatives, at least to those inspired with the revolutionary fervour of the new archaeology.

Probably all archaeologists would now agree that there have been major changes within the discipline but whether these amount to a revolution or anything really substantively new is a matter of personal belief or conviction and it is unlikely whether it can be established in any conclusive manner. Although profound disagreement is registered in this chapter and in the book as a whole with virtually every major tenet forming the 'project' of the new archaeology we wish to state that we do believe it to be a very significant development and to be of paramount importance. This has nothing to do with *content*, with what archaeologists have either said or done in specific detail. It rather concerns the act of saying itself.

Renfrew (1982a) has aptly described the period from 1900 to 1960 as the 'long sleep' of archaeology, a period in which the aims, procedures and nature of archaeology as a form of intellectual inquiry into the past were not explicitly discussed except in the work of a few scholars, most notably Childe and Taylor, and certainly did not promote many major debates. The significant feature of the new archaeology and one that remains of abiding importance is that a debate and discussion began, not among one or two, but within a whole community of scholars of what archaeology might be, what it could and could not do, how the past might be conceptualized and whether an objective knowledge of it was possible and in what way. In short it not only became respectable to theorize but this was seen as being essential for any development to take place. A large literature on theory developed, entire books being devoted to the subject, whereas few had existed before. To theorize was no longer regarded by many as an unusual activity, an adjunct to the real business of doing archaeology, but an integral component of archaeological work. If anything can be said to be truly different or revolutionary about the new archaeology it is this. However, the content of what was said is another matter.

Kuhn's influential work (1970) on scientific revolutions has been used by archaeologists to promote the view that a paradigm change has taken place and citation analyses have been used to lend empirical support and legitimate these claims (Sterud 1978; Zubrow 1972, 1980). To specify exactly what has changed and why it has changed has proved difficult in practice (Meltzer 1979). A whole host of specifics can be named such as the use of quantitative techniques, the notion of systemness or a deductive emphasis in research but these can all be either traced back to the archaeology which went before or can only be assigned 'newness' as a result of confused reasoning. For example, an emphasis on deduction in research has been opposed to a former inductive procedure (Hill 1972). However, this supposes that one could do one without the other.

Naturally all scholars like to think that advances are being made, and have been made, in their field, but it seems to have been crucially necessary to new archaeologists to mark out their work as being radically different from what had gone before and legitimate it as (i) actually being new (ii) as representing progress. Clarke (1973) identified the emergence of disciplinary consciousness as being the most promising feature of the new archaeology, the 'prize' being the possibility of radically expanding disciplinary horizons, developing alternatives to existing practices, and in so doing controlling the 'direction and destiny' of the discipline (ibid., p. 7). To Clarke this implied that the 'innocence' of traditional archaeology had been finally dispelled. The reasons for the change in archaeology have been related to a crisis in archaeological thinking, but what exactly did this crisis consist in and why should it occur in the 1960s? Was the perceived crisis merely a chance development? Hill (1972, p. 61) suggested that the crisis resulted from the failure of traditional theories and methods to solve archaeological problems. Precisely the opposite view was taken by Leone (1972, p. 21) who related the problem to the very success of traditional archaeology. Leone took the major goal of traditional archaeology as being to provide an outline of what had happened in the past. As this outline was now available what were archaeologists to spend their time doing? Trigger (1981) has attributed changes in archaeological thinking to wider social changes and attitudes over which archaeologists themselves have no control. On this account changes in archaeological theory and practice merely mirror the wider social context. Most recently, according to Trigger, the idea that technical progress would solve all social problems has been replaced with a profound pessimism and despair more or less directly expressed in Renfrew's use of catastrophe theory to explain social change (Renfrew 1978a). Whether or not Renfrew's outlook on life is indeed despairingly pessimistic is not for us to say but Trigger's formulation is hardly adequate. It relies on a conception of society as being a normative consensus between individuals and thus the theories of archaeologists, perforce, reflect the general outlook on life held at any one time. Taken to its logical extreme Trigger's position credits archaeologists with a nonactive intelligence in which they are only capable of reflecting the social conditions of their existence rather than challenging them or attempting to change them.

The contradictory views of Hill and Leone with regard to the reasons for the crisis in archaeology might, of course, be resolved by simply stating that some archaeologists believed that they had accomplished all they could by utilizing traditional theories and methodologies while to others there was a feeling that nothing of interest or importance could be established. We would suggest that perhaps a more plausible reason for the development of the new archaeology is fundamentally to do with a drive for prestige and power, but on a disciplinary basis rather than in terms of individuals *per se*. During the last two decades archaeologists have distanced their work from history, conceived as being particularistic and ideographic in character, and have characterized it as a nomothetic generalizing 'hard' science. Science, with a capital S, is the key word for understanding recent developments in archaeology. Why did the majority of archaeologists want to don the antiseptic white coat? This would seem to involve the acceptance of the myth of the supremacy of science as the ultimate mode of human understanding, the scientist as an heroic figure dispelling myths with incisive rationality. Given the increasing dominance of science and technology in contemporary society, to be cast in this image was to gain intellectual respectability and power, the power to be gained by producing or purporting to produce objective knowledge relevant to the modern world (Fritz and Plog 1970, p. 412), relevance being conceived in terms of both ethical and political neutrality and thus inherently conservative (Tilley 1985; Chapter 3 this volume). The new archaeology began optimistically; archaeology, it was asserted, could be anthropology but the limitations of traditional archaeology with respect to being able to achieve a penetrating understanding of the past were recreated as a result of the advocacy of positivist science. Drunk on Hempelian whisky and functionalist cognac the new archaeology has regressed to being able to say little more about the symbolic and social other than that which can be reduced to the effects of the technological and the economic, the initial rungs of Hawkes's ladder (1954) beyond which traditional archaeologists did not care to venture, except in rare moments of secondary speculation. It is towards a critique of the nature of the epistemology and methodology adopted in the new archaeology that the remainder of this chapter is devoted.

Grounding knowledge claims: positivism

New archaeologists not only opposed scientific aspirations to an historical understanding, but deduction to induction, positivism to empiricism. Appeals were made to the positivist philosophy of science as the royal road to success. The goal was no longer to describe the past but to explain it and explanatory structure became a central concern. Almost immediately a split developed between those archaeologists who considered their task to be the formulation and testing of laws and those who favoured functionalist explanations in systemic terms (for a critique of the latter see Hodder 1982a). This schism was first explicitly identified by Flannery who made a derisive attack on the 'law and order' archaeologists. Since the 1970s the two lines of approach have continued to be taken but the general failure to formulate any laws going beyond the trivial has resulted in a situation in which few archaeologists are now willing to commit themselves to such an approach. Common to both groups is an emphasis on the need to make generalizations and the belief that deductive testing against the archaeological record is the only way to ensure the objectivity and validity of statements made about the past.

Both those who advocated the use and formulation of laws and the functionalist systemic theorists singularly confused positivism and empiricism. Ironically they replaced empiricism with positivism, one of the most stringently empiricist philosophies to exist, and such was the general confusion that this was not recognized. A commonly accepted philosophical description of positivism is that it is systematic empiricism. Furthermore, those archaeologists who considered themselves to have totally rejected empiricist positions based their work on a very narrow reading of the philosophical literature. First, they only referred to the philosophy of science (understandable in that they wanted to become scientists), secondly, it was more or less assumed that a general consensus existed in the philosophy of science and the work of a few positivist philosophers of science, especially that of Hempel, was transferred wholesale with little or no critical consideration. Positivist doctrines were transferred to archaeology at a time when many philosophers were rejecting virtually every major tenet on which positivism was based. The unfortunate spectacle is one of archaeology embracing thoroughly discredited and outmoded ideas as the framework for its own advance. Curiously enough this trend has continued and the papers presented at the recent Southampton conference (Renfrew, Rowlands and Segraves (eds.) 1982) by those professional philosophers called in to 'advise' archaeologists, with the exception of Gellner's paper (Gellner 1982), all took a positivist, if diluted positivist line. Similarly the only semi-professional philosopher to have written a book with relation to archaeology (Salmon 1982) has retained a positivist position. This does not mean that positivism is alive and well as a viable philosophy but rather illustrates the adage that old traditions die hard. This is particularly unfortunate if it really is the case that archaeologists will believe anything told to them by a philosopher (Flannery 1982, p. 277). A current frustration with philosophy, and theory more generally, is represented by Flannery's recent paper (ibid.) and remarks made by Schiffer (1981). Flannery recommends a return to the common-sense real business of archaeology, i.e. a solid empirical culture history, while Schiffer suggests that archaeologists distance themselves from philosophical concerns which have no direct practical (i.e. methodological) implications for carrying out research.

Precisely the converse viewpoint is taken here. Ignoring philosophical and theoretical concerns is no way out. Such an approach, urging us simply to press on with the study of data without worrying about the niceties of theory, presumably inviting us to respond directly to that data, assumes that the lack of any systematic approach or procedure is somehow a miraculous guarantee of objectivity. Such a common-sense approach systematically evades any confrontation with its own premises, safeguards any methodology which is currently available and, in this manner, produces the very opposite of objective problem-free research. Empirical research presented as the obvious stuff of common sense is never called upon to guarantee its consistency, silences and contradictions and hence is entirely unsatisfactory. If philosophy has been of little use to archaeology this is because of the systematic abuses archaeologists have made of it and as a result of dabbling on the fringes of the philosophical literature. If philosophy is to be of value this will not result from calling in philosophers to tell us what to do or how to proceed. Archaeologists must themselves confront the literature, enter debates and establish positions. These will, of necessity, be philosophical positions which transcend the pragmatic concerns of the discipline but will be relevant to it. The only alternative would seem to be a blind unsystematic groping towards a study of the past, or for archaeologists to continue to find themselves subject to the comments made, quite correctly, by Morgan (1973) in relation to *Explanation in Archaeology* (Watson, LeBlanc and Redman 1971) (EA): 'In short EA seems in places reminiscent of a religious revivalist, appealing to scripture to establish his points, while surrounding his doctrine with flowery phrases and redefinitions to make that doctrine more palatable' (Morgan 1973, p. 273).

Even if it could be established – which it cannot – that philosophical issues are entirely irrelevant to archaeology, the difference between a philosophically and theoretically informed statement, and one not so arrived at, is that in the former case we do, in fact, have at least some reason to believe that we have a sound basis for what we are saying. Divorcing theory from practice is one of the fundamental features of positivism and, in itself, can only be defended or refuted on an informed philosophical basis.

We will now turn to a precise delimitation of what positivism may be taken to be, and the grounds on which it can be rejected. In constructing this critique we have found the following sources of particular use (Benton 1977; Giddens 1977; Harré and Madden 1975; Hindess 1977; Keat and Urry 1975). Two ways of proceeding are possible. The first is to consider the work of those philosophers who have actually been prepared to label their work 'positivist'. There are increasingly few of these since positivism is now more or less a term of abuse rather than a living philosophical tradition. The other, taken here, is to identify specific propositions as being positivist. We will be considering for the most part the philosophical arguments themselves rather than their direct archaeological adaptations since any use to be made of positivism in archaeology depends on whether these positions are, themselves, sound.

Naturalism

The thesis of naturalism depends on four interrelated beliefs:

(i)   human beings are principally physical and biological entities. Concomitantly, what people do and produce is, in essence, no different from the processes in the physical world in which natural scientists have their interest;

(ii)   all science forms a unity so that the principles relevant to the formulation and evaluation of statements are isomorphic in both the social and the natural sciences;

(iii)   the natural sciences provide the social sciences with a model for their procedure;

(iv)   the most certain knowledge is mathematical and deterministic in conception.

Archaeologists have explicitly or implicitly subscribed to all four of these doctrines. In fact the entire 'project' of the new archaeology is based on them and there is no need to go quotation mongering to establish this. The eighteenth-century sociologist, Charles Fourier, was so dazzled by Newton's achievements in physics, which to him consisted in the discovery of a single universal principle, that of gravitation, that he imitated Newton by proposing that social life was governed by a principle of passionate attraction. Most archaeologists would dismiss Fourier's proposition as ridiculous but, in essentials, it is no different and no more fantastic than to insist that to have any validity as a serious type of inquiry archaeology must ape the natural sciences (read physics) rather than consider social theories and model itself on the social sciences.

The thesis of naturalism can be attacked on a number of related grounds. First, as indicated above, there is no logical reason to accept thesis (iii) but, equally, it cannot be rejected on purely rational grounds and, therefore, the statement is vacuous. Theses (i), (ii) and (iv) are more crucial and will be considered together. Naturalism denies that human beings are in any way unique and claims that their actions can be explained in precisely the same manner as physical regularities in the natural world. Now it might appear open to debate whether or not a person or a society is a natural entity. After all people do possess physical bodies and are subject to the same physical forces in the world as, say, a boulder, a tree, or to use a favoured palaeoeconomic example, songbirds. There is undoubtedly a kernel of truth in such a position but it does not take us very far. People are not natural entities if we accept the primacy of sentience, intentionality, linguistic and symbolic communication. We clearly need to distinguish between physical bodily movement which can be accommodated in terms of a naturalist thesis and human actions which cannot be readily assimilated as they involve intentions, choices, dispositions and motivations. The social world is not a mirror of the natural world but a world that is always already structured and constitutes a totality which derives its nature and form from the interpretative procedures of its members. Natural phenomena, unlike social phenomena, have no inherent meaning or cognitive structure which needs to be taken account of in explanation.

Wittgenstein asks: 'What is left over if you subtract the fact that my arm goes up from the fact that I raise my arm?' (Wittgenstein 1953, I sec. 621). The implication of this question is that there is something far more important in the *action* of raising an arm than mere bodily movement, e.g. a reflex action. We subsume action not in terms of physical processes but in terms of the meanings to which it is directed. Meaning here is a crucial term. A reflex action is meaningless in that no human purpose or intentionality has caused, or can be related to the movement, but there are clear reasons why someone might raise his or her arm, e.g. to make a signal to someone. Meanings are necessarily and not contingently connected to human actions and their products. Social action, as opposed to movement, goes beyond itself. Intentionality is a crucial concept which distinguishes mental from physical phenomena. It involves a conception of people who can make distinctions, understand and follow rules, impose normative constraints on their conduct, judge reflexively or monitor their actions and be capable of deliberation or choice. This is a very different perspective from the usual view of behaviour espoused in much of the archaeological literature where actions are deemed to be propelled by various external stimuli, needs and role expectations (e.g., Plog 1974, pp. 49–53; Schiffer 1976; Jarman *et al.* (eds.) 1982). People possess the ability to act in and on the natural world and to systematically transform it and create their own world or social construction of reality. The superficial resemblances set up, in particular, by the palaeo-economic school (Higgs (ed.) 1972, 1975; Jarman *et al.* (eds.) 1982) and in forms of neo-evolutionary theory (Dunnell 1978a, 1980; Wenke 1981) between human and animal behaviour, conceals fundamental and non-reducible differences such that there is a categorical distinction between concepts such as production and foraging, ethnicity and ecological niche, property and territorality. One set of concepts does nothing to elucidate the other since they belong to fundamentally different frames of reference. Human culture is not a part of nature but a transformation of it.

Mathematization is usually an irrelevant diversion in an attempt to understand the social world. Little has been achieved in archaeology beyond the questioning of earlier work on the basis of its alleged quantitative inferiority: 'it is as if one had to board an atomic submarine for a new discovery of America, a discovery which has to be verified simply because Columbus's "Santa Maria" was technically imperfect' (Wiatr 1969, p. 23). Cooke and Renfrew (1979) develop a model to simulate the emergence of civilization. Societies are treated as systems with human beings as their 'components'. The model is operationalized by using the six subsystems Renfrew (1972) defines for the Aegean and, at this stage, the human 'components' fall irrevocably out of view. A further step is to eliminate the subsystems in favour of numerical variables between 0 and 1. Now it is only possible to ascribe a numerical variable, as in all mathematical approaches, on the basis of very clear definitions which are provided. For example the projective subsystem becomes '*either* the number of abstract concepts in use in the society relating to measure *or* the number of man-hours per head per year spent in religious observance or in facilitating them (e.g. building temples)' (Cooke and Renfrew 1979, p. 331). The authors explicitly state that the model was only a crude and prelimi- nary attempt but the specification of mathematical numerical variables can never be profitable. An analogous situation might be to ask someone to place a precise numerical variable (or even a value range), as to whether they would prefer their nose or right leg to be amputated. In essence the thesis of naturalism collapses with the counter thesis of the irreducibility of the social. Concomitantly, if the social is irreducible the statements made about the physical and natural world must take a different form and there is no need to model social processes in terms of natural processes.

Phenomenalism and the demarcation of science/non-science
The doctrine of phenomenalism and what can be taken to constitute scientific as opposed to non-scientific work remain crucial to any understanding of positivism, prob- ably more so than the thesis of naturalism. This is so because it is possible to reject naturalism while retaining a phenomenalist thesis and separating science/non-science on the basis of various criteria. In this section we will consider issues involved in explanatory structure alluded to above but not explicitly discussed.

Phenomenalism is the thesis that the only feature that can be known for certain about either the natural or the social world is what is given to human beings, as subject- observers, in the senses. Anything that goes beyond sense-perception is non- observable and therefore unknowable. It is the empiricist belief par excellence and remains at the heart of positivism. Associated with this thesis is the belief that it is possible to perform objective tests against a solid bedrock of fact and to confirm or refute statements in this manner. In an archaeological context Renfrew (1982a, p. 143) has reaffirmed the crucial importance of this 'old relationship' between theory and data: 'the hypothetico-deductive approach rightly lays stress on the passage from theory to data, by means of deduced hypotheses and of hypothesis testing'. Since the advent of the new archaeology testing statements against the archaeological record has remained the key- note of what is regarded as an objective and, therefore, truly worthy scientific enter- prise. Put very simply anything, i.e. any statement which cannot be tested, must remain a meaningless statement because there is no way of evaluating it.

No particular stress or importance is placed on where the statements come from, or the theories. They could be the result of a careful consideration of the data or previous work or, quite equally, arise from dreams or hallucinations. The first point to note, then, is that the process of arriving at these theories or statements to be tested is totally denigrated. This is of no importance and there is a one-sided stress on the testing process wherein the essence of truth is thought to arise. Secondly, it is assumed that there actually is a hard bedrock of facts or data to test against, independent of an act of subjec- tive definition. This is the proposition that all archaeologists would be able to reach agreement, in any particular case, as to what the hard facts to be tested against actually are and this will now be examined.

First, are the empirical facts non-subjectively defined? Consider the diagram below (Fig. 2.1). This is a rather famous example from gestalt psychology. Is it a young or old woman? Can we perceive what it is irrespective of an act of interpretation? The answer is no: we can either perceive it as an old or a young woman. We cannot perceive what it is supposed to be apart from a subjective interpretation of the observed evidence before us, i.e. the lines that make up the diagram. The manner in which this diagram is *described* is vitally crucial to the act of seeing what it is. The reality is not independent of a description of that reality. Hanson (1958) has argued, on the basis of such examples, that the idea of a theory-neutral observation language is untenable. What scientists see is essentially related to their theories and beliefs about the way the world is. What we observe depends on these background assumptions so there can be no objective testing without circularity. Furthermore it is not possible in a positivist framework to judge between competing theories or statements, because different observers cannot agree on what they actually see as a result of the theory-laden nature of observational statements. Kuhn (1970) has widened this position to a discussion of paradigm change within science so that at different stages of scientific activity individuals literally see things in different ways. They may generally agree on what they are seeing but this is a consensus position which has little to do with a non-subjectively defined reality. Priestley 'saw' dephlogisticated air while Lavoisier, adopting quite different assumptions, 'saw' oxygen.

Now it could be claimed that examples such as this or the young-old woman diagram are unfair. The diagram is deliberately designed to trick or deceive. It runs counter to our general intuitions and the real world of archaeological data is simply not like that. We can agree on what we see, or what the facts are supposed to be, and make our tests against them. This is a common-sense and well-established procedure. Well, the archaeologist advocating positivist science will be hoist with his or her own petard. First, the claim as to whether theories actually are independent of observations can only

Fig. 2.1 Appearance and interpretation.

be grounded on a subjective claim – a statement of belief that things really are like that. There is no reason to accept this. Secondly, science has nothing to do with common sense. It is precisely the opposite – science calls into question common-sense notions.

Consider the concept of explanation. Passmore (1962) has demonstrated how, under a variety of circumstances, a piece of information can be offered as an explanation. He adopts the pragmatic standpoint that ultimately what constitutes an adequate explanation depends on 'what I know and what I want to know'. Above all an explanation must be intuitively satisfying depending on criteria of clarity, soundness, intelligibility and precision, criteria which it is almost impossible to realistically define. According to Passmore historians use almost as liberal criteria as, to use that old cliché, the man or woman in the street. On the basis of the manner in which positivist philosophers of science have characterized their activities, natural scientists adopt an extremely specialized procedure, the deductive-nomological model of explanation: A if B (law: an atemporal, aspatial statement). Empirical case: B happened (antecedent condition). Therefore A occurred (explanadum event) (Hempel 1965). A variant on this model is the inductive-statistical mode in which laws are replaced by probability statements to the effect that if A then usually B with, ideally, a specified probability of how many times B is likely to occur if A. As discussed above some new archaeologists set out to find laws in order to make their work conform to the deductive nomological model but discovered none which were neither tautologies nor of the utmost triviality. No doubt this has promoted some of the current disillusion with the value of philosophy to the discipline. The failure to find laws has led to an emphasis on generalization as a substitute. Renfrew (1982b, p. 10) has stated that laws have always been his bête noir. However, in common with most archaeologists, he has retained the wish to make generalizations and for archaeology to be a generalizing science. It remains unspecified and unclear what status these generalizations are actually supposed to have and how general a statement must be before it counts as a generalization: two cases? three? fifty?. If the generalizations made are not laws they cannot be expected to be applicable in any one particular case so why are these generalizations of use to us? Why must the business of doing science necessarily be equated with the ability, or the will to generalize? This appears to be a procedural rule founded on the basis that generalizing, rather than considering all the particularity of the individual case, is a superior kind of activity. There seems to be no compelling reason why we should accept this.

We will now return to problems of testing theory or hypotheses against the data from a slightly different angle within positivism. So far, the only specific criticism we have made in relation to deductive nomological or inductive statistical explanation is that, in practice, archaeologists have been unable to make their work conform to these rigid self-imposed models. This may be a sufficient reason for rejecting them but it is not a necessary condition.

Historically, there has been a very strong link between the positivist tradition of philosophizing and, in particular, the logical positivism of the Vienna circle espoused in the work of Carnap, Feigl, Frank, Gödel, Neurath and Reichenbach, and the British empiricist tradition represented by Locke and Hume (Hempel belonged to a Berlin group of philosophers while Popper was never a member of the Vienna circle and has always distanced his views from theirs). Hempel's explication of the nature of explanatory structure is founded on the Humean 'regularity' view of causation according to which two events, C and E are related as cause and effect, if, and only if, they are members, respectively, of classes C and E of observable events. Thus each member of entity E regularly follows and is contiguous with a particular member of entity C. An observer experiencing E will, then, be led to expect the presence of C (Sayre 1976, p. 65). Causation, in such a perspective, is identified with regular succession coupled with psychological association. It is the psychological association made by the observer between C and E that constitutes, to Hume, the 'cement of the universe' (see Mackie 1974 for a detailed discussion). Put crudely it is the philosopher's job to provide the logical cement that links C and E. Hempel's work is one way of applying the cement. However, that this cement is required in the first place is purely a product of the empiricist's radical scepticism as to the manner in which knowledge claims can be made. It depends on a theory of perception in which the observer experiences the world as a series of independent and unconnected sense impressions and must connect these back together in terms of a logical cement between perceived regularities. This logical cement is a deductive syllogism, in the form presented by Hempel, but to Hume it was a process of induction. Real structural relationships are denied and exchanged for logical relations. We will return to this point in Chapter 5. It will suffice to state here that if we deny the belief that we experience the world solely in terms of disconnected atomistic particularities, but that real relations of structural necessity exist, there is no requirement for us to lay on thick layers of logical cement.

The logical positivists of the Vienna circle codified a distinction between analytic and synthetic statements. Synthetic statements refer to relationships existing between entities of which we acquire simple sense-perception, subject to the view criticized above, that we see the world independent of theories about it. Analytic statements are purely products of logic and only tautologies as they rest on definitional clauses, e.g. a bachelor is an unmarried man because to be unmarried and to be a man is to be a bachelor. Such statements are only correct in terms of formal logic and tell us nothing about the world. Analytic *terms* relate to entities which cannot be perceived, e.g. volume, mass, force, atoms. A scientific theory almost always involves reference to such terms. To have validity, according to positivists, it must be subject to axiomatizations. Axiomatizations of a theory must include various explicit definitions for the theoretical terms of the sort $Tx = Ox$ where T is a theoretical term and O is an observation term and the link between them is provided by correspondence rules.

Braithwaite (1968, p. 51) likened these rules to a zip which pulled together theoretical and observation statements but, true to the empiricist tradition, the theoretical language, unless it was purely tautologous and thus useless, was entirely dependent or parasitic on the observation language. The two are not on an equal footing and, furthermore, if it is conceded as even members of the Vienna circle now admit, that observation statements are not theory-free (e.g., Feigl 1970) the corollary is that theoretical and observational statements cannot at all be clearly separated. Concomitantly the latter provide, on positivist grounds, neither a conclusive affirmation or refutation of the former. Additionally W. V. O. Quine's (1961) paper 'Two dogmas of empiricism' has demolished even the difference held to exist between analytic and synthetic statements by calling into question the very concept of meaning itself construed as some kind of mystical mental property held to exist independently of the will of a speaker to assent or dissent from sentences in natural language. Quine (1960) describes science as being analogous to a force field whose boundaries (i.e. the boundary conditions) are radically underdetermined by experience, such that there is a considerable latitude of choice as to exactly which statements should be re-evaluated in the light of any single contrary experience. Thus any formal criteria for theory choice – verification, confirmation, falsification – become discredited. Positivist science is no more, no less, than a form of controlled subjectivity, the controls being that there is some sort of logic or rationality involved, but exactly where this resides except on an intra-community subjective basis is rather difficult to specify. At this point it should be noted that this kind of criterion for evaluating knowledge claims was precisely that which new archaeologists objected to in the traditional archaeology – the more famous, and inevitably the older, the archaeologist, the more reason there was to accept his or her knowledge claims as being valid, as providing a reasonable accommodation to the 'facts'.

We will return to the theory/data relationship in another and less abstract way. We have a theory and wish to test it against the data. Further, we make the assumption that the data is in some way independent of our theorization. The test is negative: is our theory falsified? Alternatively the test is positive. Do we then have any more confidence in the theory? This depends on whether we adopt a verificationist or a falsificationist strategy for hypothesis confirmation. In the early work of the Vienna circle the verification principle was upheld, i.e., statements made about the world must be empirically verifiable in relation to sense-perception data in order to have any meaning. A logical extension of this was that only scientific procedures framed in this manner could be granted meaning. Any other statements made about the world by poets, for example, or in aesthetics lacked any meaning. Concomitantly the rest of philosophy, apart from logical positivism, was also written off as meaningless activity. A concession was that statements made by others might be granted emotive meaning but little more. An immediate problem arose: a fundamental logical inconsistency. The verificationist principle itself could not be tested nor could it be granted the status of an analytic truth. Consequently, on the very grounds of logical positivism it was itself meaningless. In other words logical positivism rested on precisely the kinds of metaphysical claims about the world it shrugged off as being invalid.

The phenomenalist thesis commits positivism to the idea that there is an objective world to test or verify an hypothesis against (but see the Popper variant below). Unfortunately for archaeology, or any other area of human inquiry, the content of what is supposed to be given to the senses of the subject-observer is not independent of an operation of mind and can hardly be relied upon to point to itself. The similarities or differences between two 'given' objects of experience must necessarily be described but it is impossible to ever give a complete description. In other words every act of dealing with 'givens' in experience is dependent on a whole set of procedures not themselves given to experience and therefore not subject to meaningful discourse. If all observation is to a certain extent theoretical – objects of experience are constituted by an act of knowledge on the part of a 'knowing' subject (in our case the archaeologist) who decides what the givens are – it is illogical to maintain that theories can be *independently* tested against observations.

Popper (1959, 1963, 1974) has persistently claimed that he is not a positivist. Indeed, he has regarded his work as a critique of positivism. However, he asserts the naturalist thesis of the unity of science and maintains there is a clear demarcation between scientific and non-scientific activity and that science provides the most reliable and significant knowledge to which human beings could hope to aspire. As with the positivists of the Vienna circle, Popper's criterion of scientific activity is that statements should be subject to testing. In all these respects Popper's work remains part of the same tradition. The major points of contrast are:

(i)   the substitution of a doctrine of falsification for one of verifiability. Nothing for certain can be known about the world. All we can hope to do is to disprove statements by setting out to falsify them by empirical testing;

(ii) observation statements are in no way certain, they are theory-laden;

(iii) he has defended metaphysics and openly acknowledges that his philosophy is based on metaphysical arguments.

Surprisingly, archaeologists have not made much explicit reference to Popper's work (but see Salmon 1975; Tringham 1978) but it may accord more with their actual practices than strict logical positivism or the Hempelian position. Popper stresses an asymmetry between verification and falsification. We can never verify a law because the next test may prove it to be wrong. Scientists deal more with verisimilitude than truth (Popper 1959, p. 135). Science is carried out by a process of deduction, by testing universal statements (laws) against singular statements: 'to give a causal explanation of an event means to deduce a statement which describes it, using as premises of the deduction one or more universal laws, together with certain singular statements, the initial conditions' (ibid., p. 59). As in Hempel's work explanation is of the particular by the general and a symmetry is held to exist between explanation and prediction. Now, on Popper's account there is no compelling reason to believe there are, in fact, laws. The argument rests on the assumption that laws exist because the world can be described in terms of essential uniformities – a metaphysical assertion. Science to Popper is descriptive and divorced from language so that the 'logic of discovery' does not require correspondence rules linking theoretical and observational terms. Truth is considered to be a non-empirical concept and timeless. Corroboration is different from truth and we accept some hypothesis or statement as being provisionally 'true' in that it has not been proved to be false (ibid., p. 275). One single contrary observation falsifies a hypothesis in a falsificationist strategy. To Popper scientific knowledge is built on the shifting sandbanks of theory-impregnated observations but empirical refutations provide the basis on which knowledge is based and is supposedly a progressive advance towards more and more certainty in what we say. This idea of a progressing, but nevertheless uncertain knowledge is, in fact, only possible to defend if there were a limit to the number of conjectures and refutations to be made of a theory, but as these are infinite – there is no logical end point at which the testing procedure can stop – what basis is there to believe that any number of tests would lead us nearer to the truth? In the actual practice of testing, falsification remains unreliable. A cherished theory can always be 'saved' precisely because observation is theory-laden and Popper admits that it is. The statement that all swans are white is falsified by the discovery of a single black swan, in theory, but then, of course, we must decide whether the black swan is to count as a swan or can be defined as such. Furthermore any statement about the world or a series of statements, i.e. a theory, cannot be falsified in any simple manner since a falsifying test may not impugn the whole theory but, perhaps, an unexamined auxiliary statement. In this case we more or less have to make a choice whether to reject the statement or theory or not. In the black swan case we have to decide whether the empirical example refuting our statement is a swan. If we want to defend a theory we can simply reject the test as inadequate in some way.

Popper's response to strategies designed to save a theory from refutation, in the manner discussed above, is to claim that this is contrary to the ideals of scientists: 'we decide that if our system is threatened we will never save it by any kind of conventionalist stratagem . . . it must be left to the investigator to constantly guard against this temptation' (ibid., p. 82). So, to be a scientist, in effect, has *nothing whatsoever to do with testing*: to be a scientist is to accept some type of behavioural norm as to how to act. Popper asserts (1966) that Marxists accept no such norm and always save their theories (see Cornforth 1968 for a rejoinder). For Popper, then, it is the behaviour of Marxists that is at issue, not the conceptual structures they employ. What is observed and tested depends on the scientist's training (Popper 1959, pp. 99–104). Concomitantly, the results of tests and what then counts as knowledge depends on how scientists are trained at any one time. They can then more or less agree on basic statements about the world, but if someone doesn't agree they can be dismissed as a pseudo-scientist or a fool: 'when all else fails the danger of an infinite regression in the testing and retesting of basic statements by the scientific community may be averted by the elementary rule that might is right' (Hindess 1977, p. 175).

To maintain, as Popper does, that observation is theory-laden but that science still progresses by testing against empirical data is entirely contradictory. The basic statements, i.e. the observations made on the world, are a function of training and are theory-laden. Furthermore, a choice is always involved as to whether a test has really falsified a theory. We test our hypotheses not against any solid bedrock of fact, as the strict logical positivists of the Vienna circle once claimed, but in terms of basic theory-laden terms and observations we have supposedly been trained to know. But if theory is involved in the very act of observation then testing cannot be a rational procedure. Even if after the test we have not falsified our theory there is no reason to believe that confidence has been increased since there are an infinite number of tests which could be made. If we just single out a few 'key' hypotheses to test then, in effect, our tests only serve to reproduce the knowledge 'given' to us in our conceptual system.

In positivist philosophy, then, there are no coherent grounds for the belief that we can test against an independent non-subjectively defined reality. The testing process provides no more certainty than if we had not tested a proposition. The grounds for distinguishing scientific from non-scientific activity are far from clear and there is no reason to believe that science provides more objective or more certain knowledge than other modes of human understanding of the social world. The beliefs held by archaeologists that they can perform objective tests of their theories and choose between these theories in the framework of positivist science are undermined, likewise the belief that their activities are of a radically different nature from those engaged in by historians. Some of the arguments that have been made might well be accepted (Binford and Sabloff (1983) concur that knowledge is not to be attained by testing procedures) but with the residual retention of a phenomenalist thesis which we consider further below.

We have noted that a commitment to phenomenalism or the belief that we can only gain knowledge through sense-perception is a metaphysical statement so that there is no automatic reason to accept it. The question is: can a more plausible counter-claim be made, and on what basis? The delimitation of such a claim will be left until Chapter 5 and attention here will be concentrated on why phenomenalism provides an inadequate basis for founding knowledge claims. To use an Althusserian turn of phrase, positivism is the empiricism of the object, thought to be present to the senses, capable of isolation as such, and constituting the correct unit of study. Knowledge consists in both a radical distinction between concepts and phenomena (see the discussion of causation above), subject and object, and yet at the same time depends on a correspondence between them. There is a realm of knowledge acquired by a 'knowing' subject and this knowledge consists in propositions and concepts about the world. The realm of knowledge is opposed to the object world of phenomena passing to the subject-observer as sense data. Distinctions are set up between concepts and reality and may be linked up by correspondence rules, for example. But in positivism there can be no real difference between an object constituted in knowledge and the phenomena of experience. They become more or less isomorphic. This might be termed a form of 'subjective idealism' (Hindess 1977, p. 114) in that the investigator, as 'knower', on a priori grounds already formulates and constitutes that which is to be known. Whatever is not physically present in space or time, and whatever is general, can only be reached through inference and therefore remains uncertain. However, given that observation is dependent on theory, objects of knowledge become constituted prior to the process of knowing them. Concomitantly, knowledge is not discovered or produced from a reality but already given to that reality prior to any application of method. Knowledge consists of little more than the description of that which has already been theoretically constituted. In other words, what positivist science attempts to produce via the application of a scientific methodology has already been constituted prior to the operation of the methodology through an operation of the mind. There can be no 'logic of scientific discovery' since it has already been decided what there is to discover (see Chapter 3).

Conclusion

The fortunes of a positivist archaeology naturally depend on the philosophical tradition on which it draws, but positivism provides no coherent epistemology, no adequate ontology of the world, no means of conceptualizing the theory/data relationship which is acceptable, no convincing account of explanatory structure, asserts a crude view of the unity of science, and the spectre of science which it presents simply does not accord with actual practice, providing no basis (itself irrevocably value-laden) for claims that science is a superior mode of activity – the only really meaningful activity a scholar could indulge in. It is a tragedy that most archaeologists feel a commitment to carry on this completely discredited tradition of research in one form or another. In fact, if positivism was actually taken to its logical extreme we would have to deny the possibility of any knowledge of the past beyond pure subjectivism. Positivism would return archaeology to exactly those 'normative' traditions and that radical scepticism displayed in Hawkes's ladder of inference from which it sought to escape (Hawkes 1954). To a certain extent this has already happened.

The failure of archaeologists to discover laws reduces the explanations archaeologists make, in the positivist dogma, to mere 'explanation sketches' (Hempel 1959). According to Hempel this is because of empirical complexity more than anything else but it still seems to make archaeology a poor thinker's science *vis-à-vis* natural science if archaeologists are to accept this imperialism. Binford (1977) introduced the term 'middle range theory' into archaeology, at the same time confessing that 'in the absence of progress toward usable theory, there is no new archaeology, only an antitraditional archaeology at best' (Binford 1977, p. 9). Binford's solution to the lack of usable theory is to build it and his subsequent work (1978, 1981, 1983a section IV, 1983b) has been devoted to doing just this, but the theories are being built from the bottom up, to arrive at empirical 'facts' which are subsequently employed to invalidate the work of others. This so-called middle range theorizing is enthusiastically advocated by some (e.g., Raab and Goodyear 1984; Willey and Sabloff 1980, pp. 249ff.) and appears to be rapidly developing to the status of a new panacea for archaeological ills. Middle range theory is little more than middle range empiricism, and what is supposedly 'middle' about it is far from clear. According to Raab and Goodyear:

> One *outcome* of middle-range theorising can be the creation of a logical structure in which low-order working-hypotheses tend to confirm or negate propositions in a middle stratum and the latter in turn reflect upon the validity of yet more generalized theories . . . On the other hand a series of testable propositions can be derived from existing theories in ways suggested by Hempel (1965), Popper (1959) and others.
>
> (Raab and Goodyear 1984, p. 257, our emphasis)

Given the criticisms of positivist science presented above such a statement requires no comment other than to note that the term 'middle range theorizing' is virtually redundant as a means of differentiating the type of research that Raab and Goodyear propose from that which has been carried out without the use of it. The concept is, rather, a new fancy icing on the old empiricist cake.

In some recent discussions the terms 'objective' and 'science' take on an almost magical significance. They are so vitally important to Binford, for example, that he constantly repeats them in his publications as a means of legitimating the worth of his research programme. The commitment to phenomenalism, stridently displayed in his work in which the subject-observer must take his or her 'premises to experience and permit experience to pass judgment on their accuracy' (1983a, p. 421) results in the creation of a pseudo-science or a subjective idealism as we have argued above. This is coupled with a naturalism in which the archaeological record is considered to be purely a product of a 'complex mechanical system of causation' (ibid., p. 417), a view which is reproduced in considerations of human agency. Social action is reduced to the logistics of adaptation and maximization of resources – 'labour accommodations to incongruent distributions of critical resources or conditions' (ibid., p. 344). As will be argued in Chapter 3, such a viewpoint owes much to the value-system of the capitalist west and indirectly serves its reproduction. The adoption of positivism results in a view of the past dangerously close to Hollis's caricature. It is high time we changed stations.

3

Facts and values in archaeology

'Those who desert the world and those who sell out to it have something in common. Neither group can adopt an openly critical stance to society.'   (Gouldner 1973, p. 13)

Introduction

Chapter 2 considered archaeology's pretensions to being science through a critique of positivist doctrines accepted by many since the 1960s. In this chapter we concentrate on archaeology's pretensions to objectivity which may or may not be associated with the advocacy of a scientific archaeology. Is it possible for archaeology to be value-free? Is this a reasonable or a valid aim? Most sceptical empirical archaeologists would probably deny that archaeology can ever be an entirely objective account of the past and yet most archaeologists are undoubtedly aiming at objectivity even if it isn't thought possible to quite achieve this ideal; it is accepted that the archaeologist should aim at eliminating subjective 'bias'. But what exactly are the implications of this aim? We wish to progress beyond slippery scepticism and examine objectivity in archaeology, focussing on the relation between facts and values. Archaeologists have remained surprisingly reluctant to discuss this issue in spite of claims made over a decade ago for a dawning of critical self-consciousness (Clarke 1973). As several (Kohl 1981; Hall 1984; Miller 1982a; Ucko 1983) have noted, this self-consciousness within archaeology has largely been limited to the search for *method* to secure objective knowledge of *other* cultures. It has been methodological introspection, a concern to find an objective means of access to the past rather than reflective inquiry into the contemporary roots of knowledge in the past. We wish to examine this search for method, to look further into this discrepancy in the form and meaning of archaeology's self-consciousness of itself as investigation of the past, a discipline and practice largely untroubled by doubts and questionings with regard to social, political and moral issues which have brought about an awareness in other fields of knowledge of the manifest shortcomings of dominant patterns of thought. We argue that the notion of value-freedom, of objectivity, imports a whole series of usually unrecognized values into archaeology and contend that the separation of facts and values, an opposition lying at the heart of a complex of related theoretical standpoints, is a disabling ideology which fails to deal adequately with the past and, in however minor a way, helps to sustain and justify the values of a capitalist present.

An objective and scientific archaeology: rational method and therapy

Setting aside its more unsavoury aspects as a struggle for power in the discipline which we discuss in Chapter 2, the 'new' archaeology began as ideology critique. It aimed to

46

dispel and discredit the fact collection and humanist narrative of traditional archae-ology, to rationally reassess archaeological work and to call into question the validity of interpretations not open to such assessment and this was conceived primarily in terms of testing and quantification. Much of the introspection in archaeology during the past fifteen years is part of such a process of rationalization.

A premise of this process is that systematic observation and rational method, a term which we employ throughout this chapter as a short-hand term when referring to positivist/empiricist discourse, would provide an objective means of access to the past. The process of acquiring knowledge is viewed as being a resolution of contradiction between knowledge, located subjectively, and the objective facts:

> Knowledge starts from the tension between knowledge and ignorance. Thus we might say not only, no problems without knowledge; but also, no problems without ignorance. For each problem arises from the discovery that something is not in order with our supposed knowledge; or, viewed logically, from the discovery of an inner contradiction between our supposed knowledge and the facts. (Popper 1976, p. 88)

But the contradiction lies in the subjective side of the relation; it is a deficiency of supposed knowledge on the part of the impartial observer (Adorno 1976a). In the search for rules of method which will guarantee objectivity, reason becomes identified with the correct method, with operational rules rather than with cognitive acts. Thus the process of acquiring knowledge, of doing archaeology, is a therapeutic process. It aims to bring thought and expression, the archaeologist, into accordance with the object of archaeo-logical investigation. It aims to cure pathological thinking, contradiction within the process of knowledge.

According to rational method, reality is reasonable and the observed immediate appearance of the object is taken as being real, something existing independently of its investigation. The archaeologically observable past, the object of archaeological investi-gation is accorded epistemological and ontological priority. The basis of true expla-nation becomes an abstract conception of the fact, abstract because it does not matter which fact it is as long as it has been systematically observed, measured and recorded – processed by rational method. Objectivity is in-itself, abstracted from its context. Objectivity, which is the quality of an object, is conceived abstractly – quantitatively. Objectivity is uniform and neutral because it exists separately from the observing sub-ject. So it is objective facts which count; knowledge depends on them; they are, after all, considered to be hard physical reality. The neutrality of facts from this perspective means that they cannot be criticized; the precision and consistency with which facts are observed may be criticized, but not the abstract concept of objectivity. The fact's name, its immediate classification, exhausts its concept, describing without passing judgement.

'Value' refers to a relationship; it is a meaning, a significance for an other, for some-one. It unites, for example, an object and a person or two people. But according to rational method, values are to be separated from facts; they exist not for another but in-themselves; values are substantial, monetary. What is and what ought to be are entirely separate. Thus in affirming the primacy of the object, archaeology must positively affirm immediate appearance. Ideology comes to mean violation of objectivity or of value-freedom; it refers to the intrusion of the subjective at the level of method. So misunderstanding of the data, even systematic misrepresentation and distortion in the data must be due to the pathologically thinking analyst. Immediate reality of fact can never, after all, be unreasonable.

This is compounded by scientism – the belief that whatever is defined as scientific rationality should be the basis of archaeology. Scientism is most obviously seen in the neo-positivist law-searching new archaeology but certainly does not depend on a positivist conception of natural science. We would contend that it implicitly lies within a great deal of theoretical archaeology. If archaeology as science of the archaeological object is only contingently related to value judgements and there can be no other objective basis to a study of the archaeological past than through observation of the object, the primacy of the object leads to the identification of what is and what ought to be; the latter is reduced to the former. The way things appear immediately in fact is the way it should be.

Reification and empirical regularity

> The exchange principle, the reduction of human labour to the abstract universal concept of average labour time, is fundamentally related to the principle of identification. Exchange is the social model of the principle, and without the principle there would be no exchange; it is through exchange that non-identical individuals and performances become commensurable and identical. The spread of the principle imposes on the whole world an obligation to become identical, to become total.   (Adorno 1973a, p. 146 – modified translation)

Pre-defined rational method produces its object in advance. The particular structure of the object in the past is neglected in favour of a general method which guarantees objectivity – abstract objectivity. So the object past is not represented in, by and through archaeology but rather its representation is exchanged for universal interchangeability – a principle of identification. Objects have meaning primarily as objectivity. This means that fundamentally unlike phenomena can be equated. In particular social phenomena are reified, conceived as a set of physical processes; social phenomena as objects of rational method are part of the object world; society becomes a second nature.

This process of reification and identification is related to the capitalist mode of commodity exchange. It is through the commodification of labour and its product, through the reduction of labour to abstract labour time that non-identical individuals and practices become commensurable and identical. All practice, concrete and particular is reduced to behaviour – physical movement. Everything is identical and comparable according to the commodity form. 'Values', our subjective reaction to and appropriation of the object, are reduced to this single value of commensurability, monetary comparability. The only value allowed is that of objectivity, facts not judgements about what ought to be, explanations not 'paradigms'.

In the commodity exchange of the capitalist market we seem to be and are treated as empirical regularities governed by a natural necessity. We must adapt ourselves to the quasi-autonomous processes of the capitalist market. However, in making objective and universal this particular relationship between the individual and society, positivist/ empiricist rational method distorts society through its duplication, through the duplication of a reified consciousness. The conception of meaningful practice as physical behaviour and the symmetry held to exist between prediction and explanation has the effect of making this contemporary relationship between the individual and society seem natural:

> Predictability . . . does not lead to truth. Rather it highlights the extent to which social relations are relations of unfreedom. The more society takes the form of, and is perceived in, the categories of a second nature, the more it is shaped by the outcome of individual actions locked in relations of economic necessity, the more human agency is subjugated to 'laws' of development, the easier it is to predict social outcomes.
>
> (Held 1980, pp. 171–2, quoting Horkheimer 1968)

Thus in archaeology the widespread attempts made to predict data sets (e.g., Hodder (ed.) 1978; Hamond 1981; Sabloff (ed.) 1981) and then to think one has explained anything as a result of the outcomes of these predictions can be conceived as the imposition of a reified consciousness of the present, attesting to social relations of unfreedom, onto the past. The past is thereby recreated as the present which then becomes, in turn, naturalized by the past. Although prediction-as-explanation is logically connected with a view of explanation as subsumption of the particular beneath generalization (see Chapter 2, pp. 38–40), the former is often held without explicitly connecting it with the latter. Clarke (1972, p. 2) has claimed that 'explanation in archaeology . . . is viewed merely as a form of redescription which allows predictions to be made'. The rationale behind such redescription or model-building is that a working model – a model that *works* – is viewed as a successful explanation. The relationship between theory and reality becomes one of utility. The theory must work, and the reality it serves to define is a useful reality. Fritz (1973) and Ford (1973) have explicitly emphasized archaeology's utilitarian value, archaeology producing universal principles of human behaviour applicable to the present: archaeological theory can 'help engineers, applied scientists, government managers to control and even direct' social processes (Fritz 1973, p. 81). Past, present and future are deemed to be equivalent objects of instrumental control.

Manipulating the past as image of the present: economic archaeology

We argue that archaeology is a technology, that it is not a neutral quest for knowledge but that it systematically structures its questioning and the object it questions. It adapts the past to the exigencies of an archaeology in a capitalist present concerned with establishing the rules of a rational method to secure objective knowledge of the past, pinning it down. Such method operates on a pre-defined objectivity, a unified and abstract nature and society. This absolute reality is reduced through reification – separation of subject from object – to a quantified object of manipulation. Such knowledge aims to eliminate contradiction between subject and object, to eliminate disturbances in interaction with objective nature, to adapt the individual to nature, to produce successful expectations. As part of feedback-monitored practice the principles of knowledge become the principles of self-preservation. Immediate living – the principles of self-preservation are the principles of a free-market economy. Individuals classified as producer-consumers act 'rationally', adapting themselves to the quasi autonomous processes of the omni-historical market, satisfying need, minimizing cost and maximizing profit. But this universal market is a capitalist market within which

> The domination of men over men is realised through the reduction of men to agents and bearers of commodity exchange. The concrete form of the total system requires everyone to respect the law of exchange if he does not wish to be destroyed, irrespective of whether profit is his subjective motivation or not.
> (Adorno 1976b, p. 14)

An explicit adherence to the primacy of instrumental reason is to be found in a great deal of economic archaeology. The relation between the archaeologically observed society and its natural environment mirrors the epistemological subject-object relation of the present – a technical relation. Economic archaeology asserts the historical primacy of technologically rational behaviour. Rationality refers only to behaving in accordance with the technical recommendations of economy and efficiency – those values internal to rationality. Other value systems are non-rational and so arbitrary. History becomes the unfolding of reason, the Enlightenment dream, the curing of irrationality, of mal-adaptive behaviour. History becomes a therapeutic process.

That archaeology is to a large extent a reconciliation between the capitalist present and the prehistoric past can be seen most nakedly in the application of decision theory, game theory, linear and dynamic programming models (Jochim 1976; Keene 1979, 1981; Earle 1980; Christenson 1980). These theories represent, quite clearly, a mathematized logic of self-preservation. Such work has been hailed by Whallon as good examples of explanation and modelling and as an effective approach to theory-building of universal applicability (Whallon 1982). Underlying all this work is the notion of rationality writ large: 'the major assumption underlying all theories of choice is that of the rational decision maker' (Jochim 1976, p. 4). This rationality, we are led to understand, involves concepts such as risk and cost whether or not they were recognized by the prehistoric actors. Keene notes two assumptions on which his application of linear programming to hunter-gatherer economy rests:

> The primary goal among hunter-gatherers is to provide the basic nutritive and other raw materials necessary for the survival of the population

and

> when faced with a choice between two resources of equal utility, the one of lower cost will be chosen . . . economic behaviour is both satisfying and optimising.
> (Keene 1979, p. 370)

Virtually identical remarks are made by Earle:

> Other factors being equal, a community, viewed here as functionally equiv-
> alent to a diversified firm, should allocate its labour such that the requirements
> of the community's population are met at the lowest possible cost.
>
> (Earle 1980, p. 14)

Some remarks of Christenson may be added:

> There is no universal tendency toward profit maximization in the unrestricted
> sense. However, maximization when referring to efficiency can be considered
> a restricted kind of profit maximization where output (consumption) is fixed.
> This kind of maximization is quite relevant to understanding early human
> subsistence behaviour.   (Christenson 1980, p. 33)

These statements rather than being of great relevance for understanding the past
appear, rather, as prime examples of the *value system* of contemporary capitalist
economics projected onto the past. Optimization is a key term in all these models –
maximum profit for minimum risk and cost. Torrence (1983) has applied the quantified
time of the factory clock to hunter-gatherer societies, attempting to relate technology –
tool kit composition – to effective use of time, optimization of time – scheduling and
budgeting of time. This is claimed to provide increased reproductive fitness. This is the
value system of technocratic reason, of the company executive. As optimization has, in
such accounts, always been a fundamental feature of social life from the dawn of prehistory, such a perspective bolsters up the contemporary capitalist system by naturalizing
contemporary economic practices as the only possible ones. Mathematized decision
making is very much to be related to a capitalist rationalization of the labour process, a
rationalization which aims, of course, to benefit capital. It is no coincidence that
decision theory plays a significant part in management science.
    Rationality, in these perspectives, is not a relative concept but instead is a term that
is confined to social action in so far as it is 'satisfying', i.e. technically efficient. In effect,
rationality becomes a value in itself by means of which all other actions and values are
judged and labelled irrational. This is because the technical rationality of efficiency and
cost minimization is designated as what rationality *is* and all human beings are deemed
to be rational in just this one sense so that other 'non-rational' values not relevant to
economic maximization are reduced to dependent rather than independent, and equally
important, variables. Hence the non-economic can be reduced to the status of a random
or dependent variable (magic). The means-ends relationship from this perspective,
becomes considered in a manner which militates against the consideration of ends at all
in the last analysis. Such work is no more than a rationalization for, and assertion of the
Homo oeconomicus of capitalist theory – 'human nature' – against the timeless standards
of which all can be measured and explained. We know of little significant criticism of
this fiction in archaeology. A recent substantive criticism of optimization (Jochim
1983a) was concerned not with the assumptions of maximizing rational economic
behaviour, but with the application of the ideal model to 'reality', fitting *homo
oeconomicus* to the real world, making her work.

Systems theory, the status quo and pathology

Systems theory has become the dominant 'analogue model' within archaeology used to explain social change and social process, providing a theoretical structure, a set of modelling techniques, a source of concepts and testable propositions and a model for explanation according to one reviewer (Plog 1975). We wish to argue that it is fundamentally implicated in the search for rational method we have been outlining, in the process of rationalization within archaeology. The major theoretical exposition of systems theory in the archaeological literature remains that of Clarke (1968) and the most detailed substantive applications those of Renfrew (1972) and Plog (1974) while there are a host of other studies adopting the same general framework (e.g., Flannery 1968, 1972; Flannery and Marcus 1976; Hill (ed.) 1977) and Binford made some early programmatic remarks (1962, 1964, 1965).

Systems theory can be viewed as an updated version of the holism of Durkheimian sociology (Durkheim 1915) in which the whole, society, is greater than the sum of its parts. That is, it is not in principle reducible to the sum of the individuals which make it up. Generally, the definition used of society is of a system which functions as a whole by virtue of the interdependence of its parts. The whole system is usually divided into subsystems, the precise characterization of which varies according to the analyst. Renfrew, for example, chooses subsistence, metallurgy, craft specialization, social, projective, and trade-communication subsystems in his consideration of the emergence of civilization in the Aegean (Renfrew 1972, p. 486). The basic components of society as system are empirically defined and regularly organized behaviours of individuals. Systems analysis is based on the description of empirically given regularities. The system is to affirm, agree with immediate fact, which is pre-defined as having primacy. The concept 'system' is equivalent to pattern; it is a descriptive device. But the concept of 'system' is not part of the object of study; it is proposed in advance and cannot be empirically confirmed or refuted.

Systems theory involves analysis of the object in terms of its functional relation to the reproduction of the whole. This whole is *pre-defined* as an organic unit whose *natural state* is stability or equilibrium. Clarke (1968, pp. 48–52) defines seven different equilibrium states, in essence, different states of systems stability. Stability rather than change is the norm presupposed in systems theory and systems only change, in effect, in order to remain stable. Systems search out and converge upon desirable states. Clarke (1968, p. 52) terms this goal-seeking or homeostasis. The main explanatory concept is function (Hodder 1982a; Tilley 1981a, 1982a, p. 28).

Systems analysis as universal recipe stipulates in advance what is to be discovered. Any component of the system functions to maintain a desired state of affairs – social stability, a condition postulated in advance of any particular society. The system and its components adapt to the objective given – usually the external environment. Conservative values of persistence and stability become the norm. Change is always a contingent state of affairs while harmony is universal. Contradiction within the system is an unfortunate 'pathology' (Flannery 1972), its very abnormality revealed by the term itself. Systems theory, as pre-defined method based on immediate objective appearance, is a theory of conservative politics, conservative in that it will lend support to anything that is, the immediate 'reality' of any social form. In this sense, systems theory is not only conservative, it is immoral in its acceptance of any empirical state as a state for the good. For the sake of an abstract value of equilibrium, systems theory implicitly justifies oppression. In identifying what is with what should be, it creates a tidy, ordered and timeless world. The message of systems theory is that 'goodness' is to be found in social stability while social unrest is an unfortunate 'pathology': 'the ideal is for man to act without dislocation because this . . . communicates a set of contradictory values – capable of causing confusion, loss of cohesion and ultimately social anarchy' (Clarke 1968, p. 97). Naturally so-called 'social anarchy' is not in the interests of the ruling classes.

Cultural evolution, the politicization of time

The adoption of a systemic perspective by the 'new' archaeology involved a fresh under-standing of cultural change and permitted the development and blending of cultural evolutionary theory with a functionalist equilibrium analysis. The 'new' archaeology has generally been considered to mark a revival of interest in evolutionary theory and, in effect, the evolutionary perspective served to put the static, functionalist, adaptive, systemic perspective into operation.

Binford (1972) followed White (1959) in viewing culture as an extra-somatic means of adaptation but he was unhappy with the association of evolution with progress and instead suggested that evolutionary change was change occurring within maximizing systems which included the adaptation of the system to its environment, the more efficient use of resources and energy flux. Concomitantly, 'evolutionary processes are one form of ecological dynamics' (Binford 1972, p. 106). In addition to this ecological perspective, many archaeologists, following Sahlins and Service (1960) and Service (1975), have adopted a stadial framework according to which societies are arranged in a typological sequence of increasing complexity: bands or egalitarian societies, tribes or stratified societies, chiefdoms and states. Development is seen as the factor to be explained and most interest has focussed on the development of the state and 'civiliz-ation'. This typology has had extensive influence on social archaeology. But descriptive typology defined in advance of the object of study and 'adaptation' – the central features of cultural evolution – has a close relationship with the reductive and ultimately ideological conception of society and rational method we have been outlining.

Adaptation to socio-environmental stresses provides for Flannery (1972), as for Binford, the overall meaning and direction for evolutionary change. It provides the *rationale* for processes of 'segregation' and 'centralization'. The result is an increasing degree of efficiency and control over the environmental field. If any particular social sys-tem is unable to adapt through segregation it is no longer able to maximize its environ-mental control and resultant energy yield. In the long run it must be extinguished. The successful state is indeed a predator (Saxe and Gall 1977) in this perspective. Societies, or those that survive, attain new and higher levels of adaptive efficiency and are enabled to compete more successfully with their neighbours. Even if we do not know which socio-environmental pressures operated in any particular case, as Flannery evidently does not in the example he gives of ritual promotion and social stratification in Mexico

(Flannery 1972, pp. 414–16), these stresses 'must have been there . . . their role was to provide the selection pressures, while the actual instrument of change was ritual' (ibid., p. 416). This is not only a fundamental methodological assumption, but a metaphysical presupposition, an act of faith, for without adaptation there can be no reason for the segregation and centralization processes.

Sanders and Webster (1978) broadly align themselves with Steward's (1955) multi-lineal approach to evolution and, unlike Binford and Flannery, see an inherent paradox in trying to explain variability in culture by factors which are of their very nature non-varying. Accordingly, they state that environmental stimuli are 'basic causes of cultural evolution' (Sanders and Webster 1978, p. 251). The model they use outlines various possible evolutionary trajectories from egalitarian societies to states conditioned by the permutation of environmental variables and assumes that population growth occurs, that rates of growth remain constant, and that this is a necessary precondition for evolution: 'all processes of complex cultural evolution are processes of *growth* as well' (ibid., p. 297, emphasis in original). Adaptation accommodates people to their environment and permits the development of societal growth and higher-order social structures.

In the cultural evolutionary perspective adopted by the new archaeology the term progress is no longer used, as in earlier work; given the emphasis on scientism it is no longer acceptable. However, it has not been completely exorcized but has become conceptually shifted in relation to earlier accounts of evolutionism. It is now the more muted matter of adaptive efficiency and the ability to integrate and accommodate increasing numbers of people within the system by means of social differentiation, increasing stratification, and the emergence of higher order social regulators. The assumed need of societies to adapt to externally induced socio-environmental stresses or internally developing 'pathologies' is a differential measure of success. Societal adaptation may be efficient or inefficient, effective or ineffective, and some societies develop to become civilizations while others fall by the wayside: they never develop to the status of civilizations. Societies are like football teams with numbers on their backs and compete in the adaptive stakes – ground rules for the game which are laid out a priori before any analyses start. Some reach the top of the league and become civilizations while others are relegated to the lower divisions of bands and chiefdoms. Adaptation is the teleological cause, consequence, and measure of social development. Social change itself becomes rationalized. But societies exist in history, they are not interchangeable. However, all forms of cultural evolutionary theory treat the time of the past as homogeneous and abstract which allows the comparison of different societies, attaching labels to societies according to a pre-defined typological sequence. This is not a neutral process. It is the politicization of time. In measuring (evaluating), comparing and ordering sequences of societies according to definite criteria, we pass judgement on the past (see the discussion of time in Chapter 1).

Evolution: biology and behaviour

The only evolutionary position which does not seem to necessarily embody an explicit or implicit concept of progress is the modern theory of biological evolution combining

Darwin's theory of natural selection with Mendel's work on the nature of inheritance. The evolution of all forms of life is thought to be the result of at least five processes including inheritance, mutation, drift, gene flow and natural selection and of these natural selection is the most important. The essence of Darwinian evolutionary theory is non-directional variability on which natural selection operates in a particular environmental milieu, on individuals rather than groups. The theory provides a general and abstract conception of the mechanisms by means of which changes occur in individual organisms and remains valid whatever the concrete succession of forms actually is. Quite crucially the theory specifies no necessary direction stipulating the manner in which processes of variation and selection take place. It is an explanatory theory and is not a descriptive set of generalizations, unlike most cultural evolutionary theories. The ultimate origin of variability on which natural selection acts is mutation. This variability is transmitted genetically through either sexual or asexual reproduction. Evolutionary change is a selectional rather than a transformational process, a consequence of differential reproductive success in relation to a determinate natural environment at a specific time and place. A considerable stochastic element may be involved as regards the initial source of the variability and the types of genetic recombinations taking place through reproduction. Organisms that survive changes in an environmental milieu are not the most aggressive, fastest or largest members of a species, but forms which are biologically variant. The 'survival of the fittest' only makes any sense in relation to a specific environment. Different forms have definite relations of descent and these are always contingent as no arbitrary principles of a predetermined hierarchy of species are involved and may be explained in terms of selective processes. Sociobiologists (e.g., Wilson 1975, 1978; contributions in Chagnon and Irons (eds.) 1979) have attempted to apply this evolutionary perspective to human social behaviour while Dunnell (1978a, 1980) and Wenke (1981, pp. 111–19) have indicated it may be of value in archaeology as an alternative and more satisfactory position to cultural evolutionism.

It is by the very means of the concepts of the theory of modern evolutionary biology that we know that it simply cannot be applied to the development of human social organization except in such a problematic fashion as to completely undermine any value the attempt might have. Social relationships are not in any primary sense biological relationships and may not be explained except in the most reductionist scenario by the physical attributes of human beings in relation to different adaptive situations. Sociobiologists, and for that matter a large number of archaeologists (for example Plog 1974, pp. 49–53, 1977, pp. 16–17; Price 1982, p. 719; Schiffer 1976) write of human social *behaviour*. As argued above and in Chapter 2, 'behaviour' is the reduction of meaningful practice to physical movement, immediate and commensurable. The reduction of practice to behaviour is a central feature of capitalist social relations, of the alienation experienced on the factory floor. But we would argue that people do not behave in the sense that animals behave (see Chapter 6), they *act* and the difference between behaviour and practice or action is of fundamental significance. Humans must be conceived as sentient social beings living in a symbolically structured reality which is, essentially, of their own creation. Behaviour is to action as the immanent to the actual, as the precondition for what actually is. To reduce action to behaviour rather than leading to valid explanations in fact directly eschews anything which might be properly termed explanatory. We are left with the imagery of a plastic, malleable cultural dope incapable of altering the conditions of his or her existence and always subject to the vagaries of external non-social forces beyond mediation or any realistic form of active intervention. Sahlins (1976) has discussed at length the political and theoretical implications of sociobiology and subjected it to a lengthy critique and these arguments will not be repeated here. The 'threat' from sociobiology, especially as evinced in the work of Wilson (1975, 1978), the most widely read but least satisfactory discussions, comes from the line of argument that human social behaviour is determined by a combination of genes and environment; concomitantly the only political action which could alter social life as it is today would be eugenic. Rather than stress this aspect of the debate we will suggest that a biological evolutionary perspective, when transferred to the activities of human beings, collapses with the redundancy argument, i.e. that what people spend most of their time doing is completely redundant in terms of conferring any possible selective benefit. The sheer complexities of human social activities go substantially beyond the basic necessities of survival. Palaeolithic cave art is in no way explained by reference to cultural adaptation to climatic change (Jochim 1983b). Human social action is the product of the symbolic praxis of people in and on the world, it is inherently meaningful and 99% of this action has no direct survival value in terms of conveying any definite selective advantage. The archaeological record is, primarily, a record of *style*, i.e. ways of acting or accomplishing ends according to varying orientations to the world and with reference to individual and group social strategies and power relationships, which may not be assimilated or reduced to functional or adaptive necessity. The biological evolutionary thesis cannot even begin to accommodate or explain why people should produce elaborately decorated ceramics, create ceremonial structures, make thousands of different types of tool forms; the list can be almost infinitely extended. The perspective leaves us with such statements as 'In a cultural frame, many specific trait forms may lack adaptive value, but a reservoir of variability, some of which may ultimately acquire adaptive value with changing conditions, has a clear selective value.' (Dunnell 1978, p. 199). What is supposed to be adaptive is left on one side. In what circumstances, for instance, would a pottery vessel decorated with curvilinear lines have a selective value over one with scalene triangles? This question is not trivial or extreme or even 'suitably chosen' since similar questions can be raised in relation to the entire gamut of human culture, material or non-material. In order to work at all, the sociobiological evolutionary perspective must reduce the almost limitless variety of human action and material production to self-sameness and, in doing so, destroys that which it purports to explain. In this restrictive sense the theory *is* dehumanizing.

Statistics, mathematics and objectivity

The enormous increase in the utilization of statistical and mathematical analysis is a characteristic feature of much of archaeology since the 1960s. It is often justified as merely being a formalization of what archaeologists have always done. Naturally, according epistemological and ontological primacy to the 'facts', the objects of archaeological knowledge, provides a powerful rationale for the use of mathematics and statistics which have become part of the rationalization of archaeological practice aimed at expelling the subjective. Statistical practice is conceived as a technical and therefore neutral practice including the collection, processing, assessment and presentation of facts. It meets the need for generalization based on objective data, controlling for subjective bias, and meets the requirement for practical rules for deciding when generalization is justified or when data are inadequate. These needs accompany the conception of reality as the observable, of theory being brought into agreement with and affirming reality, of the facts being theory-neutral and intersubjectively acceptable. Above all else the use of statistics is related to the requirement for theory to be value-free.

Statistical practice is rooted in quantification, providing value-free methods of drawing conclusions from quantified data. But quantification also results in the disqualification of the object and its redefinition in terms of the primary qualities of number, extension and motion, which are readily treated mathematically. This relates to objectivity being abstractly conceived, as universal and ruled by equivalence. Quantification thus presents data – that which is 'given' – in standardized and comparable form. Adorno and Horkheimer comment that 'mathematical formalism, whose medium is number, the most abstract form of the immediate . . . holds thinking firmly to mere immediacy. Factuality wins the day; cognition is restricted to its repetition; and thought becomes mere tautology' (Adorno and Horkheimer 1979, p. 27).

Standardized and comparable data facilitate calculation. Disqualification, precision, calculability, prediction ultimately mean control. In this way quantification is dissolution of mythology – 'anthropomorphism, the projection onto nature of the subjective' (Adorno and Horkheimer 1979, p. 6). Nature is realized as universal objectivity, stuff of control; and society is second nature.

In quantified archaeology categories of analysis are necessarily designed to enable certain calculations to be made; they are methodological. In the very process of production facts are pre-censored according to the norm of the understanding which later governs their apprehension. Again the structure of the object is neglected in favour of a general methodology.

Of course statistics have long been recognized as requiring careful interpretation and being open to misuse. But the problem is seen as one of social responsibility, misuse arising from technical ineptitude or deliberate mis-manipulation. Statistical theory remains neutral, tied to objectivity. The solution is seen as being more knowledge of statistics and social responsibility in their utilization (Huff 1973; see Griffiths, Irvine and Miles 1979, pp. 347ff.).

Mathematical archaeology

Quantification, motivated by a belief in the objectivity of exactness and calculability, leads eventually to mathematization – the conception of the archaeological record in terms of neutral patterns and relations capable of precise definition and expression in terms of formulae.

The classic expression of mathematization is the volume *Transformations* (Renfrew and Cooke (eds.) 1979). Explanation is represented as the subsumption of the particular beneath generalities:

> Most of the contributors to this book would agree that the appropriate path to
> understanding is generalisation, that is, the formulation of general relation-
> ships between events and between processes, of which specific individual
> occurrences and phenomena can be seen as concrete expressions or mani-
> festations. (Renfrew 1979a, p. 5)

Mathematics provides the generalities, abstract and precise definitions of relationships.
Abstract in that it is purely formal, mathematics unifies scientific fields of studies and
overcomes the problem of scale. History becomes the unfolding of universal relations:

> We may therefore, if we wish, think of different societies, at different periods
> and localities, as being transformations of one another, with the individuals of
> society S transferred into those of society S'. (ibid., p. 38)

Renfrew stresses that this is not to deny the importance of the individual, of the human.
But the human element is strangely regarded as idiosyncrasy (ibid., p. 37) and circumstantial detail (ibid., p. 5). 'No threat is offered to the *magic* of human experience, to the
authentic force and *irrationality* of the passions' (ibid., p. 4, our emphasis). In the end
we are left with the impression that idiosyncratic and irrational human subjectivity
opposes regular, precise and predictable objectivity. It is only in so far as humans can
be transformed into regular and predictable objects that they are important. Neander-
thal man appears in modern dress (ibid., p. 38) and you wouldn't recognize him in the
street. We are all mathematically human and have been so for as long as matters. The
rest is magic and in Renfrew's light-hearted finale from Osbert Lancaster's *Draynflete
Revealed* the present becomes magically unveiled as the past, its transformation. We
rediscover our essentially mathematical selves, and in our obsession with immediacy
and factuality discover the inevitability of the present being as it is; it becomes objectively necessary.

 Transformations marks the end of the programme of the new archaeology, its logical
conclusion. Mathematical calculability has become substituted for archaeological
knowledge. This is seen most vividly in Renfrew's application of catastrophe theory
(Renfrew 1979b). It depends on the use of a purely mathematical theory, formal symbolic logic, which is true in itself. The theory can only be applied to archaeological data.
It cannot be tested in any way. The archaeological data are fitted to the theorem. This
forces Renfrew into a position with which we would agree, that knowledge of the
archaeological record cannot be reduced to the outcomes of testing processes. However,
within the framework of the new archaeology this is heresy. On the other hand, the new
archaeology has always looked to the construction of formal symbolic logic as an ultimate goal (e.g., Clarke 1968, p. 62). This goal, when reached, destroys archaeology
because it is not ultimately the data that matter any more but the internal coherence of
the statistics to which they are fitted. It is the development of the statistics that provides
the key to future work, not the conceptualization of the data. At least, the latter is placed
in very much a subsidiary and peripheral role. Mathematical coherence replaces
archaeological knowledge. Mathematization results in the dissolving of the physicality
of the objects of archaeological knowledge in terms of the logical or mathematical
relations. The very notion of objective substance opposed to subjectivity disappears.

In the quest for a unified and objective past a mathematical past becomes an ideational, subjective past. Reality is approached in an instrumentalist framework. Orton views mathematics as a cognitive instrument and a universal tool. It is not confined merely to being a technique to be used in data analysis (Orton 1980, p. 216) but 'mathematics can be used as a tool for organising one's thoughts and data, and as such is of value to any archaeologist, whatever his philosophy, and whether he works in the field, laboratory, study or armchair' (ibid., p. 13). Here reason is explicitly reduced to instrumentalism. It is an organ of calculation, of coordination, of planning. Reason becomes detached from decision as mathematical reason itself decides the means of approach to the past. The purpose, the aims of a study of the past are attributed to the calculating subject. Reason is detached from the decision to apply reason, the electronic calculator or computer from the creative impulse behind model building, from justifications. The latter can only be circumstantial detail, subjective and arbitrary. As mathematics is purely formal, it can only become meaningful when meaning itself has been discarded. Objective substance, the past, is 'the mere stuff of control . . . instrumentality which lends itself to all purposes and ends – instrumentality per se, "in-itself"' (Marcuse 1964, p. 156). In effect, this results in a suspension of judgement on what reality is, its meaning. For mathematization meaning is a meaning-less question. This is the inevitable conclusion to a belief in the objectivity of precision and calculability.

Yet the self-contained formalism of mathematical explanation is related to its opposite, totally and equally meaningless empiricism, the attempt to merely record all the facts without any subjective content or bias. Both arise as part of a seemingly unbridgeable gap between the theoretical and the empirical, between knowledge arising from within and from without; symptoms of reification: 'the abstract categorising and, as it were, administrative thinking of the former corresponds in the latter to the fetishism of an object blind to its genesis' (Adorno 1967, p. 33). In analysis subject is split from object. What in actuality must arise from the dialectical relationship of subject to object (subject-object), is instead regarded as subjectiveless objectivity (Marcuse 1978, p. 475).

Reason as method: a logistical archaeology

Reason is identified with method and as such does not decide aims or purpose but refers instead to the implementation of techniques and strategies. It excludes choice of value systems which determine ends. Thought thus becomes a form of logistics in which ends are separate from means, values from method. Reason regulates the relationship between method and pre-given aims, ends, purposes, behind the study of the past. Logistical archaeology is a radical contradiction between technique and method, and understanding, viewpoint and aim.

If reason is accepted as rational method, how are we to decide between different aims, different attitudes towards the past, different models, within the framework of rational method? Three positions can be taken on such a decision.

(1) The decision to adopt a particular approach may be attributed to irrational intuition, subjective decision. Reason as method has no way of judging between differing con-

ceptions of humanity and society. Palaeoeconomy is thus just as valid as a structural-Marxist approach, providing it adheres to rational method (adherence to immediate fact, etc.). It just assumes a different model of humanity and whether or not this model of humanity is correct is a matter not open to rational argument (Jarman, Bailey and Jarman (eds.) 1982, p. 3); such argumentation is beyond science.

The result is a passive, disabling and repressive pluralism. The question of different approaches is not just a question of differently tinted spectacles through which are seen the same facts, the same past. Some have valued such a pluralism as a strength of archaeology, stressing the final consensus (Clarke 1968, p. 21). But the colour of the spectacles matters as does who made them and who is wearing them. Pluralism cannot be indiscriminate, similarly tolerant of any approach, abstracted from society and history, passive, tolerating damaging attitudes and ideas. As such, it neutralizes any opposition to the tyranny of the majority, dismissing it as just another pair of glasses.

In Chapter 1 we argued instead for a radical, active pluralism, a pluralism which recognizes that object and interpretation are never identical and that all interpretation is time-bound, determinately related to the moment of its event, historically, socially. Such a pluralism takes sides and doesn't protect that falsity which would contradict and counteract the possibility of a liberated humanity; it is a pluralism directed towards a definite end. We argue for true discussion of alternative approaches, realizing the root of 'discussion' in the Latin *discutio* – to cut apart, smash to pieces; not consensus then, but distinguishing and cutting away false approaches, breaking neutral consensus, asserting disagreement.

(2) A different form of rationality may form the basis of the subjective decision to adopt a particular approach. One approach may be judged superior to another through an ethical argument seen as objective and perhaps given transcendental justification. This would seem to be the basis of the sort of criticism of the 'new' archaeology given by, among others, Hawkes (1968), that it is fundamentally dehumanizing. Also Winter (1984) has acknowledged that value systems apply to the practice of investigating the past. But such values, 'human frailty', are separate from the scientific, rational study of the past; 'most of our research decisions are based at least in part on value statements. It is only after these decisions have been made *on ethical grounds* that a scientific approach can be used to understand human behaviour' (Winter 1984, p. 47, our emphasis). So ethical ends are separate from scientific method, and the objectivity of the latter can be protected from consciousness-raising: 'once we have recognised the presence of value-statements in archaeology it should be possible to separate them from the scientific approach' (ibid., p. 42).

(3) The choice between different approaches may be made according to technicist recommendations of utility, efficiency, economy and comprehensiveness (technique) and objectivity (agreement with immediate empirical reality). These *values*, which are internal to technical reason, are permitted in that they are not recognized as values. So different approaches are evaluated through reference to the degree of accordance with rational method. According to Binford and Sabloff (Binford 1982; Binford and Sabloff

1983), scientific explanation is separate from 'paradigmatic understanding' – *beliefs* about the way the world is, 'everyday cultural bias' (Binford 1982, p. 126). They argue for a *rational* choice of paradigm, putting points of view to the test; paradigms can be rationally assessed according to their utility.

Any explanation produced by rational scientific method operating on neutral objectivity supposedly stands on its own; it is self-grounded. Conclusions must follow from initial assumptions and require no additional contradictory assumptions. Contradiction within this process of knowledge, as we have argued, refers to pathological thinking, defective subjectivity requiring therapy. So explanation can be divorced from the social context of its production and associated value systems. The validity of any approach can be determined independently of personal commitment, without reference to moral or political position. As Gouldner puts it, such rationalism

> entails silence about the speaker, about his interests and his desires, and how these are socially situated and structurally maintained. Such a rationality does not understand itself as an historically produced discourse but as suprahistorical and supracultural, as the sacred, disembodied word: *Logos*.
>
> (1976, p. 50)

The objectivity of scientific method is stressed as opposed to the 'psychological' objectivity of the ideal observer who eliminates bias through conscious will (Binford and Sabloff 1983, p. 395).

> The accuracy of our knowledge of the past can be measured . . . The yardstick of measurement is the degree to which propositions about the past can be confirmed or refuted through hypothesis testing – not by passing judgement on the personal qualifications of the person putting forth the propositions.
>
> (Binford 1972, p. 90)

Quantification then, and not qualification. Objectivity – a measure of value of any approach rests 'with the design characteristics of a methodology and the procedures of its implementation rather than with the characteristics of a particular observer' (Binford 1982, pp. 126–8). Rational method, empiricist science, will cure the pathology of all thought which might retain 'subjective' links with the context of its event.

But crucially, these *moral* decisions behind archaeology as science, which define the process and object of knowledge, subvert the apparent subjective freedom in choosing different approaches.

> Any prior guidelines relieve us of moral decisions; following one means surrendering both reason and freedom, for 'binding moral directives do not exist'. On the one hand, the currently dominant form of reason serves as such a guideline which suspends the freedom of autonomous judgement; on the other, its particular form makes value decisions a private matter – which lets its use appear as the voluntary choice of individuals whose decision-making ability it has just suspended. (Gebhardt 1978, p. 392)

Justifications and the meaning of archaeology

Habermas has written of an end to epistemology:

> Positivism marks the end of the theory of knowledge. In its place emerges the philosophy of science. Transcendental-logical inquiry into the conditions of possible knowledge aimed as well at explicating the meaning of knowledge as such. Positivism cuts off this enquiry, which it conceives as having become meaningless in virtue of the fact of the modern sciences. Hence transcendental inquiry into the conditions of possible knowledge can be meaningfully pursued only in the form of methodological inquiry into the rules for the construction and corroboration of scientific theories. (1972, p. 67)

In concentrating on rules of procedure, those who apply the rules are irrelevant. Rational method is independent of the archaeologist; formal logic, mathematics and statistics have universal validity. There is no questioning of the subjective constitution of objectivity; 'the meaning of knowledge itself becomes irrational – in the name of rigorous knowledge' (ibid., p. 69). In this framework, the only acceptable justification for archaeology is that archaeology is part of the 'human' quest for knowledge and truth. There is no attempt to question the meaning or function of the object of archaeology because there is no source of knowledge outside the object. Archaeology is consequently not reflexive; it is not conscious of itself as practice in a capitalist civilization. Instead it becomes a tool, an instrument, probing the past in the service of the present.

The identification of rational method with truth together with ideas of value-freedom and objectivity justify the archaeological project but as we have argued, these ideas have no meaning in a scientific sense. They are value judgements, prior guidelines. The methodological or syntactical criterion of meaning is spiritual. The origin of this spiritual meaning, the impulse to the acceptance of a commitment to rational method, was and is the success of scientific capitalism. So any justification for archaeology, any definition of the meaning of archaeological practice is, within this framework, irrational – separate from the practice it claims to justify. There is an unbridgeable chasm between the social practice of archaeology and any reason given for engaging in this practice. (See also Chapter 1, pp. 25–6.)

Facts and values, ideology and criticism

Our claim is that a great deal of archaeology is ideological practice, practice which sustains and justifies a capitalist present. Objectivity, rational scientific method, facts as opposed to subjective values and attitudes – this is an historically specific rational discourse which tends towards an argument for capitalism through appeal to the facts. There has been some criticism already of the ideology, its supportive relation to contemporary society, work which we discuss in Chapters 1 and 4. Here we emphasize the need to avoid reducing the critique of ideology to an assertion of relativism: the contention that every social group has its own equally valid way of looking at and explaining the past. It is also important to avoid making ideology critique simply a form of consciousness-raising: pointing out the inclusion of values derived from contemporary society into research that they might be the more easily isolated and excluded.

Value-freedom, as the attempt to eradicate values, precludes the very possibility of taking a critical stance on society and is consequently supportive of the status quo. The notion of value-freedom is, of course, itself a value which is by no means normatively neutral. Value-freedom commits those who wish to retain it to a rejection of a critique of the existing social order and therefore forces them to political conservatism, and so, the abandonment in and through practice of the claims for neutrality made. Consider the following statements made by those who advocate archaeology in a very explicit manner as a 'hard' positivist law-seeking science.

> A lesson which can be drawn from the study of prehistory is that wars, star-vation, exploitation and conservation are not simply moral, ethical or political issues. There is an important, indeed a primary biological component to these phenomena, *without recognition of which no really effective consideration of them can be made* . . . The possible demonstration that there are laws which govern human behaviour in the long term ought to have an effect on the way in which we view our behaviour today.
>
> (Jarman, Bailey and Jarman (eds.) 1982, p. 12, emphasis in original)

Now, this 'lesson', even in terms of the rationalist discourse in which it is situated, is hardly unequivocally established from the 'facts'. In reality the lesson is *given* to palaeo-economists in 'knowledge' since prehistory is, at the outset, viewed from a biological perspective, so that what is 'discovered' is already there in theory prior to any investi-gation having taken place. We can scarcely believe that those responsible for this state-ment would want to support it, for it has definite social and political implications which are very far from being value-free. It can be used to defend any indefensible action and results in an abrogation of moral responsibility for anything that happens. To return to the present, if the world is plunged into nuclear war this can be justified as inevitable. If a primary biological factor is claimed to be involved then the entire political process is pre-empted.

The lament of High Culture
Clark (1979, 1983) has made a claim for a radical criticism of the present from an archaeological standpoint. Archaeologists, according to Clark, are able to objectively pronounce on the past, its message to the present, its relevance, its value. The objective message, established by archaeologist Grahame Clark, is that the index of our humanity is cultural complexity and diversity which is invariably associated with social hierarchy and inequality. Egalitarian societies dominated by the illiterate peasant lower classes are dull and boring, lacking in cultural achievement. The present, increasingly subject to the 'complacent doctrines of liberal humanism' (1979, p. 5) and with an economic sys-tem based on science and technology is reverting to cultural homogeneity. What is needed is a reassertion of hierarchy and inequality.

There is nothing new in this right-wing nostalgic longing for a pre-industrial order of cultured elite and contented commons and it has nothing to do with critical reflection. It is a variation of the familiar lament for the decline of high culture in mass society.

Avoiding disputes over empirical detail, we make the following comments (*cf.* Swingewood 1977).

(1) Clark presents a simple empirical correlation between ranking and objects judged to represent cultural diversity and achievement. This is a static and reified concept of culture, a rejection of culture as praxis, as concrete production; it is an elimination of the historical roots of cultural production in that a universal aesthetic value judgement is applied uniformly across history. Cultural practice is reduced to 'cultural' artifacts. This notion of cultural value is not related to any concept of the social; the only social variable is ranking. We argue that all cultural production must be understood in relation to specific conditions of production.

(2) Clark's archaeological past is a romanticized and dehistoricized past, a myth of culturally rich and inegalitarian societies benefiting from the creative inspiration of elites. But what about poverty and the oppression of the majority? Justifiable for the sake of a high culture as defined by the Clarks of this and other societies who would attempt to shore up their crumbling political edifices with ideological props?

(3) Clark's conception of modern 'mass' society is unsophisticated in the extreme, an abhorrent affirmation of superior minorities and coarse, sub-human majorities.

Clark's is an argument for the acceptance of inequality through the *assertion* of the necessity of high culture, an *assertion* that this is represented by the immediate appearance of 'cultural diversity', an empirical observation that this is correlated with inequality and social hierarchy, and an application of this to modern society claimed to be reverting to the 'intraspecies homogeneity of a prehuman situation' (1979, p. 13). In his final years Clark has produced a statement of anti-democratic ideological commitment unparalleled in recent archaeology. But the concept of objective cultural value is not at all uncommon. Many, particularly those writing for a non-archaeological audience, would apply a universal standard of cultural value to the past, whether this is seen as cultural diversity, aesthetic quality or whatever; they would appreciate the cultural achievements of an abstract, unhistorical 'humanity'. Such value is attached to artifacts creating a cultural capital, discovered, understood, conceptually owned by an enlightened expert minority, archaeologists and others who teach us of the value of the past, who know about and therefore should make the decisions about the past, its study, its preservation and its presentation (see Chapter 1, pp. 24–6 and Chapter 4, pp. 91–3).

The valuable past
Cultural Resource Management and Rescue are openly concerned with a valuable past. The central feature of each is a 'conservation ethic' (Lipe 1977); the dominant moral issue facing archaeology is that it 'employs a non-renewable phenomenon' (Dunnell 1984, p. 64) which requires management and conservation. So an overriding concern of those planning and executing the destruction of the past is with the *value* of the 'resource base', the significance of particular features of the past. It is the question of how much money and effort should be spent on particular features. A primary conflict is between different types of value attached to the traces of the past: for example, 'scientific' importance and value to particular research programmes, as opposed to 'symbolic' value to a community.

The past is defined as valuable and must be protected from unscrupulous dealers in antiques, from detector-wielding treasure hunters and from incompetent work by inexperienced amateurs. What are needed, it is claimed, are

(1) general educative measures, inculcation of the conservation ethic – people must value the past (Lipe 1977, 1984; Cleere 1984; Fagan 1984);
(2) international agreements (UNESCO Convention);
(3) protective legislation (1906 Federal Antiquities Act and the 1979 Archaeo-logical Resources Protection Act in the USA, and the Ancient Monuments and Archaeological Areas Act 1979 in the UK; see McGimsey and Davis 1984 and Cleere 1984);
(4) professional accreditation and professional codes of ethics – it must be clear who the real archaeologists are, who truly value the past (the Society of Professional Archaeologists (1984a and 1984b) in the USA, the Museums Association and the Institute of Field Archaeologists in the UK).

At the heart of these codes of ethics and values and protective measures are traditional academic values of scholarship, objectivity, responsibility to and respect for colleagues and public, supplemented by business values of efficient management of the 'resource base'.

So value (objectified value) is attached to the objects of the past and accepted values protect the professional expert status of those who apply rational method to the past, who exert control over the past. The message conveyed by the past and revealed by the expert and the system of values associated with rational method are further legitimated in this recognition of value. The sins of archaeology (dependence on values) are confessed to salve the guilty conscience of the origins of its values in contemporary capitalism.

Conclusions: notes towards a critical archaeology

> The question whether objective truth can be attributed to human thinking is not a question of theory but is a *practical question*. Man must prove the truth, i.e. the reality and power, the this-sidedness of his thinking in practice. The dispute over the reality or non-reality of thinking that is isolated from practice is a purely *scholastic* question.
>
> (Second Thesis on Feuerbach, Marx 1970, p. 121)

We cannot cut ourselves off from questions of value, retreating into a supposedly untainted realm of objectivity, nor can we disconnect 'value' and shunt it off into a separate field of aesthetics, political or social relevance, or whatever. By attempting to ignore values we are cutting ourselves off from our work and are unwittingly denying our essential integrity as social persons living in social worlds. The distinction between fact and value arises from a fundamental error. It is a denial of the essentially active role of the subject in research. A value-free approach sets up a view of the subject as renegade or treacherous. The subject observer must deny self in order to adequately deal with the facticity of the object. This radical scepticism of the self is both impossible to achieve and, if carried through, would prevent any research at all: no values amounts to no meanings and without meanings no investigation. Because prehistoric people are dead and gone it is only too easy to treat them as mere objects to be shoved around at will, subject to the whims of technocratic reason. But in betraying their humanity we betray our own. In the instrumental attempt to create an objective past we are cutting ourselves off from sources of meaning and so ultimately destroying that which we seek to understand. Prehistoric settlement sites, for example, when transformed into spatial nodes responding to the dictates of an abstract rationality are deformed. The intentional structures of the people who lived in them and imbued them with meanings and significance are considered unimportant. Social meaning has been taken away and pure calculus substituted. We destroy the richness we want to investigate and create a world purged and divested of meaning, an unreal alienated world. This is the world of physicalism, of extension, of geometric form, of number, which has been declared as real, while everything else has been condemned as fictional magic. This is the world in which people do not matter. It is the world of capitalism.

Archaeology embraces a programme which makes of artifacts, people and their relationships objects and objective process. Subject is split from object, archaeologists from their data, past from present. Formal methods stipulate in advance what is to be discovered; the structure of the past is neglected in favour of general objective method. The abandonment of a pretence of value-freedom is vital to overcoming these problems.

To abandon objectivity based on value-freedom is to accept that meaning is not contained within the facts but arises from interaction between archaeologist and data. We have already argued in Chapter 2 that observation is dependent on theory. We emphasize here that theory is value-laden and values form an integral part of the object of study. To define or describe an artifact according to immediately given attributes is not enough because an object always has a surplus of meaning over and above any definition or description. A definition or description can never be identical with or sufficiently summarize the complexity of the overlapping relational aspects of an object. Any single definition or description applies only to a particular frame of reference which is necessarily value-laden. The particular perspective from which an object or event is viewed is an integral part of the object of study. Concepts and categories of analysis are internal to, they constitute the object of study; they are not separate from what they are categories of. So there can be no formal and general method separate from the structure of the object of study; 'methods do not rest upon methodological ideals but rather upon reality' (Adorno 1976a, p. 109).

Archaeology must become reflexive: archaeology needs to consider itself as much as the past. To recognize that meaning does not just reside in the objects of the past but in the *study of the past* is to recognize that archaeology is a *practice* today. Knowledge is not produced by passively receiving individuals acting somehow as mirrors to the world but by interacting social groups evaluating what is to count as knowledge communally. The generation of knowledge does not just arise from individual psychology but from definite social conditions. The maintenance of knowledge is not just to be explained in the manner in which it measures up to 'objective' reality. So, as we argued in Chapter 1, archaeology is a rhetorical practice, historically situated, part of contemporary society and inherently political. The social function and meaning of a theory or explanation forms part of its validity. As rhetoric, archaeology cannot be separated from its audience. There is a practical dimension to validity which is not to be correlated with the 'objective' elimination of temporal and spatial variables. It is not only what we term 'data' which constitutes evidence; practical questions must also enter into archaeological explanations. We should concern ourselves not so much with the 'truth' or 'falsity' of various statements. Rather we should ask: who are these statements relevant to and why? what kind of archaeology do they serve to produce? Truth is a practical matter not an absolute. So we may legitimately distinguish those archaeologies which give support to the existing social order, reifying people and their relationships, treating them instrumentally. These are not matters external to theory.

Values cannot be eradicated from archaeology. They are built into the very terminology and language we use and into the act of using them. We should attempt to make the values we bring to research explicit and subject the values to critical scrutiny. This will not only produce a more realistic view of the past, as history, irrevocably linked with and mediated by the present; it will also be a more honest view of what we are doing. The ideology of contemporary archaeology cannot be 'cured' by detaching an ideological dimension, by correcting cognitive failure or by making increased attempts to purge ourselves of our values. Accepting archaeology as practice, truth as constituted in practice, is to accept truth as precarious, written into political relations. It is to accept the necessity of a radical and anarchic undercutting of all those theories in search of a timeless and objective truth which would justify the present, the necessity of ideology critique. The kind of reflexive and critical archaeology we propose is not just another approach. To argue that a critical archaeology merely asks different questions and supplements already established approaches is to treat critical archaeology as another formal body of principles, a method outside history; it is to slot it on the shelf in the academic supermarket, neatly packaged next to behavioural archaeology, for anyone to take down and consume at will. A critical archaeology is not merely a way of working, it is a way of living.

4

Presenting the past: towards a redemptive aesthetic for the museum

> 'The task to be accomplished is not the conservation of the past, but the redemption of the hopes of the past. Today, however, the past is preserved as the destruction of the past.'
> (Adorno and Horkheimer 1979, p. xv)

Introduction

Chapter 3 argued for a critically reflexive archaeology which of necessity includes an assessment of the relation of the archaeologist and his or her work to contemporary capitalism, while Chapter 1 argued the necessity of taking archaeology's presentation to an audience into account, that archaeology is a rhetoric. Archaeologists present themselves and their work to a non-archaeological public through the media, publishing media, actual physical confrontation (archaeological sites, education), and the museum. This chapter considers the presentation of archaeological work, the interpreted artifact, in the museum which is probably the main institutional connection between archaeology as a profession and discipline, and wider society.

This chapter is intended as an ideology critique, a critique of the museum as an ideological institution. The museum may directly misrepresent the past, distorting it through selection and classification, creating a particular historical narrative. The museum may also restructure the past through its code of historical representation, the *way* it tells its 'story', the way the artifact is presented (*cf.* Berger *et al.* 1972; Bann 1978).

There are several effective critiques of the way museums directly distort the past as a means of legitimating present sectional interests (Leone 1981b, 1984; Wallace 1981; see also Horne 1984). We shall concentrate more on the museum's aesthetic. In presenting artifacts to be viewed by a visiting public, museums make a statement about the relation of the viewing visitor to the object world. The artifacts are assembled and presented, ordered to make a particular sense to the viewing visitor. Artifacts are mobilized in an aesthetic system (a system of presentation and viewing) to create meanings. We shall be considering this statement, this aesthetic system.

The main part of the chapter is a presentation of a series of interpretations of particular museums and displays. They are not interpretations of a random sample, but neither were the particular museums chosen to make criticism easier. We simply visited a few museums we knew. The series of interpretations builds up a critique of the presentation of the artifact in various forms of museum display. Drawing on the discussion of time in Chapter 1 we argue that the artifact is turned into a commodity and in effect removed from history. This confirms the present's relation with the object world. It is the present which is preserved, not the past.

We then move on to consider further aspects of the relation between past and present in the museum, the relationship between professional study of the artifact and its subsequent 'public' presentation. Continuing the argument of Chapter 1, we argue against the possibility of a neutral presentation of an objective past by professional archaeologist or curator. All presentation of the artifactual past is rhetorical performance, an active project of persuasion, an active mobilization of particular modes of presentation which, in the museums we considered, argue for the world as it immediately appears to us, concealing the underlying reality of past and present.

We end by drawing out ideas for a more fertile relation between past artifact and presentation, one which recognizes and assumes that the study of the past artifact and its present-ation are inseparable. We reassert that a non-ideological and critically reflexive archaeology cannot be separated from its presentation to a wider social world of people who are not archaeologists.

PART ONE: THE MUSEUMS

The artifact transformed into an object in commodified time

The Museum of Antiquities of the University and Society of Antiquaries of Newcastle upon Tyne: a small museum with two galleries. The first contains a selection of Roman inscribed and sculptured stones, mainly altars and tombstones, from the North-East. There are also models of a Roman milecastle, fort, turret, vallum, and the wall itself. Some cases are used for temporary displays. The second gallery consists of a sequence of cases presenting artifacts from the North-East in chronological order. The artifacts are sometimes juxtaposed with no implied connection other than chronological, are sometimes placed together according to similar type or site of discovery.

The format of the guidebook, a series of photographed exhibits with accompanying notes and references, clearly expresses the organizing metaphor of the museum: the artifact as chronological object, object of academic study, the artifact as specimen. In a mechanical relation of metonymy the artifacts stand for archaeological system.

In the second gallery the cases locate a collection of local artifacts in their archaeological period – prehistoric to medieval. The logical principle uniting the sequence of cases is abstract time, time as a flow divided into conventional lengths – early, middle and late Bronze Age, Iron Age, Roman, Anglo-Saxon. The only appreciable narrative behind the sequence of cases is a story of technological change. This is change abstracted from the social; it is a story of the production of variety.

The artifacts are conceptually packaged with labels indicating provenance, type and museum accession number. Any further packaging is limited to the descriptive background: some text and some small models. The artifacts stand in the cases with their academic price-tags. Price indicated by price-tag is the abstract exchange-value of goods in a shop window; the abstract exchange-value of the artifacts is their being objects for academic study, their antiquarian interest, their academic objectivity.

The objects stand solitarily. The people who made them are irretrievably out of sight and out of mind. (There are figures of Roman soldiers in cases offset from the main sequence, but significantly their armour is replica armour.) The historical subjectivity which constituted the objects is denied in their formal identity proclaimed by the labels uniting the objects according to academic exchange-principle. The objects are formally equivalent; like commodities in a supermarket their ultimate meaning lies in their formal identity, commodities to be bought, 'historical' objectivity to be decoded by the initiate, manipulated by detached academic subjectivity. The objects are before the visitor in certainty and presence, subjected to archaeological analysis.

The objects form a spatial figure rather than a temporal process; they are cartographically located according to an ontologically and temporally depthless system of archaeological referents. The past is seen, the visitor is distanced, dis-interested, 'observer of the ultimately familiar or autonomous picture in which temporality – its threats and its possibilities – has been annulled' (Spanos 1977, p. 427).

The objects are familiar: the immediate significance of the exhibited objects lies in their relation to contemporary objects, an unremarkable relation of resemblance and difference usually focussing on recognition of function (they had axes in the bronze age!), and appreciation of technical and artistic skill. But in the absence of their determinate social context the meaning of the artifacts lies in their abstract objectivity. The artifacts are objects. Archaeological history stands before the visitor as fetishized objectivity, a detached objectivity mysterious to the visitor, truly fetishistic. A typical label reads:

BELL – DERIVATIVE BEAKER
BOREWELL FARM, SCREMERSTON, N'D
Clarke 706   Class W/MR –
N/MR Hybrid   1948.7

As a coded set the objects are raw data, objective substance, ready to be worked up into descriptive archaeological narrative. This narrative is implied but almost totally absent from the exhibition. Only the models attest to its possibility.

As we have said, in the second gallery the objects are located by the cases in time, in their archaeological period. The cases themselves represent empty time, time as a container, formal and devoid of social content, but nevertheless filled with the content of archaeology – objects; objects in cases; objects in time. The cases are the content-less temporal form in which the objects are brought to exist.

But time is not a non-relational container of the reality of the past. The reduction of temporality to measured duration separated from the 'content' of the past is an objectification, a commodification of time. So History becomes rooted in empty measured duration, a rigid continuum of ephemerality, a sequence of empty instants. The past exists only in these moments, only in its present. It is over and done with, complete, an 'autonomous picture'. The past thus appears fleeting and distant from the present.

And commodified time is capitalism's factory time (Thompson 1963, 1967; Giddens 1981; Lowe 1982). As John Berger puts it: 'the factory which works all night is a sign of the victory of a ceaseless, uniform and remorseless time. The factory continues even during the time of dreams' (Berger and Mohr 1982, p. 107).

Remorseless commodified time is the mythical time of the always the same, empty, homogeneous time (Wolin 1982, p. 48; Benjamin 1973e, esp. Theses XIII and XIV).

The visitor is presented with mythical Fate incessantly piling ruin upon shattered ruin, object upon object in an inescapable and rigid continuum of empty moments. Beakers and axe-heads appear in rows; tombstones and altars stand lined up, worn with time. Commodification brings a vision of mythical compulsion to repeat, a failure of memory, a Great Myth, 'the reproduction of the always-the-same under the semblance of the perpetually new' – commodity production (Wolin 1982, p. 174). History appears as commodity production; the objects in the cases are ultimately familiar because things have always been the same. Commodified time denies remembrance, memory of difference. In this sense the reification which the objectification of the artifact represents is a forgetting (Adorno and Horkheimer 1979, p. 230). 'History no longer pays its respects to the dead; the dead are simply what it has passed through' (Berger and Mohr 1982, p. 107). People are the objects, the debris of such a history, forgotten. This is the injustice of the empty cases of objects.

'The factory continues even during the time of dreams': commodified time marginalizes subjective experience of time – individual memory and other forms of experience which have the capacity to undo, unify and deny the ceaseless passing of empty moments (see Berger and Mohr 1982, pp. 105–6). In proclaiming chronometric history's monopoly of time the museum bypasses the question of other forms of objective as well as subjective temporality (see Chapter 1) and the historical roots of commodified time.

The objects have been 'discovered'. The labels indicate provenance and information is given about circumstances of discovery of hoards and valuable objects, but not as a means of adding a geographical dimension to the understanding of the visitor – no maps are provided which indicate either distribution of exhibits or of artifacts of similar type and date. The reference to provenance communicates the idea of space as a non-relational container, an abstract existent analogous to the representation of time within which the substantive object is located. The inclusion of provenance on the labels communicates mere abstract 'discovery'. Subjectivity stands coolly apart from the objectivity of the artifact, seemingly passive yet with an instrumental relation to History, an empty screen of chronometric time onto which it projects the empirical.

But 'discovery' is fascinating. It is part of the romance of archaeology. 'Discovery' links past and present, reaching out from incessant passing of the momentary present, bridging the chasm between past and present opened up by the conception of time as an empty spatial dimension filled with artifacts locked into their respective presents, their archaeological periods.

But this resolution of the tension between past and present is a spurious harmony. The past is not *merely* discovered. 'Discovery' is not an abstract instant of capturing the past. The shock of the moment of discovery shatters the continuity of abstract, commodified time; it is a shock of discontinuity which reveals the present's practical relation to the past object.

The aesthetic artifact
The British Museum: Greek antiquities: we refer in this section to the typical form of presentation found in the great international museums – free-standing sculpture,

ceramics in cases, presented with minimum supporting information, e.g. the Parthenon sculptures.

> In the Russian ikon neither space nor time exists. It addresses the eye, but the eye which then shuts in prayer so that the image – now in the mind's eye – is isolated and entirely spiritualised. Yet the images are not introspective – that would already make them too personal; nor are they . . . mystical; their calm expressions suggest no exceptional experience. They are images of holy figures seen in the light of a heaven in which the people believe so as to make the visible world around them *credible*.
>
> (Berger 1969, pp. 20–1)

Parallel to the homogeneous spatial figure of the past found in the Museum of Antiquities, Newcastle, is the encapsulation of the past in the self-bounded, sealed-off, inclusive image – the artifact as ikon (Spanos 1977, p. 427). This aestheticization of the artifact is a romantic reaction to the commodification of the past. The lifeless, inert objectivity of analytical study is replaced (or supplemented) by the aesthetic productivity of *Homo Artifex*.

Fig. 4.1 The aesthetic artifact.

The artifact is displayed in splendid remoteness from the prosaic, from the exigencies of day-to-day life. The concrete and historically variable *practice* of production and consumption is collapsed into the 'aesthetic', an isolatable and universal human experience. Instead of abstract objectivity, the abstract experience of the aesthetic becomes the exchange-value of the artifact which is again raised to the status of a solitary fetish, a fetish of immanent 'humanity'. Now the formal identity of artifacts in terms of objectivity becomes a formal identity according to spiritual truth, universal values expressed in the exceptional artifact. History is again unified. History freezes in the ideological light of the aesthetic artifact, celebrated and exalted, elevated above everyday life.

Display of the artifact conveys the timeless ability of Man (*sic*) as toolmaker-artist. As such the visitor need only approach the artifact with finely tuned sensibilities; the artifact's universal truth is communicated via direct intuition. But whose sensibilities, whose intuition, whose 'humanity'? As the aesthetic qualities of the artifact are supposedly immediately perceptible, context and critical analysis become relegated to optional supplements.

History is differentiated only according to the unifying principle of the technical and artistic triumph of Man. It is divested of the 'trivia' of oppression, of conflict (other than inwardly spiritual), of everything social. The aesthetic artifact is an escape from the nightmare of history. But all culture shares the guilt of society. The aesthetic artifact 'ekes out its existence only by virtue of injustice already perpetrated in the sphere of production' (Adorno 1967, p. 26).

A constituting subjectivity is now recognized; Man as Homo Artifex is recognized as mastering objectivity, objective substance, investing it with a universal message. But where does he belong, where did he come from? Of course *Homo Artifex* is an abstract conception, detached from history, concealing its origins in the cultural values of particular social groups within history.

Bringing the past alive
The anti-rationalism of aestheticized objectivity is related to the secret worrying antinomies at the heart of bourgeois rationality; the success of the analytics of scientific, instrumental rationality, bringing nature and the past to order under a concealed subjectivity, foregrounds the problem of subjectivity. If science, instrumental analytics (exclusive of subjectivity), is the only firm (objective) basis for archaeological reconstruction, then what about human experience, emotion, imagination?

One answer, as we have shown, is to canonize the 'aesthetic' artifact as Art, as repository of the 'human', detached now from the analytics of archaeology, transcending history.

Another answer to this chasm in conventional approaches to the past is the humanizing narrative – setting the artifacts into their concrete 'human' context. In the museum this is represented by the narrative display which provides contextual information (usually text, diagrams, maps) and the situational display which sets the artifact in a context of contemporary artifacts and features (e.g. the period room).

From another point of view, it has been widely recognized that every visit to a museum is a hermeneutic venture and if museums are to cater for a clientele wider than an initiated elite, the artifacts cannot stand on their own. The visitor faces a slippery indeterminacy in the museum – what do the objects mean? The two forms of display which have so far been discussed implicitly propose their own answers to this question – the meaning of the object lies in its objectivity or in the aesthetic. Narrative and situational types of display approach the semiotic indeterminacy of the artifact more directly through contextual information for the visitor.

Narrative display and the artifact as information
The Museum of London: case displays, free-standing artifacts, room interiors, shop reconstructions, paintings, photographs and much written material are skilfully and efficiently combined to tell the story of London from prehistoric times to the present.

In the Museum of London artifacts are essentially used to authenticate the social description written around them. 'Written', because the museum is in many ways a book around which the visitor may wander. This makes the ultimate message of the past as descriptive information encoded in objects all the more palatable.

The narrative which was implied but absent from the sequence of cases in the Museum of Antiquities is foregrounded in the Museum of London, but again an authentic transcendence of the superficial fact is missed.

The displays convey factual information about the past of London. The Museum of London condenses past social practice and experience into information, information tied to the chronological narrative. Information – the fact – is presented as the dominant form in which social practice is stored – news. But as news belongs to a precise point in time, 'the value of information does not survive the moment it was new. It lives only in that moment; it has to surrender to it completely and explain itself to it without losing any time' (Benjamin 1973c, p. 90). Information lives only in the moment of its novelty. 'In the form of information, experience no longer has anything to teach us; it has simply become another fungible aspect of modern life, an item of momentary interest which will soon cease to be topical and then be promptly discarded' (Wolin 1982, p. 222). The visitor passes from display to display presumably absorbing 'information' and nothing more.

Indeed, 'you have to be buried alive in order to survive' (Dorfman and Mattelart 1975, p. 85). Archaeology is precisely the means to a 'living' past. The past has to be buried alive, experience killed off, stultified, pinned down to the moment of its novelty in order to be meaningful in the present as information, a permanent commodity, property, heritage, all preserved, pickled for the future.

Presence, absence, and the authenticating quote

> ὑπάρχουν, ἡ κίνηση τοῦ προσώπου τὸ σχῆμα τῆς στοργῆς
> ἐκείνων ποὺ λιγόστεψαν τόσο παράξενα μὲς στὴ ζωή μας . . .
>
> ἢ μήπως ὄχι δὲν ἀπομένει τίποτε παρὰ μόνο τὸ βάρος
> ἡ νοσταλγία τοῦ βάρους μιᾶς ὕπαρξης ζωντανῆς

does there exist the movement of the face, shape of the tenderness
of those who've shrunk so strangely in our lives . . .
or perhaps no, nothing is left but the weight
the nostalgia for the weight of a living existence

(from George Seferis 'The King of Asine',
translated by Edmund Keeley and Philip Sherrard)

The Museum of London quotes with objects. It draws on a quality of aura found in the artifact of the past, its authenticity, genuineness, authority, its unique phenomenon of romantic distance however close it might be physically, a distance located in its testimony to the past it has witnessed (Benjamin 1973d, p. 223). The aura of the artifacts, their three-dimensional reality, their facticity, all authenticate the narrative of the Museum of London. This is their purpose.

There is a subtle play of difference at work here:

Presence	Absence
Present	Past
Here now	Distant
Signifier	Signified
Trace	Substance

The objects are immediate and real before us, present to our consciousness and sight. As the concrete past, they confirm the meaning of the presentation. But the objects only represent or indicate the past. The past is the referent signified by the object. The object signifies an absent presence: of course the past is not present here and now, but absent, distant. So the objects are signs in our present. They are not the past immediately present before us but signifiers of the past (the signified), traces of the past (the absent referent). 'When we use signs, the being present of the referent and signified, incarnated in the self-present signifier, appears to us immediately, but it is delusion, misperception, dream. There is neither substance nor presence in the sign, but only the play of differences' – difference between signifier and signified, between signified and referent, between presence and absence (Leitch 1983, p. 44). The objects embody this play of difference which is tied down by the rhetorical agency of interpretation – the Museum of London producing a substantial past before us in the present, presenting a past. And it is by means of the reduction of difference that the Museum of London confirms its message.

The notion of presence is at the heart of the 'romance' of archaeology. It forms the basis of much of archaeology's appeal and popularity. The objects on view in the museum bring us face to face with the past. The objects have presence, human presence – the features of the burial mask, the thumb-print on the pot. This presence constitutes the object's authority, its authenticity. The presence of the past – the past endures and reaches out to touch us.

The authenticating, romantic presence of the museum object is a restricted, one-dimensional notion of presence which reduces the dialectic of presence and absence. It suggests that the time of the artifact can be localized, that the artifact *belongs* to the past, to a moment in time when someone made and used it. This is the romance of the object. Time is thus ultimately abstracted and reduced to a derivative of space; time comes to be composed of ultimately timeless moments on a continuum, its essence lying in the measurable 'distance' between moments. The ambiguity of the artifact – the play of semiotic difference encompassing past and present, its nature as sign in the present to and for a past – is stabilized in the name of a fixed and closed-down History.

George Seferis expresses the disturbing tension between presence and absence, the void behind the burial mask, the presence in the human features; the past is both present and absent. We must grasp the full implications of the opposition presence-absence. The makers of the artifact are absent. It is our rhetorical insistence which requires their presence.

The absent creator of the artifact is longed for – if only it were possible to meet and talk with the people of the past, have *them* present before us. But they are absent and what is left? According to some, the archaeologist is confined to describing the tangible (*cf.* C. Hawkes 1954), doomed to discover only the trivial (Leach 1973). But for the public there is the inspired popularizer, a Michael Wood (1985), a John Romer (1984), who can invoke absent humanity, bring the past alive, make it live, make the people of the past present. The presence of this past *is* our present.

As Eagleton has pointed out (1983, pp. 120–1), structuralism has exposed this humanist fallacy – for archaeology the notion that the artifactual past is a kind of transcript of the living presence of real people who are disturbingly absent. Such a notion actually dematerializes the artifact, reducing it to a mediating element in the present's spiritual encounter with the humanity of the past. Rather, meaning arises through the chronic reciprocity of presence and absence, being and non-being. Meaning is not simply present in the artifact but is in a sense also absent. Meaning is not identical with itself; the artifactual past exhibits a surplus over exact meaning. Meaning is produced in the material practice of reasoning in the present, which is, of course, in no way identical with the past.

The exhibited past

A period room in the Castle Museum, York: moorland cottage

> Typical of the North-East of Yorkshire . . . home-spun and spartan . . . The hearth was the centre of family life, providing not only warmth and comfort, but a place for the old cooking pot to simmer above the glowing peat. Bread was baked here: the dough was mixed in the wooden trough beneath the window. In front of the fire is a home-made rag or 'clip' rug . . . The country made furniture reflects a tradition of unsophisticated craftsmanship, which was about to pass away. Already, on the mantelpiece, there are factory-made trinkets and ornaments – the pair of Staffordshire pottery dogs, the fancy glass rolling pin and walking sticks, and a cheap but cheerful German clock. In the window hangs a 'witch-ball'. Its glass surface was popularly supposed to reflect from the room the stare of any witch or evil eye.   (Official Guidebook)

In situational display artifacts are brought together in an association which will supposedly enable the visitor to decode a meaning through experience of context. Such associations commonly take the form of period rooms. Figures may inhabit the rooms; they may be the intended focus of attention (e.g. costume). Situational display involves lesser or greater degrees of reconstruction to provide a window to the past.

In traditional case display the artifact demands concentrated attention according to the ritual analytics of archaeology. What matters is not so much the artifact being on view as the significance of its existence, its authenticity. Its exhibition to the public is a concession (the Museum of Antiquities, Newcastle, is a university museum). Hence the need for the visitor to be sufficiently initiated to be able to decode the objects.

The aesthetic artifact of the British Museum requires contemplation. Labelling is hardly needed. When exhibited, the aesthetic artifact is to communicate the ritual values of the cult of *Homo Artifex*. Hallowed and venerable achievement, it is the cult-image of *Homo Artifex*, ultimately unapproachable. 'The closeness which one may gain from its subject matter does not impair the distance which it retains in its appearance' (Benjamin 1973d, p. 245). It is, after all, the product of Man.

The period room focusses on the communicative-value, the exhibition-value of the artifact as opposed to cult-value (Benjamin 1973d, pp. 226–7). Situational display attempts to overcome the distance of the past. Artifacts are reassembled into 'realistic' association and no longer stand on their own. The distance between past and present is suspended in an arrested synchronism. Time is suspended and the objects are viewed through the spatial relations of the display, through their present codification (almost always in terms of function).

The visitor is drawn into the space created by the artifacts to discover their 'meaning'. The visitor herself fills the absence within the period room, the absence of a living con-stituting agent. The visitor merges with the other because of her absence, but this absence means that the absent living agent of the past artifact is all the more like the visitor. The visitor becomes the figure in a mirror of her present (see Williamson 1978, pp. 77ff.). But it is not so much the past individual who is absent as the present author.

In the period room cult-value is replaced by exhibition-value – the artifact *requires* display; it necessarily includes a communicative function. The artifacts in the period room do not of necessity require concentrated attention or contemplation. The visitor may examine the past, but absent-mindedly.

The semiotic character of artifacts is recognized. They are used as vehicles to a story of the past, as signs in the present carrying information to the visitor. They are given an explicit communicative function. They are a translucent window onto the past 'as it was', immediate, un-mediated vehicles to a 'realistic' picture of the past, a photograph of the past (*cf*. McLuhan *et al*. 1969, on the pictorial visual form of museum display).

The model of reality behind this notion of the 'realistic' is that of the photograph. The period room is set before the gaze of the omnipresent camera, the clock for making images, for capturing and fixing instants. The period room is 'reality' ready to be photo-graphed, a still life, tableau. But the period room is not so much a 'realist' as a 'naturalist' re-presentation of the past (Berger 1969, pp. 50ff.; *cf*. Lukács 1963, 1980a). The naturalistic display aims to present the immediacy of the past with maximum credibility. It aims at preserving an exact copy of 'the way things were', a replica. There is no other basis for the selection of artifacts to be included in the period room. In this sense naturalism is unselective. The period room shows what there was; it presents an inventory to the visitor and the more complete the inventory the better (Sontag 1979, p. 22). Nor is inventory a simple listing: 'inventory is never a neutral idea; to catalogue is not merely to ascertain but also to appropriate' (Barthes 1982, p. 222). Inventory fragments, lists the items the present owns. Naturalist display diverts attention away from the meaning of its inventory, from its constructed nature, from the practical *use* of artifacts as a medium to a past, a historical medium, by emphasizing immediate appearance, by appearing immediately understandable. Indeed attention is diverted from the artifacts to the empty space between them.

Knowledge of the past is presented as being informational, bureaucratic. In such a conception selection is feared. Recovery and preservation must be as complete and unselective as is inhumanly possible. The past becomes a target for surveillance. Artifacts are preserved and exhibited for scrutiny. The visitor is given the privilege of being in on the act of surveillance. The empirical detail of the past is fed into an interminable dossier (Sontag 1979, p. 156). The past is atomized, pinned down, defined, controlled.

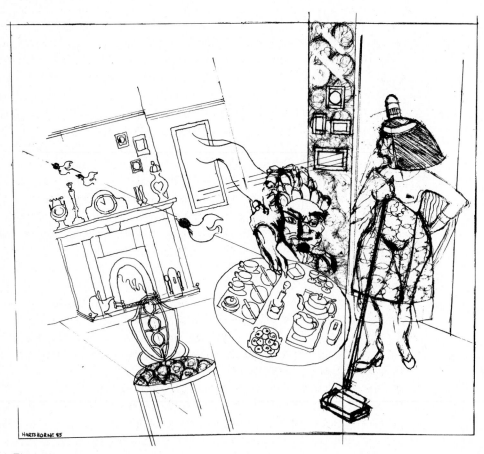

Fig. 4.2 The period room rediscovered.

The visitor is drawn into the period room to fill the human absence and in this aesthetic awareness of and proximity to the artifacts the visitor discovers the familiar. So the past seems closer, understandable, manageable. But this is a tautology. Through the period room's transparent window we recognize the familiar – the fire to relax around, old cooking pot simmering away, china dogs on the mantelpiece. In seeking such a past we must have already discovered it, hence the recognition of the familiar. The past is not explained but acknowledged.

At the same time the period room is attractively mysterious (the 'witch ball' in the window). It invites speculation about its narrative; it begs the question of the link between the artifacts other than their juxtaposition. The more complete the inventory of the period room, the more the period room tells the visitors, the less they know. The period room is a static instant, a disconnected moment. This disconnected temporality and discontinuity with the present creates the mystery. The transparency of the period room is an illusion. Atomistic, manageable, manipulated 'reality' is opaque.

In this world of commodities there is no space for experience, no space for the social constitutive function of subjectivity. There is no space for subjective experience. This also creates a problem of meaning – where is the human narrative? It must be supplied by contemporary experience of the commodity. The visitor lends the objects an experiential context. In the museum department store, the only form of subjective experience allowed is the consumer dream of acquisition and consumption, of alternative lifestyles. The visitor sees, is attracted, desires. The visitor becomes a customer of the past, a tourist of the 'reality' of the past. The past is displayed. Exhibition-value has replaced cult-value.

The arrested temporality of the period room proposes that meaning is instantaneous, located in the disconnected moment, that visible facts convey the truth. The certainty of the existence, the facticity, the 'reality' of the artifacts, the 'look' of the period room confirm this proposal. But it is precisely 'certainty' which is instantaneous. Understanding is temporal and must involve the possibility of denying immediate appearance. (See Berger and Mohr 1982, p. 89; Sontag 1979, p. 23.) This is denied in the period room. The significance of the period room is its naturalism, its pretension to immediacy. The period room is not a replica but a *simulacrum*, an exact copy of an original which never existed. The past is transformed into its own image (Jameson 1984, p. 66).

The erotics of the museum

The relation with the past based on the look of objects is an amorous one (Sontag 1979, pp. 23–4). It is a voyeuristic appreciation and celebration and a simultaneous violation of the body of the past. It is a pornography. Artifacts are promoted to virginal purity (the aesthetic artifact) or prostituted as objects for possession and consumption (the past is subject to immediate consumption in voyeuristic detail).

So the past is revealed to the visitor, exposed and uncovered to be appreciated. In this sense discovery, revelation, includes 'an idea of appropriative enjoyment' (see above). Aktaion discovers Artemis, surprises her at her bath and as voyeur enjoys her nudity, her purity and virginity, just as the visitor views the aesthetic artifact. But the sight of Artemis is her violation. What is seen is possessed; to view is to rape (Sartre 1958, pp. 578–9). So the period room invites violation. It invokes subjective emotional detachment and consumption. The visitor stands back detached (no matter how close and familiar the past may seem) and views – there is no space or time, past or present, for drawing close, for subjective experience, for finding out what lies beneath the surface. There is only the pleasure of immediate voyeuristic consumption. 'Knowledge' becomes located in appearance, in instantaneous appropriation, instantaneous consumption, rape.

Artifacts are defined as objects for scrutiny, for display, for exhibition. The past is displayed. Like the pornographic photograph, detail and clarity of reproduction bring fascination, a sense of being in on the act. The desire for certainty of being in on the act rather than understanding leads to the emphasis on explicitness, on empirical mechanical immediacy. The certainty of the 'medium', photography or artifact, confirms the 'reality' of the displayed sexual act, of the displayed past. The pornographic model is displayed, 'available', asking to be taken, to be consumed, a sexual commodity, emotionally detached.

Just as in pornography women are all equivalent as sexual commodities – reduced to sameness in relation to their display and possession in stylized, sterile sex, endlessly repeatable, so too the period room is endlessly repeatable. History is ultimately all the same, abstract temporal sequence, object of display and possession. It is a homogeneous history.

The partner of the eternal virgin Artemis is the whore of the period room brothel, instantly available, open, easily penetrated. But 'the openness of homogeneous history is both seductive invitation and frustrating refusal, since in entering its gaping void you are entering precisely nothing' (Eagleton 1981, pp. 45–6). The ease of penetration is here a sign of the sterility of the relationship.

Sex in pornography is stylized as a system of fetishistic objects – clothing, parts of body, physical acts. Sexuality is bound and immobilized, spectacular. So too with the commodified past. The visitor looks upon 'the past' in the period room. History is appreciated. For this to happen history is stylized, 'history must be complete and fully accomplished. As a process which is fully accomplished, history, with all its promise of future change and development is closed down and confined entirely to what can be exhibited as "the historical past"' (Bommes and Wright 1982, p. 291).

The George Joicey Museum, Newcastle upon Tyne: Converted seventeenth-century almshouses. The top floor of eleven inmates' cells form a sequence of period rooms in chronological order, from sixteenth to twentieth centuries.

> Is it true, do you think, that if they move us from here they will not let us keep our own furniture? I do hope they will because . . . because, well, it's home, you know.   (Inmate quoted just before the almshouses were closed in 1935:
> Brown 1934, p. 122)

> The bourgeoisie have taken possession of an appartment which they pre-leased from the moment humanity appeared on earth.
> (Dorfman and Mattelart 1975, p. 86)

In the Joicey Museum narrative is tied to situational display. Ideological distortion accompanies the formal elimination of history. The narrative is one of change in furniture. It is a chronology of antiques, the archetypal bourgeois collector's item, uniting the aesthetic and the commodity.

Temporality is again absent. It is the social practice which is utterly excluded from the sequence of rooms. This is disguised by the linear row of cells, units of homogeneous time. The cells are antique showrooms. The informational text reads like a showroom catalogue:

> In the Regency Period British prosperity grew in combination with naval supremacy and expansion of the Empire, and this is reflected in the style of furniture and the use of new woods. The mahogany table with tip-up top is flanked by a pair of dining chairs, with bowed top and reeded sabre legs. Similar in style is the armchair. The satinwood cabinet in the Sheraton tradition has a bowed central section with a panel painted in the manner of Angelica Kaufmann . . .

Time is utterly consumable. Pop round the corner after the visit and buy a piece of history – if you can afford it.

The furniture is presented in the form of period rooms, theatres without actors again. Presenting the past; the stage is set, but where are the actors? They are the audience. The actors supplied by the visitor again belong to the present. The rooms represent the nuclear family through the centuries in its living room. The past is a sequence of interior design, redecoration occurring every century or so. Change is the consumerist change of contemporary capitalism; everything changes and stays the same. This is the ideological distortion. What of the constituting reality of social practice – structures of family life, gender, patriarchy? What of the social reality of the almshouses? The past has been evicted together with all her furniture.

Shop-front commodification

The Castle Museum, York: two converted eighteenth-century prisons house a series of 'folk' collections, 'everyday' objects – agricultural implements to toys to truncheons – dating from the eighteenth century onwards. Many were collected by a local country doctor, John Kirk, at the turn of the century. There are two reconstructed streets containing shops, pub, garage, fire-station; a water-mill, many period rooms; prison cells partly converted into traditional workshops; conventional case displays.

The overwhelming metaphor of the Castle Museum is the shop front, the shop display presenting the consumable variety of capitalist society. 'Kirkgate', the older reconstructed street of the museum, consists predominantly of shop fronts displaying commodities, simply that. The objects simply evoke recognition of empirical similarity and difference to the present, and it isn't all that different (*cf.* Museum of Antiquities). The artifacts are quite literally commodified. The museum case has literally become the shop front. The museum visit has become a confrontation with empirical commodity change. (Commodification again!)

The shop front has become museum case; the shops and galleries bear the imprint of the 'collector'. Shopfronts display *collections* of gold, silver, Sheffield plate, dinner services. The guidebook proclaims: 'to many people the Castle Museum is "the museum with the street". Kirkgate is a spectacular re-creation that has caught the atmosphere of the nineteenth-century . . . It is in constant demand as a "set". But Kirkgate is not, of course, a stage-setting. It is a collection of real buildings and shop-fronts.' Kirkgate is a series of collections, not a street. The 'vivid picture of the everyday life of the past', which a plaque records as the founder of the museum's aim, is a collection of everyday objects.

The Chapel Gallery, which presents the miscellany of the museum, includes cases of horse brasses, weights and measures, model steam engines, lace, knitting, embroidery, drinking vessels, police truncheons; farm implements lie on the floor. Clock pointers, watch-keys and clock-faces: Kirk's collections of what he termed 'bygones' are the individual units of commodified time. They represent the hysterical compulsion to repeat, the failing of memory, reproduction of the always the same under the appearance of the new, the hysterical compulsion to collect and consume.

But this commodification is the reality of developing capitalism. The rhythm of the 'variety' of the objects reveals their abstract identity. The objects lose their empirical distinctions. The meaning of case after case, shop after shop of everyday objects slides into one of repetition. Meaning is no longer present in the object. This is disguised by the frequent adoption of 'realistic' situational displays; the lack of labelling and supportive material implies that the objects explain themselves.

Yet the 'realistic' display is repeatedly undermined by deconstructing details. Kirkgate's fire-station contains cases of objects; the carriage in the street is surrounded by a fence; the street is in perfect order and repair, spotlessly clean; informational text appears on walls. In the costume galleries empty suits of armour stand in a cased mock-up 'realistic' landscape. Further on, in a dark gallery with shored-up 'trench' walls, clean freshly-pressed uniforms on shop mannikins fight again in reconstructed Flanders mud. Haute couture dresses revolve in pastel pastoral landscape setting, richly furnished shop window sets.

The prisons play deconstructing counterpoint to the exhibits and displays. Peer through a slit in a door in Kirkgate (locked again) and inside is a padded cell: the hysterical historical? Just as the hysterical, delirious maniac incorporates what he or she sees and hears into his or her self-absorbed fantasizing, so too the museum seizes on manifestations of the past in order to possess them and unfeelingly incorporate them into its myth. We are in the prison of capitalist commodification. Remains of the prisons are frequently encountered: barred windows, iron-grill doors. The cells of one prison, interiors and corridors whitewashed, house workshop collections of blackened tools of Victorian pipemaker, wheelwright, blacksmith, printer. The rooms are obviously cells, some even retain grill doors; they are hardly neutral setting for 'period workshops'. The juxtaposition of blackened tools and whitewashed cells draws further attention to the stark contrast between present artificial setting and display, original carcereal use of the settings and the craftsmen's tools. The Castle Museum dismantles its own pretensions to pictorial re-presentation.

Heritage: visiting a mythical past

The North of England Open Air Museum, Beamish, County Durham: 200 acres of country-side are the setting for reconstructed and refurbished buildings, some *in situ*, most transferred from around the North-East, which are meant to represent late-Victorian north-east England. There is a railway layout, colliery, pit cottages, a farm and a town area with terraced houses, pub and co-op. A large hall houses collections and archives. Sounds of traditional fairground and brass band, the rattle of trams, the smell of engine oil and steam add considerably to the nostalgic atmosphere; the museum is animated with brass band concerts, engines in steam, passenger trams, summer fairs, whippet racing, pitmen's wives baking bread and scones, and a co-op grocer weighing sugar bags filled with sand.

> We left Gateshead to get away from houses like this.   (Visitor's comment)

'Geordie's Heyday': the declared aim of Beamish, the 'Great Northern Experience', is to preserve the North-East's heritage, the northern way of life 'about a century ago . . . when the North-East was in the forefront of British Industrial development' (Official Guidebook). Local heritage is the focus of the visit to Beamish, a visit into a mythical past. Beamish is a commemoration of a mythical past; objects never intended to com-memorate anything are transformed into monuments of mythical meaning.

Fig. 4.3 Beamish valley. A. The Hall; B. The Town; C. The Railway Station; D. The Home Farm; E. The Steam Navvy; F. The Colliery; G. Geordie (after Carmichael *c.* 1830).

Although the museum houses a reference library and photographic and sound archives, the heritage Beamish outwardly presents is property and artifacts, the property of a utopian community with all classes harmoniously in their place in Hall or terraced house, collecting mounts from stable block or working the colliery steam winder. All the dehistoricized elements of an anaesthetized past have been miraculously transported from Consett, Gateshead, Alnwick to a picturesque rural setting. It is hard to believe that this valley bottom is only a few miles from Newcastle; at Beamish history is isolated from the present.

History, objectified in property, industrial capital and the object, is the existent (as long as it is carefully preserved) and at Beamish it is eminently visitable and consumable in leisure time. Objects and buildings from the past are extracted from their present context and displayed at Beamish. History is staged as 'historical' sights, images and events. In this way 'history is abstracted from the historical and becomes an object of generalised social attention' (Bommes and Wright 1982, p. 290). History is extracted from the present.

We have noted the working of the exchange principle in relation to objects. It applies also to historical sites and to museums themselves. Beamish is eminently visitable, a place for the family to visit on August Bank Holiday. As such it is equivalent to other such places of 'historical' interest: castles, stately homes, cathedrals. The places have meaning overwhelming in relation to one another. History again becomes an 'abstract system of equivalences'. Its relation to everyday life is one of consumption in leisure time. Where should we go this weekend?

But to locate history in sites, monuments, museums, uninhabited places isolatable from the present 'suppresses at one stroke the reality of the land and that of its people, it accounts for nothing of the present, that is nothing historical, and as a consequence the monuments themselves become undecipherable, therefore senseless. What is to be seen is thus constantly in the process of vanishing' (Barthes 1973a, p. 76). Beamish does not provide a window on the past. Beamish is an agent of blindness. The past is transformed into its image, a spectacle.

The past can be visited at Beamish, but this past is another world, a fantasy, a myth, a nostalgia. It is another time; 'as in other aggressive fantasies and the dream of primal bliss, it exists in allegory rather than actual time. It is a reverse image of the weaknesses of the present, a measure of our fall' (Samuel 1983, p. ii). As theatrical spectacle replaces life so nostalgia replaces history.

Beamish nourishes a 'soft focus nostalgia' (ibid.) for times more congenial when pitmen, 'prodigious gardeners, breeders of animals, and often gamblers' (guidebook) grew leeks (the gardens are set) and raced whippets (there has been whippet racing at Beamish) and yes, took baths in front of the open fire. It must have been this way *really*, mustn't it, because people lived in the terraced cottages until 1976 and provided 'information about how *their* cottages were furnished' (guidebook, our emphasis). Jo, from number 26, died after being rehoused when his cottage was given to Beamish by the National Coal Board, but with the help of his family his cottage has been recreated. He lives on doesn't he?

Beamish capitalizes (*sic*) on the indeterminacy, the ambiguity of artifacts and through selection and relocation at Beamish presents a sentimental experience of an imprecise time and place, a utopian gratification, a euchronia. This movement from the concrete naturalism of the exhibits to imaginary make-believe 'Geordieland' is a neo-tribal gesture, an assertion of 'roots' in the face of the anonymity of everyday life in contemporary capitalism. The transformation from real artifacts to imaginary past occurs through and for the initiate, the Geordie of today. The past is pre-recognized before arrival at Beamish. Beamish confirms recognition of the myth of the past. Older people recognize objects similar to those they lived with but now anaesthetized in the terms imposed by Beamish. Younger visitors listen to their mams and dads, grandmas and grandads.

This recognition and remembrance is not wholly conditioned: 'we left Gateshead to get away from houses like this'. Positive energies of past hopes and dissatisfactions, senses of tradition and freedom are aroused. However these energies emerge in an isolated realm of leisure, that 'removed and anodyne realm in which gratification is offered for dissatisfaction in relation to work' (Bommes and Wright 1982, p. 296). As an 'experience' encountered in leisure time, the past is over, finished, relevant only in terms of a visit on Saturday or Sunday or a holiday, a day out with the kids. So why not just remember the good times – the steam engines and trams, leek shows and . . . ? Let's have a good day out at Beamish. We hope to show that such concepts of diversion and amusement – here applied to the presentation of Beamish's nostalgic mythology – are as appropriate in ideology critique as more conventional analysis which would assign Beamish's displayed past to particular sectional interests, criticizing a story mistold (see Adorno 1967, p. 30).

History is timeless through the logic of abstract equivalence. The objects and buildings also have a timeless quality because they have endured. They have defeated history's process of decay. Historical time is experienced as degeneration. We nostalgically look back from the edge of an abyss to a time of community and human dignity. This backwards look, and prospect of only further decay, is hindering: we must stop, rescue and preserve. 'Under the entropic view of history, supported as it is by High Cultural paradigms, "the past" is revalued and reconstructed as an irreplaceable heritage – a trust which is bestowed upon the present and must be serviced and passed on to posterity' (Bommes and Wright 1982, p. 291). We must preserve the past; it needs servicing, mending, fixing. But fixing is immobilizing.

The rusting items of industrial machinery scattered around Beamish are testaments to history as decay. They proclaim the need to service the past, preserve it, rescue it. They also proclaim its endurance. Together with the work in progress reconstructing buildings, these objects declare Beamish is incomplete.

However this is not a declaration that history is forever incomplete, or that history is open to human agency. It means *Beamish* is incomplete, a marketing ploy that Beamish will always be open for the visitor to return again and again to view the most recently fixed bit of the past. It means the past is still hanging on, it has endured, it is enduring, just like Jo in his cottage. It means our freedom, our agency, is restricted to being mechanics for a broken-down Gateshead tram.

The past endures, clinging to the present, weighing down the present. A sticky, slimy past sucks the present into its mire. An unfinished past of domination, unfreedom and suffering seeps into the present and drags us into a mire of compulsive repetition, unresolved conflicts, because the past is forgotten (Schapiro 1977, p. 147). The past endures with the help of the present but in being preserved in this way the past is forgotten. The truth of the past is suffocated beneath a pile of preserved objects which only proclaim a self-evident but deadened 'truth'.

Labour and discovery: the archaeologist as hero
Jorvik Viking Centre, York: an underground 'interpretation centre' beneath a shopping centre. Visitors make a 'journey in time' on talking 'time cars' to a street and alleyway in Viking Jorvik, complete with sounds, smells and models of people. A guide to archaeological excavation is followed by conventional case displays and a museum shop.

'A revolutionary concept in museum design': so claims 'Jorvik Times', an official 'newspaper' produced by the York Archaeological Trust. It is apparently so revolutionary that the label 'museum' cannot be applied to the Jorvik Viking Centre. The centre is a project of the York Archaeological Trust and aims to 'remind people of a forgotten but important and exciting piece of English history, and at the same time explain how archaeologists go about their task' (official guidebook). A visit to the centre is again an experience, the 'Jorvik Experience', a 'journey in time' to Viking Age York, Jorvik brought back to life (Jorvik Times). The experience is of discovery of the past and the labour involved in revivification.

The experience begins with a 'trip back in time', an impressionistic audio-visual presentation, after which 'time stops, history is frozen, this is Jorvik' (time car commentary). The visitor proceeds to view the reconstructed street and alleyway. The past has been discovered and reconstructed through immense archaeological labour, the scientific processing of '15,000 (or is it 30,000) objects! a quarter of a million pots! four and a half tons of bones!' (commentary). In the supporting literature and commentary, stress is repeatedly placed on the detail and accuracy of the reconstructed street, its basis in enormous amounts of factual evidence. Indeed the reconstruction is said to be so accurate, so real, that 'if the Vikings themselves were to return they would feel completely at home' (Jorvik Times). Yet the objects are made to carry meanings which would have mystified their makers: empirical detail, representational accuracy, inanimate display for educational purposes. Stress is placed on authenticity achieved through science and technology and the sophistication of the audio-visual presentation (see Wishart 1984). The stress is on the identification of empirical accuracy and 'life', the life of Jorvik. But life doesn't live.

After the street comes a jump forward to 1980 and the discovery of what lay buried. The archaeological site is preserved half excavated, a work site, labour in process, finds in a tray, wheelbarrows full. 'Archaeologists from the York Archaeological Trust are revealing the remains of the loos and wells, warehouses, workshops and homes we have just visited . . . they peel off layer after layer of soil, labelling, measuring, photographing and planning everything as they go' (guidebook).

More labour is revealed: the evidence, having been discovered, is processed. The visitor arrives at the real detective work; 'digging is only the start of the archaeologist's detective work' (commentary). The visitor passes by a desk with work obviously in process and then is presented with a reconstructed conservation laboratory complete with white-coated expert looking down a microscope. Another white-coated figure (a member of an environmental archaeology unit, we are told) sieves biological finds. On the opposite wall life-sized photographs attest to scientific industry. The commentary

Fig. 4.4 The past brought back to life. Reproduced with permission of Cultural Resource Management Ltd.

enlightens the visitor: this is biological detective work, which together with detective work on other material evidence, shows the archaeologist what life was like in the past, what conditions were like, when the enormous three-dimensional jigsaw puzzle is pieced together.

The labour of discovery and reconstructing the past: so great is the stress on authenticity that 'scientific' technique must be shown to the visitor. And science excludes the visitor – the white-coated dummy looks down the microscope, but not the visitor. We are to understand that scientific discovery guarantees the authenticity of the trip, a tourist trip into history. 'You are HERE, and you are THERE, both at the same time' (Magnus Magnusson in guidebook). Time has after all been arrested. The past is present. We are present in the past. This is the actual site of the street. These are the actual timbers. The detective work draws the visitor closer to the past. Accordingly it is appropriate that the visitor should be allowed to actually touch the past; panels of potsherds and other objects are attached to a wall.

Between the two white-coated experts is a reminder of the conceptual associate of 'labour' – 'discovery'. A marble slab in the floor records the discovery by two construction workers of the 'Coppergate Helmet' (Anglo-Saxon in date).

'Now come and see the objects'. The penultimate element in the Jorvik Experience is a conventional gallery of 500 case-displayed objects. With the supporting text they form a descriptive account of subsistence and crafts. Finally comes the museum shop where you can 'take your pick from a host of beautifully crafted mementoes of the city the Vikings called Jorvik' (Magnus Magnusson in guidebook).

Jorvik is described as an experience and like any experience it just happens, as does the thrill of discovery, discovery of treasure, of the aesthetic artifact, of the artifact laden with information. The visitor passively experiences, locked for half of the visit in a moving 'time car'. We are guided by the anonymous cultural policeman (but isn't it that kindly Magnus Magnusson?) whose precise rehearsed sentences are truly sentences – *sententiae* – acts of penal speech (Barthes 1977a, p. 191), telling us what we see, tying down the meaning of the artifacts, tying the artifact to the 'realistic'. The 'journey in time' and visit to reconstructed Jorvik is a sentence against polysemy. There is no turning back; the visitor cannot leave the 'time car'. Museum shop follows object gallery follows object laboratory follows what is presented as the life-world of the artifact. The fixed sequence culminates in the revelation of the meaning of the Jorvik Experience. Object gallery and museum shop are the commodified object of archaeological labour and the reality of commodity purchase, reified object on display followed by an opportunity to buy a memento of the purchased experience, to buy the past (1,000-year-old pieces of timber @ £1 a square inch).

> facilis descensus Averno . . .
> sed revocare gradum superasque evadere ad auras
> hic opus, hic labor est.
> (The descent to Avernus is easy . . . but to retrace your steps and escape
> back to upper airs – this is the labour, this is the toil)
>
> (Virgil *Aeneid* VI: 126–9)

> The present . . . is the bull whose blood must fill the pit if the shades of the departed are to appear at its edge.   (Benjamin 1955, p. 314)

Aeneas, Trojan hero, visited Cumae where the Sibyl prophesied his destiny and guided him into Avernus, the underworld, where he encountered Rome's destiny. Beamish is a visit to a mythical past. Jorvik is a mythical journey in the steps of the archaeologist as hero.

Like Aeneas, the archaeologist (and later the privileged visitor) is guided on a ritual journey to 'knowledge'. For Aeneas it is a fixed and irresistible destiny and future. For the archaeologist it is 'the past', finally isolated in realistic photographic detail, fixed and certain.

For Aeneas, the irresistibility, the veracity of his destiny and Rome's future is confirmed respectively by his guide, the prophetess Sibyl and her inspiration from the god Apollo, and by the supreme effort and labour required of the hero to gain access to the underworld and there discover knowledge. For the visitor the 'truth' of Jorvik is confirmed by the guides – Magnus Magnusson and other commentators – stressing the 'divine' origins of the reconstruction in scientific endeavour, and also by the supreme effort and labour required of the archaeologist-hero to discover and reconstruct the past.

But there is a striking absence. The Aeneid is Virgil's epic. Virgil, the author, is absent from Aeneas's journey. The Sibyl's and Aeneas's prophetic visions of things to come are Virgil's present, his offering to his patron Augustus. So too with Jorvik; the reconstructed street, the result of the labour of the archaeologist hero, and the guiding commentary are self-fulfilled prophecies. They too are irresistible and unavoidable because of the absent author. This is why Jorvik is described as an experience. Like any true experience, it happens, is irresistable, author-less. The Sibyl's certainty and the certainty of Aeneas's experiences belong to Virgil because Virgil is projecting his present into a mythical past. The truth of the Jorvik reconstruction belongs not in the objects, in the 'past', but in the present, in present archaeological practice, uncovering, unconcealing the fragments of Viking Jorvik.

We may take the classical analogy further. Walter Benjamin also writes: 'The soothsayers who found out from time what it had in store did not experience time as either homogeneous or empty. Anyone who keeps this in mind will perhaps get an idea of how past times were experienced in remembrance – namely in just the same way' (1973e, Thesis XVIIIB, p. 266). The ancient prophet interpreted phenomena as signs (e.g. flights of birds, hysterical ramblings of a priestess). Uncertainty and doubt existed over the status of phenomena as prophetic signs, over the meaning of the signs and the reality to which they might refer. To perform an interpretation was to arrest the present in grasping the momentary connection of the signs with the future and reduce the doubt over meaning in a prophetic reading. Reservation was repressed, meaning assigned and then asserted – interpretation was open to criticism and debate within the community. So the prophet's experience of time is not empty duration χρόνος but καιρός – the critical moment, conjunction of present and future (Kermode 1967, pp. 46ff.; *cf.* Leitch 1983, pp. 3–6). To interpret the past is also to play the prophet. Jorvik, or rather its creators, read the fragments of the past and tie them to a particular un-mediated meaning, descriptive, empty, its connection with the present forgotten but not absent.

PART TWO: PAST AND PRESENT IN THE MUSEUM

The museum's aesthetic eliminates the concrete author of history; it suppresses the concrete authorship of the past in the present. And this is in spite of the museum's frequent use of a linear 'book' format – using artifacts to carry or support a story line. In presenting the archaeological and/or historical process of acquiring knowledge as one of passive discovery and subsequent description of the past, history is presented as being written by the white-coated expert, a faceless author, a universal author, god or science. The present's implication in the past is one of objective contingency.

On another level, the present is accepted as being implicated in the museum as an institution. First, the museum is an active intervention in the past as it conserves and preserves artifacts which originated in the past. Secondly, it presents these to the public – the objects are exhibited. Authorship refers to the creativity of interpreting the past for the public – the exhibition is designed. The present's implication in the past is here one of subjective contingency.

At both levels the link between past and present is contingent. The past is fixed and complete; the present turns to the past according to its own subjective decision. The decision is made to turn to the past because it is conceived as valuable to the present, as value-laden. But this is an abstract monetary value: it doesn't really matter what the past was like in its details. The decision is to turn to a past pre-conceived as fixed, complete, in-itself.

This contingent relation between past and present determines the themes open to discussion concerning the museum as an institution.

(1) Does the museum materially preserve the past with efficiency? The management and conservation of collections. Research and collections.

(2) The museum and the commodity. Services *for* the community – information services, object identification. The relation of museums to other institutions and bodies (such as local government, planning departments, English Heritage, government departments, local societies, adult education). The museum's contribution to tourism.

(3) Education and the museum – museums and educational institutions (schools, universities), loan services. The museum and its message – educational theory and museum applications; traditional knowledge areas (art, history, natural history) and the museum.

(4) Is the museum effectively getting across its message? Communicative effectiveness and 'interpretation' in the museum. ('Interpretation': 'an educational activity which aims to reveal meanings and relationships through the use of original objects, by first hand experience and by illustrative media rather than simply to communicate factual information' (Tilden 1957, p. 8).) Exhibition design and layout – use of supportive 'interpretive' material (labels, models,

text, diagrams, maps); static and interactive display; object-based and concept-based display. Formal and technical matters.

The majority of work and discussion on museums is confined to these themes (see the comprehensive bibliographies produced by the Department of Museum Studies, University of Leicester).

As a means of critique, we will now consider two particular debates concerning archaeology's relation with the present.

Entertaining the public: 'real' and 'popular' archaeology

The display which aims at the uninitiated visitor and sets out to stimulate, entertain, divert, but ultimately to educate, is the shadow of a 'real' archaeology which is isolated from its determinate context, an autonomous archaeology which searches desperately among the debris of the past for the immediacy and meaning it has overlooked in the present. The popular exhibition is the social bad conscience of 'real', serious archaeology (Adorno and Horkheimer 1979, p. 135). Archaeologists dig up the past, lodge their finds in the museum and *may* speculate according to their theoretical models as to the meaning and significance of what they have found. Presenting any of this to a public – those who do not belong to the community of archaeologists – is entirely contingent, a separate matter from 'real' archaeology. Popular presentation is split from the real work of archaeology. The link between archaeology/artifact and public becomes 'interpretation' of archaeology/artifact/history. Interpretation is the function of the museum. The museum becomes a service manned by professionals.

So the museum presents *for* the public, the uninitiated ('knowledge', 'concepts', 'ideas', artifacts – it doesn't matter in this purely technical relation). Experts supply cultural goods, cultural capital for the visitor, manufacturer for customer. The supermarket-museum is simply the physical locus for this transaction.

Archaeology 'is in the end reduced to mere communication. Its alienation from human affairs terminates in its absolute docility before a humanity which has been enchanted and transformed into clientele by the suppliers' (Adorno 1967, pp. 25–6). Reduction to communication, reduction to broadcast: the only form of creativity and agency within this technical relation is the 'creativity' of the curator-entrepreneur, supplying his inventiveness to the marketing of the past, the design of displays. All that can be said to the visitor concerning her agency is 'you too could be an expert'.

Those museums and commentators who draw on progressive educational theory and advocate interactive displays – displays which involve the visitor in some active way, which centre themselves on the visitor – do not alter this relation. They merely comment on the presumed efficiency of the communication, that an interactive display will convey more of its 'message' to the visitor. They are equally manipulative of the visitor (*cf.* critiques of progressive educative techniques, e.g. Elshtain 1976, Entwistle 1979).

To entertain, inform, educate the present, the past must be presented in an accessible way. Hawkes (1968) has voiced the conscience of humanist as opposed to scientific archaeology. Decrying the inhuman works of scientific archaeologists shored up 'behind ramparts of jargon and other specialist defences' (p. 260), Hawkes wants an accessible humanist archaeology, 'historical (i.e. descriptive-narrative) writing of the quality and humanity of the work of the young Gordon Childe, Mortimer Wheeler, Christopher Hawkes, Stuart Piggott, or even, in his more austere way, Grahame Clark' (p. 256). Hawkes wants historical synthesis, extraction of 'historical' meaning from disparate facts.

For Hawkes, a return to, or re-emphasis of humanist writing would overcome the split she perceived between inaccessible scientific archaeology and traditional archaeology. The link between the archaeological artifact and popular accessible writings is the imaginative *personality* trained in the humanities (p. 261). There is still a split between real archaeology concerned with the past and popular archaeology for the present. The link is the imaginative personality instilling human values into dusty dry artifacts, writing historical synthesis. Clarke also acknowledges the split between real and popular archaeology. For Clarke, vulgarizing archaeology is the last refuge of the humanities-trained archaeologist unable to deal with real analytical archaeology and seeking material gain (1968, p. 22).

Both of these positions rely on a conception of an autonomous archaeology. For Hawkes, archaeology's autonomy from contemporary society is its basis in eternal human values; archaeology is a pursuit of the cultured (Childe read Pindar after dinner? Hawkes 1968, p. 261). For Clarke, archaeology is archaeology is archaeology. Analytical archaeology is autonomous in that it is a scientific discipline in quest of knowledge coming to its maturity. Archaeology as culture, archaeology as analytical discipline: both oppose the notion of archaeology fundamentally being for-something-else. Primarily archaeology exists in-itself.

In these conceptions archaeology has no *necessary* link with the public, with a clientele, with its social context. The links that are established between archaeological artifact and the public are due to the social responsibility and sense of social duty of the archaeologist or curator, the personality of the archaeologist or curator.

All the discussion of the reasons behind the archaeologist's quest for the artifact and its eventual residence in the museum is a vacuous rhetoric, a marketing ploy to justify the ideological work done in the name of culture, science or whatever other reified and alienated realm. Why dig up and preserve the past? Because of natural curiosity, the human will to knowledge and understanding; as an aesthetic quest to secure beauty and variety; to establish symbolic links with the past, a sense of national or human identity; because humans need a past, a communal memory, a sense of the past; because of a sense of social duty – the past is being destroyed; for personal satisfaction; to entertain and divert; for nostalgic reasons – a search for more congenial times; to learn from the past and educate the present; to find a model for inspiration; to reconcile East and West and solve the world's problems (see also the discussion in Chapter 1, pp. 25–7).

The answer lies in the split between real archaeology and its presentation and/or justification to a public. The error is in posing the question after the act of separating real and popular archaeology. Discussing and considering the presentation of archaeology, or its relevance to the present, or justifying archaeology to the present with entertaining or diverting popular works and exhibitions presupposes the gap which such rhetoric is to bridge. The relation between archaeology and the present remains arbitrary because archaeology is absolutized as though grounded in the inner nature of knowledge; it is justified in an ahistorical way by reference to eternal human qualities or values. Archaeology is reified, separated from the present (Horkheimer 1976, p. 212).

Archaeology is reified, rooted in the antinomies of a fragmented capitalist society. This brings a secret source of comfort in the split between real and popular archaeology. That the fatal fragmentation might some day end is a fatal destiny, nemesis – retribution for archaeology's pretension to autonomy, its hubris (see Adorno 1967, p. 24). Reification, involving those eternal values of humanity and objectivity must not end. Archaeology must not be contaminated by society's materialism, the mob armed now with metal detectors, wrecking the past in search of material gain. Archaeology must counter this growing barbarism with educative measures, popular works and exhibits accessible to the mob, to justify its civilized alternative, to appease the mob.

Archaeologists as creatures of their times

> Was fällt, das sollt Ihr stossen   (Nietzsche)
> (If it's falling down, give it a shove)

The autonomy of archaeology is potentially violated by the archaeologist and curator who address the public with justifying and entertaining works. The archaeologist and curator are, of course, members of society, but what is the significance of this? Is the autonomy of archaeology compromised?

Fowler writes: 'as a factor in our use of archaeological evidence, the meaning we give to it, the fashion of the times remains potent . . . The archaeologist is a creature of his own time . . . There is no ultimate, finite truth to be revealed by archaeological evidence . . . all interpretation of it is relative' (1977, p. 136). Fowler separates the artifact, the evidence, from its interpretation by the fallible archaeologist, a creature of his (*sic*) times.

Clarke's controlling models locate the archaeologist in society determining his or her confrontation with, his or her interpretation of the past (1972, pp. 5–10).

Daniel expresses scepticism regarding 'new' archaeologists – they will realize that the past is something to be recorded, described and appreciated. Their deviations from this empiricist truth are due to their (defective?) personalities, their subjective experience and disposition (1981, p. 192).

So from these points of view archaeology's autonomy lies in its object. Archaeology is further abstracted from its determination in the present in the assertion that its practitioners belong to the present. Archaeology is judged according to its practitioners who are subsumed, assimilated in an administrative manner into the prevailing constellations of power *which the intellect ought to expose* (Adorno 1967, p. 30). The 'artifact' retains its purity and integrity in spite of the potential violation. The present though is absolved from guilt in this absolutization of an immediate relativity.

But the present is not absolved from its duty to the past. Archaeology's autonomy, its truth, lies in the artifact, patiently enduring time and subjective interpretation. The past is objectified as property. The obvious conclusion is that the object past must be preserved, protected. Property is sacred. In the devaluation of the practical confrontation of archaeologist and the past to a universal relativism, the artifactual past is the historical constant, our Heritage to be preserved for interpretation in the future. Every present needs a past to be interpreted. We must preserve the sacred past for the future (Fowler 1977, p. 192). Museums preserve the future's sacred heritage, its private property. Objectivity is sacred fetishized property. Whose property? The property of Man?

'Disputing the decay of works in history serves a reactionary purpose; the ideology of culture as class privilege will not tolerate the fact that its lofty goods might ever decay, those goods whose eternity is supposed to guarantee the eternity of the classes' own existence' (Adorno 1964, p. 62, translation by Susan Buck-Morss). We remain hidden in the labyrinth of a commodified past, a labyrinth of deadened and preserved objects. De-struction is necessary to create openings to get out, for the sake of liberation. A way out must be uncovered. In this sense truth is the Greek ἀλήθεια, a practice of uncon-cealing. The way out has been forgotten (reification is a forgetting), it is hidden behind a heap of decaying objects (see the discussion in Chapter 1).

What is the nature of the relation between curator and his or her society? In an analysis of the National Air and Space Museum, Washington D.C., Meltzer makes use of a concept of 'ideology', which he claims to derive from Althusser, 'to view our society's manner of reinforcing and reproducing its economic structure' in the museum. 'The Museum is about air and space, but only on a superficial level; it is more properly about us' (1981, p. 125). Meltzer utterly neutralizes the concept of ideology in what he recognizes as an apolitical analysis (ibid. p. 125). For Meltzer, the museum as ideo-logical institution means that it tells 'us' about 'our' economic structure. 'Our' use of artifacts of the past tells 'us' about 'ourselves'. 'We', presumably, are citizens of the democratic U.S.A., good American capitalists.

Mediating past and present

It is necessary to mediate these two related poles, to mediate a metaphysics of history where history is identified as the past, and a relativization of history where history is a reflex of present social and material reality, present social conditions.

Leone suggests one form of mediation. Drawing on Bloch's proposal (1977a, 1977b) that discussions of the past among most peoples have little or nothing to do with the facts or processes described but are entirely about the present, being models of how society ought to work, Leone claims that the scientist's social structure is replicated when his or her work is presented to the public, in the ritual of public performance. The archaeol-ogist is concerned in his or her professional work with giving the objects accurate mean-ing (1981a, p. 12). This search for objective accuracy produces boredom when pre-sented to the public because it ignores the link between past and present. The way out is to 'allow the past to be the image of the present it must be by its very nature in a ritual setting' (p. 13). The professional and private work of archaeology is separate from its ritual and public performance. A bored reception indicates lack of meaning in the original work, an unrealized connection with the present. The solution is to credit the public performances with their private-professional authors. Let the public settings based on interpretations change, 'show them changing and teach how they are changed and what they change in response to' (p. 13; *cf*. Schlereth 1978).

Leone locates the determinate link between archaeology and the present in its public presentation. The professional-private work of the archaeologist must respect the present's creation of the past if the ritual of presentation, of performance is to be meaningful.

However we would argue that there is no homogeneous present creating the past – the present is fragmented and contradictory. Secondly, professional archaeology and its public presentation are both forms of performance.

Presentation as performance

There can be no 'realistic' objective representation of the past. We have argued that actual past history is not identical to its representation in archaeological reason. There is no genuine past to be brought into harmony with archaeological thought and neutrally re-presented to the public. Archaeology does not provide a mirror to the past nor does it provide an abstract system which expresses the 'reality' of the past. This is to identify reason with the past and does not do justice to the material practice and suffering of human subjects in the past. Such an identification justifies the tyranny of thought over individual human existence, 'it is the triumphant tyranny of the concept, the relentless sublation of discrete particulars to a system radically closed in its very dreary infinity' (Eagleton 1981, p. 120). The qualitative meaning of the past is lost in the universal authors' quest for the objective past. Reified, commodified objectivity, empty quantified detail, communicating universal 'truths' of history as progress, decay, or simple objectivity yielding to present reason, destroys the historical meaning of the artifact, its temporality.

The past is not a three-dimensional jigsaw puzzle buried beneath the archaeologist, or a palimpsest. All such conceptions reduce the past to a monolithic structure, a synchronic structure of spatial relationships. Artifacts are not neutral elements with a frozen meaning ready for defrosting, but fields of contention and contradiction with constantly shifting significance and connotation, shifting according to their inscription in past and present social *practice*.

The past is not a tangle of factual details to be decoded, presented to and appreciated by those with an educated 'sense of the past' (Fowler 1981), 'but consists rather of the numbered group of threads that represent the weft of the past as it feeds into the warp of the present . . . The subject matter of history, once released from pure facticity, needs no *appreciation*. For it offers not vague analogies to the present, but constitutes the precise dialectical problem that the present is called upon to resolve (Benjamin 1979, p. 362).

So the museum exhibition is not so much representational or referential as figural and rhetorical. It is the rhetorical performance of the museum, its *act* of interpretation and persuasive intention which opens up meaning.

There are several implications of the notion of presentation as rhetorical performance.

Archaeology and its presentation in the museum cannot begin with an abstractly defined objectivity or a priori method but must begin *in medias res* with the artifact in its present historical circumstance, riddled with error, contradiction, doxa (Benjamin 1973b, p. 103). The primary question is not ontological or methodological but strategic, political. Not what is the past and how should we approach it, but what do we want to do with the past and why? (*cf.* Eagleton 1983, pp. 210–11).

Archaeology does not receive its meaning from the artifact. The artifact surrenders and receives meaning in the practice of archaeology and presentation in text or in the museum. This does not sacrifice truth in a relativism whereby it is impossible to decide between rival explanations and presentations if each springs rationally from a particular way of life, from particular social conditions in the present. Such a relativism is only a problem if the concern is with the relation of an *abstract* consciousness or subjectivity in general, formulating explanations and creating presentations, and an abstract object of study. The abstract subject's explanation and presentation of the abstract object is relative to present social context. This problem 'disappears in the concrete process in which subject and object mutually determine and alter each other' (Adorno, quoted by Buck-Morss 1977, p. 51). Objectivity itself is heterogeneous, not abstract. The artifact cannot be completely defined in terms of abstract, ahistorical, objective qualities such as form, dimension and all related categories of type. It is the insistence and agency of the act of interpretation, explanation, presentation which restricts the ambiguity of the artifact to meaning and understanding. Artifacts have endured and are authentic materially, but they are vulnerable. Their truth is precarious and in constant need of re-articulation. Truth is time-bound, temporal, historical.

The material reality of the artifact is not mythically permanent. The artifactual past is not eternal abstracted objectivity to be appropriated by archaeological reason. The artifact is time-bound, transitory. Non-chronometric time enters into the meaning of the artifact. Material reality is in a permanent state of historical becoming. The past is irreversible, discontinuous, particular and thoroughly mediated objectivity. The past is not a systematic array of objects and their relationships, a fixed reality of commodified objectivity towards which archaeologists are groping and which may be represented in museum display. Such a conception is a denial of temporality; the past is here presented as an eternal image or myth. The past instead must be realized as the 'subject of a construction whose locus is not empty time but the particular epoch, the particular work' (Benjamin 1979, p. 352). The artifacts must be broken from historical continuity.

We must renounce all abstract closedness and totality in definitions and re-presentations of artifacts. There is no unified identity behind all artifacts. As such there can be no universal method, no formal principles of interpretation and display.

The contradictory present

Why go to a museum? To see the past because it exists, to be educated? The answers to the question offered by the museum exhibition are inadequate in their masking of aporias, contradictory relations lodged in contemporary social experience. We have tried to show how these contradictory relations lie within the museum's aesthetic, its presentation of the artifact:

spatial	temporal
closed, completed past	open, unfinished history
eternity	history

reified	relational
repetition	particularity
identity	difference
presence	absence
homogeneous	heterogeneous
coercive	explorative
passive	active
monologic	dialogic
forgetting	remembrance
conservation	redemption

The museum manipulates these relations, suppressing contradiction, fixing the past as a reflection of the appearance of the present. The present recognizes itself and is justified. The museum as ideological institution suppresses difference and heterogeneity in advertisements for the world through its duplication in the artifactual past. The museum suppresses temporality and agency. In the museum the past becomes the death mask of the present.

Conclusion: towards a redemptive aesthetic

Some implications can be drawn from our argument:

(1) We must retain heterogeneity and difference, the fragmentary and discontinuous reality of the past as a means of overcoming the ideological effects of a reified object world, past and present. The presented artifact is a reified object in the museums we studied. Social relations which provide meaning to the artifact are transformed into an appearance of relationships between objects. The exhibited object's pretence of trans-parent naturalism is a rendering of society as opaque, of history as homogeneous, always-the-same. Opaque homogeneity, running in a continuous flow through history, conceals the antagonistic and contradictory class-structured present and imposes an image of the present on the past. We must resist the power of reification, shatter the homogeneous past, reveal the social relationship of past and present in a true realism, a social physiognomy which embodies objective social contradiction, which embraces contradiction, discontinuity and conflict in a dynamic totality (Adorno 1967; Jameson 1977).

(2) We must oppose professional preservative History with its archaeologist-curator speaking for a monolithic and murdered past. We should democratize and personalize authorship in an attempt at avoiding the absorption of author-archaeologist and visitor into the product (display, book) (see CCCS Popular Memory Group 1982, p. 215). This involves an active reconciliation of production and reception of the past, a renunciation

of the conventional relationship of professional producing the past *for* a consuming public, of experts presenting an elitist high culture.

(3) We must recognize the full implications of authorship and fully embrace reflexivity. So all presentations are to be understood as being precisely that – intimately tied to the present. Their truth is to be found in the present's specific encounter with particular aspects of the past. We must present a specific and unique engagement with the past, an engagement original to every new present (Benjamin 1979, p. 352). We must present specific acts of construction, work in progress, varied forms of relationship with the artifactual past instead of a fixed relation of representation of a completed past. The museum can allow the visitor to construct a past along with the archaeologist-curator: participation not as a means to a pre-given, pre-discovered end, but as an open process of constructing different pasts.

(4) The artifact must not be reduced to uniform abstract objectivity. The artifact is not reducible to a one-dimensional representational sign of the past. The past is not fixed, to be represented, but changes according to its specific engagement with the present. So we must detach the artifact from its 'self-evident' meaning as object of scientific study, reveal the artifact as non-identical with its apparent meaning, strip the object of its pretension to being-in-itself, strip the object of its immediacy in order that it might be released from the sterile continuum of the homogeneous history of the always-the-same (Wolin 1982, p. 125). This may involve enabling the artifact to gesture to its own material inscription in social practice, its own material existence, at the same time as it conveys a meaning in the context of a museum display. It certainly requires considering recent work on the symbolic meaning and use of artifacts – the style of function (see Chapter 7).

Techniques for achieving these ends:

(1) Introduce political content into conventional displays – show how the past may be manipulated and misrepresented for present purposes.

(2) Break artifacts from fixed chronological narrative and from their original contexts and reassemble them with contemporary artifacts similarly decontextualized: juxtaposition, montage (a) as a means of drawing attention to and engaging with official cultural meanings of the artifact and effecting an ideological critique of commodification, and (b) as a means of illustrating alternative (non-commodified) meanings.

(3) Supplement 'objective third person narrative' with exaggeration, irony, humour, absurdity, as a means of stripping the self-evident meaning of the artifact of its power.

(4) Avoid permanent displays, emphasize authorship and changing perceptions of the artifactual past.

(5) Encourage the use of artifacts of the past outside the institutional space of the museum. Allow community use of museum artifacts, people constructing and presenting their own pasts in the museum.

Perspectives for a social archaeology

5

Hermeneutics, dialectics and archaeology

> 'Above the *subject*, beyond the immediate *object*, modern science is founded on the *project*.'   (Bachelard, 1978, p. 11)

Archaeology as interpretation

In this chapter we attempt to provide some preliminary groundwork for a revitalized philosophy of archaeology which moves beyond traditional notions of a split between archaeologist and data, between subject and object, subjectivity and objectivity. These opposed and dichotomous terms and others related to them (e.g. intuitive–deductive; theory–data; idea–fact; abstract–concrete; theory–practice; present–past) pose a primary epistemological obstacle to understanding past and present and the connection between the two. Any philosophy which sets up and maintains a radical disjunction between such polarized terms is a philosophy of NO (Bachelard 1975), which constrains, sets limits, attempts to legitimate the notion of fundamental foundations to thought beyond which we must not stray. It is a rigid framework which were it to be actually adopted by scientists in their *practice* would stultify thought. Virtually all existing epistemologies or theories of the grounds for making knowledge-claims are philosophies of NO. Their correlative is the archaeology or archaeologies of NO which aim to constrain research and lay down a priori frameworks of that which can or cannot be legitimately said. Such are the archaeologies which have been discussed and criticized in the previous four chapters of this book, archaeologies rooted in closed philosophies. Positivist/empiricist discourse is a closed philosophy. By this is meant that it supposes that there is only one correct and proper manner of approaching, describing and explaining reality – by granting primacy to the empirical object of study through sense-perception, elevating the general over the particular and putting faith in testing strategies leading to verification or falsification (see Chapter 2). We have challenged these suppositions and here argue instead for an open philosophy of archaeology – a philosophy which does not set limits, create areas beyond which research should not stray.

Archaeology, we contend, is an interpretative practice, an active intervention engaging in a critical process of theoretical labour relating past and present. It is entirely misleading to pose the problem of understanding and explaining the past in terms of either a purely factual representation tied to the past and purged of subjective 'bias', or a presentist quest for liberation from the dogmatic burden of the archaeological record through unrestrained fictionalizing and mythologizing. Interpretation is an act that cannot be reduced to the merely subjective. Any archaeological account involves the creation of *a* past in *a* present and its understanding. Archaeology in this sense is a performative and transformative endeavour, a transformation of the past in terms of the present. This process is not free or creative in a fictional sense but involves the translation of the past in a delimited and specific manner. The facts of the case become facts only in relation to convictions, ideas and values. However, archaeology would amount to an exercise in narcissistic infatuation if it *only* amounted to a deliberate projection of present concerns onto the past. The archaeological record itself may challenge what we say as being inadequate in one manner or another. In other words, data represents a *network of resistances* to theoretical appropriation. We are involved in a discourse mediating past and present and this is a two-way affair.

The hermeneutic circle
The hermeneutic circle may be described as consisting of

> a laborious construction of the totality of life, which is simultaneously unknown and not available to direct insight, out of the odds and bits of life which are sentiently accessible, but yet incomprehensible. The circle starts from the divination of the totality to which the confronted element belongs; if the guess is correct, the element in question reveals part of its meaning, which in turn gives us the lead toward a better, fuller, more specific reconstruction of the totality. The process goes on, in ever wider circles, until we are satisfied that the residue of opacity still left in our object does not bar us from appropriating its meaning.
> (Bauman 1978, p. 31;
> *cf*. Heidegger 1962, pp. 150ff.; Gadamer 1975, pp. 235ff.)

We can suggest that any interpretative account of the past moves within a circle, perhaps more accurately, a widening spiral, and involves changing or working theoretically upon that which is to be interpreted. One cannot understand anything about the meaning of material culture-patterning in the past (or the present) unless one is willing to make conceptualized interventions by means of using social, ethnographic or other starting points about the manner in which the past social totality was constituted. If these conceptualized interventions are more or less correct we will gain insight and understanding. If not we will be left with an uninterpretable mass of observations. Additionally we cannot obtain a grasp of that totality which we seek to investigate until we have some understanding of the contextualized matrices of social life into which the material culture-patterning fitted and acted. Interpretation thus seeks to understand the particular in the light of the whole and the whole in the light of the particular. To make sense of the interconnections between diverse areas of material culture-patterning – burial, artifact use and disposal, ceramic designs, faunal remains, architectural directional placement, etc. – requires some prior or anticipatory understanding of the social totality in which the material culture acted as symbol, code, or structure. What makes the archaeological data speak to us, when we can interpret it, when it makes sense, is the act of placing it in a specific context or set of contexts, and the project of making sense of the data involves the intrinsic variability apparent, and the full use of this variability in an examination of possible meaning-structures. The concepts of a correct or an incorrect understanding do not rely upon a preconceived set of methodologies (hermeneutics is not an alternative methodology) but make sense only in terms of the past context being investigated. The fullest understanding is irrevocably context-dependent and context-confined. This means that the nature of archaeological understanding is relational to the context being investigated and involves a dialectical movement back and forth between the parts and the totality. This means that the nature of archaeological understanding is inextricably linked to the determinate context being investigated and stands diametrically opposed to an urge for a technical control of the past using laws or generalizations which are not context-dependent.

The notion that an interpretative account of the past moves within a contextually dependent circle, or spiral, removes the very possibility, the myth, that simplistic falsificationist or verificationist testing approaches can be applied to break out of the circle and establish whether or not the interpretations are correct at some stage or other of inquiry. Corrections take place by a dialectical process within the circle itself. The data has no 'pure', bedrock-like refuting essence but is itself indelibly part of the circle (see Chapter 2, pp. 36–43, and further discussion of this point below). However, it should not be too simply concluded that the circle is in some way self-referencing and this leads us on to consider the role of the interpreter.

The role of the interpreter

In Chapter 3 it was argued that a value-free archaeology was an impossible enterprise and we attempted to demonstrate that contemporary archaeology can hardly be claimed to be devoid of social and political values. Here we wish to link in that discussion with the role of the interpreting subject, discussing the hermeneutics of Gadamer.

Gadamer (1975, pp. 235–6) quotes the following passage from Heidegger's *Being and Time* (1962, p. 153), in which he refers to the hermeneutic circle:

> It is not to be reduced to the level of a vicious circle, or even a circle which is merely tolerated. In the circle is hidden a positive possibility of the most primordial kind of knowing. To be sure, we genuinely take hold of this possibility only when, in our interpretation, we have understood that our first, last and constant task is never to allow our fore-having, fore-sight, and fore-conception to be presented to us by fancies and popular conceptions, but rather to make the scientific theme secure by working out these fore-structures in terms of the things themselves.

A number of important implications can be drawn out from this passage (*cf.* Gadamer 1975, pp. 236ff., 1979, pp. 148ff.; Bernstein 1983, pp. 136ff.):

(1) Interpretation is not an optional choice such that 'objective method' can ever be regarded as a substitute for it in the manner, for example, that empiricist discourses might claim. Interpretation resides in our Being or existence in the world. There is no way in which we can escape interpretation. This is an ontological and not a methodological point. The circle or spiral of interpretations is not something which should be regretted and therein resides a positivity, i.e. possibilities are opened out for us.

(2)   Fore-having, fore-sight and fore-conception or presuppositions provide the foundations for any understanding, truth, or knowledge-claims. In this context it is worth noting with Sellars (1963, p. 169) that 'in characterizing an episode or a state as that of *knowing*, we are not giving an empirical description of that episode or state; we are placing it in the logical space of reasons, of justifying and being able to justify what one says'.

(3)   'The things themselves' (i.e. the data on which we work) exist only in so far as they are conceptualized. To move back to an earlier statement made in this chapter, reality is human, objects are not.

(4)   In the attempt to understand the past we have to open ourselves up to it and the claims to truth that reside in that which we study, truth claims which only we, the interpreters, can bring out and emphasize. This is not the 'truth' of empiricism nor does it imply an act of empathy (see the critique of empathy in Chapter 1). What it does mean is that we situate our opinions, ideas, presuppositions, fore-knowledge, our presentism, in relation to the past. We cannot purge ourselves of values but these can be productively mediated by that which we study. It is impossible to radically bracket off the self. Equally, that studied is not a subjective creation. Interpretation is what Gadamer refers to as 'fusion of horizons' (1975, p. 273) involving an active conjunction of past and present, object and subject.

This conjunction of subject and object or interpreter and data requires further amplification. As we have seen, in the hermeneutic circle the interpreter approaches a set of materials in the fullness of their contextuality, and presuppositions permit an initial understanding of the meanings of these materials. In a sense they anticipate their form and nature. In the light of contact with that studied, these preconceptions are inevitably modified in a progressive way to eventually permit a *satisfactory* understanding. Gadamer (ibid., p. 238) suggests that

> meanings cannot be understood in an arbitrary way. Just as we cannot continually misunderstand the use of a word without its affecting the meaning of the whole, so we cannot hold blindly to our own fore-meaning of the thing if we would understand the meaning of another . . . All that is asked is that we remain open to the meaning of the other . . . this openness always includes our placing the other meaning in a relation with the whole of our own meanings or ourselves in relation to it. Now it is the case that meanings represent a fluid variety of possibilities . . . but it is still not the case that within this variety of what can be thought, i.e. of what a reader can find meaningful and expect to find, everything is possible . . . The hermeneutical task becomes automatically a questioning of things and is always in part determined by this.

Now this notion of 'a questioning of things' is of essential importance. We are not attempting to mirror the past but to probe into it, to move beyond surface appearances to underlying structures beneath the data we empirically 'see'. A satisfactory understanding is, as the words suggest, never a complete understanding but is itself embedded in our praxis as interpreters. It involves our mediation of the data. It does not claim to be the reflection of the past. Understanding both *reproduces* and *produces*. It is not a recovery confined to original meaning. The meaning comes into being through understanding. The corollary to this philosophical hermeneutics is that knowledge is practical and in part depends upon what we do and what we want to do, a corollary that will be discussed below. Before initiating that discussion it is, perhaps, worth emphasizing the difficulty of archaeology as a hermeneutic enterprise because this leads us to understand fully the importance of theory construction as the key towards disciplinary development.

Archaeology as fourfold hermeneutic

Giddens (1982, 1984, p. 374) has written of a double hermeneutic as being involved in social science, through a contrast with natural science:

> The hermeneutics of natural science has to do only with the theories and discourse of scientists, analysing an object world which does not answer back, and which does not construct and interpret the meanings of its activities . . . But social theory cannot be insulated from its 'object-world', which is a subject-world. (Giddens 1982, pp. 12–13)

> The social scientist studies a world, the social world, which is constituted as meaningful by those who produce and reproduce it in their activities – human subjects. To describe human behaviour in a valid way is in principle to be able to participate in the forms of life which constitute, and are constituted by, that behaviour. This is already a hermeneutic task. But social science is itself a 'form of life', with its own technical concepts. Hermeneutics hence enters into the social sciences on two, related levels. (ibid., p. 7)

It has been argued that interpretation in archaeology is a process of overcoming the distance between one frame of reference (the present) and another (the past) and that this distance is productive of discourse (on the notion of distance see Chapter 1, esp. pp. 17–18). The process of coming to understand the past is an extremely complicated one and not susceptible to being simply boiled down to a single procedure or set of procedures which can be reproduced by others in the manner of a rote formula or recipe. Archaeology, and history, we wish to suggest, are the most difficult of all disciplines because the process of acquiring a historical understanding involves a quadruple act of interpretative endeavour. Natural scientists are only involved in a single hermeneutic, since they deal with inanimate objects and processes such as chemical reactions which in themselves have no human meaning, but to which meaning may be ascribed. Any theoretical scheme which gives meaning to these objects and processes is itself a form of life involving sets of concepts and procedures and experimentation which have to be mastered, and a mode of practical activity generating specific types of descriptions. Sociologists are involved in a double hermeneutic in that they both live and work within a form of life, a set of contemporary practices from which they cannot escape, and a world of pre-interpreted meanings. The sociologist both shares a form of life and through theory construction and language use or extension attempts to throw light on the participatory meaning frames in which he or she is imbricated. Anthropological work involves a treble hermeneutic in that the anthropologist lives within a pre-interpreted universe in the light of which his or her problematic and outlook is framed and yet attempts to understand alien cultures inhabiting other meaning frames. The archaeologist and the historian are involved also in this treble anthropological hermeneutic, with the additional intersection of the past, a form of life not directly accessible, but one which must be reconstructed. So, archaeological work involves:

(i) the hermeneutic of working within the contemporary discipline of archaeology;
(ii) the hermeneutic of living within contemporary society as an active participant, put broadly, gaining knowledge of that which is to be human, to interact and participate with others and to be involved in struggles about beliefs and social and political values;
(iii) the hermeneutic of trying to understand an alien culture involving meaning frames radically different from his or her own;
(iv) the hermeneutic involved in transcending past and present.

The difficulty involved in archaeology as fourfold hermeneutic is what makes the discipline potentially so exciting and worthwhile. It undoubtedly goes some way to explain the public fascination with archaeology. However, it is worth underlining once more that the difficulties involved should not lead to any romanticism or nostalgia for the past, to think by some transcendental human effort we can get back inside it. This was the major failing of the hermeneutics of the late-nineteenth century, especially as expressed in the work of Dilthey and more recently by Collingwood (1946). Equally, the apparent ease with which contemporary scientistic archaeology claims stringent objectivity, via a restricted set of simplistic methodologies, has to be rejected. It can, in fact, only claim to do this at all by a remarkable set of reductions in which human beings are virtually exorcized from the project. The fourfold hermeneutic involved in any and all forms of archaeology undermines any attempt to fix for once and all the manner in which the past should be understood in terms of methodological rules for procedure. It rather requires the use of a multivalent plurality of approaches. A concomitant of the intellectual difficulty involved in understanding the past should be that archaeology must have a highly developed theoretical structure. Arguably, it should be the social science with the most sophisticated and highly developed set of theories. In actual fact archaeology remains the most weakly theoretically developed of all the social sciences. A curious inversion appears to have occurred – the discipline most in need of theory by and large appears to think that it can get along quite nicely without it.

Thought as embedded in historical process
Archaeological interpretations of the past are not secondary to the physical reality of the past, the objects in the archaeological record. Understanding the past is a dialectical process occasioned by continual adjustments of ideas, concepts and representations and is not something that could be fixed by a single method such as the hypothetico-deductive method. In essence, this is a method which is designed to leave us, as interpreters of the

past, speechless and powerless because it attempts to take away the responsibility for *choice* between competing ideas and concepts in a purely mechanical manner. It embodies a hope that the burden of choice, of evaluation, will pass away from us. The notion of the hermeneutic circle allows us to realize that we can never shed this burden of choice. Any interpretation of the past is multiple and constantly open to change, to re-evaluation. In essence the attempt to privilege a way of reducing all possible descriptions of the past to one methodology is an attempt to escape from humanity, from the fact that the past is produced in the here and now, in the present, by men and women. To suggest procedures could be developed leading to a totally objective view of the past (e.g. Binford 1982) is, as Sartre suggests (1982, p. 37), to place oneself in the image of God. Rorty nicely develops the point:

> Such a being does *not* confront something *alien* which makes it necessary for him to choose an attitude toward, or a description of, it. He would have no need and no ability to choose actions or descriptions. He can be called 'God' if we think of the advantages of this situation, or a 'mere machine' if we think of the disadvantages. (Rorty 1980, p. 376)

Now, as all archaeologists know, or should know, there are a multitude of possible competing descriptions of an artifact, an assemblage, or any set of remains encountered in the archaeological record. The choice involved in the description of these remains is related to the theories used to understand them.

The result of the archaeological project is that a vision of the past is produced and presented through publication. Archaeological work is historical in at least three ways: the archaeologist is concerned with the past, the archaeologist creates a past, in turn the past once created itself becomes historical. The implication of this 'historicism' (for the want of a better term) is that a critical attitude must be maintained in relation to archaeological practice. As we argued in Chapter 3, archaeological practice is, in part, political practice. To refuse to treat past social actors as mere 'objects' resulting from analysis to name just one area, does have political and social implications for the present. The manner in which the past is conceptualized, the data interpreted, and the analyses performed all provide meanings for the present. The kinds of explanations archaeologists give provide messages to other archaeologists and the non-archaeological public as to what archaeology *is* – the essence of its practical transformative activity on the past. Archaeology does not simply provide a conception or view of the past. It is also a discipline which should inform us of the nature of the human condition and the possibility of social transformation. In this sense we can agree firmly with Bernstein that what is required is 'to learn to think and act more like the fox than the hedgehog – to seize upon those experiences and struggles in which there are still the glimmerings of solidarity and the promise of dialogical communities in which there can be genuine mutual participation' (Bernstein 1983, p. 228). For the archaeologist to think like the fox rather than the hedgehog (perhaps slug would provide a better dramatic referent) is to realize that his or her work does have social and political implications and to act in conformity with this, i.e. to think clear-headedly about the nature of contemporary society in which he or she is inevitably embroiled and to ask whether the presuppositions he or she employs in trying to come to terms with an essentially alien past will either challenge or help to sustain the contemporary social order. No political position is neutral on this issue and there can be no neutral archaeology. We cannot and must not just describe dominance, power, hierarchy, inequality, exploitation and oppression but must engage in a critical perspective on the past. Archaeology is not, then, just some kind of resuscitation of the past in the present, but must involve a critique on the particular past that leads to our concrete present. For this critique to be successful, to have force, we cannot afford the essential irrationality of subjectivism or relativism as this would be cutting the very ground away from under our feet. What is needed is a transcendence of these through our practical work as archaeologists, through our own historicity. The guiding light which Gadamer's reconstruction of hermeneutics provides is that as far as archaeology or any other social science is concerned there is no simple choice to be made between a subjective or an objective account of reality unless one is to abandon science altogether and write novels instead. The post-empiricist philosophy of science seems to be arriving at a similar conclusion (see, for example, Hesse 1978; Bhaskar 1978; Harré 1979; Putnam 1978; Harré and Madden 1975; Papineau 1979).

Beyond hermeneutics, towards dialectics

Up to this point we have stressed the nature of archaeology as an interpretative hermeneutic exercise. However, this is not sufficient. There are certain well-known problems with hermeneutics – the lack of a notion of structure and of adequate consideration of power and ideology amongst others. While archaeology is inevitably an hermeneutic exercise and should be hermeneutically informed, it is not simply reducible to hermeneutics. In discussing the hermeneutic circle, we have already referred to a dialectical process of the interpretation of data binding it to theory. In the following section we wish to draw out the implications of this more fully.

A dialectical approach to the past involves at least three conceptions of the use of the term 'dialectic' and the language associated with it, terms such as 'moment', 'mediation', 'contradiction':

(i) a mode of theoretical appropriation of data;
(ii) a method of analysis and criticism transcending subject/object divisions;
(iii) a theory of social reality as a set of internally connected relations in a process of flux.

Here we focus on points (i) and (ii). In Chapter 6 we consider point (iii).

In an investigation of the past we are necessarily involved in making the elementary presupposition that there is an objective reality which exists beyond the realm of experience of any individual human subject. A real past exists but the pure essence of the objectivity of that past, i.e. how it really was, eludes us in that to begin to deal with the past involves us in decisions or choices as to how we might conceive of it. This is simply an extension of saying that we are inevitably involved in a process of selection and subsumption under some description. There are real past 'facts' but the facts that the archaeologist deals in are not these. The facts employed in any study of the past are not independent of their theorization. They are in no sense given to us but a product of the process of knowledge acquisition. Ideas, or the means for the factual constitution of the past, do not fall from heaven, but like all cultural products of human activity are formed in given circumstances. The facts of the archaeological case are 'real' as opposed to 'ideal' constructions in that they involve a transformation of aspects of data. The facts are thus theory-laden constructions constrained by resistances in the data. To understand any past object of study, be it a tomb or a potsherd, we need to ascribe meaning and significance because the data studied is a product of meaningful and symbolic human action. The meaning of an object is not given to it for us to directly perceive, nor is it solely constituted by a knowing subject. The meaning resides in, and is internal to, the dialectical relationship between the two. The interpreter conceptualizes the object of interpretation (that which has been created by subjects), and in turn, the object affects that conceptualization. Subject mediates object and object mediates subject in a reflexive process resulting in knowledge of object by subject. Following from this we must reject any naive distinction between the object conceived as concrete hard fact and theories or ideas about it conceived as abstract. Theory works on empirical objects which are theorized, brought into the account, through the subject-object reflexive relationship. Theory does not, then, work on a completely independent real object but on a *theoretical object*. The theoretical object on which theory works pertains to the real, to the data available in sense-perception, i.e. it takes or develops some aspect of it and is empirically constrained, but the theoretical and the real object are not one and the same thing but have a relative autonomy from each other. The data thus becomes a theoretical appropriation of the real, and theory works on this data through its further conceptualization. There can be no question, then, of testing in terms of either a verificationist or a falsificationist strategy. This is because there is literally *nothing independent of theory* or propositions to test against. Any test could only result in a tautology. At this point it is worth noting that such a position does not call into question the use of statistics and what are incorrectly termed statistical tests (e.g. chi-square, rank scales and other standard procedures). What we are saying is that these and any other statistics do not confirm, refute or falsify propositions. All they can be used to do (and this is the manner in which they are used in Chapters 7 and 8) is to redescribe data patterning. We still have to make sense of the redescription or grant it meaning and significance. The redescription provided by the use of statistics may be more or less useful to us in our attempts to conceptualize the past. They may help conceptualization as aids to description and redescription, interpretation and reinterpretation.

If one rejects an account of archaeological knowledge grounded in processes of testing, in a confrontation between subject and object, the question arises as to how great is the distinction between a data-based account of the past and a fictionalized account. It would be common to differentiate archaeology from literature on the grounds that archaeology deals, at least nominally, in a realm of fact while literature moves in the realm of fiction. It is true that the archaeologist may not invent facts at will while the literary writer may and has a much greater freedom in exploring relationships. On another level the distinction between archaeology and literature breaks down in that archaeologists construct what may be termed facts and all archaeologists use heuristic fictions or models to organize and orientate the archaeological record and make it meaningful, to sort out that which appears most pertinent to understanding. The idea of a purely factual archaeology, a totally objective account of the past, is itself an ideal type or a heuristic fiction. Even if some archaeologist were to achieve this impossibility it would remain unrecognized by either the investigator or others. The paradox is that to appreciate an objective mirror image of the past for what it is we would already have to know what the past was really like. The alternative, the way out of this paradox, is as argued in Chapter 1, to accept the presence of the past and that in the present and the future new pasts will be created.

Explanation

Explanation can only take place at the level of the theoretical object because it is only here that meaning is conferred. As the theoretical object is inextricably related to the real object, this is also explained, but only through its theoretical mediation. Explanation and understanding of the archaeological record consists in:

(1) Making conceptual links between the theoretical objects such that they can be shown to be related to each other in a coherent fashion. This is a process of conceptual extension and translation between the theoretical objects;

(2) Showing the manner in which the interlinked theoretical objects can be generated by underlying principles related to the life-world of the past. These principles are formulated by the analyst as a result of his or her knowledge, a knowledge dialectically produced through conceptual labour working on theoretical objects, and the conceptual links made between them. It represents a third and final level of theoretical appropriation of the real. The plausibility or conditional truth of the account, resides in the logical links established through the stages of the theoretical appropriation of the past and has nothing to do with a correspondence in any direct or simple manner with external facts. The entire process of analysis and explanation of the real moves in a dialectical process in which theoretical analysis results in the formulation or understanding of structuring principles of social life which are then referred back in order to explain data via conceptual links (Fig. 5.1).

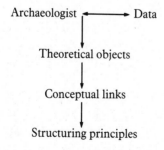

Fig. 5.1 Stages in theoretical appropriation.

We support the realist point (Bhaskar 1978, 1979) that the observable is generated, and thus at least in part explained, through unobservable processes or relationships.

This is the single most important realist proposition which sets it up in direct opposition to positivism/empiricism and it involves the rejection of the Humean conception of causation discussed in Chapter 2, in which the world is presupposed to consist of atomistic particulars or cause-effect regularities known through sense-perception by the subject who then applies a thick layer of logical cement (inductive or deductive reasoning) to link together cause and effect which, at the outset, have been separated. A realist position, by contrast, asserts that regularities which are observable through sense data are the result of unobservable generative mechanisms which link them together. These mechanisms are real, that is they possess ontological status, but exist independent of thought:

> The realist view of explanation can be conveniently summarised in the claim that answers to why-questions (that is requests for causal explanations) require answers to how- and what-questions. Thus if asked *why* something occurs, we must show *how* some event or change brings about a new state of affairs, by describing the way in which the structures and mechanisms that are present respond to the initial change. To do this, it is necessary to discover *what* the entities involved are: to discover their natures or essences.
>
> (Keat and Urry 1975, p. 31)

This means that we need to pay attention to the underlying logic governing the apparent visible logic. We are involved in a search for structures underlying the real. Now, social structures differ from natural structures in a number of important ways. Social structures are relations of production and reproduction which are both constraining and enabling (see Chapter 6). Social structures, unlike natural structures (i) do not exist independently of the activities they govern; (ii) do not exist independently of the agent's conceptions of what activities they are carrying out; (iii) are in a chronic state of structuration and are only relatively enduring (Bhaskar 1979, pp. 48–9; Giddens 1984, 1979, chapter 2). The notion of structure is taken up further in the next chapter and all we wish to note here is that these structures are composed or constituted by structuring principles. These structuring principles are to be related to theoretical objects and are partially explanatory in so far as they can be shown to generate them. The data is thus explained by a necessary step of shifting away from it and the dialectical interplay of theorized data takes place within the hermeneutic circle.

Knowledge
Knowledge is propositional; it resides in making statements about the world and being able to justify these statements. Standard epistemologies rely on either (i) making a transcendental claim or a metaphysical statement which we can either accept or reject, or (ii) are forced to move backwards in an infinite regress (see Rorty 1980, for an excellent exposition). We do not reject the concept or notion of knowledge but wish to take some of the unjustified 'glamour' away from the term by adopting the position that knowledge arises from the practical activities or *praxis* of men and women in the world (*cf.* the consideration of truth on pp. 20–2). This is not a roundabout way of

suggesting 'all knowledge is relative' since a relativist claim of the latter sort is contradicted by the universality of the clause employed to argue for it.

Theory is not something which can be merely 'applied' to empirical data. Statements and interpretations or propositions about the past result from practical actions or theoretical labours linking subject and object and going beyond both. Hence theory is practice and knowledge is a production. This conception of knowledge as a production has a number of distinct advantages and we owe it in one form to the work of Althusser (1977). Viewing theoretical work as social practice sharing features with other social practices (e.g. economic, political, technical, ideological) characterized by a distinctive means and mode of production and type of human labour working on raw materials to create a product, removes the untenable notion of knowledge being reducible to a product of pure flights of genius – we just need a few archaeological Einsteins to tell us how the past was or how to set about research! The raw materials from which knowledge is created are concepts, notions and facts (theoretical objects) which for archaeology are either the work of prior discourse inside or outside the discipline or are themselves produced and then further reworked. Returning to the notion of the historicity of thinking discussed above, the idea of knowledge as production leads us to understand that this production always takes place at a particular time and place in a field of power relations and politics. Involved in the production of knowledge is *conceptual struggle* and concepts, more broadly conceptions of the past, may have *effects* as interventions today in the present. In this sense the past is real and not dead and gone: through archaeological and historical production it is an active part of the present.

Conclusions

We have argued that archaeology is a hermeneutics, an interpretative practice, and have outlined a conception of archaeological research as dialectical and knowledge as practical. These conceptions were supported by an emphasis on historicity and critique. A critical archaeology is both reflexive (critical of itself) and critical of the past. It aims to explain meanings and ideologies by disclosing the social conditions, social relations, interests and structures from which they arise. This permits the possibility of being able to disclose the manner in which meanings may be constructed and imposed by dominant groups. A task of a critical archaeology providing a critical explanation of the past is to study the manner in which material culture may be employed to foster 'distorted' communication and used in power strategies (see Chapters 6–8).

In this chapter we have made a brief set of philosophical remarks which are only intended as possible guides towards the fully fledged development of a hermeneutic, reflexive, dialectical and critical non-empiricist philosophy of archaeology. There can be no final answers to the problems we have discussed; as with the book as a whole, the end of this chapter is arbitrary: it signals a beginning. We finish with some summary points.

(1)   The task of a philosophy of archaeology should be to offer potentialities rather than to foreclose them.
(2)   Archaeology is characterized by a fourfold hermeneutic and, as a hermeneutic process, is an attempt to make sense of the past in its contextual embeddedness.

(3) We need to escape from the notion of 'hard' facts and 'weak' theories and put both on an equal and dialectical footing.

(4) It is necessary to go beyond surface appearances in understanding the past.

(5) It is important to distance being empirical – considering data in all its potential fullness and complexity – from being empiricist – granting primacy to that data.

(6) Archaeology is neither subjective or objective; it transcends this dualism.

(7) We should see the gap between past and present as productive of discourse and dialogue rather than as a troublesome barrier.

(8) Archaeology is historically and socially situated – a political practice.

(9) An archaeology which is involved in an active interpretation of the past reveals the potential of the notion of critique in relation to past and present.

6

Social archaeology: the object of study

'A little formalism turns one away from History . . . a lot brings one back to it.'
(Barthes 1973b, p. 112)

Introduction

In previous chapters we have considered archaeology as a practice in the present, a writing and production of texts about the past. We have argued that the past is not identical to its representation; reality is irreducible to facts, is not information to be objectively, quantitatively defined, but is a field of polysemy, is informed by values, is constituted in practice. We have emphasized archaeology as being indelibly hermeneutically informed, as dialectic, and as itself embedded in historicity. We have also criticized the reduction of meaningful practice to behaviour – the descriptive treatment of meaningful and historical practice as bodily movement. We have emphasized instead individual agency, that archaeology as practice is a rhetoric produced in definite social conditions and social circumstances. In our criticism of various positions adopted in the archaeological literature we have elaborated how they may be construed as ideological – related to contemporary structures of inequality. Archaeology has in so many ways become not a reawakening or remembering of the past, but an apology for the present.

In this chapter we build on this conception of practice and ideology in considering the object of archaeology. In accordance with previous chapters, we reject the possibility of making a methodological prescription of what we are to find in theory, but instead concentrate on a series of ideas and concepts which we consider can overcome the disabling fissures running through conventional approaches.

Archaeology is unavoidably social not only in the sense that it is produced by men and women in and outside institutions but because its data are the products of social practices. Such practices are structured and structures have a dual nature: they are the medium and outcome of practices which constitute social systems in a reflexive manner. This separates structure from its practical constitution – system – and emphasizes the spatiality and temporality of practices. We stress that practice, in its structuring, spatiality and temporality, is political and historical, and social systems are contradictory, not homogeneous entities, but characterized by political relations of dominance and subordination. Individuals are competent and knowledgeable while at the same time their action is situated within unacknowledged conditions and has unintended consequences.

The concepts presented in this chapter have been outlined elsewhere (Tilley 1982a; Miller and Tilley 1984b; Shanks and Tilley 1982; Hodder 1982a; Rowlands 1982; see also Bhaskar 1979; Bourdieu 1977, 1979, 1984; Giddens 1976, 1979, 1981, 1984: we have also found stimulating Ollman 1971; Hindess and Hirst 1977; Cutler *et al.* 1978; Gregory 1982a, 1982b; and Laclau and Mouffe 1985). Our aim here is not to provide an exhaustive treatment of the conceptual apparatus (which would require a considerable work now in preparation; Shanks and Tilley (in press)); to avoid undue repetition we present instead more of a resumé.

Artifact, culture, system

Focus on artifacts and the labour of typology and classification as an end in itself is a long-discredited antiquarianism. 'The archaeologist is digging up, not things, but people', claimed Wheeler (1954, p. 13), arguing for a 'seasoning of humanity', that the dry and dusty remains be brought to life by the archaeological imagination. For most of this century the concept of *culture* has provided the link between artifacts and peoples. Developed by Childe to mean regularly associated material culture traits in the same time and place (Childe 1956, p. 33), 'cultures' were assumed to represent peoples or societies and have been the basic object of study for prehistoric archaeologists. Once classified, prehistory could then be described in terms of the interaction of such entities – diffusion of ideas, migration, invasion or internal innovation.

Much criticism has been made of the correlation between cultures and peoples. Clarke (1968) emphasized that cultures were archaeological rather than ethnic entities, polythetically rather than monothetically defined. Renfrew (1978b) has questioned the existence of homogeneous assemblages, arguing that cultures are arbitrary taxonomic categories imposed on a continuum of change, and Shennan (1978) has skilfully elaborated the spatial variability which makes the Beaker phenomenon meaningless as a coherent cultural tradition.

Binford (1972) has criticized the definition of artifacts as expressions of social norms specific to distinct groups. Instead of distinct cultures and their particular interactions, the object of archaeology was to become culture systems, behavioural and adaptive, in terms of which variability in the archaeological record could be explained. In contrast to the pessimism of traditional 'normative' archaeology which despaired of being able to specify supposedly non-material aspects of society (religion, beliefs, politics), a fully social archaeology became accessible according to a framework permitting a mechanistic relationship between society and environment with material culture mediating as an extrasomatic means of adaptation.

The optimism of new archaeology with regard to the object of archaeology has led to an extensive interest in reconstructing past societies and with schemes of social evolution, even if some of the claims have been discarded or never been accepted (e.g. formulation of laws of culture process, rigid hypothetico-deductive procedures).

However, the concept of social or cultural system within the ecological functionalism of the new archaeology has been effectively challenged (Hodder 1982b; Tilley 1981a, 1981b). The idea of a social system as developed by Renfrew (1972), Clarke (1968), Plog (1974) and others, is based on a biological analogy, either explicitly or implicitly, that society can be conceived in some sense as an organism in homeostatic equilibrium within its environment. Much archaeology has thus been concerned with defining and investigating relations between social system and environment or ecosystem in relation to technology and population levels. But with the natural system state being defined as stability and absence of change and with a radical separation of what is internal and external to the system, change has usually been viewed as deriving from outside the system parameters, and there is a separation of statics and dynamics, synchrony and diachrony, the latter being associated with change. As a reified whole, the social system has no place for individual action. The major problem is the dependence on *function* as the explanatory concept – that any social element can be explained by reference to the part it plays in maintaining the survival of the social whole. Things said to have functions are attributable to an enormous variety of categories, e.g. pencil sharpeners, record players, cars, parts of organisms, social institutions, specific events or relationships. Questions of the form 'What is X for?' almost demand a functional answer in everyday discourse. For example a reply to the question 'What are shopping bags for?' might be 'for holding articles purchased while out shopping'. Now this is fairly innocuous and we might think it a fairly reasonable reply. The crux of the problem is that when such answers are given to explain social relationships they become manifestly inadequate, and the more complex the practices which are to be explained, the more inadequate the answer. The subsystems of a society are claimed to function together via negative and positive feedback mechanisms in much the same way as the parts of an organism, such as the heart or the kidneys, function to keep it alive. When certain practices or institutions are present in a social system these are explained as part of its functioning. For example, Rappaport (1967, pp. 224–42; 1971a) proposes that ritual is an information exchange device communicating cultural, ecological and demographic data across the boundaries of social groups. On his account, other rituals regulate the dispersal of human populations, preserve a balance between farmed and fallowed land, and keep domestic animals within an adaptive goal range (Rappaport 1971b). In archaeology such ideas have been used by Thomas (1972) and Flannery and Marcus (1976) among others. However, such a functional explanation for the presence of rituals in all these cases tells us nothing whatsoever about their form and content – all it purports to explain is why these rituals occurred at all. We are left with an empty shell of an explanation in which content is reduced in favour of instrumental logic. Moreover, we have no glimmering of an account of why one particular type of ritual should occur rather than another. The reference made to practical interest, utilitarian value, adaptive expedience (adaptation to the environment) in such a framework entails a radical separation of function and culture, objective expedience and style, function and style (*cf.* Dunnell 1978b; Schiffer 1979). What functional value can the style of a pot possess? – little can be said of particular meaning, of the specific way things are made and done, that is style, which is so much of what archaeologists are concerned with (see Chapter 7). When what matters is simply the 'objective' and 'adaptive' aspects of what is done, meaningful social practice is reduced to behaviour – bodily movement.

For systems analysis in archaeology, the system, environment and subsystems are essentially descriptive categories, patterns of empirical regularities tied together through functional links. Much effort has gone into investigating pattern in the archaeological record (settlement distributions, distributions of exchanged items, resource distribution, artifact distributions and distributions of features within sites). Once the patterns are depicted then they are presumed to fit into a behavioural functional whole. A functional explanation always presupposes some needs, wants, interests or goals. In other words it is teleological in form. Something occurs as the result of reaching towards or pertaining to a desirable state. Individuals may be very well said to have needs. Indeed this is an essential characteristic of humanity: to have aspirations and desires. By contrast social systems themselves have no needs, they have no need to function, to survive, to attain a goal range or to seek out homeostatic states. The needs of the social system cannot be independent of the actors which make it up, so the notion of system function or the function of rituals or other institutionalized practices is entirely irrelevant and misplaced. Feedback processes cannot be conceptualized except in terms of some goal unless they are just random, but to anthropomorphize such processes is an invalid procedure.

It is a misconception to conceive of the object of archaeology as artifacts in themselves, the archaeological culture concept, or as a functionally defined social system. An alternative proposed by some (e.g. Schiffer 1976, 1981, 1983a) is that archaeology should be a science of material culture, its object being the remains and artifacts, their relationships and processes of the formation of the archaeological record. But the ultimate aim is to specify links (usually mechanical) between material culture patterning and 'society'; the aim is to reach a description of society, either defined in terms of a functionally adaptive system or in terms of a generalized, atemporal, aspatial 'culture process'.

Some archaeologists, through a reading of Marxist work, especially Marxist anthropology, have drawn on the concept of the mode of production, looking at the archaeological record in terms of social relations of production, involving especially considerations of ranking, kinship structures and ideology within social formations characterized by contradiction and conflict rather than homeostatic mechanisms (e.g. Bender 1978; Friedman and Rowlands 1978; Gledhill 1981; Gledhill and Rowlands 1982; Frankenstein and Rowlands 1978; Kristiansen 1984; Gilman 1984). While fully supporting the aims of this work to overcome the inadequacies of systemic approaches with a valuable emphasis on contradiction, reproduction and change, we wish to question the adequacy of the concept of mode of production and social relations of production as predetermined objects of archaeological analysis.

Against essentialism: social system as relational whole
We have argued in previous chapters that the artifact cannot be isolated from its relational context in both present and past. We would thus agree with Lukács's (1971 [1923]) programmatic proclamation made in the early days of Western Marxism, of the centrality of the category of totality (see Jay 1984 for an excellent review of historical changes in the use of the concept). Any archaeology which argued for the existence in the past of entities larger than the individual or interactions between individuals and their artifacts, would seem to, at least nominally, conform to this position: culture, society, social system or mode of production are all holistic units differing mainly according to the definition of constituent parts and the characterization of their inter-

relations. Rowlands, in particular (1982), has reaffirmed that the idea of totality is a strength of archaeology, concerned as it has been for so long with aggregate units, but does point to problems with the idea of 'society' – that bounded units within the archaeological record which might be equivalent to society don't exist (referring to Shennan's work, 1978), that the unitary notion of 'society' is historically derived, part of the emergence of nation-states in Western Europe (Rowlands 1982, pp. 163–4). We wish to build on this position and contend that there is no underlying principle or principles unifying the concept of 'society' good for all times and all places, principles which would remove the category of society from history. The category of totality cannot be pre-defined. We wish to argue against the object of archaeology being any particular and abstract object, *society* or *system*, sometimes defined in theory, sometimes distilled from the empirical, essentially existing beyond history. We argue that there can be no general structuring of society or of the social world with pre-defined subsystems, with one or several principles or 'essences' (the economic, environment, technology, population, social relations of production) producing effects (as in, for example, the Marxist base–superstructure formula). Such essentialism is mechanically deterministic, reductionist – reducing empirical detail to the effect of a principle – and naturalizes and legitimates a *particular* and historical conception of the structuring of social reality which has the effect of removing it from the historical process. Neither individuals nor the theoretical systems they construct can miraculously escape from the historicity of human existence (see Chapter 5).

Nor is there an essence 'human nature', such an entity as homo oeconomicus (Chapter 3) or homo artifex (Chapter 4). We do not criticize such objectifying values with reference to another set of absolute 'human' values (deemed to be superior in some way), but rather wish to emphasize the ambiguity and fragility of human values, their perversion through association with other values and their restriction to particular sections of the population often held to be enlightened and especially perceptive (see the discussion in Chapters 1 and 3 of Cultural Resource Management's conservation ethic which must, it is claimed, be transmitted to the general population; and see the discussion in Chapter 3 of Clark's assertion (1979, 1983) that human cultural value is dependent on the presence of elites).

Such essentialism also reproduces a whole series of disabling dualisms, aporias, conceptual dead-ends which it is vital to avoid:

essence	–	appearance
necessity	–	contingency
interior	–	exterior
abstract	–	concrete
concept	–	fact
object	–	properties
subiectum	–	*accidentes*
substance	–	attributes
society	–	individual
reality	–	consciousness
body	–	mind

The terms of each pair are radically separated and often, explicitly or implicitly, the first term is privileged, made to have primacy over the second. The whole complex forms a labyrinth of contradiction encompassing archaeological explanations.

The specification of a principle or essence unifying, underlying and explaining data depends on the idea that it is possible to radically separate that which is primary and constituting from that which is secondary and contingent on a priori grounds. Many conventional approaches to the archaeological past specify an underlying principle or essence (adaptation to environment, systemic homoeostasis, economic necessity, social relations, function) which can be separated from the contingent, which produces effects, effects which are determined by the underlying principle (it may be empirical detail, 'superstructures', 'style', social change, artifact variability). Archaeology becomes the viewing of the transcendental signified through its expressions or signifiers (social structures through burial practices, through material culture patterning). The essential is viewed through its appearances.

The search for an underlying principle implies a definitional obsession: marking the boundaries of the essential, defining 'real' entities, evolutionary stages, 'cultures', 'subsystems', according to which the past might be explained. Such definition (often disguised as neutral classification) depends on a separation of interior and exterior – that which is internal to the transcendental signified and that which is external, separating the essence from the appearance.

A redefinition of necessity is required. It does not refer to an underlying and externally defined determinant principle but refers to the nature of structural relations. So in a total system with each element specified and related within the whole, all relations are necessary, all elements and relations depending on each other. Such a total system of synchronous necessity is a political project, a totalitarian project of a perfectly defined and administered society, timeless, lasting a thousand years. This is the project implied in the separation of synchrony and diachrony. It is considered possible to make a slice through time and read the social structure of the moment, the static essence of its empirical development – the events of history. As Althusser (1977, pp. 94–6) points out, this essence-development duality is based on a conception of time as a continuity of present (synchronous) moments, homogeneous measurable duration, empty, a conception we have criticized in Chapters 1 and 4. Such a conception makes history a problem; the 'essential section' of the social, the synchronic as contemporaneity itself, timeless presence, has primacy over practice and history.

For Althusser, the totality, the social whole is *overdetermined*. So the totality is not some external structure or some essence, reference to which explains surface phenomena, concrete effects; structure is neither internally nor externally separate but is present in its effects. There is no barrier between abstract concept and the empirical-concrete (Althusser 1977, pp. 188ff.). Laclau and Mouffe (1985) emphasize the potential significance of this contention; the social is a symbolic order. So there is no ultimate and primary substance represented in a separate realm of (contingent) signification; the social is always already a symbolic order. In such a symbolic order meaning is realized through the system of differences; meaning does not reside within any element in-itself but each element means or exists only in so far as it relates to other elements, differing, deferring or delaying absent elements. There can be no self-sufficient or self-identical element. In supporting the idea of the social being overdetermined in this way we reject the search for an ultimate object of archaeology which can be defined literally and its secondary effects or properties read off.

This involves a rejection of the concept of an object being separated into underlying materiality (*subiectum*) and properties or attributes attached or possessed (*accidentes*) (see Chapter 1, pp. 9–10). This idea of discrete objects of analysis with definable and quantifiable attributes is obviously encouraged in archaeology by the character of remains of the past – many apparently discrete units: pots, tools – and also by the applicability and 'success' of mathematical and statistical procedures. Time is not a dependent variable or attribute: empty measured duration according to which the substance of the past can be plotted. The social does not exist *within* time so it is not possible to separate synchrony from diachrony, static definition from temporal development, as we have just pointed out in another context.

This viewpoint entails a rejection of conceptions of middle-range theory (see Chapter 2), the idea that a set of mechanical and universal principles can be defined, and according to which dynamic culture process can be read-off the static archaeological record which, in effect, becomes contingent, unnecessary, accidental. Equally inadequate are structuralist attempts to reduce all explanation to the structure behind the appearance, essences of that which is empirically observable. Structure and its realization cannot be radically separated out in so far as structure exists only in its realization in space-time – is present in, through and by its effects (see below).

Instead of discrete objects defined according to attributes, a flux of internal relations: it is to this relational complex that the category of totality refers. The relations between elements are *internal* (Ollman 1971); it is not a case of discrete elements joined by external relations. There is no totally internal element, a fully constituted identity, in-itself, identical with itself; any part of a social order is always subverted by internal relations with other elements in a system of differences. The presence or trace of some elements in others prevents identity being fixed; there is always a surplus of meaning which cannot be pinned down. So it is not possible to separate environment from society, external from internal; each defines the other. The economic cannot be separated from the political, from ritual; there can be no literal differentiation. Each is subverted by a polysemy which prevents stable, self-contained definition. The economic is both present and absent in the political and ritual, is structured as political and ritual space. In addition to rejecting a base-superstructure conception we reject any simple a priori separation of economy, politics, ideology.

The object of archaeological study is always partial and incomplete, pierced by contingency; a total system would be a system of total necessity and regularity with all meaning fixed, all action predictable, all intentions fulfilled. Necessity in a relational sense refers to the fixation of meaning, the establishment of regularity in difference, in the contingent; necessity and contingency define each other.

Agency and social practices

What place is there for human agency in a conceptualization of the social totality as consisting of a flux of internal relations? Of all the dualisms mentioned above one of the most damaging and disabling is the individual/society; subject/structure couplet in which the two sets of terms are radically opposed to each other. It is no exaggeration to state that the problem of how to conceptualize the relationship between individual or group agency and wider social processes has been a primary problem of both the philosopher and the social theorist since the Enlightenment and beyond. Conceptualization of the relationship may amount to little more than 'taking sides': either the individual and social practices or society and social structures become effectively annulled. In part this is a debate about free will and determinism. Is society determined by the will of individuals or individuals by society? It is also a debate between idealism and materialism, between preconceived categories of a human essence and a view of subjects being constructed in the social.

One extreme is to assert individualistic voluntarism in which individuals are regarded as creating societies. The latter becomes more or less a residual term: the sum of the individuals who through their actions make it up, a doctrine sometimes termed methodological individualism (Brodbeck 1966; Watkins 1970; Weber 1964, p. 101). Subjectivist sociology (phenomenological sociology, e.g. Phillipson 1972; and ethnomethodological perspectives, Garfinkel 1967; Johnson *et al.* 1984, chapter 3) bears a family resemblance to the same general approach in which human actions are thought to depend solely upon how subjects interpret and account for the social conditions in which they are situated, the meanings such situations have for them as agents and the languages and symbolic forms of discourse they use and construct to explain these states. Human actions flow from subjective intentions, and social structures become subjectively inhabited or based. Such a view also finds expression in much historical narrative in which history is effectively boiled down to the doings of great men and women. The fact that Caesar crossed the Rubicon becomes an essential historical detail distinguished from the crossing of the Rubicon by anyone else.

On the other hand, functionalism, structuralism and post-structuralist approaches effectively eliminate the individual from the analysis in various ways. Individuals become statistical detail (Redman 1978b, p. 330), props for the structure (Althusser and Balibar 1977, p. 180) or bourgeois illusions which require decentring (Coward and Ellis 1977, p. 94). Foucault (1979, 1981) is always much happier when referring to 'bodies' rather than 'people'.

In the position taken here we wish to refuse this dualism, to acknowledge that without individuals and the social practices of individuals societies would not exist but that at the same time the individual human subject requires a thorough decentring from the stage. We can agree both that 'man is a myth of bourgeois ideology' (Althusser 1976, p. 52) and that 'it is only from the face-to-face relationship, from the common lived experience . . . that the intersubjective world can be constituted' (Schutz 1972, p. 166). This requires a materialist dialectical conception of the relationship between subject and structure, the agent and society. Considering the agent as an active decentered subject enables a position transcending mechanistic reduction and voluntaristic idealism. All subjects are *positioned* in relation to other subjects, groups and institutions or collectivities, power, ideology and social structures. To state that the subject is positioned does not require that he or she becomes a mere component or a prop.

The following points may be made about agency:

(1) All action is social action.
(2) The primary characteristic of such action is a realization of teleological positing.
(3) All social actions are determined actions because (i) some actions may be forced by violence or its threat; (ii) most actions have a habitual basis; (iii) some actions are influenced and promoted via ideology; (iv) actions which seem to be free in the sense that they involve a choice on the part of the subject, involve interests and values. However, these interests and values are themselves situated in a socially constructed field so that the choices are not free-floating. No child born in Britain makes a choice of whether or not to speak English if the act of speaking has a communicative intent in relation to other English speakers.

To regard all action as social action is to recognize the constitution of action in sociability and in socialization processes. A child brought up in complete isolation could hardly be subsequently regarded as being a competent member of society. There is no principle of action which can be regarded as being a distinctive property of an individual if by this is meant some intention, purpose or quality originating entirely outside social life. Actions make sense in relation to the social context in which they are situated as does language. Robinson Crusoe may have been alone on his desert island but in another sense he took his entire society with him. The practices of individual subjects and their relational effects in the social totality take place both *in* language and *in* the materiality of Being. The individual is both constructed through language use and the materiality of his or her social being but also has a certain reflexive efficacy in that construction process. When an agent makes a statement about a situation or produces or uses an object the statement made or the particular type or form of production or usage is a product of past experiences, intentions for the future and the particular language or material object involved. Through agency, praxis, language and consciousness become conjoined and there can be no sharp division between language and the manner in which social reality is constructed. Reality is conceived through language and through acting on that reality such that language, thought, reality and action all become contextually interbedded. The role of language and action is less to reflect or picture or operate in reality but to actively shape that reality, reproduce it or transform it.

The distinctive quality of action and agency is that it is purposive. Societies as a whole are not purposive and neither are animals, birds or plants. The latter may be held to be characterized as being 'purposive without a purpose' (Kant). Lukács underlines the point that 'only in labour, in the positing of a goal and its means, consciousness rises with a self-governed act, the teleological positing, above mere adaptation to the environment – a stage retained by those animal activities that alter nature objectively but not deliberately – and begins to effect changes in nature itself . . . Since realization thus becomes a transforming and new-forming principle of nature, consciousness, which has provided the impulse and direction for this, can no longer be simply an ontological epiphenomenon' (Lukács 1980b, pp. 22–3).

When we speak of agency, the vocabulary used to consider actions and their results involves terms such as wishes, desires, interests, intentions, purposes, dispositions, motives, principles, irrespective of whether or not these wishes, etc. ever actually were effected. Reasons may be regarded as causes of actions but not in a limited cause and effect type sense. Von Wright (1971, p. 107) puts forward the following scheme, in tenseless form, for understanding action:

> From now on A intends to bring about p at time t.
>
> From now on A considers that, unless he does a no later than at time t', he cannot bring about p at time t.
>
> Therefore, no later than when he thinks time t' has arrived, A sets himself to do a, unless he forgets about the time, or is prevented.

This is a scheme of practical inference or reasoning capturing notions of time, place, consciousness and teleological positing, emphasizing that intentions, goals for action, knowledge of the circumstances in which the agent finds him or herself and the means by which action is effected or done are all interdependent and changing or, in other words, relational. Such a formal scheme has a fairly limited area of application in the sense that it is an 'ideal type' and in most practical situations in the ongoing stream of daily life agents do not formally reason in such a manner. Wittgenstein notes that the 'game of giving the reason why one acts in one particular way does not involve finding the causes of one's actions' (Wittgenstein 1969, p. 110). To make sense of this statement requires a consideration of the relationship between action and consciousness.

A stratified model of agency

Faced with a choice between alternative goals and modes of conduct an agent may undertake a process of reasoning in some sense equivalent to the model of practical inference discussed above. Similarly, apparently spontaneous actions may be rationalized afterwards in such a manner. The ability to be able to talk about action or provide reasons for conduct involves discursive consciousness of the event. The game consists of being able to make the action intelligible in terms of the stream of other actions in daily life, forms of conduct implicitly or explicitly known to all social actors in any particular socio-historical context, knowledge which may readily be drawn upon for justifying or explaining actions. Discursive consciousness is thus a *rationalization* of and for action.

Characteristics attributable to agents always go under some sort of description. Typical terms include selfishness, greed, laziness, altruism, caring, industriousness, etc. Such attributes do not so much originate in the actor but are only possible or intelligible in terms of the particular social totality under consideration and in other situations the same actions might be described or understood in another fashion. In other words, there are no basic existential characteristics of 'humanity' such as these, good for all times and places. Actions have to be understood in terms of the context(s) in which they take place. The vast majority of social action is not normally open to discursive discussion but takes place on a level of practical consciousness or knowing how 'to go on' or proceed in a certain situation. Driving a car while not thinking about traffic rules, speaking while being unaware of the grammatical basis for language, eating dishes in a certain order are all examples of the same general phenomenon and practical consciousness pervades all practice from bodily hexis to the types of material goods found in an individual's home to the type of drink he or she chooses to take and the manner in which it may be consumed. Actions are performed in one manner rather than another because the social world is fundamentally a symbolically structured reality and inherently meaningful. The knowledge of the world on which agents draw in their day to day encounters and labour is largely implicit or taken for granted knowledge, and social life involves the constitution and transformation of meaning-frames through which agents orientate their conduct to others and the social and natural environment in which they are situated or positioned. Practical consciousness forms, typically, the primary basis for understanding that most action is overdetermined in that a host of unacknowledged conditions may underline any action or set of actions. Similarly actions, more often than not, may have unintended consequences. For example: *A* approaches *B* to greet her while holding a knife in his hand (because at the time he was gutting a fish). The intention of *A* was to greet *B* but at the last moment *A* trips over an unobserved boulder and stabs *B*: an unintended consequence of action. To make matters even more complicated another scenario might be: *A* actually intends to stab *B* and moves towards her with this end in view but trips over the boulder. Was the knife entering *B*'s body an intentional act or not? Had *A* not tripped over the boulder might he not have changed his mind at the last moment? The latter example is introduced to emphasize that the outcome of any action is always uncertain until it has been effected and that actions take place in an infinite variety of different circumstances which influence their outcome and result. Bourdieu (1977) and Giddens (1979, 1984) both emphasize that action sequences are typically monitored and that actors are not in any sense motivated cultural dopes but aware of their conditions of existence, although for the most part this is an intuitive, practical awareness. The boundary between discursive and practical consciousness is constantly shifting and sliding according to the time, the place, and the actors involved. The division between practical and discursive consciousness 'can be altered by many aspects of the agent's socialization and learning experiences. Between discursive and practical consciousness there is no bar; there are only the differences between what can be said and what is characteristically simply done. However, there are barriers, centred principally upon repression, between discursive consciousness and the unconscious' (Giddens 1984, p. 7).

To assert that action is determined is not to propose any mechanical determinancy but to acknowledge that actors find themselves in a life-world not of their own choosing and operate in that life-world and may reproduce or transform it through their activity. However, the motivations (unconscious desires, or formulated or unformulated reasons) for actions are contextually created in a determinate sociohistorical situation.

Structures, structuring principles
So far we have emphasized the notion of active agency but, given the rejection of any position which attributes the properties of social totalities as being derived solely from the activities of agents as individuals or in groups, institutions and collectivities, the

position that we wish to adopt here is that the social totality as a network of internal relations embraces the concepts of system and structure. By the former is meant the net-working of relations between individuals and groups in a field of existence embracing the categories of the economic, the political, the ideological and the symbolic which together constitute conditions of existence for the social strategies of individuals and groups situated in time-space. The social totality as a system networking of internal strategies and relations between individual groups is also a structured totality. Action and meaning becomes orientated or fixed at specific spatio-temporal conjunctures in that economic, social, political and ideological/symbolic relations are ordered by struc-tures which constitute and are constituted in and through social practice and social strategies deriving from that practice (Fig. 6.1).

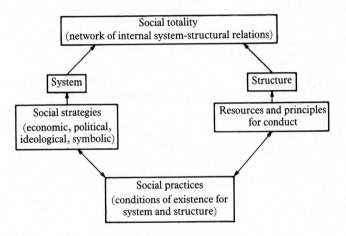

Fig. 6.1 Model of the social totality.

The conception of structure employed here may be summarized by the following points:

(1)   Structures are atemporal, aspatial entities yet chronically subject to change in time and space. They are present only through their effects, at their points of constitution via human agency and the social practices and social strategies which arise as a result of this agency.

(2)   Structures are constituted by principles and resources orientating social prac-tices and which are, in turn, orientated by those practices. These resources for conduct may involve sets of operations for ordering the social world such as left/right, back/front, inside/outside, pollution/purity; oppositions as rules or norms for conduct. At the most abstract level the principles involved which structure structures (structuring principles) are basic grounding oppositions such as that between socialized production and private appropriation in the capitalist state.

(3)   Structures as dynamic entities embrace contradictions and non-correspondences. There are no structures common to any society but only

particular structures located determinately at specific moments in time-space. Internal contradictions in structures are a necessary potentiality for change and such contradictions can only be dissipated through change.

Structuration

The practice of individuals is both structured and structuring, articulating meaning and conduct in a system of *difference*, creating meanings for action and conduct and conditions for the interpretation of those meanings and reproducing of transforming structures. Structured practice is produced according to the form or *modality* of the articulation of the structuring or generative principles and resources composing structure. The mediation of social practice via structure and the constitution, transformation or reproduction of structure via the medium of practice is embodied in the concept of structuration (Giddens 1979, pp. 69–73; 1984, pp. 1–40) which is akin in some respects to Bourdieu's use of the term 'habitus' (Bourdieu 1977, pp. 72–94; 1984, pp. 101–2, 169ff.). Both concepts play a similar role in linking social practices and social structures in a dialectical fashion.

The concept of structuration usefully encapsulates the chronically incomplete and 'imperfect' (see Chapter 1, pp. 9–10) nature of the social as lived, that structures are not hermetic and permanently fixed entities but are in a constant process of reproduction and transformation in practice. Structures form a medium for practice enabling and constraining it and, at the same time, are the outcome of practice and are reproduced or transformed by that practice. The process of structuration is both a temporal and spatial process. Time is not empty duration and space is not a vacant container, but both serve to constitute the form and nature of social practices and are relative to particular practices. So there is no objective measure (such as annular chronology) according to which all variation may be referred and classified and there is no way of distinguishing long and short-term change on an a priori basis (as palaeoeconomy, for example, assumes in its separation of the biological-evolutionary from the social-historical, the former being identified with long-term, underlying change).

The concept of structuration and the notion of habitus defined by Bourdieu as: 'the durably installed generative principle of regulated improvisations . . . [which produces] practices which tend to reproduce the regularities immanent in the objective conditions of the production of their generative principle [i.e. structure]' (Bourdieu 1977, p. 78) overcomes the duality of individual and society: the atomism of an individualism, a voluntaristic idealism which specifies motivations as the determinant factors in social practice, facing the reified and mechanical change of a holism in the face of which the individual is powerless (although, according to the apparently collective nature of archaeology's data, atomistic individualism has hardly appeared in archaeology, it is present as the absent opposite of mechanical holism). From the perspectives that all action is social action and that individual actions are mediated by structure which is in turn actively reformulated and reconstructed through individual agency, people do not consciously produce society; the social always already exists as social structures which enable and constrain action but do not determine it mechanistically. People act knowledgeably in terms of intentions and choices upon which social structures or unintended consequences of action depend. People are knowledgeable with the capacity to define themselves, and practice is open to discursive and practical consciousness; knowing *that* and knowing *how* to act. The social is a negotiable field and practice is inherently political with actors pursuing particular sociopolitical strategies.

That the social is overdetermined – always preconstituted as a symbolic field – and that structure has a duality enabling rather than determining in a mechanistic sense the practice of knowledgeable actors, means that there is an internal relation between activity and consciousness, body and mind. There is no primary substance – the object-world, reality – or behaviour, which produces effects in consciousness, determining a field of ideal signification. Action always goes beyond itself; it cannot be treated as movement, i.e. as behaviour. To explain an action, reference must be made to the social positioning of agency and to the context of practice. The object world and social world are always already symbolically constituted as part of language, symbolic systems, consciousness. This is not opposed to objects (and social structures) existing external to thought or language or consciousness; it is rather to assert that objects cannot produce themselves as objects (social structures as structures) outside language and consciousness. So categories, concepts, signification, representation are internal to, constitutive of the objects to which they refer. Products of labour, including material culture, embody mental operations, just as ideas have a material existence. Another important point is that symbolization, metaphor, metonymy, paradox, rhetoric are not aspects of thought and discourse which add additional sense to a primary literal meaning of the social or object world – there is none. They are part of the chronic process of negotiating meaning, of subverting the necessary character of positioned social relations.

Contradiction, power, ideology, change

The seeds of change need no sowing. Structures, dynamic and partial, are a unity of oppositions, a fixation of difference, chronically subject to change in their reproduction in practice. Actions may also have unintended consequences which react on the generating structures. The social is open, incomplete; the identity of any element in the social order can never be fully defined or found in a particular case, but exists as a field of relations. This system of difference is domesticated and arrested in structures. But structures do not fix meanings in a haphazard manner. We have pointed out the thoroughly political nature of social practices; structures enable and are produced in practices which are organized around political relations of dominance and subordination, power and control.

Productive power, power as the capacity to act in and on the world is an integral element of social life, a component of all social practice. Such *power to* can be distinguished from *power over*, social control and domination. So power is both productive, a positive force intimately involved in the reproduction and transformation of the social order and reality, and power may be a repressive and negative element, supporting social inequalities. Productive power draws upon and creates resources, material and non-material (forms of knowledge). Repressive power works within institutions and mechanisms which ensure subservience to the social order (forms of legitimate authority) and ultimately rests on a sanction of violence, direct physical coercion. Power then has no unitary form, no essence which can be possessed by individuals or groups, but is lived, is an aspect of practice and structure.

Social structures embody contradiction; structures are never total, never fully articulated with each other, never fixed and reified, but in a state of constant reproduction and change which may result in contradiction within and or between structures. This is particularly the case with a disjunction between intended and unintended consequences of action. Contradiction between structures results in antagonistic beliefs and meanings regarding practice and clearly relates to social relations of inequality. Contradiction translated into antagonistic interests and open social conflict generates social change.

But this translation into conflict between social groups, political struggle, is not automatic. Particular contradictions may not appear in the know-how and knowledge of a particular social group – they may not be aware of the context, meaning and consequences of a particular practice. We have already noted that repressive power may be used to exert control and forcibly prevent political struggle. However, such direct physical repression is rarely fully effective and is usually supplemented by ideology.

Ideology does not refer to a body of ideas, views, beliefs, held by a group of people, but is an aspect of a limited practice, an aspect of relations of inequality. Ideological practice misrepresents contradiction in the interests of the dominant group and may exhibit the following properties:

(1) it represents as universal that which is partial;
(2) it represents as coherent that which is contradictory;
(3) it represents as permanent that which may be in flux;
(4) it represents as natural and necessary that which is cultural and contingent.

Above all, ideology serves in the reproduction rather than the transformation of the social order: a strategy of containment and social closure.

Social totality, social practice, social strategies, structure, structuration, contradiction, power, ideology, conflict: this constellation of concepts provides a means of understanding and explaining reproduction and change within a field of sociopolitical relations of knowledgeable social agents.

Material culture: objectification and social strategies

> The objectification of man places a seal on the inert. He *comes to know himself in the inert* and is therefore a victim of his reified image, even prior to all
> alienation.   (Sartre 1982, p. 72, *n*. 32)

Material culture is an objectification of social being, a literal reification of that social being in the co-presences and absences embodied in the material form. Inert matter is transformed by social practices or productive labour into a cultural object, be it a product for immediate consumption, a tool or a work of art. Objectification – the serial transformation of matter into a cultural object – is the inevitable consequence attached to and flowing from labour. The image of humanity inscribed in material culture is, of course, not a phenomenal image of the self but of the powers involved in transformative social practice. The practice of individuals is 'written' and imprinted in the world leaving traces of varying degrees of solidity, opacity or permanence – material culture. Every act of social production is always one involving an interconnection between inert materiality, consciousness, action and thought. If there were no teleological positing on the part of agents there would be no material culture. Material culture results from a productive process and as a production it is the result of purposeful activity: it bears the indelible stamp of the positioned subject, positioned in relation to social structures and social strategies.

The social labour congealed in the object is inherently meaningful labour, labour which takes place in relation to a symbolically constructed social field. Just as the practice of agents is both structured and structuring so material culture is structured by agency and once the labour becomes objectified in material form it acts back to structure practices. Obvious examples are buildings which channel movement, both enabling certain patterns and constraining others – exerting influence. The objectification of practice in objects binds the two spheres together inextricably and the link is conceptual and internal to the objectification process. Structured patterns of action and consciousness become retained in objects as significations of the practice that produced them. A dialectical movement is involved in objectification in which activity transforms matter and negates its original form in the process of that transformation while at the same time the objectified object is a stabilization or negation of the action which produced it (see Sartre 1982, pp. 159ff.). Material culture retains the significations involved in its production as inscriptions intertwined into its nature and form. This gives these significations their efficacy in the ongoing stream of social conduct. The objectification of practice results in the creation of a form which confronts future practice yet is subject to future transformative activity at a material or interpretative level. The positioned agent or subject is always a social subject and in precisely the same way material culture is a social and socialized production even if the work of a single individual.

Material culture as an objectification of social practice and social structure does not directly reflect these practices and structures, but it may serve to mediate them via the logic of its own form. Material culture may operate simultaneously in a number of social fields. It may

(1) facilitate interventions in the natural and social world as technology;
(2) provide a communicative medium of symbolic significance in a structure of difference and signification;
(3) provide a medium for social domination as an expression of power and ideology.

Meaning in material culture
The major challenge confronting archaeologists is that of being able to confer meaning and significance to a world of otherwise meaningless and non-significant objects in terms of the social. The traces of the past are meaningless in the present and they require decoding (see Chapters 1, 5, and the discussion above and in Chapters 7–8). We argued above that social practice engraves meaning in material culture and structures it and that

material culture is active (it affects practice) and may operate three-dimensionally. In this section we wish to build further on this conception.

Material culture as a social objectification is charged with meaning and structured in relation to social strategies. People symbolically construct and organize their activities in a pre-constituted social field and simultaneously effect an ordering of the representation of those activities in language and in material objects as a symbolic scheme or modality for action in the world; activities can neither be understood nor explained apart from these. Meanings are not simply ethereal essences or reflections of the extant material conditions of existence and the social relations necessary for social reproduction and/or transformation, but are embedded in the materiality of day to day existence. The ability to use, meaningfully constitute, and manipulate systems of signification is a distinctively human quality which makes ideation and consciousness possible, the basis for all social interaction.

Material culture, as a structured and structuring resource, as an integral element actively and recursively involved in social life, plays an important role in the constitution and transformation of meaning frames. Any determinate social totality is characterized by distinctive practices, strategies and structures which are temporally, spatially and socially situated and articulated. Material culture is part of this articulation. This means that material culture can only be realistically interpreted once it is contextually situated in a double moment. First, explanations must be related to the field of internal relations of individual social totalities, and this invalidates cross-cultural approaches. Secondly, they must be contextually situated in the spatio-temporal moments of the totality. There is no point in attempting to formulate a highly specific general model of the significance of particular aspects of material culture-patterning such as types of burial practices, good for all time and all places. Material culture only has significance within the context of a particular social totality and the structures, structuring principles, conditions for social action and the nature of social practices which will differ from one particular case to another. People in particular situations operate in a form of life which needs and requires no justification other than that it has been tacitly agreed upon, and play different kinds of material culture games:

> I was asked in Cambridge whether I think that mathematics concerns ink marks on paper. I reply: in just the same sense in which chess concerns wooden figures. Chess, I mean, does not consist in my pushing wooden figures around a board. If I say 'Now I will make myself a queen with frightening eyes, she will drive everyone off the board' you will laugh. It does not matter what a pawn looks like. What is much rather the case is that the totality of the rules of the game determines the logical place of a pawn.
>
> (Wittgenstein *in* Kenny 1973, pp. 160–1)

The agreement in 'game rules' is not, in essentials, a decision open to any individual agent and neither is the form, content and nature of material culture and the significations it embodies. These are pre-given but may be transformed in a field of political and social strategies. The rules, then, of the material culture game are not fixed like those of chess but mutable and continuously subject to the possibility of change even though for the most part they may tend to be reproduced. Meaning is not a matter of an immutable relationship between signifier and signified but the spatio-temporal fixation of a chain of signifiers to produce an interpretable meaning.

Material culture can be considered to be a mode of non-verbal communication, at one and the same time both simpler and more complex than written or spoken language. The syntactic links are likely to be more explicit and fewer in number, and differences between right and wrong more clearly defined than in speech acts. At the same time material culture is more complex because it is polyvalent and can act in multidimensional channels. Material culture as a sign system serves power in social strategies as a producer and organizer of consensus and thus takes on an ideological dimension. The domination effected through ideology does not consist in the control of ideas by a ruling social class or group with particular sectional interests. It rather is effected as a result of the positioning established by agents in various social strategies in relation to meaning. A materialist theory of material culture as an embodiment of power and ideology involves an analysis of the processes by which fixed relations of meaning are produced in a symbolic field *for*, *in and by positioned subjects*. Material culture, as a structured and structuring sign system may be particularly productive in serving power strategies at a practical or non-discursive level of consciousness. That which is contingent may appear to be natural. Social actors may not realize in many instances that they are employing a series of embedded codes and in this case the sign system will use them rather than vice versa. Concomitantly, consensus may seem not only to be natural but actually spontaneous. Hence contrasts and relationships can be exploited as part of a semiotic code to structure, restructure and reproduce specific sets of social practices and relations.

What is present to the senses in the symbolization of material culture has to be actively produced by agents and therefore the conditions, context and form of its production and subsequent use will relate strongly to phenomenal form. So, material culture should not be conceived of as something passive merely reflecting social relations but as dialectically related to these social relations. Once created, produced, material culture forms a powerful medium for acting back and restructuring social practices. Material culture may be a particularly effective medium through which to legitimate the social order precisely because of its materiality, its fixation of the practice embodied in it allowing a relative permanence and efficacy in the structuring of subsequent practice.

As material culture is polyvalent acting in multidimensional channels any simplistic interpretation of it (e.g. as an extrasomatic means of adaptation) is bound to be inadequate. Material culture can neither be taken to be a direct mirror of society, nor are different aspects of material culture-patterning necessarily compatible with each other in terms of what they represent. We need to deal, ideally, with a wide range of different types of evidence in order to work out in precisely what manner they operate together or contradict each other in a field of social, economic, political and ideological relations. Differing representations may, as often as not, relate to contradictory ways of structuring social reality in relation to power strategies. In some contexts, as opposed to others, material culture may be used to create on an imaginary plane a universe whose content and form differs entirely from social reality, but whose components are akin, recognizable and therefore acceptable.

Conclusions

It is important to realize that in this chapter we have not been concerned simply to provide an alternative conception of the social and of material culture. We are instead asserting a social field which is thoroughly historical in the sense that definition of 'society' must be particular, related to particular historical conditions and events. There can be no universal definition of society (or any other object of archaeology) which would apply across history and across geography. Any such definition is the equivalent in theory of an absolute state fixing the place of every phenomenon in a totalitarian order, to a hegemonic paternalism, a repressive pluralism, an incorporative conservatism which effects a closure of the social in a monumental formalism. Through the denial of the search for essence we open up meaning and the question of the particular object of archaeological theory and practice. Through the notion of structuration and an active conception of situated or positioned practice we affirm the social negotiation of meaning in a destabilization of the supposedly concrete and solidly stable positivity of the world, affirm the permanence of the potentiality for social change, and the agency of individuals and that it is stability which requires explanation and understanding as much as the trajectories of any particular social transformation.

Material culture is the result of productive activity; it is an objectification. As such it is always actively implicated in the structuring of social practices. It is not a simple reflection of the totality or extant social relations but forms a set of resources, a symbolic order within practice, drawn upon in political relations, activated and manipulated in ideology. Chapters 7 and 8 further examine the role of material culture and situate it within both past and present social practice and structural relations.

The object of study of a fully social archaeology is, then, on the basis of the framework advanced above, the relation of material culture-patterning to social practices, social strategies and social structures in determinate social totalities in the past and in the present.

PART III

Material culture and social practices

7

Style and Ideology

'The first principle of a materialist analysis would be . . . productions must not be studied from the standpoint of their unity which is illusory and false, but from their material disparity. One must not look for unifying effects but for signs of the contradictions (historically determined) which produced them and which appear as unevenly resolved conflicts.'   (Balibar and Macherey 1981, p. 87)

'Like private property, the [work] thus appears as a "natural" object, typically denying the determinants of its productive process. The function of criticism is to refuse the spontaneous presence of the work – to deny that "naturalness" in order to make its real determinants appear.'   (Eagleton 1976, p. 101)

Introduction

Questions concerned with stylistic and functional attributes of material culture-patterning lie at the heart of much archaeological theory and practice. Pots and broken pots constitute a major type of archaeological data. But once they are recovered from the ground, what are we to do with them? Put them in a glass case and admire their aesthetic qualities, comment on their crudities? Speculate as to their function? Or simply treat them as another 'type fossil' – signifiers of chronological location, degree of social contact, diffusion or migration? The designs on pots vary in an almost infinite number of forms and this chapter sets out to tackle this most basic problem, the problem of the style of ceramics and stylistic variability. We first consider how archaeologists have treated the style of pots, discussing among other things, the traditional use of pots as a means of dating sites, as supposed signifier of groups of people, the notion of the separation of style and function involving the assertion of the primacy of function and the relegation of style to an irrelevant or mute peripheral feature, the idea of style being adaptive and as reflecting social relations. We argue that conventional theories are inadequate in accounting for many aspects of stylistic variability either because of their limited scope and scale of application or because they rely on a reductive form of functionalist analysis which either subsumes or fails to account for the variability of designs. Our criticisms rest on the argument that pots are made and decorated by knowledgeable social actors. In accordance with previous chapters we stress that the production of material culture is a social practice, a signifying practice situated within social, political and economic structures, structures which enable action. The style of ceramics may ultimately be ideological – an imaginary solution to social contradiction. This alternative contention is investigated in an analysis of 70 middle neolithic funnel neck beakers from the entrance to a megalithic tomb in southern Sweden.

How archaeologists have dealt with style

Seven accounts of stylistic variation will be discussed and their implications examined:

  (i)   the 'normative' theory characterizing the majority of archaeological research until the 1960s;
 (ii)   stylistic drift;
(iii)   theories of regional adaptation and vessel form;
 (iv)   social interaction hypotheses;
  (v)   motor habit variation;
 (vi)   information exchange;
(vii)   isochrestic variation.

Normative theory

Since the birth of archaeology as a serious and distinctive field of academic inquiry the primary concern has been, and still is in many studies, to analyse ceramic design variability not specifically to infer aspects of past social organization but as a means to date sites and as a signifier of groups of people. That some aspects of design change through time is axiomatic but there is no reason to assume a priori, as many archaeologists have done in the past, that all or most of the variation discernible in ceramic design within and between sites has a primary temporal dimension or that time is merely an abstract reference dimension. Spatial commodified time (see the discussion in Chapter 1, pp. 10–11) provides the background to a great deal of the treatment of ceramics both in 'normative theory' and the theories of the new archaeology. In archaeological studies pre-dating 1960, aspects of ceramic design were primarily used as 'index fossils' to date sites in a relational series. Concomitantly, the meaning and explanation of changes in ceramic design attributes was almost entirely circumvented. An unremitting flow of spatial time provided the background determinative variable. Dating the site or the sites was deemed to be an end in itself and so stylistic variation became relegated as the means to establish the passage of time rather than something which could provide information about past societies. Such studies are so ubiquitous in the older literature it hardly seems worthwhile citing specific instances (Piggott 1954; Krieger 1944 and Malmer 1962 provide a few 'classics' of this genre). The problem of why changes in stylistic attributes might occur was never directly addressed and was simply assumed to be the result of fashion, innovation, or a form of drift in which small deviations from the norms governing ideation and action gave societies a form of stochastic in-built dynamic more or less directly reflected in a continuous fluctuation in ceramic design attributes and in which pots or other artifacts were virtually ascribed properties such that they could generate other series of pots or artifacts without reference to human agency.

Discontinuities were assumed to result from specific historical events such as invasions, migrations, the diffusion of religious or other ideas or as a result of an extension of exchange networks. Such accounts assumed a statics/dynamics model of cultural process in which change was assumed to be either non-directional or accretional (stability) or short and sharp. The implicity or explicitly inferred reasons for change were all essentially non-explanatory in that they failed to account for the processes underlying the event, e.g., why a migration should take place and, more specifically, why this should result in the occurrence of one design configuration rather than another. Ceramics were held to signify people, and the spread of ceramic designs into a region directly represented a group of people or a particular set of ideas moving with them. As the meaning of style was supposedly self-evident it was never really investigated.

Stylistic drift

Binford (1963) adopting the position that changes in sociocultural systems should be understood in terms of the demographic structure of the human group and the integrative stresses which enable it to adapt to a particular environmental milieu, suggests (a) that in any given social unit variation exists in the execution of stylistic norms, and (b) that this is a pool of variability subject to sampling error analogous to the gene pool of small isolated populations or those undergoing demographic change or segmentation leading, according to him, to the following expectations:

(i)   with demographic increases daughter populations are likely to bud off from parent communities with the result that random sampling error may arise in relation to some attribute classes, consequently covariation relationships should overlap in regular spatial patterns discernible in radiating or linear distributions;

(ii) in stable demographic situations sampling error or drift might result because of discontinuity between generations in learning and enculturative behaviour in a region. Sub-regional social segments would, therefore, be characterized by vagaries in the execution of any given design attribute state and each attribute subject to drift would tend to have a non-complementary distribution in relation to others. Such changes could either remain statistical permutations or under selection for maximizing group identification be objectified and elaborated with the result that real formal differences would arise between sub-regional units.

A further suggestion made by Binford is that cultural content alone would be subject to such a process or series of processes and that this would not affect the overall nature of the sociocultural system, i.e., the particular form of environmental adaptation and the particular functional tasks carried out. The entire thesis assumes that the execution of stylistic attributes (and style in general) is of no particular importance to social groups simply because it has no adaptive importance or functional significance. Style is considered to be peripheral, opposed to an asserted primacy of function, and therefore unlike functional traits of material culture, is subject to the vagaries of random permutations which lack meaning but might be statistically registered in the process of research. A style/function dichotomy is assumed (*cf.* Dunnell 1978a, 1980; Jelinek 1976 and see Chapter 3, pp. 55–6) and material culture is relegated to a passive role in the change process. If, on the other hand, style is considered to be an active element of social relations, drift, in the manner in which Binford envisages it, either will not take place at all or will account for such minor modifications in stylistic form that they are unlikely to be modified or seized upon by social groups to play a role in group differentiation.

Regional adaptation and vessel form

In this perspective (Martin and F. Plog 1973; Cohen 1977; S. Plog 1978, 1980) populations are viewed as adapting to specific regions so that sites will vary formally and spatially with regard to the nature of the functional tasks carried out and the social composition of the units performing these tasks. Different decorative fields of a single vessel or a series of different vessels may have different designs and the choice of where designs are placed on the vessel surface are assumed to be contingently related to vessel form, so that form is the independent variable and decoration the dependent variable. Primary characteristics of vessel form are governed by vessel function. So if different functional activities are carried out at different sites or in different areas of the same site or if more tasks of a particular type are carried out on some sites as compared to other sites this will affect the nature of design similarities and differences both in different areas of one site and between sites (S. Plog 1978, p. 155; 1980, pp. 18–19). Changes in ceramic design are then related to an assumed need to adapt through time to different environmental conditions (Martin and Plog 1973, p. 256). Sherratt (1981, p. 280) relates the widespread similarity of certain vessel forms in the later European neolithic to the broadening of the resource base in the form of a 'secondary products revolution' and the use of vessels in the processing and storage of these secondary products, primarily milk and cheese.

However it is problematic to what extent primary characteristics of vessel form are to be related to their function. In practice, function is a vacuous category for analysis. For example, storage vessels may perform the 'function' of storage equally adequately irrespective of whether they are large or small or have a curved, angular, rounded, regular or irregular profile. The functional argument is entirely mute because it is quite incapable of specifying why one form rather than another should be adopted. Vessel shape may very well constrain where certain types of designs may reasonably be placed but shape itself is primarily a stylistic rather than a functional feature. The only functional parameter that can reasonably be ascribed to shape is that if vessels are to contain anything then they must envelop and contain a volume of space. This specifies virtually nothing about the *form* of that envelopment of space. Even if we were to accept the argument linking environment to adaptation to vessel function to vessel shape to vessel design, we would be left with the realization that we were still incapable of specifying why one design rather than another might be chosen.

Social interaction

From the interaction perspective (Deetz 1965; Engelbrecht 1978; Frankel 1978; Hill 1970; Longacre 1970; S. Plog 1976; Redman 1978a; Whallon 1968, amongst others) stylistic attributes are viewed as being more or less directly related to the degree of interaction between social units, and this proposition has been used to infer aspects of prehistoric social organization either on the basis of the degree of stylistic similarity within and/or between sites. The essential premise is that if more interaction takes place between residential units then the higher will be the degree of stylistic similarity between them and, concomitantly, the lower the degree of homogeneity within sites. Individuals produce similar designs in accordance with the degree to which they interact. Various spheres of interaction are themselves determined by the type of residence unit and thus degrees of stylistic similarity are reflected at varying spatial scales. Through time, changes in inter-site and intra-site design variability reflect changes in the types of organizational units or changes in marital rules such as village endogamy or exogamy, matrilocal or patrilocal residence patterns.

S. Plog (1978, 1980) has examined several sets of archaeological data which purport to support the social interaction hypothesis, and has shown that in almost all cases there is no empirical evidence to suggest that similarity either within or between sites actually does decrease with distance. More conclusively Hodder's ethnoarchaeological studies (Hodder 1977, 1981, 1982a) have demonstrated that the degree of social interaction between individuals and groups has no necessary or direct correlation with the amount of stylistic similarity. It is possible to have distinctive social groups with distinctive stylistic forms in situations in which between-group interaction is very frequent. There is no reason whatsoever to assume that stylistic similarity falls off in any clear or regular manner with distance. It is simply not possible to set up predictive models of this sort.

Motor habit variation

Hill (1977, 1978) and others (papers in Hill and Gunn (eds.) 1977) have suggested that differences in the motor habits or motor performances of individuals are always slightly divergent and this will result in small stylistic variations in the manufacture and/or use-wear patterns of particular items of material culture. As much of this variation is subconscious it cannot be taught or transmitted, and this makes it possible to identify the work of individual artisans. Hill has attempted to demonstrate that these motor habits or performances do not vary significantly during the life of an individual. He specifically suggests that the most sensitive variables by means of which we can identify individuals are such features as the angles at which parts of a design come together, distance measures such as line thickness, distances between lines, relative heights or lengths of a portion of design (Hill 1977, p. 100). While we do not deny the importance or interest of this work, it obviously only accounts for very minor aspects of stylistic variation and it is questionable to what extent the approach would be able to lead us to insights into long term change or the form and meaning of stylistic variation in ceramic design as regards within and between-group social strategies and social practices.

Information exchange

Information exchange theory as put forward by Wobst (1977) and applied, in part, by Hantman and Plog (1982), Braun and Plog (1982) and Weissner (1983), views style as having considerable adaptive importance directly contributing to human survival. According to Wobst, stylistic messaging is adaptive because it makes social interaction more predictable and less stressful by serving to summarize the economic and social situation of an individual (*cf.* Weissner 1983, p. 258) broadcasting the potential advantages or disadvantages to be realized from an encounter between individuals who may not know each other intimately before such an encounter has taken place (Wobst 1977, p. 327; Weissner 1983, p. 258). Wobst and Weissner suggest that style becomes of particular importance when sending messages to socially distant receivers, i.e., those beyond the immediate kin group or residence unit. Concomitantly, the utility of stylistic messages is deemed to decrease the more closely the emitter and potential receiver are acquainted, but also with increasing social distance beyond a certain point the ability for other individuals to either encounter or be able to decode a message cannot be ensured. Stylistic messaging is, therefore, only an efficient mode of information exchange with relation to a target group of socially distant members of a social unit and as social networks increase in size and complexity the need for stylistic messaging becomes more and more important. Those artifacts seen by most individuals are the most appropriate for transmitting stylistic messages since they are the most accessible (Wobst 1977, p. 350). The messages most likely to be signalled, according to this framework, are those of group and individual identity and affiliation, status, wealth, religious beliefs and political ideas, because the cost of decoding and signalling messages via the medium of stylistic attributes would be too great to transmit a wide variety of information.

This approach, although in many respects considerably more sophisticated than other theories of stylistic variability, fails to provide an adequate framework for understanding style, first because material culture is assumed to passively reflect individual or ethnic identities. It is quite possible that precisely the contrary situation may take place, in which style is actively manipulated to invert, disguise and misrepresent social practices. Furthermore, style cannot be held to simply mirror social strategies and practices but can also *mediate* and therefore serve to actively reorientate those strategies. Secondly, the theory tells us little or nothing with regard to why particular messages should be signalled with one set of stylistic features rather than another – both form and content are overlooked. Thirdly, there is no reason to believe that ethnic or other identities should be signalled by the highly visible, the overt, the obvious, as Wobst claims. Hodder (1982b, pp. 54–6) has shown how even intimate and everyday aspects of material culture such as hearth position may play an active part in stressing social relationships and group identities.

Style as isochrestic variation
Sackett (1982, 1985) has developed a particularly interesting and provocative framework for understanding the nature of style in material culture variation. He addresses three central questions fundamental to any consideration of style:

(i)   where does style reside?
(ii) are stylistic objects or attributes anything else but stylistic?
(iii) what is the style/function relationship?

He argues that once the effects of post-depositional alteration have been accounted for, style and function 'share equal responsibility for *all* formal variation observable in artifacts' (Sackett 1982, p. 68). Style and function are so thoroughly embedded that neither can be understood except in relation to the other. Artifacts may play either a utilitarian (e.g. technological or extractive) role or a non-utilitarian role in the social or symbolic realm. Most if not all artifacts simultaneously operate in both, and their purpose is functional in a broad sense in that they either enable populations to obtain or utilize resources or signal social relationships and ethnic identities. Cross-cutting utilitarian or non-utilitarian objects or attributes is what Sackett refers to as 'adjunct form'. The paradigm is pottery decoration which displays no obvious advantage in most cases in procuring or processing resources at least from the archaeologist's outsider point of view. By contrast, stone tools, with which Sackett is primarily concerned, possess no obvious adjunct form comparable to that found on decorated ceramics. He goes on to argue that there exists a great range of alternative forms of tools which may function in an equivalent manner for achieving a certain set of ends whether these concern the design of a weapon to kill a reindeer or the execution of a design on a pot to symbolize ethnic identity (ibid., p. 72). This is isochrestic form. Isochrestic form is to be found embedded in all artifacts and resides in all their attributes from overall morphology down to features such as retouch on lithics. Isochrestic variation requires no explanation: 'it neither suggests nor requires an explanation of why any given kind of attribute does or does not have stylistic significance in any given situation' (Sackett 1985, p. 157).

That isochrestic form requires no explanation depends on the argument that it is habitual. Any one society tends to 'choose' only one or a few of the potentially infinite ways in which to produce, for example, a projectile point and chance dictates those forms which actually are utilized. The same specific shape, technique of retouch, etc., is unlikely to be chosen by people not ethnically related in some manner and chance alone dictates if two unrelated societies employ exactly the same isochrestic form(s) for accomplishing the same ends. This is because material culture and its fashioning is a product of learned behaviours, i.e., socialization (Sackett 1982, pp. 73–5). So isochrestic variation occurs across time and space and the formal variation of artifacts reflects ethnic identity:

> choices must be made with regard to every functional end served by material objects. It follows in turn therefore that style is no more than function writ small, that is, function as it happens to be expressed within a culture-historically specific, ethnically meaningful segment of the archaeological record . . . Formal variation in short is an inherently dualistic province of which function and style constitute fully complementary aspects. The functional aspect resides in the manner in which form serves given ends, while the stylistic aspect resides in the specific context-determined ethnic variant of isochrestic 'choice' which this form happens to assume. (Sackett 1982, p. 75)

Sackett's position in relation to the understanding of 'adjunct' form or that which can be clearly delimited as decoration is not all that clear. On the one hand, his argument seems to suggest that whether one pot design rather than another is chosen depends on socialization and, therefore, represents isochrestic form or time-space variation. On the other hand he seems to accept that such variation may be used to *actively* mark out and symbolize sets of social relationships (whether at a conscious or subconscious level) and that what he terms an 'iconological' approach to style is appropriate (ibid., p. 81).

The position we wish to take in relation to Sackett's argument is as follows: We agree that style is to be found throughout the entire gamut of morphological variation in material culture from the macro to the micro level. In other words, style is not to be conceived of as a residue left over when functional parameters have been taken into account. Variability which could be termed 'isochrestic' does exist and may have a habituated basis in the structuring of material culture-patterning in relation to the social construction of reality by any particular social or ethnic formation (*cf.* the discussion of practical consciousness in Chapter 6). However, the meaning of this variation cannot be sidestepped and shifted to some unspecified expression of ethnicity which just happens. Style is made to happen in different social and historical circumstances in relation to social, political and ideological relations and in order to understand style – more broadly, the meaning of material culture-patterning – we have to understand the social conditions of its production. Claiming that ethnicity provides a necessary *and sufficient* explanation for style is inadequate because it is a non-explanation which completely evades the question of meaning and is clearly meant to do so in Sackett's framework, which is founded on an essential scepticism: 'No doubt iconology also structured . . . life. But it seems to lie beyond our grasp, at least in the realm of stone tools and at least if its search is to entail reasonable canons of procedure and evidence. This is to be regretted, as is the loss of any part of the fabric of prehistoric life' (Sackett 1982, p. 105). Sackett's view of isochrestic variation as compared with iconological variation (the production of specific designs) depends on a distinction between style which occurs because it is embedded in the consciousness of artisans at an essentially non-discursive level, and style with intended effects in terms of specific social strategies or iconological variation. The latter is regarded as purposive and therefore amenable to explanation, the former as non-purposive and non-intentional in the sense of being actively used to produce a result, and not amenable to or requiring explanation. This distinction might be re-framed in terms of practical and discursive consciousness discussed in Chapter 6. We pointed out that there can be no rigid division posited between the two and that actions have unacknowledged conditions and unintended consequences. Both practical and discursive consciousness are intimately linked in the production, reproduction and transformation of social life and the boundaries are shifting and sliding: outcomes of a specific form of life and sets of social relations and social strategies. If we are to understand style of whatever form and at whatever level it must be related to the social matrix from which it arises. Even if certain aspects of style are not produced at a level of discursive consciousness the corollary that they are not actively implicated in the structuring of social life does not follow – style, any kind of style, produces effects, symbolically meaningful effects, forming part of the social conditions for life and structured and restructured, negotiated and renegotiated.

While Sackett usefully stresses the embeddedness of style and function, it certainly does not follow, as he claims, that 'style is function writ small' but rather the reverse – function is style writ small. Given that artifacts may take an almost infinite number of forms while fulfilling the same task, the world of material culture is primarily a world of style and not function – function adheres to or is embedded in the style. A couple of examples may be given to underline this argument: pot shape and projectile point form, the latter being an example Sackett himself gives. A primary function of pottery vessels in an everyday domestic context could be said to be for holding either liquids such as water or wine, or solids such as grain or berries. So long as the pot possesses a bottom and walls, it can perform these tasks irrespective of the particular shape of the bottom or the walls (see the discussion above). In other words, the function of the vessel as a container explains virtually nothing with relation to its form. The style of construction is primary and the function inheres in this style. All that is presumably required of a projectile point in terms of its functional operation is to pierce and enter the flesh of an animal and wound or kill it, or allow poison to enter the bloodstream. In order to fulfill this task, projectile points need to be both pointed and sharp and 'pointedness' and 'sharpness' may be created in a very large number of different ways. As Sackett suggests (1982, p. 73), attempting to measure degrees of efficiency in terms of Western technological, social or ideological standards is a dubious exercise at best. Again, the function would seem to be secondary in relation to style (although both aspects cross-cut and enmesh each other); possibly more so than in the pot shape example.

What Sackett refers to as 'adjunct style' (e.g., pot decoration) is no more nor less active in social strategies than morphological form (pot shape). In terms of morphological form or the production of designs we need to know how to distinguish between individual motor habit variation and isochrestic variation. This is basically a question of suitable forms of analysis. We do not consider isochrestic variation to be 'passive' in some manner as opposed to a more 'active' area of iconological style signalling social relationships. Such an arbitrary distinction lies at the heart of the debate between Sackett (1985) and Weissner (1983, 1985) in relation to Weissner's data on San arrowhead morphology.

Weissner (1983) was able to demonstrate that arrowheads exhibit clear stylistic differences at the level of the language group among the San, distinguishing the !Kung, !Xo and G/wi who speak mutually unintelligible tongues and occupy distinct territories (ibid., p. 268) but share similar material culture inventories. No clear-cut stylistic variation was apparent at the level of the band, but dialect groups could be distinguished amongst the !Kung and band clusters among the !Xo at a low level of resolution. Weissner could find no coherent principles lying behind the choice of attributes for differentiation which widely vary (e.g. point size or variations in tip and body shape). She suggests that 'the choice of attributes in which to invest style appeared to be the result of historical events, rather than following coherent principles' (ibid., p. 273). That style is not clear-cut at the band level is explained as the result of actively suppressing it, since bands do not have a coherent and unchanging membership but are characterized by social fusion and flux. The development of distinct styles symbolizing band membership would contradict this process. Sackett (1985) suggests that Weissner's data are more parsimoniously explained in terms of passive isochrestic variation which signals ethnic identity but is not actively manipulated to do so. At the band level he argues that style is 'simply inhibited in expression by the very fact that [people] . . . do come together' (ibid., p. 159). In relation to the band level of social organization, we would suggest that the reason why there is no distinctive stylistic differentiation is quite simple. Bushman bands have no coherent social basis in terms of individual membership and therefore as bands have no ongoing basis but are characterized by a fusion and flux of social relations there is no distinctive identity to symbolize or repress: the point made by Sackett. At the level of the linguistic group, stylistic attributes would seem to be implicated in the structuring of social relations as Weissner insists. Whether or not this is at a level of practical or discursive consciousness is not an issue which, if it could be settled on the side of the former, would make style any less active in terms of those social relations – the implication of Sackett's argument.

In this brief review of some theories of stylistic variation with reference to ceramics (see S. Plog 1983 for further discussion of some related issues) a number of individual criticisms of different perspectives have been made. To summarize, the major criticisms that can be made of these approaches are:

(1) Material culture in general and stylistic variation in particular are considered to play a purely passive role in the social world reflecting, alternatively, types of adaptation to the natural environment, ethnic groupings or degrees of social interaction.

(2) The theories advanced are dependent on a functional type of argument in which, as in the case of stylistic drift theory, stylistic attributes are assumed to be of peripheral importance because they are thought to have no adaptive significance or, as in information exchange theory, are viewed as being of adaptive significance, specific stylistic forms being related to different social identities. In neither case do we have even the beginnings of an account or explanation of why some stylistic elements rather than others should permutate randomly or signal ethnic identity. The notion of isochrestic variation specifically denies the question of meaning altogether and style is relegated to an expression of function. In the frameworks advocated, content tends to be overlooked and, in practice, the arguments advanced become little more than tautologies, e.g. a certain set of stylistic traits or design configurations are 'explained' as relating to the need for an exchange of information in an efficient manner between or within groups, therefore the existence of these traits is explained.

(3) There is no adequate account of stylistic change except in terms of adaptive expediency which in itself cannot specify why changes in stylistic attributes should take one form or another. The statics/dynamics split implicit or explicit in all these theories has the effect of identifying time with change rather than seeing it as being imbricated in both stability and change.

(4) There is no adequate conception of the *social production of style* and *active* human involvement in its form and use, in the negotiation of structures of meaning within the context of definite social practices and social strategies.

An alternative perspective

Style is such an elusive term that attempts to define it are always likely to remain partial and inadequate. As Muller (1979) points out, the manner in which, historically, style has been conceptualized and defined, redefined and reconceptualized, is virtually identical to the multitudes of attempts to come to grips with the word 'culture'. It is almost as if to try and think about 'style' or 'culture' is to try and think a category which refuses to be categorized, to be tied down to any single essence. While recognizing that the word 'art' refers frequently in contemporary society to the production of 'works of art' which is considered by many a distinctive social practice, in the following discussion the terms 'style' and 'art' are used, to a certain extent, interchangeably. One cannot consider style without considering the nature of art and vice versa. It does not seem to be useful to maintain a radical separation between the two terms. Art mediates style just as style inheres in art. The question of where art and style 'begin' and/or 'end' is not one which we wish to address, since it always involves a dubious line-drawing exercise between various cultural products which cannot but be founded on practical interest and cultural preference. Style or the production of form in the most general sense inheres in all products arising from human activity. Style is, in a very real sense, everywhere and whether one wishes to term any particular product 'art' is open to considerable debate. Our primary interest is in what manner style or art relate to the social as meaningful modes of expression and as ideology.

De-centring the individual: style as a social production

> To all those who still wish to talk about man, about his reign or his liberation,
> to all those who still ask themselves questions about what man is in his essence,
> to all those who wish to take him as their starting-point in their attempts to
> reach the truth . . . we can answer only with a philosophical laugh.
>
> (Foucault 1974, pp. 342–3)

> A text's unity lies not in its origin but in its destination . . . The birth of the
> reader must be at the cost of the death of the Author.   (Barthes 1977b, p. 148)

Foucault's 'philosophical laugh' at the announcement by Barthes of the death of the author are part of an important trend in post-structuralist thought to de-centre or challenge the notion of the individual as mystical and transcendent creator of culture, a position which as we noted in Chapter 6 (pp. 122–6) is not necessarily at odds with a notion of active and knowledgeable human agency. The view of the artist as somehow transcending society to produce an autonomous comment on it can be traced back to the rise of the myth of individual freedom associated with the development of industrial capitalism which through the progressive division of labour has tended to marginalize artists, giving them an aura of being removed from the social in some sense. To de-centre the individual is to view artistic production as a social and material rather than an individual and psychological process and to explain the work of art with reference to its location and reception in society, to the institutional sites of its production and consumption. Traditionally the study of style in art history has been dominated by a study of individual artists, just as in literary criticism the study of texts has been dominated by consideration of their relationship to the individuals who signed them.

It is not realistic to regard the artist as a supreme creator or free founder of the work he or she produces. The opposed 'structural' account of the artist as a virtually expendable medium through which a work reveals social and economic determinants is equally unsatisfactory. De-centring the individual does not require abolishing him or her from the analysis. Viewing the artist as cultural *producer* rather than cultural *creator* (Macherey 1978; Eagleton 1976; Bennett 1979; Wolff 1981) requires that artistic production, rather than being conceived of as a form of practice radically different from other cultural practices, deriving from a unique creative impulse, should be regarded as being in principle a form of production in essentials no different from others. The artist is a material agent acting in a particular time and place under social conditions and constraints he or she has not created, and located in relation to social contradictions which, by definition, cannot be individually controlled. Art works are not something deriving from divine inspiration or explicable in terms of their producer's individual psychology. This view fails to take into account the manner in which subjects are themselves constituted in society and, in part, mediate it.

Art is primarily an historical rather than an aesthetic form (Wolff 1984). This means that to consider art is to consider a particular practice of labour structured by and in turn structuring particular sets of material, economic, political and ideological relationships. As argued in Chapter 6, all production is located in and affected by social structures, such that all productive activity must be viewed as social labour arising in conjunction with multifarious structural conditions and constraints which do not just post limits but are also enabling. Even individuality is constructed in socialization and the artist is always subject to societal preferences, ideas, values and aesthetic codes. Audiences or consumers play an active or participatory role in creating the finished product, in that they 'read', interpret and so transform it. Whether or not these readings or interpretations correspond to the producer's stated or actual intentions is irrelevant. Works of art are not, then, self-contained and transcendent entities but products of specific historical practices on the part of specific social groups or individuals in given conditions. Therefore they embody the imprint of the ideas and values and the social conditions of existence of these groups.

The ideas, beliefs and values expressed in artistic production may be considered as being ideological in the sense that they are always likely to be related in a systematic way to the social, political and economic structures in which the artist is situated. The world view of any individual is not only, or even most importantly, to be related to his or her personal biographical development but is also a mediation of group consciousness. What is stated in a work of art is the manner in which particular social groups actively construct social reality. Styles, genres, rules of design and aesthetic codes are always already established and confront the artist and so delimit and constrain the modes in which ideas can be expressed in any particular material form. Hence artistic practice is situated practice – the mediation of aesthetic codes, values and ideologies. The artist forms the locus of the mediation of the ideational into the material, and so facilitates a particular way of expressing the nature of social constructs. In other words, art is a practice which gives rise to a definite type of cognitive appropriation of reality. It can be viewed as a practice of transformation working upon and transforming pre-given modes of representation giving rise to distinctive social effects which can be subject to political manipulation.

To summarize, art (or style) operates on a number of levels to create a tripartite vision of the social. First, art can be held to present a vision of the habituated stocks of knowledge present in society and on which artists draw. This reflection is never immediate but transformative. The collective social character of artistic production derives from the fact that social structures are, in part, homologous with the mental structures of individuals and groups, or that at the very least these are intelligible in relation to each other. The individual work of art is a transformative reflection of social consciousness but is active in that it can help to constitute and structure social consciousness. The reflection is never direct. The idea that art merely reflects social reality is inadequate as it suggests a purely passive mechanistic relationship between art and society as though the art work merely registers inertly what is going on in the external world. If the image were to correspond wholly to reality it would cease to be an image at all. No one-to-one relationship can therefore be held to exist between art and the social. The relationship is always transformative and analagous to the manner in which a dramatic production 'reproduces' a written text. While formally linked to the text, the dramatic production nevertheless creates something new which is not reducible to that text but transcends it.

Secondly, art, by the transformative process which it creates, tends to restructure reality away from normal terms of reference which condition access to the social and is thus capable of producing new and unexpected visions of the social reality to which it relates. In this sense art can challenge existing and habituated social forms.

Thirdly, artists are located in relation to social contradictions which, by definition, are not subject to individual control. As ideology, art, by virtue of its own formal internal operations, can effect a further transformation and produce an imaginary solution to implacable social contradictions and through its materiality bolster up strategies by means of which the dominance of individuals and groups over others is achieved. Ideas are not independent of the social and material conditions to which they relate and this relationship is not haphazard but structured and systematic. The relative uniformity of ideas in any given society rests on a successful claim to the universality and naturalness of what is, in fact, a partial perspective structured by those in positions of authority who possess the power to define what is real. Similarly, the relative uniformity of works of art may derive their content by virtue of producing an illusion of a reconciliation of the irreconcilable. Art as a sign system and a signifying practice produces definite effects delimiting the manner in which people come to think about and approach social reality, actively playing a role in shaping social consciousness. Art may thus speak for certain interest groups in society and towards the end of maintaining existing systems of power. The ideological element in art provides a link or nexus between the social practices of which the art speaks and the maintenance of power through denying the existence of contradictory social practices.

In order to arrive at a more specific and concrete consideration of the three levels in art which we have referred to above, we will consider some discussions of the social nature of art in the anthropological literature.

Level 1: Art as a mediation of habituated forms of social consciousness
The majority of anthropological work on art styles has conceived of them as being primarily modes of expression at either an individual level or in terms of collectivities, but there has been much less concern than among archaeologists to tie style into a reductive adaptational and functional model of culture process. Art styles are sometimes viewed as being simply beyond the realm of social practices, a medium through which the limits of everyday experience can be transcended and external values and truths expressed: 'visual art, like music is a form of communication and is concerned especially with communicating the ineffable, that is truths, values, feelings, etc., for which the normal channels of communication such as speech are unavailable or inadequate' (Fagg 1973, p. 155). This view has been criticized above and will not be considered further. Munn (1966, p. 936) regards art as a mechanism for ordering experience of the world and segmenting it into manageable categories. Because this is the case, visual representations are culturally standardized and may serve to organize social experience in the fields of knowledge, the emotions, and the activities of the social group. So, art helps to orientate people in relation to their social world and to come to terms with that world, often at an unconscious level. Conkey (1978), following Gombrich (1960), regards style as the projection of similar thoughts, feelings, and orientational constructs of those taking part in the sociocultural context of production. Thus a style embraces common encoding and decoding strategies: 'a style like a culture or a climate of opinion sets up a horizon of expectation, a mental set, which registers deviations and modifications with exaggerated sensitivity. In noticing relationships the mind registers tendencies' (Gombrich 1960, p. 53). From this perspective, art can be viewed as a form of communication, a material manifestation of ideas held collectively and expressed individually by different members of a community. It is thought in visual form, a concrete expression of abstract ideas serving the purpose of transmitting across and within groups concepts, values, and the interrelationships of those concepts and values fundamental to the society in question. It may exist and operate because the principles that are expressed are not verbalized and possibly not able to be verbalized. Munn (1973) has demonstrated how a particular visual form widely used in the iconography of the Walbiri, an aboriginal group in northern Australia, the circle-line figure,

> presents certain fundamental concepts of world order and thus provides an
> easily reproducible vehicle for their transmission over time . . . philosophical
> premises about the macroeconomic order are continuously brought into the
> sense experience of the individual Walbiri man through the agency of this
> iconic symbolism.   (Munn 1973, pp. 215–16)

Her specific interpretation is that the circle-line figure provides an image of a 'world theory' built on the notion of 'coming out' or 'going in', male/female oppositions and centre/periphery contrasts making up a spatial model of the relationship between the past and the present, the world of the ancestors and the world of the living. It expresses multiple and convoluted referential social meanings about the way social reality is constructed and organized.

While expression of habituated social meanings relating to the manner in which the social world is organized must be a necessary element in any attempt to understand the nature of art in society, the perspective remains insufficient as it stands because art works are still only very weakly conceptualized in terms of social practices and their social conditions of existence. Sackett's view of isochrestic variation as habituated expression of ethnicity denies the need to conceptualize these conditions of existence. Presupposed in the views discussed so far is some kind of consensual unity of values projected into the medium of art so that the meaning of art or style tends to be equated with consensual value orientation.

Meaning is always culturally specific and negotiated. No cross-cultural connection can be held to exist between the meaning ranges for even the simplest graphic elements (*cf.* the meanings associated with the circle in Walbiri art (Munn 1966, p. 938) or in Abelam flat painting (Forge 1973, p. 187)). Munn (1966) attempts to make a distinction between graphic elements with discontinuous meaning ranges and those with continuous meaning ranges. The first term embraces those graphic attributes with multiple meanings such as a circle which can, for example, refer to a waterhole, fruit, fire, a yam or a conical hill. The latter term indicates that in a set of possible meanings for a representation of a tree only different species of trees would be included. In a similar vein Humphrey (1971) uses the Saussurian concept of motivated and non-motivated signs in language. Translating these concepts into the field of graphic design, a motivated visual sign would look like the thing it refers to whereas non-motivated signs could take any visual form. Such work provides us with very limited insights as to how social meanings are embedded in designs and glosses over many difficulties. As Korn (1978, pp. 165–6) points out, in societies in which feathers indicate virility and are worn by young men a feather design might be chosen to represent virile men and would, as such, be motivated even though it obviously does not resemble a man. The nature of visual art as a transformative mediation of the social is too complicated to be adequately embraced by such a simplistic analytical framework. Similarly, whether any particular graphic element can be considered to have a discontinuous or continuous meaning range depends to a great extent on the level of conceptual abstraction one uses to interpret the meaning of graphic elements. The problem of what social meanings are being referred to in designs is so complex and difficult that some anthropologists openly dismiss the question. Faris, in his early work (Faris 1972), regards the only importance of Nuba body designs as the embellishment of healthy bodies, while Korn (1978) conducts a purely formal analysis of Abelam painting without reference to meaning.

The search for the social meaning in design is unlikely to be fulfilled if we conduct an analysis with each element, design segment, or pattern standing for or representing one or a number of things. As Forge has suggested, it is an ethnocentric assumption for us to think that the meaning of a work of art in an alien culture actually should be able to be verbalized, and to set up rigid dichotomies between representational and abstract features of design is misleading. To be able to identify any single representation is not to find out what a work of art means. An alternative position is that meaning resides in the relationship between the elements used to create a work of art:

> in an art system such as Abelam flat painting, elements, in this case graphic
> elements modified by colour, carry the meaning. The meaning is not that a
> painting or carving is a picture or representation *of* anything in the natural or
> spirit world, rather it is *about* the relationship between things.
>
> (Forge 1973, p. 189, emphasis in original)

Gombrich (1979, p. 151) has noted a conflict or tension between what he takes to be
the two major functions of perception: the perception of *things* and the perception of
order. Repetition can detract from, and isolation enhance, potential meaning. A row of
eyes in a series is no longer anybody's particular eyes:

> as soon as a shape is identified as a thing or a creature it becomes transformed.
> No wonder non-figurative artists fight the tendency of looking for represen-
> tational elements in their shapes or colours, for such projections can have the
> most disruptive effects on the dynamics of form. Meaning can subvert order,
> just as order can subvert meaning.   (ibid., p. 158)

The majority of art in small-scale societies, it can be suggested, is to do with principles
of order and how order should be. That is to say the art rather than representing particular aspects of the social world and their symbolic referential qualities such as an association between males, feathers and virility is to do with principles of social order,
principles which in the widest sense structure society and make it what it is. These
principles become embedded in the art through the practical operation of the consciousness of the artist in the process of the production of the art work. To conclude, the
habituated forms of consciousness which art projects are principles of order, the structuring principles upon which society operates. This is the primary level of meaning in
the art irrespective of its particular execution in terms of representative or non-
representative designs.

Level 2: Art and the restructuring of social reality
We have argued above that art by its very nature does not directly reflect or project
reality into a material form. In the process of production that social reality to which art
relates becomes transformed. The consciousness which art transforms is a consciousness, usually unable to be verbalized, of principles structuring the social order. These
principles are transformed and related to each other through the particular graphic
medium employed. They are inscribed within the frame of reference of a formal graphic
vocabulary. In order to begin to understand what principles in society are given visual
form in any particular set of designs, it is necessary to adopt a form of structural and
formal analysis which goes beyond 'surface' compositional features to the underlying
principles imprinted in the work. To undertake a formal structural analysis is not
sufficient on its own, because such an analysis attempts to seek an interpretation 'within'
the work which will supposedly reveal its secret and result in the discovery of the rationality underlying the work. To be successful, such an analysis needs to be related to
within and between-group social relations and the manner in which other aspects of
material culture, in various social contexts, are produced and structured.

A number of anthropological studies clearly suggest that several basic structuring principles to do with social order underlie disparate aspects of material culture-patterning and also serve to orientate the form and nature of social relations. The art provides a formal set of relations whereby these principles are both distanced and revealed. Adams (1973) has shown that the same principles serve to structure the composition of designs on textiles, the spatial organization of village ground plans and in social practices such as marriage, gift exchange and formal negotiations in a small-scale society, which are presented in the formal order of a dyadic/triadic set. She suggests that the same principles used in the ordering of composition of textile designs run parallel to and are a formal transformation of the structuring principles orientating social interaction. Hodder's ethnoarchaeological study amongst the Mesakin Nuba, Sudan, suggests that structuring principles underlying disparate aspects of material culture-patterning can be related to a common conceptual scheme whose principal elements are a concern with group purity and boundedness (Hodder 1982b, pp. 125–84). Vastokas (1978) has interpreted the art and architecture of the North-west coast Indians as embodying in visual terms a tension between opposites or conflicting forces: 'visual images, therefore, reveal themselves as mechanisms for the expression of these latent cultural-cognitive tensions, the rivalry between one principle of order and another and a striving for integration and balance, never perfectly achieved' (Vastokas 1978, p. 257). She goes on to relate this tension in the art to other aspects of North-west coast society – economically located between a subsistence and a surplus economy, in social organization between relative egalitarianism and rigid class structure, in religion between individualistic shamanism and organized priesthood. Structural features of the art are thus seen as formal transformations of tensions and ambiguities in society as a whole.

The studies mentioned above and others (Fernandez 1966; Lévi-Strauss 1968, 1973, p. 255; Layton 1981) have all lent support to the proposition advanced above that there is a link between principles of order in art and principles of the social order, a transformative formal link to be discovered in the art itself and also underlying social relationships.

In order to locate principles of order we need to undertake a formal analysis of design configurations which is both detailed and can be carefully controlled. We have already suggested above that meaning resides in order and in relationships between the elements and attributes making up a design. We need to pay particular attention to combinations of attributes and their arrangement in space and may, in this manner, derive the rules or principles which underlie the graphic vocabulary. Certain combinations of design attributes or elements may conflict with principles of order and should not, therefore, occur. Others may only be produced in clearly specifiable sequences and constellations.

Level 3: Art and the insertion of ideology
In the perspectives discussed so far in relation to Levels 1 and 2, insufficient attention has been given to the role of artistic style within the context of power relations in society, clashes of interest between individuals, and contradictions between different structuring principles orientating and giving meaning to social production and action in the world.

If we accept the position that style in art and other areas of material culture is about the relationship (in graphic transformation) between ordering principles of life rather than merely being a representation of important elements in the natural and social world, this leads us to some interesting possibilities. Artists may manipulate designs and graphic elements to create associations between disparate aspects of social relationships and practices which may be contradictory. Art and artistic style may be considered to be ideological when they are actively utilized in order to resolve contradictions which have their basis in social practices. If the principles on which society is based (principles which mediate social action and define social reality) exist in a contradictory relationship, these contradictions may be displaced or 'resolved' through the medium of graphic style.

Lévi-Strauss has stated that in the face of social contradictions between different principles of social order, the graphic art of Caduveo women 'is to be interpreted, and its mysterious appeal and seemingly gratuitous complexity to be explained, as the phantasm of a society ardently and insatiably seeking a means of expressing symbolically the institutions it might have, if its interests and superstitions did not stand in the way' (Lévi-Strauss 1973, p. 256). In other words the art expresses, embraces and suggests an ideal, the way things might be rather than the way they actually are. The art is speaking not in a neutral voice but in terms of power strategies in the hierarchically organized Caduveo society with a hereditary aristocracy, an organization of social relations in terms of endogamous castes, with women subservient to men and exploitation also based upon age divisions (for other analyses of the role of artistic style in relation to social competition and power strategies, see Braithwaite 1982; Faris 1983; Miller 1982b; Welbourn 1984).

Expanding this position the expression of an ideal through the medium of graphic arts, or indeed any morphological variation in stylistic attributes, may in clearly specified circumstances be considered to have the important ideological effect of mystifying or denying the contradictions between the structuring principles on which society is based. Oppositions and tensions are denied and society is presented in an imaginary fashion as a unified harmonious whole. The immediate ideological effect of a work of art may be to dissolve oppositional elements present in that art, themselves graphic transformations of contradictory structural principles in society, into a spontaneous whole so that what is in fact in contradiction is brought together through the graphic medium to form an inseparable unity as a form of signifying practice in which contradictions between structuring principles are denied to create on an imaginary plane a universe whose content and nature differ entirely from social reality but whose components are akin, recognizable, and therefore acceptable. Contradictions in society can be simultaneously displaced into the realm of visual imagery and dispelled through this form of signifying practice. In this way graphic design can contribute to the reproduction of the social order. So style can be actively manipulated within the context of within and between-group social strategies. This means that we must take a relational view of stylistic or artistic production in which it provides an object for subjects (i.e., individuals in society) and in turn the subject actively relates to the object (artworks). As art is produced in a definite social context it may have the effect, within the context of social strategies, of negotiating, mediating and transforming that context according to the interests of the individuals concerned.

Style: a summary

Building on the discussions above, style in material culture will be defined as the mode of existence of particular attributes of material culture arranged in a series, displaying regularity, and having specifiable social conditions of existence in terms of the constraints placed upon discourse within a determinate set of social relations mediating and transforming the form in which those social relations are, alternatively, conceptualized, represented and misrepresented. So style plays an active role in the relation of the subject to the object world. Style can also only be adequately explained by relating it to its social conditions of production residing in relations of power and social strategies. Style is a form of social rather than individual practice offering a triple vision of the world in terms of habituated forms of social consciousness, principles of structural order, and can be manipulated so that it has the ideological effect of misrepresenting and re-presenting strategies of social dominance.

Style as ideology in southern Swedish middle neolithic ceramics

The data set used to investigate some aspects of the theoretical perspective put forward above consists of 70 completely restored or restorable vessels attributable to the southern Swedish middle neolithic funnel neck beaker (TRB) tradition, datable to between *circa* 2600 b.c. and 2280–2140 b.c. (3370 BC – 2950/2750 BC) (Bakker, 1979, pp. 142–5; Davidsen 1978, pp. 170–1; Nielsen 1977; calibration after Clark 1975). The sherds of these vessels were discovered around and immediately outside the entrance to one megalithic tomb, Fjälkinge No. 9, in the north-east of the southernmost province of Sweden, Scania (Figs. 7.1, 7.2). Fjälkinge No. 9 was excavated by Hansen in 1927 (Hansen 1927) and the find material was published by Bagge and Kaelas (1950). In the chamber and passage of the tomb, disarticulated remains of around 20 individuals were discovered (Hansen 1938, p. 25) but no osteological analyses were carried out. Associated with these human remains were amber beads, a few bone implements, animal teeth and flint blades. No pottery was discovered in the tomb chamber and only seven sherds in the passage. Contrasting with the sparse finds of artifacts from inside the tomb was a huge accumulation of fragmentary ceramic material around and outside the passage entrance extending over 40m^2. These sherds were packed in a layer about 5 cm thick overlain by large stones and a 50 cm sterile sand layer and, according to Hansen, 'not a single bit [of pottery] had been disturbed by a plough' (Hansen 1927, p. 2). Of the approximately 14,000 sherds recovered, a high proportion (62%) are decorated. Bagge and Kaelas (1950, p. 72) estimated that the original number of vessels, as represented by the sherd material, amounted to 1,256. It is unusual to find all the sherds belonging to the same vessel and impossible to fully reconstruct more than a relatively small number of the pots. Bagge and Kaelas (ibid.) put forward a four-phase relative chronology for the ceramics which will be adopted here. Unfortunately the radiocarbon chronology at present available for the middle neolithic is too shaky to assess the relative duration of these temporal phases. The vast majority of the ceramics are all datable to phases II and III with a comparatively insignificant deposition taking place during the initial and final phases of the TRB. Bagge and Kaelas were only able to securely date 260 (about 20%) of the estimated original total number of vessels. For the purposes of this study it was essential to have more or less completely reconstructable vessels which could also be dated. These criteria limited the sample size to 70 vessels or a 5.6% sample of the estimated total number of vessels recovered. All these pots are illustrated by Bagge and Kaelas (1950, Figs. I–XIX) along with more incomplete reconstructions which were excluded from the analysis. Of these 70 vessels, ten can be assigned to the earliest phase of the TRB, 25 to phase II, 31 to phase III and 4 to phase IV. This numerical temporal distribution more or less mirrors differences in the rate of vessel deposition at the tomb through time, although phase I is over-represented. All the pots were studied in 1980 and examined again in 1984 in order to check the reconstructions of Bagge and Kaelas against the originals. The resulting data set, although by no means ideal, was the best it was possible to obtain in the circumstances and it is beyond the scope of this chapter to extend the analysis to also consider material from other sites.

Describing the designs

In the discussion which follows we will first present a series of analyses of the designs on these vessels and then go on to interpret the results in terms of the sociocultural context of the production and use of the pots. Fig. 7.3 shows some representative examples of the pots from each of the temporal phases and Fig. 7.4 a number of distinct levels of

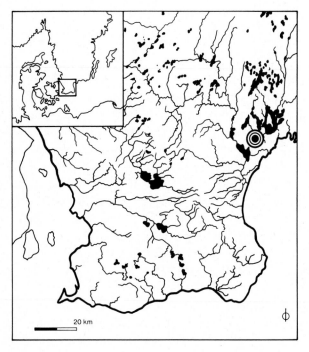

20 km

Fig. 7.1 The location of the passage grave Fjälkinge No. 9.

a hierarchical classification system for a formal analysis of the designs based on previous work on Swedish TRB ceramics (Tilley 1983, 1984). At the most inclusive level, two attributes were recorded – whether individual motifs were bounded or unbounded. The distinction made here is between the closure or non-closure of any particular design. A bounded design is defined as having lines or boundaries on all sides with or without internal infill, e.g., lozenges. By contrast an unbounded design serves to break up the continuous or empty space of the vessel surface without entirely enclosing any area of it, e.g., zig-zag lines. This is a basic distinction dependent on the formal properties by means of which the 'carrier' space of the originally undecorated vessel surface is broken up (for further discussion see Tilley 1984, p. 129). At level 2 of the classification system, ten primary bounded or unbounded forms were distinguished. These form the major elements utilized to create the overall design structure of the vessels analysed and may be combined, infilled or have secondary appended forms in some cases. For three of these primary forms a further level of division is shown (Fig. 7.4).

Establishing order in the designs
The sequence of designs in zones down the pots from the rim to the base was recorded at level 2 except for banded forms (Fig. 7.4: 13) and lines which were differentiated at level 3 (Fig. 7.4: 23; 24) in order to take account more fully of basic horizontal/vertical distinctions in the overall organization of the designs on the pots. The design occurring

Fig. 7.2 The passage grave Fjälkinge No. 9 (photo: Karin Tilley).

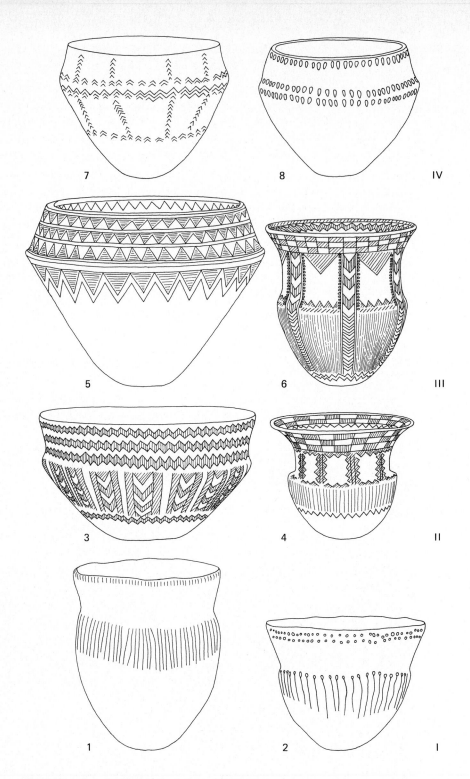

Fig. 7.3 Pots from the four temporal phases at Fjälkinge No. 9.
Pots 1 and 2: funnel neck beakers
Pot 4: funnel neck brimmed beaker
Pots 3, 5, 7, 8: biconical bowls
Pot 6: cylinder neck brimmed beaker

in the top zone of the vessel on or immediately below the rim was coded as A. The following design was then also coded as A if it was the same as the top design or B if it was different. A series of alternative zones can thus be described in terms of alphabetical sequences, e.g., ABCAD (Fig. 7.5). In carrying out this type of analysis we are not interested in the particular empirical sequences of the various primary forms defined at levels 2 and 3, but in their structural relationships.

Table 7.1 gives the frequencies of TRB vessels possessing particular design sequences according to temporal periodization. Looking more closely at these sequences, a number of generative principles may be singled out. Using seven simple generative principles it is possible to construct 64 (about 90%) of the recorded sequences on the individual vessels. Combining these principles is sufficient to generate the sequences on the remaining six vessels (Table 7.2). Rule 1 stipulates simple repetition of the same design on different areas of the vessel surface, rule 2 requires a contrast between two different designs, while rule 3 requires the sequential addition of one different design to another. These are the three simplest principles and account for 41 of the vessels (58.6% of the total number). Rule 4 stipulates an additive sequence 'broken' by the repetition of the first design in the middle of the sequence. Rules 5 and 6 are variants on rule 4 – an additive sequence with a double 'break' created by utilizing the first design (rule 5) or an additive sequence with a 'break' created by repeating the second design before the end of the sequence (rule 6). Finally, rule 7 stipulates an additive sequence 'offset' by the repetition of the third design at the end of the sequence.

All except one of the vessels from phase I can be generated using rule 3. One design is simply followed by another different design. All but two of the vessels from phase II can be generated by using rules 3, 4 and 7. The pots from phase III with longer design sequences are considerably more complex with only rule 1 not being utilized, while for phase IV the designs on the vessels can be generated by stipulating rules 1 and 2. The overall impression to be gained from the analysis is one of developmental complexity in design generation from phases I to III with a simplification in phase IV. In other words, specific generative principles for design, while appropriate at one temporal phase, are no longer appropriate at another.

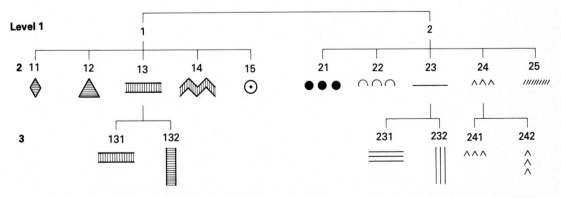

Fig. 7.4 A hierarchical classification system for the designs on Swedish TRB ceramics (initial classification levels only).

Another way of considering the generative structure of the level 2 design sequences is to reduce the primary forms distinguished at level 2 to two basic contrasted forms and then to investigate their interrelationship. We have already put forward such a division in the discussion above of bounded and unbounded forms. The sequence of bounded/unbounded designs was coded from the rim to the base of all the vessels. Table 7.3 gives the frequencies of the various sequences for the data set and Table 7.4 shows how the individual empirical sequences can be generated by a number of simple rules, alone or in combination. Virtually all the individual design sequences on the pots can be generated using four rules. All vessels from phases I and IV can be accounted for simply in terms of the repetition of unbounded designs (U′) or by alternating bounded and unbounded designs (UB′/BU′) while the principles required to generate design sequences during phases II and III are considerably more complex in form.

The vessels from phases I and IV can be considered to be more or less equivalent being characterized by a predominantly unbounded design structure (Fig. 7.6) either

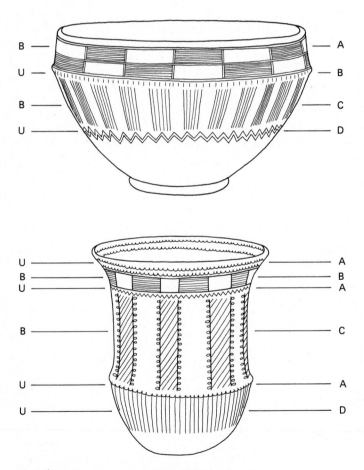

Fig. 7.5 Design sequences on two pots from Fjälkinge No. 9
(U: unbounded design; B: bounded design).

Table 7.1. *The frequency of alphabetically coded design sequences according to a four-phase temporal division of the TRB*

Sequence	Phase				
	I	II	III	IV	Total
A	1	—	—	—	1
AA	—	—	—	2	2
AAB	1	—	—	—	1
AABAB	—	1	—	—	1
AB	7	3	—	—	10
ABA	—	—	2	1	3
ABAACA	—	1	—	—	1
ABAB	—	—	—	1	1
ABAC	—	2	3	—	5
ABACAD	—	—	3	—	3
ABACADE	—	—	1	—	1
ABACBBA	—	—	1	—	1
ABACD	—	3	—	—	3
ABBAAB	—	—	1	—	1
ABC	—	3	8	—	11
ABCA	—	—	1	—	1
ABCB	—	1	—	—	1
ABCAD	—	1	—	—	1
ABCBD	—	—	2	—	2
ABCD	1	4	2	—	7
ABCDBE	—	—	1	—	1
ABCDC	—	1	2	—	3
ABCDE	—	3	2	—	5
ABCDEC	—	1	—	—	1
ABCDEF	—	1	1	—	2
ABCDEFC	—	—	1	—	1
Total	10	25	31	4	70

Table 7.2. *The frequency of vessels generated according to different design rules in relation to a four-phase temporal division of the TRB*

Rule	Example	Phase				
		I	II	III	IV	Total
1	AA	—	—	—	2	2
2	ABAB	—	—	2	2	4
3	ABCD	9	14	14	—	37
4	ABAC	—	6	3	—	9
4	ABACAD	—	—	3	—	3
6	ABCBD	—	—	3	—	3
7	ABCDC	—	3	3	—	6
Total		9	23	28	4	64
% of vessels		90	92	90	100	91

Table 7.3. *The frequency of bounded and unbounded design sequences according to a four-phase periodization of the TRB*

Sequence	Phase				
	I	II	III	IV	Total
BB	—	1	—	—	1
BBB	—	1	2	—	3
BBBBB	—	—	3	—	3
BU	—	1	—	—	1
BUB	—	—	2	1	3
BUBU	—	1	2	—	3
BBU	—	2	3	—	5
BBUU	—	1	1	—	2
BBUUU	—	2	—	—	2
BBBUU	—	1	—	—	1
BBBUUU	—	—	1	—	1
BUBUU	—	2	1	—	3
BBUBB	—	—	1	—	1
BUBBUU	—	1	—	—	1
BUUBUU	—	—	1	—	1
BUBUBUUU	—	—	1	—	1
U	1	—	—	—	1
UU	5	2	—	2	9
UUU	1	—	—	—	1
UUUU	—	—	—	1	1
UUUUU	2	—	—	—	2
UB	—	—	3	—	3
UBU	1	1	3	—	5
UBUB	—	3	1	—	4
UBUBU	—	1	—	—	1
UUBUU	—	1	—	—	1
UBUUU	—	1	—	—	1
UBUUUU	—	1	—	—	1
UBUU	—	1	—	—	1
UBBUU	—	1	—	—	1
UBBBU	—	—	1	—	1
UBUBUU	—	—	1	—	1
UUUBUB	—	—	1	—	1
UBBBB	—	—	1	—	1
UBUBUB	—	—	1	—	1
UBUBUBB	—	—	1	—	1
Total	10	25	31	4	70

being generated by repetition of one or two primary forms or by additive sequences. Through time there is an increasing stress on boundedness and the generative principles become more involuted no longer involving simple repetition or addition but instead the structured combination of unbounded and bounded forms in sequences of variable length with 'breaks' and 'offsets' added to a process of repetition or sequential addition of primary forms.

Having arrived at this description of the nature of the design structure from a process of analysis 'within' the observed designs we need to go on to assign meaning to these changes in the structural order of the ceramic designs. So far we have investigated the

Table 7.4. *The frequency of TRB vessels captured by various generative rules for the combination of bounded and unbounded designs according to a four-phase temporal division of the TRB*

		Phase				
Rule	Example	I	II	III	IV	Total
U′/B′	BBBBB	7	4	5	3	19
UB′/BU′	UBUBUB	3	7	12	1	23
(UB′)U′/(UB′)B′/(BU′)B′/(BU′)U′	UBUBUU	—	5	5	—	10
B′(U′)/U′(B′)	BBBUU	—	6	6	—	12
Total		10	22	28	4	64
% of vessels		100	88	90	100	91

U = unbounded design   B = bounded design   ′ = repeat *n* times   / = or

formal limits of some aspects of the graphic vocabulary of TRB ceramic design. Comparing and contrasting the curtailment or extension of graphic possibilities at any one temporal phase is illuminating since it leads us to ask why are some graphic possibilities exploited rather than others? Given those forms that do occur why are some used frequently as opposed to others?

Interpreting the meaning in the order

TRB ceramic design is strikingly abstract in form. It does not represent anything that is immediately interpretable in the manner in which an oil painting may clearly depict people, landscapes, etc. The very geometricity of the designs defies conventional interpretations in that there is no immediate reference point for 'translation', i.e., whether any particular design such as a lozenge stands for or represents a specific feature of the natural or social world such as snakes or houses, women or men. If the meaning resides in the order, as suggested in the first part of this chapter, we are forced to ask: what meaning has order? In order to reach an understanding of the meaning of the order in the ceramic designs the pottery must be related to its context of production and use.

The social location of this ceramic art at and around the entrance to the tomb has important implications. The pottery was almost certainly specifically produced for use in a ritual context as contemporary settlement ceramics contrast in the use of a very restricted number of primary forms and their design structure is almost always sequential and unbounded (Tilley 1983). The character of the deposition of the pots around the entrance to the tomb has theatrical connotations. This pottery was very obviously displayed for the benefit of the living and their relationship to the dead. Now in small-scale 'traditional' societies in which artistic production is highly ritualized, little room is left for individual expression or innovation in form or the introduction of new or radical content, hence the potential effectiveness of art to challenge the social order is severely restricted. The art tends to legitimate a particular and partial social construction of reality serving the interests of particular interest groups. Another feature of the TRB pottery which should not go unnoticed is not only its geometricity but its strikingly constrained character – the graphic vocabulary is very restricted and the similarities between individual pots in terms of their overall design structure and appearance, or aesthetic effect, are much greater than their differences. Temporally, the same primary forms are combined, recombined and manipulated in various sequences over a period of about 600 absolute years. In this sense the designs clearly transcend time whilst also being transformed through time. While the structural sequences change through time, that which is being structured – the primary forms at levels 2 and 3 – remains the same. A limited number of graphic elements are being structured and restructured through time with this structuring reaching a peak of complexity during phase III with a drastic simplification in phase IV. The disarticulated human remains in the tomb suggest that the individual human being is being subsumed in a cultural order (Shanks and Tilley 1982). Similarly, individual expression in the art is subsumed beneath a formal geometric order.

The structural order in the ceramic designs occurs in the dramatic ritual context of the deposition of the pots outside the entrance to the tomb. It would seem appropriate to develop a dramaturgical conception of the space-time axes structuring and being structured by patterns of interaction of the social actors using the tomb. The area outside the tomb entrance may be considered to be a structured ritual space and we may conceive of this space in terms of its relational qualities: areas to the left or right of the passage entrance or directly in front of it, and areas at the front or close to the tomb or at the back farthest away from the tomb. The space in front of the tomb is thus conceived as a relational contextualized space for action sequences involving pottery deposition – a stage for conduct.

Hansen excavated an area of 71 m² outside Fjälkinge No. 9 and the spatial distribution of the sherd material was recorded by 1 m² excavation units for a 47 m² area. Material from a further 24 m² area was lumped together (Fig. 7.7). The spatial distribution of the sherds for the individual excavation units is shown in Fig. 7.8. Fig. 7.9 shows,

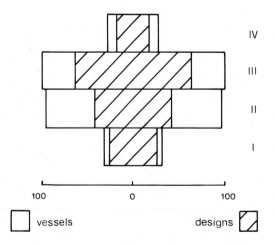

Fig. 7.6 The percentage of vessels possessing bounded designs and the percentage of bounded designs on vessels for the four temporal phases at Fjälkinge No. 9.

respectively, the total aggregated frequency of sherds (excluding Hansen's area 31) across the entire excavated area by 1 m bands from left to right in relation to the passage entrance and from the metre band immediately in front of the passage entrance to the limits of the excavated area farthest away from the tomb entrance (*cf*. Figs. 7.7 and 7.9). From these diagrams, even when taking into account that Fig. 7.9 is partially influenced by the extent of the excavated area, it is evident that there is a strongly asymmetrical distribution of sherds in relation to the passage entrance. Considerably more sherds are to the right of the entrance than to the left and sherd frequency tends to increase with distance from the passage entrance until after six metres they start to decline. Such a spatial distribution of sherds is characteristic also of other tombs in

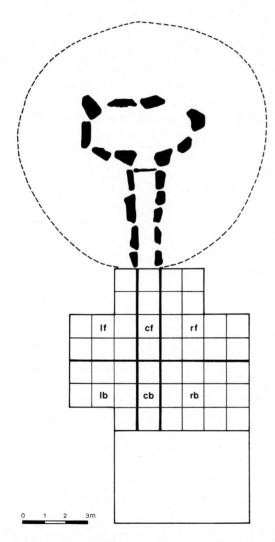

Fig. 7.7 Plan of Fjälkinge No. 9 showing the excavated area and the six analytical space regions
lf: left front space   cf: centre front space   rf: right front space
lb: left back space   cb: centre back space   rb: right back space

Scania (Tilley 1983, 1984, p. 127). The sherds belonging to individual vessels are in most cases scattered over most or a large part of the excavated area. No complete vessels were recovered, either complete or crushed, *in situ*. In view of the total lack of plough disturbance this strongly suggests deliberate vessel crushing which has been documented at other tombs in Scania (e.g., Strömberg 1971, p. 351). The assumption was made that the excavation square or squares possessing the largest number of sherds from an individual vessel provides an indication of its original position or site of destruction. The excavated area outside the entrance to the tomb was divided into six *analytical space regions* (Fig. 7.7). These were labelled using the terms left, centre, right and front and back according to their position in relation to the passage entrance. Each of the 70 pots used in the analysis presented above were then assigned to one of these analytical space regions after a study of the sherd distributions. Fig. 7.10 shows the relative frequencies of the vessels occupying these areas through time. In the earliest phase, the majority of the vessels are located in right front and back space. In phases II and III right back space is the major area for deposition but this has also spread into all other areas with particular emphasis on centre space in phase II and back space in phase III. All the

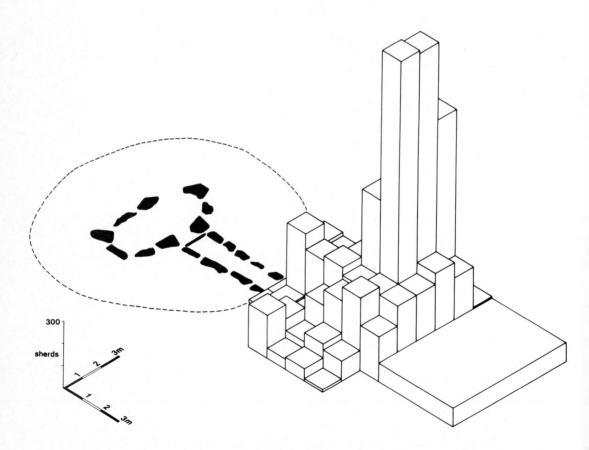

Fig. 7.8 The distribution of potsherds at the entrance to Fjälkinge No. 9.

vessels are confined to right back space in phase IV. Generalizing, there appears to be a trend towards a shift of deposition into back space. Left space is only utilized during phases II and III when vessel deposition reaches a peak and the generative rules governing design are most complex, and it is only during phase II that centre front space appears to have been important. Now these changes in time-space axes for the deposition of the pots in relation to the tomb entrance with a trend towards greater complexity can be viewed as a transformation or rearticulation of the complexity of the generative rules used to structure sequences of designs on the pots. The stress on unbounded design forms in phase I occurs at the same time as a stress on the utilization of right space (this also occurs in phase IV). In phases II and III, characterized by convoluted sequences of unbounded and bounded designs with 'breaks' and 'offsets' in the

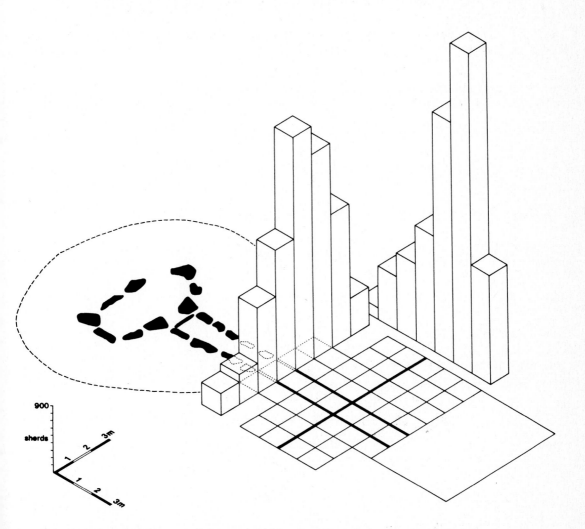

Fig. 7.9 The number of potsherds for 1 m bands right to left and front to back at the entrance to Fjälkinge No. 9 (entire frequencies combined into the 1 m bands).

structuring of the sequences, the use of space outside the tomb for vessel deposition and destruction becomes similarly complex. The contention being made here is that the *graphic order* and the *spatial order* are linked together on a temporal axis. Further confirmation of this can be found on a micro scale – in certain of the infill types utilized for the four primary bounded forms (Fig. 7.4: 11–14). Fig. 7.11 shows the frequencies of oblique lines, left to right, top to bottom, and right to left, top to bottom, for each of the primary bounded forms. Oblique infill: right to left, top to bottom, clearly predominates in all cases and irrespective of the particular primary bounded form in which it occurs. There is no left to right, top to bottom symmetry in the utilization of oblique infill for the primary bounded forms. Instead there is a preponderance of right to left sloping forms. This right/left distinction is a graphic translation of the overall distribution of the sherds and the individual pots in relation to the passage entrance of the tomb.

Following from this, we put forward the proposition that the distinction between

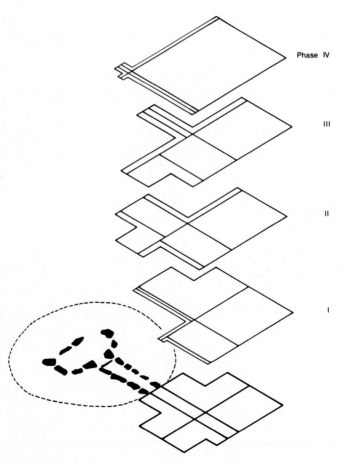

Phase IV

III

II

I

Fig. 7.10 The changing relative frequencies of vessels found in the analytical space regions outside Fjälkinge No. 9 (*cf.* Fig. 7.7). The area varies with the percentage of pots of each phase found in the excavated analytical space regions.

bounded and unbounded primary forms can be linked with the dramaturgical utiliz-ation of space outside the tomb in terms of left and right. In turn, these structured oppositions can be linked with other principles structuring social practice in the ritual context of the tomb.

The deposition of the ceramics outside the passage entrance suggests that the entrance to the tomb, as one might expect, had a special symbolic importance and it would seem to symbolize an inner/outer distinction, an opposition between the world of the living outside the tomb and the interior world of death, the ancestors, and the spiritual cosmos. It is significant that cereal impressions occur in relatively large quantities in the sherds of the pots deposited at the tombs despite the fact that these pots were not used in an everyday domestic context. This suggests an intimate connection between grain and the pottery, and the vessels very possibly contained grain and other products. So, there appears to be an association being made in the ritual stage of the tomb entrance between human bones disarticulated and deposited inside, death, pottery and the ancestors in relation to life, grain and fertility. The deposition and destruction of the ceramics is thus linked with the fertility of grain, disarticulation of bones, life, death and the continuance of the social order. A number of conceptual and relationally interlinked dualities are being mediated at the tomb:

living	ancestors
life	death
outer	inner
right	left
boundedness	unboundedness
production	destruction
fertility	barrenness
individual	cosmos

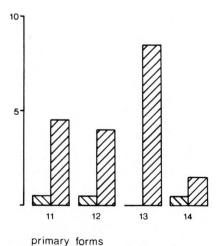

primary forms

Fig. 7.11 The frequency of oblique infill for each of the primary bounded forms of the classification system (*cf.* Fig. 7.4).

where the reproduction of the social order is presented as being dependent on these oppositional elements as structuring principles of the overall social totality.

We have no direct access with regard to the nature of social relations existing during the TRB and rejecting empathy (see Chapter 1) we are forced to use the anthropological literature for an anticipatory understanding of the past social totality we are investigating. This is not a question of taking one present day small-scale society and then overlaying it on the archaeological record as theoretically constituted through the formulation of conceptual objects and the creation of conceptual links between them (see Chapter 5), the process we have been engaged in up to this point. It is rather a question of using some generalized insights and working within the limits of a dialectically conceived hermeneutic circle (see pp. 104–13).

The most suitable model would seem to be a 'lineage' type social system with a group of people associated with a tomb and using it in ritual activities in which asymmetrical within-group and between-group power relations are played out, represented and misrepresented. Each individual social unit is not structurally independent but linked to others through feasting, marriage, exchange and other practices. Such societies are very far from a utopian egalitarianism, but are characterized by socially exploitative practices with a hierarchical set of social relations based on age and/or sex (Tilley 1984).

Elsewhere we have argued at length (Shanks and Tilley 1982; Tilley 1984) that an emphasis on boundedness serves to express an us/them, insider/outsider dichotomy between different social groups. Through time, at the Fjälkinge tomb, we have seen that there is an increasing stress on boundedness in ceramic design, or spatial and social closure, which directly contradicts another principle expressing unboundedness or non-closure and that such a distinction is also correlated in terms of right/left, inside/outside, etc.

In order to maintain internal social cohesion or to reproduce a social order with definite conflicts of interests between individuals and groups, an us/them distinction is a cogent strategy since it tends to direct antagonisms and social conflicts of interest outside the local group. However, since individual social groups are not self-sufficient or autonomous socially independent units, an expression of closure conflicts with and contradicts an expression of non-closure or social interdependency. The generative principles governing the sequences of bounded and unbounded primary design forms on the pots deposited outside the tomb during phases II and III can be seen as an attempt to resolve on an imaginary (because graphically displaced) plane the contradiction entailed by an assertion of social boundedness and non-boundedness at the same time. The denial of the contradiction between these structural principles serves the interests of those who benefit from the reproduction of the social order rather than its transformation. The style becomes a material form of ideology attempting to transform the relationship between oppositional elements into a spontaneous whole with the overall aesthetic effect of unity rather than opposition. The particular manner in which design forms are structurally conjoined is thus used to resolve contradictions which have their basis in social practices. The formal structured sequences of designs form on an imaginary basis an inseparable unity as signifying practice in which oppositions between structural principles orientating the social construction of reality become 'resolved'. Increasing temporal stress on boundedness necessitates greater generative complexity in the manner in which social closure and non-closure are tied together. This is mediated through the utilization of ritual space outside the tomb.

Summary

In the theoretical perspective advanced for an understanding of style, or art, we noted three levels in which style or art relates to social reality. To recapitulate: style displays

(i)   a mediation of habituated forms of social consciousness;
(ii) a restructuring of social reality in material form;
(iii) an insertion of ideology at specific historical moments.

The brief analysis of TRB ceramic design has attempted to work through these ideas in practice, through a process of working conceptually on theoretical objects (e.g., boundedness) and establishing links between these theoretical objects. Generative principles producing order in the design sequences were located by means of formal analyses going 'beneath' the empirical sequences of individual design motifs (lower-order theoretical objects). Aspects of the formal ordering of design were then related to the sociocultural context of the deposition of the pottery. Embracing a dramaturgical conception of the tomb setting as stage, a linkage was suggested between principles structuring the graphic order of the ceramic designs, the spatial ordering of their deposition at the tomb and changes in this ordering through time, and principles of the social order. We attempted to show that the graphic, spatial and symbolic/social orders can be conceptualized as partial transformations of each other. Finally, the interpretation considered the ideological import of the ceramic designs and suggested that they played a role in the maintenance and reproduction of the social order.

8

Social values, social constraints and material culture: the design of contemporary beer cans

'Systematicity is found in the opus operatum because it is in the modus operandi. It is found in all the properties – and property – with which individuals and groups surround themselves, houses, furniture, paintings, books, cars, spirits, perfume, clothes, and in the practices in which they manifest their distinction, sports, games, entertainments . . . In the ordinary situation of bourgeois life, banalities about art, literature or cinema are inseparable from the steady tone, the slow, casual diction, the distant or self-assured smile, the measured gesture, the well-tailored suit and the bourgeois salon of the person who pronounces them.'   (Bourdieu 1984, pp. 173–4)

Introduction

We agree with Rathje (1981) that archaeological investigation of the present is of prime importance. Unfortunately, the majority of modern material culture studies carried out in Arizona and elsewhere (see Gould and Schiffer (eds.) 1981, with references) have worked from an empiricist and functionalist perspective which has had the deleterious effect of strictly limiting the insights to be gained so that the conclusions tend to verge on the banal, e.g., the observations of Schiffer *et al.* (1981) on re-use and re-cycling of items, or the details reported by Rathje that a study of material items at isolated dirt road ends revealed concentric rings of beer bottles and, in areas secluded from car headlights, sex related objects which 'conformed to the activities that were assumed to occur at road ends' (Rathje 1981, p. 52). Perhaps more importantly, the majority of the studies which have been conducted have failed to realize the potential of the study of modern material culture as a critical intervention in contemporary society, an intervention with trans-formative intent.

Some approaches using insights from semiotics and structuralism (for example, Bath 1981; Hebdige 1983) and critical theory (e.g., Miller 1984) have made illuminating and pertinent contributions to the study of the symbolic, social and economic structure of contemporary western society. Miller, for example, shows how architectural styles may mediate social strategies legitimating dominance and power between various interest groups. Notwithstanding the general interest of Miller's study in common with other sociological studies of the present, it has one major drawback from the point of the study of material culture and the way in which it is used as a resource in relation to ideology and power – that it is not architectural forms or buildings in themselves that are analysed in any detail but, rather, discourses about them. Similarly, Barthes's study of fashion (Barthes 1985) is only concerned with written fashion rather than actual garments. If we are to demonstrate that archaeology really can make a distinctive contribution towards an understanding and critique of the present then, we feel, reference must not only be made to discourses but must pay detailed attention to the material culture-patterning as well.

This chapter is an initial attempt to achieve an understanding of a common and everyday item of contemporary material culture – beer can and beer bottle design. How can the designs on cans and bottles be explained? Our approach to this problem involves an investigation of the social meanings attributed to alcohol consumption and in particular those connected with beer drinking; we contend that the designs are embedded in the social and symbolic structures of everyday life. Our analysis extends to can design in two countries, Britain and Sweden. Even superficial observation reveals a fundamental difference in social attitudes towards drinking in these two countries. Whereas in Britain alcohol is not generally considered an item of key public or individual concern, in Sweden alcohol consumption is generally regarded as one of the most pressing of social issues, at least in governmental circles. If material culture-patterning is structured in relation to social processes in a systematic manner, as claimed throughout this book, then we might expect some considerable differences to exist between British and Swedish beer can design which can be meaningfully related to social strategies.

THE DESIGNS ON BRITISH AND SWEDISH BEER CANS

Sampling strategy

There are certainly over 1,000 beers retailed on the British market. *The Brewery Manual and Who's Who in British Brewing and Scotch Whisky Distilling 1983* records 727 brand names. There are many varieties of ale such as bitter, mild, scotch, brown ale, stout; however, in our analysis of can and bottle design we focus on a more fundamental distinction, between beer and lager. Although there are perhaps only 60 lagers brewed in Britain, lager sales accounted for about 25% of the market at the time of the survey in 1983. Lager takes its name from the continental brew, but is rarely, if ever, brewed in the same way as on the continent. It has been presented by the breweries as new and distinctive and has been heavily advertised (lager sales accounted for 2% of total beer sales in 1958, 8.6% in 1972 (Brewers' Society figures)).

Swedish beer (in Britain it would all be termed 'lager') is divided into three classes on the basis of alcoholic strength. Class I beer, with the lowest alcohol content, is not officially regarded as an alcoholic drink and is sold in supermarkets with Class II beers. Class III stronger beers are only available in the Systembolaget shops – government controlled outlets for all alcoholic drinks other than Class I and II beers. At the time of the survey we conducted there were 27 different Class III beer brands on the Swedish market which were either brewed by Swedish companies or foreign brands brewed under licence in Sweden (Systembolagets prislista 3, 1983). We were unable to find out exactly how many different Class I and Class II beers were marketed in Sweden. No official statistics exist and the breweries we contacted were either unwilling or unable to provide this information. Based on a search of retail outlets in all parts of the country from Malmö in the south to Kiruna in the north, we estimate that the number of different brands does not exceed 100 and is probably within the range of 80–90.

The following procedures were used to provide a representative sample of beer cans for analysis:

(1) Sampling was confined to a two month period: September and October 1983.
(2) Sampling was restricted to one British town, Washington, and one Swedish town, Lund.
(3) Sampling was stratified according to different types of retail outlets.
(4) All imported beers were excluded from the sample. Beers brewed under licence from a foreign company were included in the sample since it was found that in the majority of cases different can designs or bottle labels were used according to the country in which the beer was marketed.
(5) An identical number of British and Swedish cans or bottle labels was collected. If the same brand was marketed in a can and a bottle, the can was chosen in preference.

For the British data the cans (hereafter the term 'cans' is to be taken as an abbreviation for cans and bottle labels) studied were bought from four shops belonging to different supermarket chains, Savacentre (Sainsbury's / British Home Stores), Presto, Co-op, Liptons and one off-licence (Cellarman). For the Swedish data cans were collected from five different supermarkets, Vildgåsen Livs, Fokus (independent stores belonging to the ICA marketing chain), Konsum and Domus (both belonging to the Swedish Co-op) and Tempo for beer classes I and II. Class III cans were purchased in the three Systembolaget (government alcohol monopoly) shops in Lund. These shops varied in size from the very largest to the smallest. An initial survey of all the different brands, or differently designed cans on sale in these shops was made. For Sweden a total of 60 different brands, irrespective of beer class, were available for purchase, and 78 from the British shops. All 60 of the Swedish cans were collected and 60 (or a 77% sample) of the British. Of the 60 British cans 37 were beer cans and 23 lager cans. For Sweden the sample included 10 Class I cans, 29 Class II cans and 21 Class III cans. Since the number of Class I cans was small, in order to facilitate statistical comparison five additional cans were collected from retail outlets outside Lund. These were only used in internal statistical comparisons of the Swedish data in relation to beer class.

Finding pattern in the variety
How do the cans differ? Do the cans differ significantly between British beer and lager types, between British and Swedish cans, and between the three classes of Swedish beer? We recorded 45 variables for each can, variables which cover different aspects of can design: the number of colours employed over the entire can surface and for the lettering, the background colour (if any) on which other colours, words or designs are superimposed, the frequency and substantive content of the wording (excluding legally required or purely technical information (e.g., wort strength)), the language used, lettering style, field orientation of the wording, the frequency and form of representational and non-representational designs and major surface divisions in the design. Since all the cans are a standardized shape and size, this factor was ignored (Fig. 8.1).

Differences between British and Swedish beer can designs
Colours

Of the British cans, 37% possessed more than four different colours on the entire can surface as compared with 52% of the Swedish cans. The Swedish cans are not only more colourful but there is also more variability between them in terms of the numbers of colours utilized (variance of British cans 0.76; for the Swedish 1.32). As we might expect, this distinction is replicated in the numbers of different colours used for the lettering. No British cans utilize more than three different lettering colours while 20% of the Swedish cans do so. The choice of background colour also differs significantly. Black and red are the colours most frequently chosen for the British cans (35%), white and blue for the Swedish (58%). The British and Swedish cans were assigned a rank

General
1 name of beer
2 class of beer (Sweden only)

Colour
3 number of different colours on can
4 number of colours used for lettering
5 background colour
6 silver
7 gold

Wording
 8 number of words
 9 company name
10 storing/serving conditions
11 quality of raw ingredients
12 source of raw ingredients
13 character/type of beer
14 strength of beer
15 place of origin of beer
16 reference to past/tradition
17 foreign name

Lettering
18 printing
19 italics
20 handwriting
21 old-fashioned writing
22 3-D lettering: one colour
23 3-D lettering: two colours
24 3-D lettering: three or more
25 flat lettering: one colour
26 flat lettering: two colours
27 flat lettering: three or more

Field orientation of words
28 horizontal
29 vertical
30 diagonal: left to right
31 diagonal: right to left
32 oval/circular

Designs
33 number of representational design elements
34 representational design elements
35 number of abstract design elements
36 oval/circular panel
37 band around middle
38 band around top
39 band around bottom
40 diagonal band: left to right
41 diagonal band: right to left
42 reference to past/tradition

Surface division
43 top v. bottom
44 right v. left
45 back v. front

Fig. 8.1 The variables recorded for each beer can.

Table 8.1. *Ranks of the British and Swedish cans according to the frequency of the occurrence of background colours*

Colour	British	Swedish
black	2	9
red	1	4.5
yellow	5.5	6.5
green	3	6.5
brown	7.5	9
blue	4	2
orange	9	9
white	5.5	1
gold	7.5	3
silver	10	4.5

$r_s = -0.10$

according to the frequency of colour choice for various background colours and Spearman's coefficient of rank correlation proved to be non-significant (Table 8.1). So, colour choice differs significantly not only in terms of frequency but also in relation to rank of preferred colour choice. Colours most commonly associated with luxury and status – silver and gold – are utilized more frequently on the Swedish than the British cans both as a background colour and/or for representational or non-representational designs.

Wording, lettering style and field orientation of wording
A clear difference exists between the number of words displayed on the British and Swedish cans (Figs. 8.2A and 8.3). No British cans employ more than 50 words whereas 15% of the Swedish cans possess this feature. Most British cans use one to ten words (60%). Use of the company name for the beer name, reference to storing/serving conditions, beer type (brown ale, etc.), place of origin (e.g., Newcastle Brown Ale), and to the past and tradition are more frequent on the British cans. The quality of the raw ingredients used and the strength of the beer are more frequently described on the Swedish cans, on which product 'information' is much more detailed and descriptions more lavish. Foreign languages used for the beer name or to describe the product are a common feature of the Swedish cans but unusual for the British. Use of different lettering styles such as handwriting rather than printing occurs more frequently on the Swedish cans as does the use of three-dimensional lettering and two or more colours for flat lettering. The use of a vertical or a diagonal field for the orientation of the wording/lettering is virtually restricted to the Swedish cans, while in Britain word orientation is confined to a horizontal or oval/circular field.

Designs
The number of both representational and non-representational elements in the designs are far greater on the Swedish than the British cans (Figs. 8.2B, 8.2C and 8.4), and chi-square tests, adopting an arbitrary division between the numbers of cans with three or

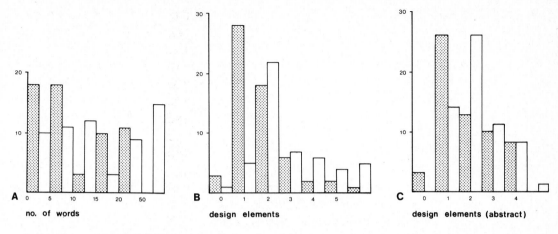

Fig. 8.2 British and Swedish cans
A: the frequency of words on the cans (legally required and technical information excluded)
B: the frequency of different representational design elements on the cans
C: the frequency of abstract design elements on the cans.
British frequencies are shaded.

Fig. 8.3 Writing on Swedish and British beer cans.

more or less than three representational/non-representational designs were very significant (p = 0.01). Surface division, rare on the British cans, is a fairly common characteristic of the Swedish data. Table 8.2 gives the frequency of various types of representational designs on the cans. For both the British and Swedish cans a fairly restricted range of motifs are utilized, but with differing frequency. These can be divided into those specifically to do with the product, i.e., illustrations of the raw materials used, people, illustrations connected with its manufacture, distribution or consumption, symbols of distinction and depictions of nature or the natural, e.g., birds or landscape scenes, and other designs (usually trade marks on the British cans). In considering these designs it is important to notice what is not depicted as much as that which does appear. Raw ingredients (hops and barley) are more frequently depicted on the Swedish cans. In both countries these appear in stylized form, in a natural state, rather than in the form in which they are actually utilized for brewing (e.g., barley is depicted rather than malted grains). While the dry ingredients are shown, water, constituting between 90 and 98% of beer, is never depicted. Beer, the weakest of alcoholic drinks, is thus symbolically differentiated from water. Indeed in the brewing industry the water used for beer making is referred to as 'liquor' while water is a term reserved for the stuff used to wash equipment and utensils. There is thus emphasis on beer as a natural product and beer as alcohol rather than water. The representation of beer as a natural product is stressed more in Sweden than in Britain as is alcoholic content, expressed both in the use of a class system based on beer strength, and in descriptions on indi-

Fig. 8.4 British and Swedish beer cans (see text).

Table 8.2. *Representational designs on British and Swedish beer cans and bottle labels*

	British		Swedish	
	N	%	N	%
Raw ingredients				
hops	5	8.3	19	31.7
barley	8	13.3	14	23.3
People				
men	16	26.7	7	11.7
women	1	1.7	1	1.7
historical figure	8	13.3	4	6.7
hand	1	1.7	—	—
Manufacture, distribution, consumption				
picture of brewery	1	1.7	—	—
oast houses	2	3.3	—	—
dray	2	3.3	2	3.3
beer barrel	—	—	5	8.3
brewing equipment	—	—	4	6.7
mugs/glasses	2	3.3	—	—
Symbols of distinction				
crown	3	5.0	16	26.7
scroll	11	18.3	13	21.7
medals	1	1.7	18	30.0
seal	2	3.3	6	10.0
trophy	1	1.7	—	—
star	2	3.3	1	1.7
royal coat of arms	6	10.0	8	13.3
other coat of arms (e.g. town, county)	16	26.7	13	21.7
flag	—	—	5	8.3
castle	1	1.7	—	—
'Nature'				
landscape scenes	3	5.0	9	15.0
foliage/flower/tree	11	18.3	8	13.3
animals/birds	12	20.0	21	35.0
Other				
magnet	1	1.7	—	—
milk churn	1	1.7	—	—
chain	1	1.7	—	—
rope	1	1.7	—	—
ship	2	3.3	2	3.3
horseshoe	1	1.7	—	—
globe/map	1	1.7	—	—
harp	2	3.3	—	—
bell	—	—	1	1.7

vidual cans. People are more commonly depicted on the British cans and in both countries there is an emphasis on masculinity and the past. If people are depicted they are invariably male and often historical figures such as cavaliers and vikings for Sweden, blacksmiths, brewery workers and cavaliers for Britain. Similarly, when the motifs are associated with the manufacture or distribution of beer, drays, rather than articulated lorries, wooden rather than metal barrels, are depicted. Symbols of distinction such as medals, crowns, scrolls or coats of arms (real or fictitious) are common on both the British and Swedish cans in differing combinations as are depictions of foliage or animals and birds. The latter are invariably the male of the species and aggressive (e.g., falcons, eagles, lions, panthers). The major difference between the Swedish and British cans is not in the form of the representational designs but the employment in Sweden of a much wider range of combinations of the motifs on individual cans (Fig. 8.4).

On the basis of the discussion above it is clear that there is a considerable difference between the British and Swedish cans for virtually all the variables recorded. This is not an either/or distinction in terms of the individual variables but one of complexity and elaboration. The Swedish cans tend to be both far more complex than the British and clearly differentiated from each other. The results of this simple statistical analysis were confirmed by multivariate analyses of the cans. Fig. 8.5A shows the results of a principal components analysis for all the cans using standardized frequencies of variables 3, 8, 33 and 35 (see Fig. 8.1) as input data. The first two components accounted for 65% of the total variability, 36% on the first component. Variables 3 and 33 made approximately equal positive contributions to the first component with variables 8 and 35 contributing negatively. All variables contributed approximately equally to the second component, 3 and 8 positively and 33 and 35 negatively. On the plot of the first two components (Fig. 8.5A) a fairly clear separation exists between the Swedish cans clustered to the left and the British cans to the right due to the higher frequency of different colours, numbers of words, representational and non-representational designs used on the Swedish cans, especially Class II. It is mainly the simpler Class III Swedish beer cans which tend to cluster with the more complex British beer and lager cans. Internal differences between the British beer and lager cans and the Swedish beer classes are largely obscured, as we might expect, by the overall differentiation between the British and Swedish cans. However the majority of the lager cans are high on the second component, separated from the majority of the beer cans on the basis of the possession of more colours and a greater number of words (see discussion below).

A similar result is apparent on the basis of a principal coordinates analysis conducted on a similarity matrix computed using the Gower coefficient for 26 independent quantitative and presence/absence variables (Fig. 8.5B). Again the majority of the (more complex) Swedish cans are clustered to the left of the plot, with the British cans to the right. Differentiation between British beer and lager cans, and the Swedish cans according to beer class, is more blurred than the overall British/Swedish distinction.

Differences between British beer and lager cans
Colours

Beer cans tend to use more colours than lager cans. Background colour also differs significantly with predominant use of black, red and yellow for beer, and green, blue and white for lager (Table 8.3). Silver only appears on the lager cans and gold appears roughly twice as frequently on the lager as it does on the beer. In terms of background colour and use of silver and gold, British lager cans are more similar to Swedish cans than to British beer cans.

Wording, lettering style and field orientation of wording

More words are used on lager cans (Fig. 8.6A) and the content of the wording also
differs significantly. The company name is used more frequently (86% of the cans) for
beer than for lager (52%). While reference to the type of the beer occurs on all the beer
cans only 52% of lager cans possess such descriptions of the character of the lager. The
place of origin of the beer, mentioned on almost half of the beer cans is only noted on a
few lager cans which frequently make reference to storing/serving conditions and
alcoholic strength – features rarely described in connection with beer. More beer cans
make reference to the past or tradition while the use of a foreign 'language' only occurs

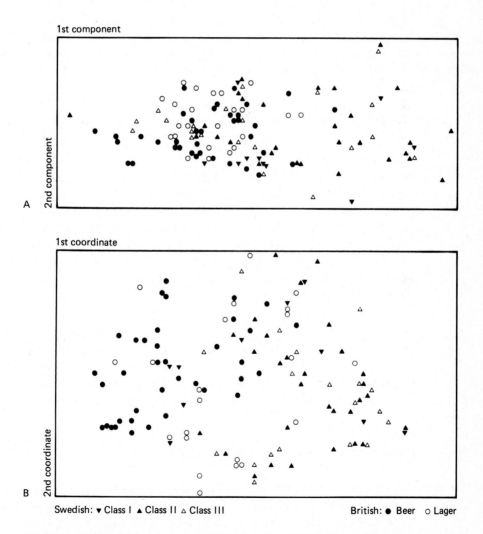

Fig. 8.5 A: principal components analysis of British and Swedish beer cans (input variables: 3, 8, 33, 35;
  cf. Fig. 8.1).
  B: principal coordinates analysis of British and Swedish beer cans (input variables: 3, 6–17, 29, 32,
  33, 35–39, 42; *cf*. Fig. 8.1).

Table 8.3. *Ranks of the British beer and lager cans according to the frequency of the occurrence of background colours*

Colour	Beer	Lager
black	1	9
red	2	4.5
yellow	3	6.5
green	4.5	1.5
brown	4.5	9
blue	7	1.5
orange	7	9
white	7	3
gold	9	4.5
silver	10	6.5

$r_s = -0.17$

for lager: 35% of the lager cans have foreign-sounding names, many purchased from continental breweries. A wider range of lettering styles are generally employed for beer cans, particularly the use of handwriting and three-dimensional lettering.

Designs

Beer cans possess a higher frequency of representational designs (Fig. 8.6B) while abstract designs tend to be employed more often on lager cans (Fig. 8.6C), especially bands around the middle and bottom of the can. As one might expect, reference to the past or tradition is a more frequently employed characteristic of the beer cans. Use of surface division only occurs on the lager cans. Almost all representational designs occur more frequently on the beer cans except for crowns and mugs/glasses. The virtual absence of depictions of people on the lager cans is particularly noteworthy.

On the whole there appears to be less clear-cut differentiation between British beer and lager cans than between both these sets of cans considered together and the Swedish material. However, in some respects such as colour, frequency of wording, use of abstract designs and surface division some of the lager cans are more similar to the Swedish ones, while others have a more British style. This is borne out by the results of a principal components and a principal coordinates analysis (Figs. 8.7A and 8.7B respectively). On the plot of the cans against the first two components, the lager cans, as opposed to most beer cans, cluster on the first component on the basis of relatively higher frequencies of words and abstract designs. The lager cans are dispersed on the second component according to numbers of representational designs. This differentiation of the lager cans can be seen more clearly on the principal coordinates plot (Fig. 8.7B) in which they are not only differentiated from each other in terms of complexity, but also from most of the beer cans (Fig. 8.8).

Differences between Swedish beer classes
Colours
A negative correlation exists between increasing use of colours and beer strength such that the Class III cans tend to be least colourful (Fig. 8.9A). However, use of four or more colours for lettering is most common on the Class II cans. The use of different background colours is most restricted on Class III cans (81% utilizing blue, white or gold) and most variable for Class II cans. Gold is most common on the strong Class III beer cans and least frequent on Class II, while silver occurs with roughly the same frequency for all the beer classes.

Wording, lettering style and field orientation of wording
Descriptions are much lengthier on the Class II cans than for Classes I or III (Fig. 8.9B). The descriptions used (Fig. 8.1: variables 9–17) either do not differ significantly in frequency between the beer classes or are more common on Class II cans, except for strength, most frequently referred to on Class I cans, and reference to the past or tradition most frequently stressed for Class III beer. A wider range of lettering styles are employed for Class II cans and three-dimensional lettering is not frequently employed for Class I as opposed to Classes II and III. Field orientation of the wording is most variable for Class III cans with comparatively high percentages of cans with diagonal field orientation, right to left or left to right.

Designs
Class II cans possess more representational and non-representational designs than Classes I and III. Class I cans have larger numbers of representational designs than Class III cans which possess more abstract designs (Figs. 8.9C and 8.9D). Surface division is a more common characteristic of Class II than Class III cans and is rarely used for Class I. Depictions of raw ingredients are more common for Classes II and III while people are confined to Classes I and II, particularly Class I cans on which virile males occur

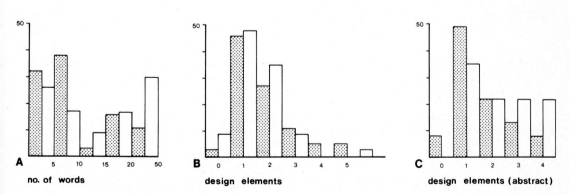

Fig. 8.6 British beer and lager cans
A: the relative frequency (per cent) of words on the cans (legally required and technical information excluded)
B: the relative frequency (per cent) of different representational design elements on the cans
C: the relative frequency (per cent) of different abstract design elements on the cans.
Beer frequencies are shaded.

(Fig. 8.10). Symbols of distinction are common for all beer classes with particular emphasis on crowns for Class II and medals for Class III.

The class variation between the Swedish cans is not as clear as that between British beer and lager cans on a multivariate basis (Figs. 8.11A and 8.11B). Some aspects of design, such as colour or depictions of people, are negatively correlated with increasing beer strength. Class III cans tend to be less elaborate than Classes I or II (Fig. 8.12), while the most complex designs occur on the medium strength Class II beers. The lack

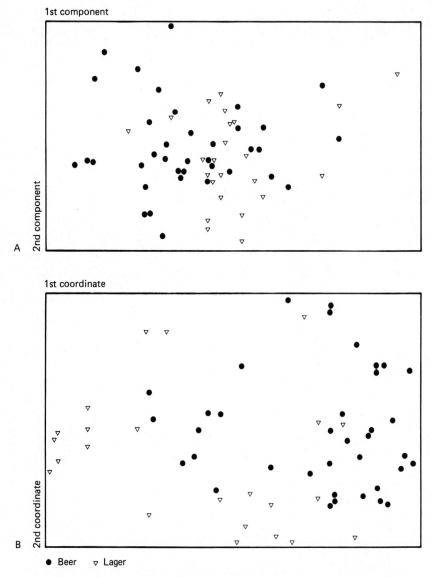

Fig. 8.7 A: principal components analysis of British beer and lager cans (input as for Fig. 8.5A)
B: principal coordinates analysis of British beer and lager cans (input as for Fig. 8.5B).

Fig. 8.8 British beer and lager cans.

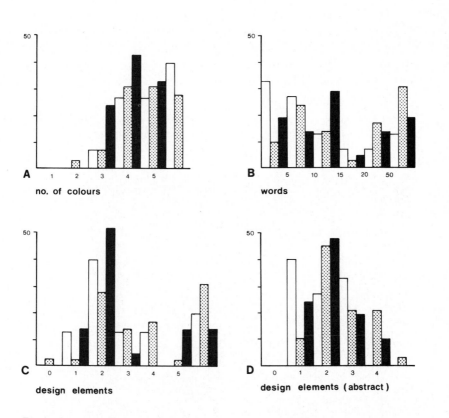

Fig. 8.9 Swedish beer cans
A: the relative frequency (per cent) of different colours on the three classes of Swedish beer cans
B: the relative frequency (per cent) of words on the cans (legally required and technical information excluded)
C: the relative frequency (per cent) of different representational design elements on the cans
D: the relative frequency (per cent) of different abstract design elements on the cans
Class II can frequencies shaded; Class III can frequencies black.

of a very clear-cut distinction across the classes on the plots can partially be accounted for by the fact that for a number of beer brands virtually the same designs are used for Classes I, II and III or Classes II and III with only minor differences such as background colour, the rest of the design remaining unaltered.

How is the structure of difference we have discussed above to be explained? To explain can design, the meaning of the difference, reference must be made to the location of the cans within social structures and social practices; can design is related to the meaning of the consumption of alcohol. This makes necessary an investigation of brewing and the marketing of its products, consumerism and the consumption of drink, and, because alcohol is a drug, the relation of drinking to images and conceptions of health and the body. So in the next section we look at the growth of the brewing industry within the development of the capitalist nation states of Britain and Sweden.

DRINK, THE STATE, CONSUMERISM, DISCIPLINE

Early industrial capitalism and alcohol production

The development of industrial capitalism involved the transformation of labour, distribution, and consumption, relations previously embedded in non-economic social forms, into relations mediated by the abstracted goals of commodity exchange and capital accumulation. With use-value subordinated to exchange-value, the commodity form became dominant. The associated commodification of labour, the institutionalization of wage-labour, made necessary the expropriation of the worker from the means of production with the latter now subordinated to the logic of capital accumulation

Fig. 8.10 Swedish Class I beer bottle label (see text).

rather than the satisfaction of need. Such changes developed at an early stage in the British and Swedish alcohol industries.

In Britain in the eighteenth century an increasing farm acreage, an effect of the enclosure movement, created a grain surplus of which much was converted into spirits. Distilling gin from such surplus grain was recognized as a very effective means of capital formation (Park 1983). So too was commercial brewing. With the aim of maximization of profit the characteristic features of industrial production – processing raw materials on a large scale using a wage-labour force concentrated in one place and distributing the

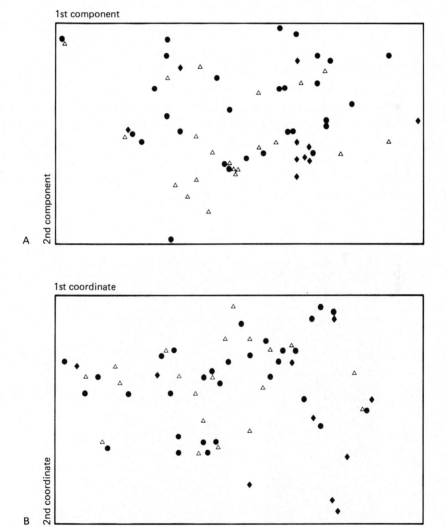

Fig. 8.11 A: principal components analysis of Swedish beer cans (input as for Fig. 8.5A)
B: principal coordinates analysis of Swedish beer cans (input as for Fig. 8.5B).

product to a large number of wholesale and retail outlets – developed at an early date in brewing (Harrison 1971, p. 65; Park 1983).

The products of distilling and brewing were supplied to a growing urban population. Together with the increase in the relative importance of commercial as opposed to domestic brewing, it is such economic developments which form the determinate background to the dramatic increase in alcohol consumption from the eighteenth century in Britain and the associated problems of 'Gin Lane' and after.

By the mid-eighteenth century in Sweden, *brännvin* or distilled spirits had largely displaced beer as the national drink. Alcohol rapidly grew in importance as a commercial item in the agrarian economy. Distilling from grain and potatoes became a widespread domestic industry flooding the country with *brännvin*. According to a survey conducted in 1756 there were a minimum of 200,000 stills in operation. At least every seventh adult possessed a still (Svensson 1973, p. 17). In urban centres such as Stockholm and Göteborg consumption was public and conspicuous as in British cities (Mathias 1959, p. 127; Järbe 1971, p. 58).

In 1855 the Swedish parliament introduced the *brännvin* reform measures which laid the basis for subsequent political reforms concerning alcohol. This reform abolished small stills for domestic use, setting the smallest quantity to be distilled at 300 kannor (780 litres) per day. On this produce the government received a substantial excise duty. This measure resulted in a drastic reduction in the number of stills operating to 451 in 1869 (Carnegie 1873, p. 5). In effect the 1855 reform transferred the right to produce

Fig. 8.12 Class differences between the Swedish beer cans: left to right Classes I–III.

brännvin to those already owning large factories, or with the means to invest capital. A concern for public temperance provided a general justification for the reform bill rather than its primary motive. With a system of widespread and unregulated production, taxation to provide state revenue could never be very successful but with production confined to a relatively small number of rationalized factories taxation could be very effective. State income from *brännvin* increased tenfold after the reform, making up more than one fifth of the total state revenue (Nycander 1967, p. 11). The *brännvin* reform thus provided a great increase in revenue and an extension of state control. It also provided the conditions suitable for capital formation on a large scale in a period in which industrialization was developing at an ever increasing pace. It was at this time that the brewing industry, in part stimulated by government incentives, rapidly developed. By 1880 brewing had become the sixth largest industry in the country (Svensson 1973, p. 47).

So, in the eighteenth century in both Britain and Sweden drinking reached an unprecedented level. While in Britain this developed hand in hand with rapid urbanization, in Sweden it was largely among an exploited and depressed peasantry. The development of industrial capitalism in both countries stimulated and impelled consumption. We would wish to argue with Park (1983) that consumption of alcohol is not encouraged simply in that brewing and distilling are means of profit making and capital accumulation, but that drinking was (and still is) promoted and encouraged in a progressive way.

The profits from the industrial production of alcohol and its increasing consumption by a demoralized population detached from pre-capitalist social controls on heavy drinking (see below) enriched a significant number of the emergent bourgeoisie and the British and Swedish state coffers. Those owning the means of alcohol production formed a socially prominent and politically powerful interest group in both countries (Harrison 1971, pp. 58ff., pp. 340ff.; Nycander 1967, pp. 14ff.).

Changes in experience of work and leisure

By the nineteenth century, urbanization and the concentration of wage-labourers in towns and cities in Britain brought about changes in the character of daily life. Such developments occurred significantly later in Sweden and on a smaller scale. Dominated by the experience of industrial labour, the social communities of pre-capitalist society were increasingly replaced by occupational communities.

In such communities all aspects of daily life were permeated by the experience of labour and class contradiction in a class culture of work (Alt 1976). This collective experience was for most unskilled workers one of long hours and low pay. Generally the labour process tended to be harsh and exploitative under the inexorable impulse to maximization of profit. Profit accrued to capital owners and derived from the surplus value created by wage-labourers. Although increasingly separated from work, physically and institutionally through the commodification of labour, leisure was internally related to work in that recreation served to reproduce the occupational community and its group cohesiveness.

In Britain, beerhouse and gin palace provided escape from harsh labour. In contrast to the traditional village alehouse and traveller's inn where classes mingled (Harrison 1971, pp. 45–6; Park 1983) these new drinking houses were located in working-class areas and were patronized by an urban working class (Smith 1983, pp. 370–2; Harrison 1973). With leisure dominated by the experience of labour, the pub provided a distinctive *class* experience, the social infrastructure for relief from industrial labour, but also an environment for the creation and reproduction of social solidarity (Alt 1976, p. 64). The public house was (and is) a colonized institution (Clark 1979, p. 245) embodying a contradiction between acting as a marketing mechanism for the capitalist enterprise of the brewing industry, inciting consumption for the profit of capital, and through colonization by the working class acting as the focus for the social reproduction of working-class solidarity. 'Leisure served the social reproduction of the working class, which gave them the capacity to labour, but it also created the internal social solidarity necessary for affirmative class action' (Alt 1976, p. 55).

Harrison (1971, chapter 2) has outlined the social relations of drinking in early nineteenth-century England (*cf.* Park 1983; Smith 1983, pp. 377–9). Drinking and drink sellers were tightly related to wider social relations. They were closely associated with labour and recreation especially in that alcohol was one of the few safe beverages and in that drinking houses were practically the only public meeting place apart from the church. Public houses were a focus for entertainment, acted as labour exchange and trading centre. The publican often had responsibility for wage payments. Such were the positive social and commercial incitements to drink.

Thus the settlement of a wage-labour force around particular capitalist industries resulted in a 'determining relation between labour and leisure, mediated and reproduced through the associations of leisure' (Alt 1976, p. 65). Such associations centred on the public drinking house.

This centrality of the public house and drinking in the life of the industrial proletariat and the earlier inseparability of drink and labour and recreation needs to be stressed in opposition to the moral and later medical attacks on heavy 'problem' drinking (the definition of 'problem' drinking arising out of the very labour process which established the occupational community and its vehicle of social reproduction – the drinking house). Public house and drinking were (and to a lesser extent still are) inscribed in practice as opposed to the normative attacks on them.

In Sweden the smaller size of urban communities, together with their later growth (see Scase 1977), restricted the development of working-class sub-cultures. The drinking house played a similar role to that outlined above for British industrial communities (Magnusson 1985). However, the life-styles of Swedish workers tended to be more privatized than in Britain but, in part, this greater degree of privatization was a direct result of social control and disciplinary power.

Drink, social control and disciplinary power

It is no coincidence that the development of a temperance movement in Sweden ran almost exactly in tandem with industrialization, or that increasingly restrictive legislative controls on the sale of drink and the 'problem' of alcoholism developed as the nation rapidly industrialized between 1850 and 1950. The development of a fully fledged occupational community reproducing its labour power through leisure time spent in the drinking house was, in part, broken with the advent of the so-called Göteborg system. The period from 1855 to 1900 in Sweden is characterized by the gradual enforced transference of drinking from the public to the private sphere, from the drinking house to the home.

The new methods of industrial production in Britain and Sweden with division of labour and removal of control of the labour process from the labourer required a new worker, disciplined and passive. Such an occupational role is incompatible with undisciplined drinking. Thus emerged a contradiction between the fostering of a market for the commodity drink and the incompatibility of drink with the new industrial labour process. This contradiction is not merely determined by changes in mode of production but is also related to developments in the technology and strategies of power. The factory-based labour process depends on discipline, a modality of power which renders bodily behaviour routine and repetitive, subject to codifiable rules, accessible to surveillance, to calculation (Foucault 1979). Disciplinary power is the capillary imposition of a heteronomy of the body aiming at the transformation of individuals and related to the requirements of capital for a new labour force (Foucault 1980, p. 158; 1981, pp. 140–1; Smart 1983, p. 122). Thus the factory system developed not as a functional means of increasing productive efficiency but as a means of implementing a disciplinary control over wage-labourers (Marglin 1976). The logic of the factory is political not economic; it is more efficient and profitable in terms of an economy of *power* (Foucault 1980, p. 38). The contradiction thus presupposes the class difference between capital owner and wage-labourer; the new methods of production created a capital-owning class with a direct interest in curbing working-class drunkenness (Harrison 1971, p. 40).

There was also the drunken 'mob'. Urbanization and demographic expansion was creating from the eighteenth century a large economically redundant population: the 'mob' – dangerous, unsupervized, escaping surveillance, drunk. Hence a further necessity for coordination and integration through discipline (Foucault 1980, p. 171). Thus social control, the subjection of people to normalizing judgement, is inscribed in the logic of disciplinary power (Foucault 1979, p. 304). It is worth noting in this context that the concern with working-class drunkenness is not necessarily related to an actual high incidence of drunkenness but is as much a sign of a moral and political challenge to the association of work and recreation with drink (Harrison 1971, p. 40).

So working-class leisure became an object of administrative and moral interest to the middle classes. Their capital, the means for creating wealth, lay in the hands of the workers; disciplined workers – capital and wealth was to be protected by a moralization of the population, by the 'administration of a cultural lobotomy and the implanting of a new morally superior lobe' (Storch 1977, p. 139).

With respect to drink, temperance reformers aimed at inculcating self-improvement and domesticity, privatized leisure dominated by bourgeois values and centring on the family home, at physically or psychologically separating the worker from the communal focus of the occupational community (Storch 1977, p. 149).

Excessive drinking was often blamed on the absence of the moral example of the upper classes, ignoring the fact of drunkenness among the latter (Park 1983). Class segregation of drinking was connected with a concern for restoring 'wholesome personal contact between men of different social stations' (Storch 1977, p. 147) – disciplinary surveillance.

This disciplinary surveillance and a concern to improve the morality of the working classes was particularly strong in Sweden. The Göteborg system began as an extralegal communal development and was later made compulsory through legislation and brought under increasing state control. In 1850 a group of the middle-class bourgeoisie with a philanthropic interest in the alcohol trade organized a company in Falun which took over the operation of all drinking houses in that town giving up all revenues to the disposal of the municipal authorities. In the company charter it was stated that 'the morals and welfare of the working classes in our community have their worst enemy in the pub . . . [Consequently] in these places a close scrutiny will be exercised in order that intemperate drinking may be checked instead of encouraged; that brännvin will never be dispensed on credit or account or to minors or persons already intoxicated . . . and that cleanliness and order will be striven for to the highest possible degree' (quoted in Thompson 1935, p. 13). In other words the supposedly loose morality of the proletariat was to be checked by constant surveillance and the imposition of middle-class standards of morality. Order was to be drawn into the disordered world of the drinking house. The method eventually spread over the entire country becoming obligatory through legislation in 1905. Carnegie, a Scot who visited Göteborg in the early years of the operation of the system, noted the difference between the Swedish company drinking house and the British gin palace: 'the fittings of the public houses rented by the company are not in the style of drinking palaces, resplendent in vulgar taste, with plate glass, mahogany, polished brass, and glittering with gilding, paint and flaring gas; but are simple and inexpensive . . . nothing could be more orderly, sober, and respectable than the whole scene' (Carnegie 1873, pp. 10–12). One of the measures of the 1855 *brännvin* reform had been to enforce an association between food and drink in that food had to be available in licensed houses. Now the old disorderly drinking houses were not only to be cleaned up but also converted into cafés and restaurants. The pub was to become a thing of the past and consumption to be either privatized or 'civilized'.

The social embeddedness of drinking meant that temperance reform had little impact on levels of consumption in either Britain or Sweden (Harrison 1971, p. 306; Nycander 1967, p. 19) (Fig. 8.13). 'To abandon drink was to abandon society itself' (Harrison 1971, p. 50). Despite the advent of the Göteborg system in Sweden consumption rose to a maximum in the 1870s. Privatized leisure in Britain was unlikely to supersede communal drinking until more readily available consumer goods enabled an enriched home environment and until the values of consumerism could be fostered (ibid., p. 46). In some respects in Sweden the Göteborg system actually stimulated drinking because it was possible for the towns to make large profits from the sale of *brännvin* and pay for all the poor relief with this income.

The temperance movements had very different effects in Britain and Sweden. The one in Britain failed and became discredited. Harrison draws attention to the rebuttal of its central premises especially by the socialist movement: the notion that individual *personality* was responsible for undisciplined drinking and the sectarian attack on the drink trade which became a scapegoat for more deeply rooted problems such as the centrality of drink in relation to poverty (ibid., ch. 17). The period from 1880 to 1920 was one of political struggle in Sweden between right and left, fanatical prohibitionists and advocates of personal freedom, between the bourgeoisie and the developing socialist movement. The first lodge of the Order of Good Templars was opened in Göteborg in 1879. This new temperance movement rapidly grew in strength stressing total abstinence and demanding prohibition. Despite internal divisions amongst its supporters, especially the middle-class and religious factions of the Order and the socialists (Jönsson 1946), the question of prohibition was a live one at the turn of the century. A referendum on prohibition was narrowly defeated in 1922. That prohibition was not introduced was partly due to the development of an alternative, the Bratt system of alcohol control, named after the Stockholm doctor Ivan Bratt who, with the backing of an influential lobby, put forward an alternative plan in pamphlets and newspaper

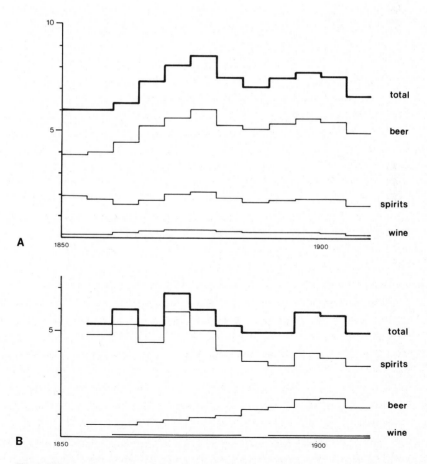

Fig. 8.13 Per capita consumption (litres) of pure alcohol according to drink type for Britain (A) and Sweden (B) 1850–1910 (*Sources:* Wilson 1940; Svensson 1973).

articles published between 1909 and 1912 (see Nycander 1967; Svensson 1973; Bruun 1984, for discussions).

The Bratt system was made obligatory under law from 1919. The two principles on which the system operated were removal of the private profit motive from the alcohol trade and control of the individual consumer by means of a rationing system. This system lasted until 1955.

The sole rights to the wholesale trade were vested in a state-controlled company coordinating the manufacture, importation and distribution of all alcoholic beverages with the exception of beer (see below). The retail trade was vested in a series of localized system companies in the style of the old Göteborg system. Such companies could only be established in towns with a population greater than 5,000 inhabitants and most rural districts were entirely 'dry'.

The Bratt system permitted an unprecedented degree of disciplinary control and surveillance over the individual, almost perfect in its calculation and precision. In order to purchase spirits or wine it was necessary to obtain a ration book (*motbok*) from the local system company within whose control area the applicant resided, and to which purchases were confined. Permits to buy alcohol were not granted to citizens who were

  (i)   not over 21 years of age;
 (ii)   married women;
(iii)   persons who had more than once during the last three years been found guilty of drunkenness;
 (iv)   individuals convicted of crimes involving drunkenness;
  (v)   persons committed to correctional institutions for alcoholics or those prohibited from drinking by the local temperance board (see below);
 (vi)   persons convicted of selling, manufacturing or purchasing alcohol illegally.

The maximum spirit ration obtainable was four litres/month (reduced to three litres/month during World War II). Wine was not rationed as consumption was low, but all purchases were carefully noted down in the *motbok*. In practice very few individuals received the full ration after the first few years of the operation of the system. At the beginning of 1920, 20% of men and 77% of women received less than the legal maximum. By the end of the 1930s, the corresponding figures were 77% and 99% (Thompson 1935, p. 112). The allocation of spirits was 'means tested' according to individual 'needs'. Applicants for a *motbok* were required to state on a special form their name, sex, age, occupation, place of employment, the parish in which they were registered, their income, capital, the amount of taxes paid and whether they had been in arrears for the past three years, the size of their family and the names, ages and dates of birth of all those members of the household in which they resided over 21 years of age and their record and reputation for sobriety. On the basis of this detailed personal information the allocation of spirits for each applicant was decided by personnel of the local system company. The allocation of spirits varied widely with the social standing of the individual applicant. Although the legal age to purchase spirits was 21 it was unusual for anyone to receive a *motbok* until they were 25 or older. A married man had, in principle, the possibility of increasing his allocation, with age, to the maximum, provided he did not fall into debt, receive social help, or be found guilty or suspected of temperance offences. As noted above it was impossible for a married woman to receive a *motbok* and self-supporting women rarely received more than one or two litres of spirits/quarter (Systembolaget 1965; Thompson 1935; Socialstyrelsen 1952).

The *motbok* resembled a cheque book in which the maximum spirit allocation and associated purchasing restrictions were stamped. Detailed files on all consumers were kept at the local system company offices against which the signature of the holder of a *motbok* could be checked together with his/her ration allocation. These files were also open to the police and other public officials such as members of temperance boards. By means of the *motbok* and the files of the system company it was possible to keep a minute and precise registration and control of the drinking habits of every individual consumer, and any 'irregularities' could be investigated. For example, a man taking out his full ration of spirits within the first few days of the month and thereafter purchasing a large quantity of wine would almost certainly be subject either to an investigation or to surveillance by officials of the local system company in conjunction with checks by the police and the temperance boards for actual or suspected incidence of non-sobriety. Persons convicted of temperance offences would have their *motbok* confiscated for a shorter or longer period.

The *motbok* system was grossly discriminatory in terms of

(i)   sex – women were actively discriminated against both in terms of the possibility of obtaining a ration book and allowances allotted to them;
(ii)   social class and standing – a close correlation existed between those holding the highest quotas and their social status (e.g., 1% of farm labourers received the full ration, 30% of businessmen in trade and communications);
(iii) income – the larger one's income, the more likely one was to receive a larger allowance (detailed statistics in SOU 1951: 43). In 1930 the Stockholm system company rejected 136 applications solely on the grounds of 'miserable living conditions' (Thompson 1935, p. 116). Persons who did not pay their taxes on time were in danger of losing their ration books and those receiving social help were unlikely to obtain a ration;
(iv)   place of abode – persons living in rural areas generally received a lower ration.

Under the old Göteborg system social patterns of drinking had been largely transformed so that in the early years the Bratt system operated entirely in relation to sales for consumption off the premises. The result of this was that consumption in restaurants began to increase, and these were consequently brought under direct managerial control of the system companies and an elaborate system of rules was introduced intending to regulate consumption according to the time of day, the class of restaurant, the sex of the customer and the type of drink ordered. These controls on public consumption replicated those on private consumption in terms of both sexual and social discrimination. They ensured the continuance of privatized drinking if only to avoid greater surveillance in public: checkers were frequently employed to inspect restaurants and to ensure, for example, that those ordering a drink also consumed it rather than giving it to someone else (Socialstyrelsen 1952, p. 271).

The Swedish brewing industry was not nationalized but brought under indirect state control. Breweries were spread over the entire country, strongly localized to towns and their rural hinterlands in which they had a virtual monopoly on sales promoted by legislation and an elaborate complex of cartel agreements with regard to area divisions and sales quotas (Gabrielsson 1970). The legislation was designed to restrict competition in the interests of temperance so that the effects of sales competition between breweries would not increase consumption. In 1919 a tripartite class system for beer was introduced on the basis of alcohol strength and in 1923 the strongest beer (Class III) was banned altogether on the domestic market and was only obtainable on a doctor's prescription.

It is clear that the Bratt system was directed in force towards underprivileged groups (women and the working classes) and especially tried to control the individual 'deviant' drinker. In addition to the moralizing forces of temperance attempting to 'uplift' the British and Swedish working classes another aspect of disciplinary interest, displayed most stridently again in Sweden, was a general concern with public order, with bringing the dangerous classes under institutional surveillance (Fig. 8.14). The imposition of an extensive penal discipline centring on the prison created a criminal class segregated from the general populace and constituted as dangerous to both rich and poor. This permitted the emergence of police and other predominantly state authorities exercising disciplinary and surveilling power (Foucault 1979, 1980, p. 47). Just as the Swedish *motbok* system has no parallel in Britain the treatment of those individuals socially defined as alcoholics has no counterpart in British penal legislation.

The first Swedish 'alcoholic law' was eventually passed in 1913. It was primarily a public order measure aimed at the protection of society from unwanted alcoholics, using

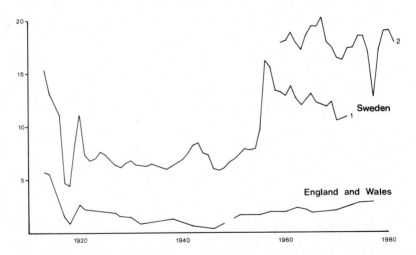

Fig. 8.14 Convictions for drunkenness in England and Wales and Sweden per 1,000 inhabitants over 15 years of age (England and Wales 1913–48 convictions per total inhabitants). For Sweden the number of people taken into custody for drunkenness is also shown (2). Drunkenness in Sweden was decriminalized in 1977. *Sources:* Royal College of Psychiatrists 1979; SOU 1952: 53; SOU 1974: 90; *Alkoholstatistik* 1973–82. The higher frequencies for Sweden are probably as much a result of increased police activity as indicating an objectively greater amount of drunk and disorderly conduct.

compulsory internment as a means to this end if necessary. According to the 1913 law, temperance boards were to be set up in every town, their duties being to promote temperance and take action against abusers. Changes in the alcoholism laws in 1922, 1931, 1938 and 1954 permitted earlier interventions on the part of the temperance boards. The duties of the temperance boards, originally confined to the most visible and obviously 'chronic abusers' were thus continually extended and their powers widened such that 'preventative measures' and 'investigations' could be undertaken prior to the internment of the most intractable offenders (Fig. 8.15). Detailed records were kept of actual or suspected temperance infringements. In the case of a report of an individual for temperance infringement, 'preventative measures' (Fig. 8.15) might include talking

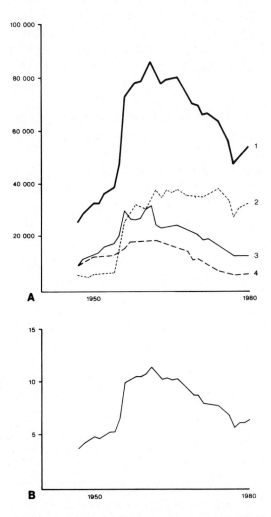

Fig. 8.15 Activities of Swedish temperance boards 1945–80. *Source: Socialvårdstatistik.* A: (1) total number of investigations (2) number of people only subject to an investigation for an alleged breach of temperance (3) number of people subject to 'slight preventative measures' (4) number of people subject to 'more severe preventative measures' including coercion and imprisonment. B: the number of people per 1,000 inhabitants against whom a temperance board has proceeded.

to the individual, threats of committal, placing him or her under 'supervision' or giving aid to change his/her personal environment or place of work. An individual not influenced by these 'remedial' measures would then be interned (Wiklund 1948; Sjöhagen 1953; Bremberg 1973). A whole variety of institutional treatment became available for committal, ranging from internment in 'total institutions' (often converted prisons) to labour camps in the countryside, boarding with private persons of 'impeccable moral character', to hostels in which leisure hours away from work had to be spent (Sjöhagen 1954; Malmén 1966; Bremberg 1973).

Class contradiction formed the determinate background to these controls and the development of the 'problem' of working-class leisure in Britain and Sweden. Working-class leisure moved into the space of inter-class relations where 'the discovery and emergence of disciplinary techniques of power cast the dominant classes as collective teacher prompting the people to learn and observe the one way of life considered properly human' (Bauman 1983, p. 36; see below on the teacher-judge). And drinking a lot just wasn't properly human: 'socially, they [alcoholics] do not fulfill the demands that are usually made on citizens . . . a high degree of alcoholic indulgence causes social unfitness' (Dahlberg 1939).

Just as the penal system tends to produce criminals and delinquents (new prisons are invariably rapidly filled), a system such as the one in Sweden designed to cure alcoholics invariably finds, or creates, people to treat. More broadly, 'problem' drinking with its moral and/or medical connotations is related to the expansion of disciplinary interest in the use of the body in leisure time and its health. The determinate relation between discipline and the capitalist labour process means that heavy drinking (however defined) and 'alcoholism' are defined as being problematic, as 'deviant'. This is in turn related to the contradiction between the behavioural consequences of drink and the disciplined way of life *required* of the capitalist worker. This is not to belittle the often severe personal and physical distress which may be associated with heavy drinking. It is, however, to question the identification of such drinking as deviant, as an object of societal intervention in the form of disciplinary (educative, medical/psychiatric, penal) and legislative (taxation, restrictions on availability and drinking hours) procedures.

Consumerism, the welfare state and the medicalization of drinking practices
Since the Second World War the British and Swedish nation states have produced highly developed welfare systems. The desire to maintain a healthy working population for capital accumulation and the consumption of consumer goods has led to an increasing degree of medicalization of drinking practices. The moralizing focus of the nineteenth and early twentieth-century temperance movements involving the inculcation of bourgeois values centring on family-based leisure has become augmented in the welfare state by an increasing degree of medical intervention and definition of the perceived problem, that of alcohol addiction or alcoholism. Enforced disciplinary procedures such as the restriction of the availability of alcohol in Sweden or restrictions on drinking hours in Britain have become supplemented by a bio-politics of life focussing on the regulatory control of the health of the population. This regulatory 'goal' of the state increasingly conflicts with and contradicts the fostering of consumerism.

With the commodification of labour in capitalism and the institutionalization of disciplinary power in various state apparatuses the worker lost direct control of the labour process. The wage form of industrial capitalism created the consumer of alienated products of labour. The worker was 'free' to spend his/her wage and consume in leisure time. Such a freedom acted as a compensation for loss of control over the labour process and, increasingly, this *economization of power* led to the notion that freedom lay in leisure-time and leisure-space, consumer needs for leisure consumption being satisfied by appropriating marketed goods (Bauman 1983, pp. 38–9). The maintenance of class hegemony required, however, that the 'acceptable arena of human initiative is circumscribed by the act of purchasing' (Ewen and Ewen 1982, p. 75). This entailed that a socially privatized existence, mediated by consumerism, came to supersede the mediation of social relations and consciousness by the conditions of class experience of labour (Alt 1976).

The exploitative and harsh nature of labour as a determinant of political struggle has given way, through higher wages and reduced work time, to the aim of improving at an ever-increasing pace the standard of living, primarily by providing extended possibilities for consumption. Consequently labour becomes culturally devalued as a source of values. Individual freedom is defined symbolically through commodity consumption, through *style*. Consumable leisure is ennobled as a subjective answer to the discipline of the machine (Ewen and Ewen 1982, p. 35).

And indeed the development of new bases for stable economic growth in monopoly capitalism has involved an expanded use of disciplinary technology in industry related to a rationalization of the labour process. Deskilling and replacement of craft skills by specialized machine operations have accompanied the separation of mental (administrative) and manual (operational) labour in corporate capital organizations (Braverman 1974). The disciplined, atomized body of the worker, treated not as a unit but as a mechanism made up of separately usable parts is economically more efficient.

The development of consumerism and the extension of hegemonic concern to consumption as well as production means that the worker is no longer considered as merely a unit-in-production. Increasing attention has been paid to the prediction and control of the worker-consumer through companies' personnel management and marketing policies, aggressive advertising and a cultural apparatus directed at the shaping of a consumer consciousness (Ewen 1976; Ewen and Ewen 1982; Featherstone 1982; Inglis 1972; Packard 1981).

Already, in the nineteenth century new forms of distinct and specialized recreation – libraries, music halls, museums, for example, developed as diversions. In Britain these increasingly began to remove the public house from its central place within the recreation of the occupational community. In addition a mode of *rational* recreation developed which has encouraged the replacement of unstructured sports and activities, which required unspecified amounts of space, time and participants, by spectator sports with a codified set of rules – consumable sport. Legislative and disciplinary control in Britain regularized and restricted drinking hours. Improved housing and the increasing availability of consumer goods meant that the home was in process of becoming the origin and physical setting for leisure – increasingly privatized leisure.

Class segregation in public drinking meant that private as opposed to public drinking began to be seen more and more as a mark of respectability.

Regarding conceptions of the body, the belief that fatness signified health was challenged. The healthy body became the athletic body. The athletic physique associated with the new leisure sports required disciplined training and was incompatible with heavy drinking. The relation between work and drink (drink imparting strength and energy) was also weakened in that reduced working hours and better working conditions meant alcohol was less needed as a restorative.

These processes tended to sever the relationship between drink and work and weaken that between drink and recreation while the relationship between drink and socializing remained. These changes have continued in Britain with the increasing dissolution of the occupational community with its determinate structures of working-class localism, especially since the 1940s through the effects of changes in the production process and through the state's social and political policies (Clarke 1979, p. 240; Clarke *et al.* 1976, pp. 35ff.).

In 1955 the popularly termed 'October revolution' occurred in Sweden – the Bratt system of alcohol rationing was abolished following the findings of a special government investigative committee (the 1944 Temperance Committee, which published seven lengthy volumes reviewing the entire system of alcohol control). The Bratt system had never been popular from its inception. Popular support for the temperance movement declined drastically after the 1920s. In an increasingly affluent consumer society developing after World War II a special alcohol rationing system stuck out like a sore thumb. Although in the 1950s only about one fifth of *motbok* holders were allowed the maximum ration of spirits the system was, ostensibly, only meant to restrict excessive and not moderate drinkers. Most damning of all was the realization that the system was a failure. Alcohol consumption had increased because of the rising ratio of people taking out their full ration to those who did not (there was a widespread popular belief that failure to take out the full ration might lead to reduced entitlements (Thompson 1935, p. 113, note 12). The system of individual control of the excessive drinker was largely ineffective. For example, by far the greatest number of drunkenness offences were committed by precisely those individuals denied a *motbok* (Dahlberg 1951, p. 38). The very irregularity in which alcohol was treated in relation to other consumer goods stimulated and incited consumption (and still does).

The post-Bratt liberalization of alcohol control policies substituted individual control for an attempt to control total consumption, via a system of progressive taxation of drinks in relation to alcohol content. This was accompanied by an increased emphasis on the dissemination of information (e.g. in schools) and via advertising strategies intended to produce healthy drinking. Commercial advertising for alcohol was initially restricted and finally banned altogether (see below). Healthy drinking was promoted by an attempt to persuade people to consume drinks of lower alcohol content (i.e. wine and beer rather than spirits). Alcohol-free drinks were (and are) promoted and there was a general attempt to sever the connection between drink and leisure, drink and sociability – to promote a drug-free culture especially amongst the young (SOU 1974: 91; Socialstyrelsen 1983, pp. 52–3). These techniques are supplemented by continued restrictions on the availability of alcohol, with strong beer, wine and spirits being sold only in the government alcohol monopoly (Systembolaget) shops. Sales in restaurants remain very closely regulated at a local government level. Permits to sell alcoholic drinks for consumption on the premises are comparatively few in number compared with Britain (Fig. 8.16) and generally only given if food is part of the service. Prices of drinks in restaurants are so high that the sheer cost of public drinking ensures

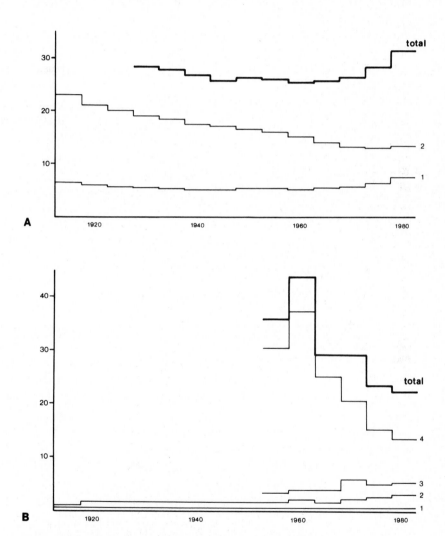

Fig. 8.16 The number of outlets per 10,000 inhabitants for alcohol
A: England and Wales
  1: alcohol for consumption off the premises
  2: alcohol for consumption on and off the premises
B: Sweden
  1: Systembolaget (government alcohol monopoly retail shops)
  2: restaurants
  3: restaurants (Classes I and II beer only)
  4: sales outlets for beer Classes I and II.

privatized consumption (Fig. 8.16B). An entire micropolitics of power is involved in processing applications to serve alcohol (Fig. 8.17) which may be compared with the situation in Britain in which power is vested in local licensing magistrates. The wording of the Swedish law concerning licence applications is so ambiguous that, in practice, almost any grounds may be used by the numerous authorities involved to refuse permission to serve alcohol (Vatanen and Tengvall 1983). An age restriction forbids the purchase of alcohol in the government monopoly shops, set at 20, despite the age of majority being 18. The present day restrictions in Sweden appear liberal in an historical perspective but contrast markedly with those in Britain where restrictions have, since the nineteenth century, been confined to granting licences for the sale of alcohol and, since 1828, with imposing restrictions on opening hours of public houses (see Wilson 1940; Monckton 1966, 1969).

In relation to the development of consumerism and increased leisure the consumption of alcohol in both countries has risen markedly since the 1940s (Fig. 8.18) and in Britain all alcoholic drinks have been made freely available in supermarkets since the 1960s. Despite the far wider range of restrictions in Sweden, as compared with Britain, throughout the twentieth century the perceived problem of alcoholism has remained. Alcohol is still considered 'one of our greatest social problems' (Proposition 1976/77: 108 (Swedish government white paper)) yet consumption is considerably higher on a per capita basis in Britain (Fig. 8.18) where government interest is still primarily fiscal, alcohol control a matter of minor interest and public opinion indifferent (Bradley

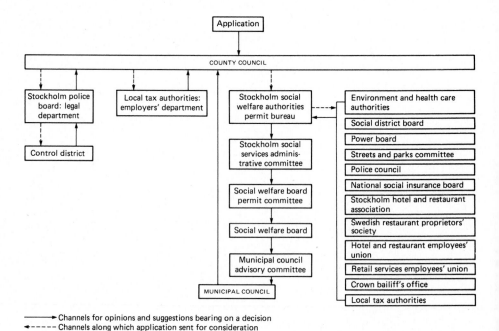

Fig. 8.17 The micropolitics of power involving an application for a licence to serve spirits in Stockholm (after *Dagens Nyheter*, 14 July, 1983, p. 21).

and Fenwick 1974). Indeed in Sweden alcohol consumption is on a per capita basis one of the lowest in the industrialized world yet it is one of the leading countries involved in alcohol research.

The exceptional concern with alcohol 'problems' in Sweden, very closely tied up with disciplinary power, is intimately related to a massive proliferation of discourses on

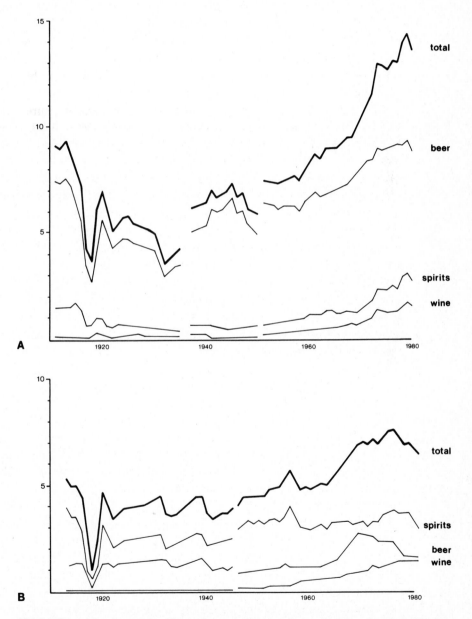

Fig. 8.18 Per capita consumption (litres) of pure alcohol according to drink type for Britain (A) and Sweden (B). *Sources:* Brewers Society; Wilson 1940; SOU 1952: 52; SOU 1974: 90; *Alkoholstatistik* 1973–82. (Britain after 1951 per inhabitant over 15 years of age, Sweden after 1946 per inhabitant over 15 years of age).

alcohol and statistics concerned with every conceivable aspect of alcohol use, or potential use (e.g., attempts to estimate the degree of home distilling on the basis of the ratio of yeast sold to that required to make bread on the basis of the quantity of flour sold, the remaining yeast being assumed to be used in distilling (SAMO 1981: 21, pp. 14–15) to the investigations of the 1944 Temperance Committee concerning the frequency of venereal disease in relation to alcohol consumption (SOU 1951: 43, pp. 109–24). The exercise of disciplinary power produces both knowledges and their object. It is certainly not the case that a simple objective high incidence of problems associated with alcohol 'naturally' gives rise to a legitimate and objective concern. The very close connection between temperance agencies and research work done on alcohol and alcoholism attests to this.

To a great extent, both in Britain and Sweden, the intervention of the law as a mechanism of control has been displaced by attempts to produce a normalization of the population, both moral and medical. The universal reference has become the norm rather than the law: the normative judgement of the doctor-judge, the social-worker-judge, the teacher-judge imposing homogeneity while measuring and observing individual deviance (Foucault 1979, pp. 304–5). The medical imperative of health has complemented the notion of the disciplinary body. The worker, the body-machine, is to be maintained as well as controlled. These techniques of power relate to the insertion of a capitalist conception of the worker-unit into the production-consumption cycle.

Since 1982 the old alcoholic laws in Sweden have been replaced by two acts, the Social Services Act and the Act on the compulsory care of abusers. Social aid has thus been separated from the means of coercion, still maintained as a last resort. Significantly, the old-style temperance boards are no longer separate administrative agencies of state control but are integrated with the welfare services as a whole (social welfare, child welfare, welfare for the aged, etc.). This has broadened the means of social control of deviant drinkers in that the chances of them being 'recognized' are extended through the entire gamut of welfare services.

Despite the impossibility of constructing any universally applicable definition of alcoholism (see e.g., Christie and Bruun 1968, p. 65) it nevertheless is the case that people do and have applied the terms 'alcoholic' and 'alcoholism' to what, at any historically contingent moment, appear to be clearly delineated persons or types of states. The alcoholic, far from being a social fact is, rather, a social accomplishment (Schneider 1978), a product of discourse, classification, definition and struggle between various interested parties. In the welfare state, medical definitions of 'problem' drinking as mental 'illness', rather than as a sign of a lack of essential moral fibre, tend to objectify drinking, removing it from its determinate, constitutive context. The consumption of alcohol as drug and its physical consequences may then be treated by experts sanctioned by science and the state, observing all according to the healthy norm and treating the unhealthy, dysfunctioning, deviant individual. The development of the welfare state is bound up with the transference of the power to detect and define the alcoholic from civil to medical authorities, involving the repudiation of the idea that the alcoholic was simply a social degenerate and the perception of alcoholism as an illness or a problem. The apparent irrationality of excessive consumption becomes explained in the new medical framework not only as illness, but as mental illness. It is not surprising, therefore, to find ever increasing proportions of deviant drinkers treated in mental or psychiatric hospitals or wards or, given the much greater concern with alcohol in Sweden, that the Swedish figures should dwarf those for Britain (Fig. 8.19). In the welfare state, to drink excessively has become linked to madness so the lunatic and the drinker become grouped together. The hospital has become a major agency of regulative social control (Fig. 8.20) and the treatment or control of deviance is rooted in techniques of power over the body and in transformations of its conception (*cf.* Szasz 1975; Doyal 1979; Bologh 1981).

Consumerism is internally related to the techniques of disciplinary power discovered and increasingly exercised from the seventeenth century. While partly a resistance to, a compensation for institutional discipline, both consumerism and discipline form a

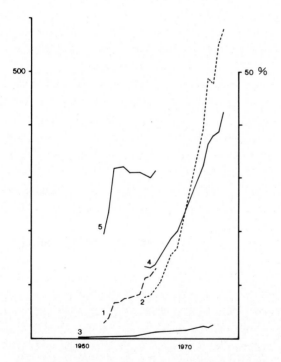

Fig. 8.19 The frequency of alcoholics in mental hospitals or psychiatric wards in Britain and Sweden per 100,000 inhabitants
(1) Sweden: frequency of patients with disorders associated with alcoholism in mental hospitals and psychiatric departments in general hospitals. *Source:* Herner 1972.
(2) Sweden: frequency of discharges (transferred and deceased excluded) of patients with disorders due to alcoholism from mental hospitals and psychiatric wards of general hospitals. *Source: Statistika Meddelanden* HS 1981: 6.
(3) England and Wales: admissions to mental hospitals and units under regional hospital boards and teaching hospitals where the primary or secondary diagnosis was alcoholism or alcoholic psychosis. *Source:* Royal College of Psychiatrists 1979.
(4) Sweden: the percentage of diagnosed patients who were alcoholics. *Source:* Herner 1972.
(5) Sweden: the percentage of diagnosed male patients who were alcoholics. *Source:* Herner 1972.

determinately contradictory nexus of meanings and attitudes focussed on the human body. This nexus also includes the regulatory interest in the health of the body.

Consumerism is not about freedom from control but is about self-imposed 'autonomous' discipline: 'it is about the joy of controlling the body of one's own individual will, with the help of sophisticated products of technology which offer the visibility of the formidable power of one's controlling agency' (Bauman 1983, p. 40). So the body needs to be trained, cultivated, taught, and thus brought into line. In training the body is an object of both institutional heteronomous discipline and individual autonomous self-surveillance. In such discipline, the body is viewed both positively and negatively, some aspects to be developed, some suppressed; the body is both redeeming and sinful. Consumption of a product either magically brings about a desired end or acts as recompense for lack of it (*cf*. Williamson 1978, on advertising the product as magical agent and/or substitute for a desired end). Consumption opposes prohibition: cookbooks and diet books; drinking and temperance and health education.

Health education demands constant vigilance of the body as machine, self-responsibility for maintenance of health and appearance. This appeal of the health educationalist to the rationality and hence value-freedom of self-preservation masks the influence of the consumer culture's idealization of youth and beauty (Featherstone 1982, p. 25) – consumerism's norm.

So according to the imperative of health, the body must remain an object of constraint and drill however much it consumes in displaced compensation for the capillary operation of institutional discipline.

Such consumption is abstract in that the use-value of the product is suppressed in relation to its abstract exchange-value. So 'the body is trained into a capacity to will and absorb more marketable goods, and . . . routines are instilled through a self-inflicted drill which makes possible just that' (Bauman 1983, p. 41). The body is not to discern

Fig. 8.20 View of Lund, Sweden, from the south. In *Ceremonial Chemistry*, Szasz (1975) writes of the transference of the power to define deviants in capitalism from the theocratic (religious/Christian morality) to the therapeutic (scientific/medical) state. The decline of religious/civil power to define the deviant and the rise of scientific/medical power is symbolized in the architecture of Lund (and other Swedish cities). The huge modern building dominating the skyline and visible for miles around from all directions is the hospital. The cathedral with its twin towers, to the right, is scarcely visible. Pure chance? The hospital is the largest employer in Lund and for all Sweden no less than 10.5% of the working population is employed in health care. (Photo: John Duncan)

and appreciate but merely to absorb. It doesn't matter *what* is consumed but merely the style and symbolism of the act of consumption.

The brewing industry

It is in the context of a consumer society that the general activities of the British and Swedish brewing industries, and their products, since the 1950s needs to be viewed. In both countries rationalization, mergers and take-overs have dramatically diminished the number of breweries with a national rather than regional distribution network for their products (Fig. 8.21). This trend is particularly marked in Sweden with a reduction in the number of factories from 223 in 1903, to 16 in 1983. The repeal of legislation restricting competition, occurring at the same time as the abolition of the Bratt system led to one company, Pripps (now 75% state owned) establishing a virtual monopoly over the entire beer market, accounting for 74% of all beer sales by 1977 (DsI 1978: 34; Anell and Persson 1984, p. 58). In 1983 one of Pripps' brands (Pripps Blå) had a 33% market share of all beer brands (*Prippsnytt* 1983, p. 2; PLM 1983).

In Britain a similar development occurred with six breweries dominating the market. Increasingly oligopolist, the larger British breweries rationalized pub design, altered the product on sale and replaced tenants with managers producing a tendency towards centralized rather than local control over the context of public drinking (Hutt 1973; Boston 1977; Protz 1978). Such a development was related to attempts to open up the drinking market to a new customer: a young (*cf.* Featherstone 1982, pp. 21f.), classless 'consumer' rather than a 'member'. As Clarke notes 'this newly forged interpellation dissolves previous patterns and habits of "how to drink" and substitutes for them preferred "styles" of drinking' (Clarke 1979, p. 245). With the decline of the British

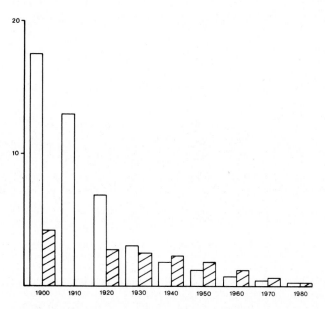

Fig. 8.21 The number of breweries in Britain and Sweden (shaded) per 100,000 inhabitants. *Sources:* Brewers Society; Annell and Persson 1984; Mårtensson 1961 (no data for Sweden 1910).

occupational community, the pub is less patronized by occupational peers with the fetishized status of wage-labourers reproducing their relationship to work in the public bar, than by consumers seeking entertainment and symbolically affirming their mobility and freedom (Alt 1976, p. 72).

Emphasis on styles of drinking and consumption has the concomitant that it matters less what the product is or tastes like than what it means. The original use-value of the product becomes submerged beneath its exchange-value in a market of images. The individual is on display, is self-conscious, exercising self-scrutiny, self-surveillance, measuring appearance and performance against the norm (Featherstone 1982, pp. 19–20).

The old tripartite class system was retained in Sweden for beer following the abolition of rationing and the strong Class III beer was made available in the government alcohol monopoly (Systembolaget) shops. The weaker Class I and II beers were sold freely in food shops as before. The introduction of a fourth class of medium strength beer (mellanöl – Class IIB) in 1965 was related to an attempt to radically alter the image of beer. Prior to the 1960s beer was widely regarded as a drink associated with older working-class males. The advertising campaign associated with the new beer was directed to making beer classless and to appeal both to the young and women (see below). Image was all that mattered, the advertising images were numerous and provocative to those concerned with temperance. The effectiveness of this campaign and the rapid increase in beer consumption, especially amongst the young, eventually led to the withdrawal of this beer from the market through legislation in 1977. However the image and style-value of beer remained and continues to be promoted by the breweries, as it does in Britain.

So beer is marketed by brewery companies like any other product and such companies have not failed to exhibit all the features of the capitalist corporation – vigorous advertising programmes and market creation, especially in the last 20 years. But beer is not just any consumable item; it has strong historical and social links with community life and socializing in both Britain and Sweden, although after legislative and social intervention, most beer in Sweden is drunk in the private home. Beer is also an alcoholic drink, a drug. Alcohol, in its many varieties, may be consumed as intoxicant, as food, as medicine, social lubricant, or as religious sacrament. This density of alcohol's social and historical mythology (*cf.* Barthes 1973c), the multiplicity of use and exchange values, resonate with the contradictory nexus of the meanings of the human body in contemporary capitalism. Drinking is inserted into structures of disciplinary power, consumerism, and a health imperative of a biopolitics of the population.

We have aimed to show how the capitalist state may be held to relate to the production and consumption of alcohol through a number of relatively autonomous institutions. To summarize, the major fields of relation are:

(1) (a) the production of alcohol as a commodity bears on commercial, industrial and agricultural policies and interests;

     (b) production of alcohol contributes substantial revenue to the treasury through exaction of excise duty.

(2) The consequences of alcohol consumption bear on
   (a) public order,
   (b) industrial productivity,
   (c) the health of the population

(*cf*. Mäkelä and Viikari 1977; Mäkelä *et al*. 1981; Bruun *et al*. 1975). State intervention may occur through reference to four major forms of power:

(1) legal-juridical power which creates restrictive or enabling legislation;
(2) disciplinary power focussing on the body as a machine to be supervised and placed under surveillance;
(3) techniques of power focussing on the health of the population (Foucault 1981, Part 5);
(4) techniques of power channelled through modes of information dissemination, gathering and processing, e.g. television, radio, publications, computer technologies (Poster 1984).

We have attempted to avoid a simplistic conception of the state as a unitary repressive power, as a coherent set of institutions performing a pre-given role in the reproduction of capitalism. A lack of coherent functionality is contained within the logic of the capitalist state. The state fosters consumerism, pursues policies which enable the production and consumption of alcohol as a commodity in the capitalist economic cycle, while exercising various forms of power in dealing with the consequences of drinking on the population. Consumption opposes and contradicts control, discipline and health. In returning to the can designs we shall consider two related forms of everyday material culture – advertisements and newspapers – as a way of refining and elaborating this fundamental contradiction we have noted as structuring drinking practices, preparing the ground for explaining the structure of difference which the can designs exhibit.

ALCOHOL IN THE MEDIA AND ADVERTISING

Drink and the news

Newspapers, as ideological vehicles, to a large extent 'produce' as much as 'reflect' public opinion not only expressing but also repressing and excluding certain issues from discussion. The mass media and the formation of a public and public opinion are, historically, mutually supportive. As Gouldner has put it, a public is formed when the links between culture and social interaction are, in essentials, attenuated so that people can share something (e.g., news) without being involved in a process of interpersonal interaction (Gouldner 1976, p. 109). Newspapers, and the mass media more generally, actively create and facilitate a process by which a *public*, as opposed to a *community*, is formed by dramatically increasing the exchange of information at a distance. Newspapers thus mediate a relatively abstract experience of the social world varying in terms of social and spatial distance from the readership (local, home, international news, etc.) and produce a diffuse but nevertheless structured set of meanings for consumption. Their overt content owes much to competition for readers and advertisers within the general field of cultural production, endlessly seeking to increase their readership at the expense of competitors, involving the production and subsequent interpretation of information which, by its very inclusion, becomes identified as 'news'.

We are concerned in this section to investigate the sets of meanings newspapers present as associated with drinking, to ascertain to what extent alcohol rates as a news item, and the meanings associated with this news coverage. We again undertook a comparative study of Britain and Sweden, analysing newspapers over a four-month period from September to December 1983. Since it was beyond the scope of this study to analyse a whole range of different types of British and Swedish newspapers and magazines it was decided to choose two 'serious', as opposed to tabloid, daily papers with a similar political outlook and a national distribution. For Britain *The Guardian* was studied and for Sweden, *Dagens Nyheter*. Both of these papers are of identical page size with similar circulation figures and both put forward an 'independent liberal' political position. In Britain the press is far more centralized than in Sweden or for that matter most other European countries (see Williams 1979). Although *Dagens Nyheter* has its primary circulation in Stockholm and the surrounding area, it is also read in all parts of Sweden and may be held to fulfill a dual role as a Stockholm and a national newspaper. At the time the analyses were undertaken *Dagens Nyheter* had larger circulation figures than any other daily morning newspaper in Sweden. By contrast the circulation figures for *The Guardian* by British standards are small but truly national. Since *Dagens Nyheter* has a periodicity of seven issues a week and *The Guardian* only six a week, a British 'liberal' Sunday newspaper, *The Observer*, was also analysed to further facilitate adequate comparison. Although, inevitably, there are differences in the amount of editorial and non-editorial matter published in the British and Swedish newspapers, whether articles are written about alcohol or advertisements inserted is a matter of choice largely independent of overall newspaper size.

Table 8.4 gives the results of the survey of the number of articles written about alcohol and the number of adverts. An obvious and striking contrast exists. While 58 articles were written about alcohol in the British newspapers over the four-month period, 203 appeared in *Dagens Nyheter*. When the number of adverts is considered the situation is reversed. *The Guardian* and *The Observer* contained 95% more adverts than *Dagens Nyheter*. This difference is, however, a result of differences in alcohol control policies between the two countries rather than a reluctance on the part of those concerned with marketing alcohol to advertise in Sweden. Since 1979, advertisements in the press, apart from trade journals, have been banned in Sweden for spirits, wine and strong beer. No such restrictions exist in Britain and for the four-month period analysed there was an interesting trend in the British data – the number of articles about alcohol declined from September to December while the number of adverts increased significantly, a trend obviously geared to persuade consumers to buy alcohol for the Christmas/New Year holiday period.

A contrast in the visibility of alcohol exists between the British and Swedish newspapers. In Britain alcohol is primarily visible as a concrete marketed product available for consumption through the medium of advertisements. In Sweden alcohol is highly visible but in another way – as an abstract product to be discussed, dissected and

Table 8.4. *The frequency of articles written about alcohol and alcohol adverts in British and Swedish newspapers for the period September–December 1983*

month	A G+O	A DN	B G+O	B DN	C G+O	C DN	D G+O	D DN	E G+O	E DN
Sept.	21	45	40	6	—	4	14	—	8	3
Oct.	15	49	70	4	1	4	15	—	9	1
Nov.[1]	12	59	89	3	—	6	29	—	21	—
Dec.[2]	10	50	111	3	—	4	32	—	29	2
Total	58	203	310	16	1	18	90	—	67	6

G: *The Guardian*, O: *The Observer*, DN: *Dagens Nyheter*.
A – number of articles written about alcohol (editorial matter)
B – number of adverts
C – number of front page articles
D – number of front page adverts
E – number of colour adverts
1 – Two issues of *The Guardian* and one issue of *The Observer* lost because of an industrial dispute.
2 – Five issues of *The Guardian* lost because of an industrial dispute and one issue of *The Observer* and two issues of *Dagens Nyheter* lost because of Christmas holidays.

debated. This contrast in the forms of visibility of alcohol is replicated when we consider differences between the newspapers in terms of the number of times alcohol rates as a front page news item, front page adverts, and the sizes of the articles and the adverts. Alcohol was only given front page coverage once in *The Guardian*, never in *The Observer*, but no less than 18 times in *Dagens Nyheter*. Adverts never occurred on the front page of *Dagens Nyheter* while being inserted on the front page of 90 editions of *The Guardian* and *The Observer*. Similarly, a high proportion of Swedish articles about alcohol (about 20%) tend to be lengthy, occupying more than 26% of a newspaper page whereas only two articles in the British newspapers were of any length, this difference being reversed in relation to advert size.

The survey thus reveals a much higher degree of news coverage of alcohol in Sweden than in Britain but what of the content of the articles? The topics discussed were classified according to 14 general content categories, in terms of newspaper classification, and attitude expressed toward alcohol consumption (Table 8.5). The results of this analysis (Table 8.6) indicate that the major topics discussed in the British articles concerned alcohol production, consumption and sales figures and articles about wine as a cultural drink in association with food preparation accounting for 67% of the total number of articles. This correlates with an emphasis in terms of the newspaper classification on women, personal, consumer affairs and finance. Put in another way the emphasis is on alcohol in relation to capital investment and profit making (e.g., articles about investing in vintage wines or brewery profits rising during the long hot summer of 1983) and as a product intimately related to leisure time activities (e.g., knowledge of the correct wine to serve with such and such a dish). The articles in *Dagens Nyheter* are more evenly divided across a whole range of issues. Aspects of legislation, alcohol and crime, temperance organizations and pubs and restaurants, topics not discussed in the

Table 8.5. *Variables recorded for the newspaper analysis*

Var.	*Topics discussed* (variables 1–14)
1	Health (e.g., alcohol related diseases)
2	Alcoholics and alcoholism (case studies of individuals, etc.)
3	Welfare and social policy
4	Legislation and issues arising from it (e.g., restrictions on sale of alcohol)
5	Drinking and driving
6	Alcohol and crime (e.g., thefts of alcohol; smuggling)
7	Illegal trading or production of alcohol (e.g., home distilling)
8	Temperance organizations, teetotallers, temperance related organizations
9	Alcohol production (breweries, vineyards, finance, etc.)
10	Alcohol marketing (e.g., prices; selling wine; new initiatives; Swedish Systembolaget alcohol stores)
11	Alcohol consumption (consumption and sales figures)
12	Wines and food (cultural issues)
13	Pubs and restaurants
14	Other
	Articles in terms of newspaper classification (variables 15–21)
15	Home news
16	Foreign news
17	Arts
18	Women / Personal / Consumer affairs
19	Financial
20	Sports
21	Letters
	Articles in terms of attitude to alcohol (variables 22–24)
22	Positive
23	Neutral or not made explicit
24	Negative

British articles, were given fairly substantial coverage in Sweden (about 35% of the total number of articles). While a substantial number of articles were concerned with alcohol marketing (13%) the main object of discussion was the Systembolag government alcohol monopoly with articles about mundane features such as experiments in queuing systems for customers, and detailed accounts of price rises. Illegality was a favourite topic for discussion, no less than 25% of the articles being concerned with drinking and driving, illegal production of alcohol (home distilling) and trading (illegal drinking clubs) and crimes involving alcohol. Most of the crimes reported were not acts of physical violence following drinking but thefts or smuggling of alcoholic beverages. Corresponding with these topics the majority of the articles rated, in terms of newspaper classification, as home news. Attitude of the articles to alcohol was difficult to record without a very detailed semantic analysis. Unless very obvious it was recorded as 'neutral or not immediately evident'. As we might expect, in those articles written fairly explicitly a greater number of those in Britain expressed a positive attitude toward alcohol consumption while in Sweden a larger proportion were negative or restrictive in tone.

We know of no comparable study in Britain but in Sweden a similar survey was carried out during 1970 using a sample of 56 newspapers and magazines (Englund, Solberg and Svensson 1974). This survey showed a similarly high number of articles

Table 8.6. *Results of the content analysis of numbers of articles about alcohol*

Topics discussed													
Variables: 1		2		3		4		5		6		7	
month	G+O	DN	G+O	DN	G+O	DN	G+O	DN	G+O	DN	G+O	DN	G+O	DN
Sept.	3	1	—	4	3	4	—	3	3	4	—	4	—	5
Oct.	—	1	1	4	—	4	—	3	—	1	—	3	1	4
Nov.	—	2	2	3	—	5	—	3	—	2	—	11	—	5
Dec.	—	3	—	3	—	1	—	4	1	5	—	2	—	5
Total	3	7	3	14	3	14	—	13	4	12	—	20	1	19
% Total	5	3	5	7	5	7	—	6	7	6	—	10	2	9

	8		9		10		11		12		13		14	
month	G+O	DN	G+O	DN	G+O	DN	G+O	DN	G+O	DN	G+O	DN	G+O	DN
Sept.	—	—	2	1	2	4	1	3	7	4	—	—	—	8
Oct.	—	3	3	3	—	9	5	2	5	5	—	6	—	1
Nov.	—	7	4	3	2	11	—	1	4	4	—	1	—	1
Dec.	—	4	2	3	—	3	—	7	6	5	—	—	1	5
Total	—	14	11	10	4	27	6	13	22	18	—	7	1	15
% Total	—	7	19	5	7	13	10	6	38	9	—	3	2	7

Newspaper classification													
	15		16		17		18		19		20		21	
month	G+O	DN	G+O	DN	G+O	DN	G+O	DN	G+O	DN	G+O	DN	G+O	DN
Sept.	6	37	1	1	1	1	9	6	3	2	—	—	—	—
Oct.	2	18	3	3	—	—	7	11	3	1	—	—	—	3
Nov.	2	41	—	—	—	—	6	16	4	2	—	—	—	—
Dec.	2	36	1	2	—	1	4	6	2	5	—	—	—	—
Total	12	132	5	6	1	2	26	39	12	10	—	—	—	3
% Total	21	65	9	3	2	1	45	19	20	5	—	—	—	1

Attitude					
	22		23		24	
month	G+O	DN	G+O	DN	G+O	DN
Sept.	9	4	10	35	2	6
Oct.	5	10	9	32	1	7
Nov.	4	4	6	43	2	12
Dec.	1	6	8	37	1	7
Total	19	24	33	147	6	32
% Total	33	12	57	72	10	16

G: *The Guardian*, O: *The Observer*, DN: *Dagens Nyheter*. Variable numbers refer to Table 8.5.

about alcohol in the Swedish press, especially in daily newspapers and an advertisement frequency of between 8.42 and 4.10 adverts per issue (ibid., pp. 19–22, Tables 1–4) in the large daily newspapers; 5.49 adverts per issue during a 'normal week' and 8.42 adverts per issue in the two days immediately preceding the June midsummer holiday. This advertising rate is considerably in excess of a 'normal week' for the 1983 sample of British newspapers (1.43 to 3.17 adverts per issue) and were it not for the legislative restrictions in operation in Sweden today we might expect to find not only a considerably higher number of articles about alcohol but a higher advertising rate.

In general, then, the newspaper survey highlights the contrast between Britain and Sweden regarding the social meaning of drink: in Britain, primarily a product for consumption, in Sweden, alcohol as an abstract product, topic for concern and discussion.

Advertisements

As Williams (1980, p. 184) has noted, advertising is, in a sense, 'the official art of modern capitalist society: it is what "we" put up in "our" streets and use to fill up half of "our" newspapers and magazines'. Advertising is increasingly conspicuous, permeating all areas of social life from the public and political to the private arena. The material products sold through advertising are never in themselves enough, even in the simplest of adverts, but imbued with denotative and connotative social meanings, meanings in part created through the advertising medium, and assigned to different products through play on underlying structural principles, through reference to and elaboration of ideas and practices of our capitalist society: 'advertisements are selling us something else besides consumer goods: in providing us with a structure in which we, and those goods are interchangeable, they are selling us ourselves' (Williamson 1978, p. 13). So adverts create systems of difference, distinguish one product from another in the same category, assigning distinctive meaning to products for sale.

Advertising may have a profound effect on influencing drinking and public knowledge about alcohol, for example by strengthening or weakening the association in people's minds between alcohol and lifestyles or desirable activities. In a more general way advertisements may have an effect on the social acceptability of alcohol and of the industries that produce and market it. Many analyses of alcohol advertisements have been concerned to reveal such factors as play upon individual susceptibilities (e.g. Bromme 1971; Breed and DeFoe 1979; Strickland, Finn and Lambert 1982). Our concern here is more to develop a critique of alcohol advertising obliquely, while concentrating on analysing the range of social meanings associated with drink in British and Swedish advertisements.

We are interested in three sets of questions:

(1) To what extent are different meanings associated with drinking in British and Swedish advertisements?
(2) To what extent do these meanings differ according to the type of drink being advertised, i.e. wine, spirits and beer?
(3) How do these meanings relate to an understanding of contemporary beer can or bottle label design?

Sampling – problems

Before presenting the results of a series of analyses it is necessary to consider the nature of state alcohol policies in relation to advertising in Britain and Sweden. For Britain the situation is quite simple. There are no statutory restrictions whatsoever on the advertising of alcoholic drinks other than those which apply to advertising in general. Only a few voluntary limitations exist with a limited degree of legal backing: television companies do not usually accept advertisements for spirits, some publishers restrict alcohol advertising in magazines intended for young people, alcohol advertisements should not be aimed specifically at the young or associate drinking with driving (CPRS 1982, p. 56).

In Sweden, since 1917 with the advent of state control over wholesale and retail distribution of all alcoholic beverages, with the exception of beer, alcoholic drinks produced in Sweden (i.e., spirits and some wine) have not been advertised. All advertising was therefore initiated by agents for imported brands and by the Swedish breweries. This advertising was effectively free and increased steadily in frequency (SOU 1974: 91, pp. 265–6, Tables 20.1 and 20.2). In association with the abolition of alcohol rationing in October 1955 a six month temporary ban on advertising was introduced and during the 1960s and 1970s a series of voluntary agreements were made between the government alcohol monopoly, the Swedish brewers association and agents for foreign wine and spirits importers. Flagrant disregard for these guidelines might lead to an import ban on the part of the government alcohol monopoly or enforced withdrawal of a particular advertisement. The main feature of these voluntary agreements was an agreement on the part of the brewers not to advertise strong beer (Class III). This permitted a virtually free hand in advertising beer not sold in the government liquor stores (Classes I, IIA and IIB). During the late 1960s and early 1970s a flood of unrestricted advertisements for beer, especially the new middle strength 'mellanöl' appeared.

Since the early 1970s an extensive series of restrictions, voluntary and compulsory, on advertising alcohol in Sweden (SOU 1976: 63, Bilaga 3; SOU 1974: 92, Bilaga 6, pp. 53–6) poses problems for a valid comparison of the meanings ascribed to alcohol and different classes of alcoholic drinks in British and Swedish advertisements since any differences noted might be the result of different restrictions on advertising content rather than choice on the part of the advertiser. In 1976 in Sweden a restrictive code of practice prompted by prevalent abuses of previous voluntary agreements, restricted wine and spirits advertisements to a picture of the product, raw ingredients used to manufacture it and such features as glasses and serving equipment. The wording of such advertisements was similarly restricted.

After a series of government investigative committees and much debate, advertising for all alcoholic drinks, except beer Classes I and II, was eventually banned by law in 1979. Beer advertising was virtually restricted to newspapers and magazines. The fact that advertising for certain of the weaker classes of beer was still permitted was, no doubt, due in part to an extensive propaganda campaign on the part of the Swedish breweries who consistently argued that, in effect, to advertise beer (of the weaker kinds) promoted temperance, since if people drank beer this might encourage them to drink spirits and wine, drinks higher in alcohol content, less frequently (Hamberg 1978; *Fakta* 1978, pp. 12–13).

In order to mitigate some of these problems it was necessary to obtain a sample of Swedish advertisements prior to 1979 when the spirits and wine advertising ban came into force and over a long period of time before the fairly stringent voluntary agreement on wine and spirits advertising was introduced in 1976. A systematic sample of wine, spirits and beer advertisements was taken from a monthly periodical, *Det Bästa*, for the period 1966–1979 (1966–1980 for beer advertisements). *Det Bästa* (the Swedish language version of *Readers Digest*) was chosen for two reasons; first it contained a consistently high number of alcohol advertisements per issue, and secondly, circulation figures were high (*c*. 230,000–350,000 copies sold every month during the sampling period). This sample of old advertisements was supplemented by a collection of beer advertisements from 1983. Of the 16 adverts which appeared in the Swedish newspaper survey from *Dagens Nyheter* (see above) only ten were beer advertisements. The remaining six adverts were placed in the paper by the Systembolaget alcohol monopoly, designed to improve its public image or warn people of the 'dangers' of alcohol consumption, especially the young. No temperance adverts appeared in the British newspapers sampled. Since the number of adverts was so small an additional random sample of twenty different adverts was taken from the evening newspaper with the largest circulation figures, *Expressen*, and six different monthly or weekly magazines (see Table 8.8) with large circulation figures which might be expected to appeal to different social groups or interests. This sample, although small, is representative of the types of beer advertisements being produced during 1983. Since these advertisements are somewhat restricted in content as a result of governmental regulations, in the comparisons which follow between the British and the Swedish advertisements the older beer advertisements are used in preference to those from 1983 if significant differences occur.

For Britain a 50% random sample of the 310 advertisements from the British newspaper survey was taken, stratified according to drink type as spirits advertisements were roughly twice as frequent as wine advertisements. A weakness of the British data is that only three advertisements for beer appeared during the four-month period. Most adverts for beer occur on TV, radio and on billboards. All billboard adverts in the Newcastle upon Tyne area were photographed in January 1984 and again in April 1985 to provide 25 different adverts for analysis. In spite of the difficulties in obtaining the sample, we are confident that it is adequate for our purposes.

The advertisements

Table 8.7 gives the variables recorded for a content analysis of the adverts and is based, in part, on discussions of advertising in Andrén, Ericsson, Ohlsson and Tännsjö (1978), Chapman and Egger (1983), Dyer (1982), Millum (1975), Williamson (1978) and Winship (1981). As all the adverts were coded jointly no problems of inter-coder reliability arise and any possible biases in determination are at least likely to be consistent. Table 8.8 gives the results of this analysis.

In assessing the results of the analyses presented in Table 8.8 of the 405 advertisements we considered (i) invariant features of the advertisements, i.e. those features associated with alcohol in general and not differing significantly in relation to the type of drink advertised or the country, (ii) features showing a systematic difference between the British and Swedish advertisements but largely irrespective of the type of drink being advertised, (iii) features displaying considerable variability both in relation to the drink being advertised and the country, and (iv) the specific meanings attributed to beer both in Britain and Sweden using the results of Table 8.8 and individual analyses of a number of specific advertisements.

Invariant features of alcohol advertising

One striking feature of Table 8.8 is how few invariant features there are connected with drink in general. Those that do occur are primarily related to sex and age. Men are always more frequently depicted than women, either as models or as 'cropped' depictions, e.g., a male hand. Young or middle-aged men are preferred to old men. If women are depicted they are invariably young and in the company of men. While males may be depicted individually, or in groups, groups of female friends drinking never occur. If women are depicted as role models they are more likely to have eye contact with the viewer of the advertisement than male models. Drinking is never associated with families, and hierarchical relationships between those drinking are also virtually absent (one Swedish beer advertisement). So, the main features of the advertisements displayed for drink *in general* may be summarized as:

Appropriate to alcohol in general		*Largely or totally inappropriate*
men	:	women
young/middle-aged men	:	old men/women
single males/groups of males	:	families/groups of females
convivial relationships	:	hierarchical relationships

Features showing a systematic difference between Britain and Sweden

Those features displaying systematic variation between Britain and Sweden, irrespective of drink type, are similarly limited and confined to packaging, the quantity of drinks displayed and patterns of consumption. The drink packaging is always displayed more frequently in the Swedish advertisements and depictions of more than one package and glasses filled with drink are more common. Advertisements showing consumption in an ordinary home or with a meal only occur in Sweden. The British advertisements tend to make more use of familiar, everyday props while those used in Sweden are more frequently of a luxurious or expensive nature. While British advertisements tend to make heavy use of slogans, jokes or paradoxical use of language, the Swedish ones have a more 'serious' intent with much use of value-transference, flattery and temptation as techniques of persuasion. These differences may be summarized as:

Britain		Sweden
qualities of the drink	:	quantities of the drink
public drinking	:	private drinking
drinking as isolated activity	:	drinking connected with food
drinking normalized	:	drinking problematized
packaging less important	:	packaging more important

Table 8.7. *The variables recorded for a content analysis of the British and Swedish alcohol advertisements*

Var.	*The product itself*
1	alcohol content specified or referred to
2	packaging (bottle or can) shown
3	more than one package shown
4	glass shown
5	more than one glass shown

People: appearance

6	people or person present
7	young man/men
8	middle-aged man/men
9	old man/men
10	young woman/women
11	middle-aged woman/women
12	old woman/women
13	working-class man/men
14	middle-class man/men
15	upper-class man/men
16	working-class woman/women
17	middle-class woman/women
18	upper-class woman/women
19	beautiful man/men
20	beautiful woman/women
21	ordinary-looking man/men
22	ordinary-looking woman/women
23	formal clothing (including working clothes)
24	casual clothing
25	eye contact with female
26	eye contact with male
27	cropped picture of female (i.e., only parts of body shown: head, hands, legs, etc.)
28	cropped picture of male

People: groups

29	single male
30	single female
31	couple
32	family
33	group of friends: mixed sex
34	group of friends: male only
35	group of friends: female only
36	reciprocal relationship (persons depicted concentrating on each other)
37	semi-reciprocal (one person concentrating on another whose attention elsewhere)
38	divergent relationship (each person's attention directed towards something different)
39	people object-orientated towards the product advertised
40	people object-orientated towards something else (e.g., TV)
41	hierarchical relationship (including sexual domination)

People: activities

42	handling the product
43	drinking the product
44	relaxing with drink
45	working

The setting

46	home (ordinary)
47	party
48	meal
49	pub or restaurant

Table 8.7 (*cont.*)

50	countryside
51	working place
52	setting opulent or idealized (usually a home)
53	setting fantastic (anything that could not happen in ordinary life, e.g., a room with all furnishings, etc. in the same colour with only the drink advertised being a different colour)

Props used[1]

54	familiar, everyday
55	idealized, wishful or expensive
56	fantastic

Techniques of persuasion

57	eye catcher (picture more than 50% of advert)
58	sexual connotations
59	emphasis on slogan
60	paradox or syntactic/semantic peculiarity
61	value transference (some quality, person or phenomenon is made to seem obtainable through using the product)
62	popularity (suggestion that the product is in great demand)
63	nature (suggestion that the product is natural and therefore it is self-evident that one should consume it)
64	flattery (if you're clever or possess good judgement or taste you will consume the product)
65	temptation (owner of the product can achieve some generally desirable state or status)
66	testimonial (some person states the product is good)
67	newness
68	gift (the product makes a good gift)
69	entertainment (the advert contains a joke or a pun)
70	narrative (the advert tells a story)
71	reference to history or tradition
72	reference to art or culture
73	product is cheap
74	product is expensive or exclusive
75	one is initiated into a secret

[1] I.e., anything in advert not a person or the package of the product advertised.

Variability between drink type and country

Alcohol content is only specified or referred to in Swedish advertisements for spirits and especially beer (33–63% of the ads). In both countries the packaging is more frequently depicted for wine and spirits than for beer but when more than one package is illustrated this is rarely in connection with spirits but for wine or beer. When glasses are shown these tend to be in connection with beer rather than wine or spirits but the inclusion of many glasses tends to be in connection with drinking wine or spirits rather than beer. Young men and women in the British advertisements are most frequently depicted drinking spirits or beer rather than wine. However, middle-aged men are least frequently depicted in relationship with beer drinking. In Sweden young or middle-aged men are most commonly shown in relation to beer or wine consumption, especially beer, while middle-aged women (never depicted in the British ads) are most commonly shown drinking wine. Working-class men in both countries are primarily associated with beer drinking, never with wine consumption, and only in relation to spirits in

Table 8.8. *Results of the content analysis of British and Swedish alcohol advertisements. Figures in rounded percentages. Numbers of adverts also given for British and Swedish 1983 beer adverts.*

Var.	Wine % British	Wine % Swedish	Spirits % British	Spirits % Swedish	Beer British N.	Beer British %	Beer Swedish (1966–80) %	Beer Swedish (1983) N.	Beer Swedish (1983) %
1	—	—	—	4	—	—	33	19	63
2	36	96	54	91	7	28	75	21	70
3	26	32	4	21	3	12	20	7	23
4	18	60	14	32	12	48	84	17	57
5	8	28	24	28	3	12	24	3	10
6	16	24	43	25	5	20	45	4	13
7	2	10	18	3	5	20	25	3	10
8	10	10	16	4	1	4	19	—	—
9	—	—	—	3	—	—	5	—	—
10	—	10	10	3	1	4	23	—	—
11	—	10	—	1	—	—	4	—	—
12	—	—	—	—	—	—	1	—	—
13	—	—	6	—	3	12	15	3	10
14	8	16	13	3	2	8	16	—	—
15	2	6	21	7	—	—	1	—	—
16	—	—	—	—	1	4	4	—	—
17	—	16	7	4	—	—	11	—	—
18	—	4	7	1	—	—	—	—	—
19	—	6	17	—	—	—	5	—	—
20	—	6	10	—	—	—	9	—	—
21	2	8	8	4	2	8	40	2	7
22	—	8	—	—	1	4	17	—	—
23	6	20	34	7	1	4	15	1	3
24	—	4	5	3	3	12	27	1	3
25	—	—	4	1	—	—	7	—	—
26	—	—	5	1	1	4	9	—	—
27	—	4	10	3	—	—	3	1	3
28	4	6	17	15	1	4	4	3	10
29	4	—	22	16	2	8	17	1	3
30	—	—	—	1	—	—	7	—	—
31	—	8	12	1	—	—	8	1	3
32	—	—	—	—	—	—	—	—	—
33	—	14	1	1	—	—	12	—	—
34	2	—	—	—	2	8	5	1	3
35	—	—	—	—	—	—	—	—	—
36	4	6	—	—	—	—	3	—	—
37	—	6	2	—	—	—	12	—	—
38	—	6	4	—	1	4	7	—	—
39	2	—	10	—	1	4	5	—	—
40	—	—	5	—	3	12	1	1	3
41	—	—	—	—	—	—	1	—	—
42	2	6	10	11	3	12	1	2	7
43	4	8	2	3	3	12	1	2	7
44	—	10	6	1	—	—	19	1	3
45	2	—	9	—	1	4	7	1	3
46	—	4	—	—	—	—	12	2	7
47	—	10	1	—	—	—	1	—	—
48	—	4	—	1	—	—	33	3	10
49	—	—	2	—	3	12	13	—	—
50	16	2	17	3	1	4	9	3	10

Table 8.8. (*cont.*)

Var.	Wine % British	Wine % Swedish	Spirits % British	Spirits % Swedish	Beer British N.	Beer British %	Beer Swedish (1966–80) %	Beer Swedish (1983) N.	Beer Swedish (1983) %
51	—	—	2	—	1	4	8	1	3
52	4	22	9	5	—	—	16	4	13
53	4	—	1	5	—	—	—	—	—
54	10	6	24	4	19	76	64	7	23
55	4	26	12	16	1	4	13	—	—
56	8	8	4	4	2	8	—	—	—
57	60	72	70	37	22	88	93	24	80
58	—	4	10	1	—	—	5	—	—
59	38	30	48	4	12	48	23	9	30
60	8	2	27	1	7	28	7	4	13
61	4	24	4	29	1	4	45	5	17
62	6	8	12	32	4	16	13	3	10
63	24	8	25	8	—	—	17	3	10
64	—	2	—	5	—	—	1	—	—
65	4	14	—	24	—	—	29	2	7
66	6	—	5	—	—	—	—	—	—
67	—	—	—	4	—	—	4	1	3
68	—	2	5	1	—	—	—	—	—
69	8	—	12	4	10	40	8	1	3
70	2	16	25	15	2	8	4	—	—
71	2	8	44	18	4	16	9	—	—
72	2	—	14	—	1	4	—	—	—
73	26	6	1	—	—	—	4	1	3
74	44	42	56	33	3	12	15	10	33
75	10	—	3	4	—	—	3	—	—

Variable numbers refer to Table 8.7. British wine and spirits data from *The Guardian, The Observer* and *The Observer* colour magazine, Sept.–Dec. 1983. Swedish wine and spirits adverts from *Det Bästa* 1966–79. British beer adverts 1983–5 from billboards in Newcastle. Swedish beer adverts 1966–80 from *Det Bästa*. Swedish 1983 beer adverts from *Dagens Nyheter, Expressen, Hemmets Journal, Allt om Mat, Året Runt, ICA Kuriren, Månadens Journal, Det Bästa* July–Dec. 1983.
British and Swedish wine N = 50, British spirits N = 100, Swedish spirits N = 75, British beer N = 25, Swedish beer (1966–80) N = 75, Swedish beer (1983) N = 30.

Britain. Middle-class men may be depicted drinking wine, beer or spirits while the upper classes are never associated with beer drinking. Attractive looking men or women are primarily associated with spirits in Britain and wine in Sweden whereas ordinary looking people, irrespective of sex, are generally associated with beer drinking. Similarly, formal clothing is shown as most appropriate for spirits consumption in Britain, wine in Sweden. Casual clothing (never shown on British wine advertisements) is most frequently shown in relation to beer.

As regards groups of drinkers single males in both countries are shown drinking spirits or beer rather than wine. In Britain single females are never depicted in relation to drink but occur in Sweden on beer advertisements. Couples, in the British advertisements, are only shown drinking spirits whereas in Sweden they are associated with beer or wine consumption. Groups of friends of mixed sex are virtually never shown in the British ads (one example for spirits) but occur in Sweden in relation to wine or beer drinking. Groups of male friends in both countries are primarily shown beer drinking. Reciprocal relationships tend to be associated with wine and divergent or object orientated relationships (e.g., people admiring the drink) occur largely in relationship to spirits or beer.

The activities associated with drinking differ very considerably both in relation to country and drink type. In Sweden only beer is associated with work whereas in Britain beer, wine or spirits are shown in work situations, especially the latter. In Britain people relaxing with a drink are only shown in relation to spirits whereas handling the drink or drinking it is primarily associated with beer. In Sweden relaxing is most frequent for beer, handling for spirits and drinking for wine. Consumption in an 'ordinary' home or at a party is only shown in Sweden in relation to beer or wine. Drinking with a meal is shown for Sweden in relation to all drink types, but especially beer. Food is not associated with drinking in the British ads, the preferred locations being the countryside for wine and spirits or opulent 'home' surroundings. Beer drinking in both countries is shown in pubs but not for wine or spirits. Opulent settings (usually the home) are primarily shown in relation to spirits consumption in Britain and for wine or beer in Sweden. Ordinary props are most frequent for beer and expensive props for spirits and wine in Sweden.

Heavy use of visual imagery is common to all drink types in both countries. Most of the ads are designed to catch the eye. Reference to the expensive or exclusive nature of the product is the second most common technique employed for wine and spirits. For British beer much emphasis is placed on the slogan, while value-transference is employed for Swedish beer. Suggestions that the product is popular are most frequently used for Swedish spirits and British beer advertising.

The complex sets of images in the British and Swedish ads in relation to drink type may be generalized as:

	British wine	*Swedish wine*
Age and sex	middle-aged men	young or middle-aged men and women
Class	middle class	middle-class men or women, upper-class men
Appearance	ordinary, formal clothing	ordinary or beautiful, formal clothing
Groups	single male or male friends	single male, couples, friends of mixed sex
Relationships	reciprocal	reciprocal, semi-reciprocal or divergent
Activities	drinking	handling drink, relaxing, drinking
Associations	countryside	party or opulent surroundings
	British spirits	*Swedish spirits*
Age and sex	young or middle-aged men, young women	young, middle-aged or old men, young women
Class	working, middle or upper-class men, middle or upper-class women	middle-class men or women, upper class men
Appearance	beautiful or ordinary men, beautiful women, formal clothing	ordinary men, formal or casual clothing
Groups	single male or couple	single male
Relationships	orientated to product or something else	none
Activities	drinking, relaxing or handling drink	handling drink
Associations	countryside or opulent	countryside or opulent

	British beer	*Swedish beer*
Age and sex	young men	young, middle-aged or old men, young women
Class	working or middle-class men, working-class women	working or middle-class men and women
Appearance	ordinary, casual clothing	beautiful or ordinary, casual or formal clothing
Groups	single male, groups of males	single male or female, couples, groups of males or mixed sex
Relationships	orientated to something other than product	divergent or orientated to product
Activities	drinking or handling product	handling product, drinking, relaxing
Associations	pub	home, meal, pub, working place, country-side or opulent setting

These, then, are elements of particular life-styles which advertisers tend to consistently project or associate with specific types of drink in Britain and Sweden in addition to those features we noted associated with alcohol in general and those distinctive to Britain or to Sweden largely irrespective of drink type.

Meaning in beer advertising
A statistical analysis of advertising, as presented above, is an incomplete technique for uncovering the specific meaning structures associated with drink. Here we employ some specific analyses of individual advertisements, in combination with the results of the previous analysis, to look a little more closely at the denotative and connotative meanings associated with beer consumption.

Both Swedish and British adverts refer to relationships and meanings commonly associated with drink – masculinity and conviviality, as opposed to family life and hierarchical relationships. Such conventional meanings and associations serve to legitimate the product on offer as do the techniques frequently found in advertising generally: associating the product with the countryside, with the 'natural', with nostalgia and tradition, and claiming a product is popular.

However, the differences between Swedish and British adverts are striking. Swedish beer adverts, as opposed to the British, consistently indicate a concern for establishing the consumption of their products as a normal practice associated with many types of relationship. Swedish adverts also indicate a different pattern of consumption – packaged private consumption: quantity in private surroundings as opposed to public conviviality. They also avoid light-hearted punning.

The British beer adverts establish links between their products and tradition, consumption with friends in the pub, and with locality through reference to a whole mythology of 'Geordieland' North East England in the particular cases we considered. Lager adverts, in contrast, attempted to link the product with conceptions of 'style'. Drinking is on the whole accepted as a normal activity; there is no need to establish it as such. It is thus possible to have light-hearted, tongue-in-cheek adverts using slogans, jokes, puns. British wine adverts make reference to a more restricted set of meanings than Swedish wine and British spirits and beers: the consumption of wine is relatively low in Britain (Fig. 8.18A) and is associated particularly with middle-class cultured consumption.

Fig. 8.22 McEwan's Best Scotch   *Newcastle upon Tyne, Jan. 1984*

Notes
An express return, first class too, from the south of England (with its poor beers) back home to the real stuff
– McEwan's Best Scotch in Newcastle (the train is crossing one of the Tyne bridges). However it's not an
Intercity 125 of the 1980s but the Flying Scotsman (depicted in traditional oil painting) from the good old
days of steam when Geordieland north-east England was more distinct than now. The beer is thus associated
with tradition and local community. The connection is further emphasized by McEwan's Best Scotch
appearing on an engine name plate – all the qualities of steam engines (traditional, wholesome) are transferred
to the beer. But to remind you that McEwan's Best Scotch is available now down at the local off-licence and
pub, the pump decoration of the 1980s pub, showing the marketing design, appears within the engine plate
together with a freshly poured pint.

Fig. 8.23 Pripp   *Det Bästa*, 1969
Translation of caption

A beer which awakes memories

This is Pripp. A beer which stirs memories.
What do you remember?
We ourselves remember tankards with hops engraved on the glass and oak barrels
in cool cellars and bottles that you have to open with a cork screw
and beer labels with long rows of gold medals.
We have achieved a lot over the years.
Now we're old and big and broad in the stomach
which suits a proper brewer.
Now we have stainless steel barrels, thick as the hull of a ship
And the bottles have crown corks
and the cans have ring-pulls.
Because just as in the old days there is a rush for good beer when you're thirsty.
We remember.
This is why we brew Pripp.

Notes

The beer is given significance through reference to tradition and nostalgia. The use of 'we' is deliberately ambiguous and the reader is left uncertain as to who it refers to – the company Pripp or a fat brewer. The brewer referred to is presumably the embodiment of Pripps brewery which in turn gives substance to the brewer's body. Thus the modern mechanized brewing process is humanized in terms of an unspecified person. While we are told certain details such as the substitution of metal for wooden beer barrels, the reality of the modern brewing industry and the alienated labour involved in the production process, in short the social relations of brewing in monopoly capitalism, are carefully left unmentioned. While we are told of changes, it is the past which is depicted – wooden barrels and engraved tankard – but connected with the present via the open modern bottle of Pripp. So although ostensibly about change, the advert in fact fuses past and present through its imagery. By drinking Pripp today, you're drinking the past; indeed we are challenged 'what do you remember?'. In the advert history is empty, devoid of any content apart from changes in beer containers. The insecurities of technological change are smoothed over. Even if we don't remember the old beer bottles and tankards, Pripps do. This assures us that the beer produced, Pripp, is the same as produced in the past. Through drinking Pripp we can get back to the past, the good old days. Shown a nostalgic past of old beer barrels and tankards and challenged to remember it as our past which we reconstruct through remembering to buy Pripp, the gap between past and present can be filled and reconciled by the product.

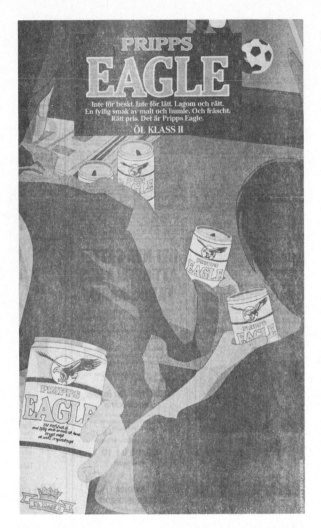

Fig. 8.24 Pripps Eagle   *Dagens Nyheter*, 13 Oct. 1983
Translation of caption

Pripps
Eagle
Not too bitter. Not too weak. Just right.
A full bodied flavour of malt and hops. And fresh.
Right price. It's Pripps Eagle.
Beer Class II

Notes
A group of young men are watching TV. We are drawn into the picture as if we're there watching TV with them, sharing the sociability of the occasion, for it is sociability of males which is being indicated in the advert: informal clothing, watching a typically male sport – soccer. They're drinking at home from the can; informally dressed, they're drinking informally from the can (soccer – a male consumer sport; Pripps Eagle – a male consumer product). Eagle is presented as a beer to be consumed in leisure time (*cf.* Fig. 8.31, Lyckholms), and it is implied that sociability can be achieved with this beer. Everyone is drinking in quantity. The advert is concerned to stress the packaging; our attention is drawn to the can in the foreground, from can to can and to the TV screen. The caption replicates the central area on the can. The room background is insignificant in relation to the cans, the young men and the soccer on the screen, the Eagle life-style, just right.

Fig. 8.25 Carling Black Label   *Newcastle upon Tyne, Jan. 1984*

Notes
This is part of an advertising campaign using the slogan 'I bet he drinks Carling Black Label' representing the exceptional qualities of the Carling Black Label drinker. Mocking and humorous reference is made to those adverts which claim their product will bring about a magical transformation of the consumer. The point is not that Carling Black Label drinkers are superhuman (the humour is to entertain and so involve the viewer in the set of meanings of the advert) just special, one of a clan, those who drink Carling Black Label and, as implied in this advert, enjoy soccer. The link between Carling Black Label and soccer is emphasized by the orange, white and black colour connections between football sock and boot and the Carling design in the corner.

Fig. 8.26 Harp Lager　　　　*Newcastle upon Tyne, Jan. 1984*

Notes
It is claimed that the pint of Harp Lager stays sharp-tasting to the end; this is conveyed by a simple reference to musical notation, associating, in the process of decoding, the drink with a pre-existing set of meanings. It is implied that sharpness is a desirable quality in drink: not warm and soft, but cold and sharp (Lager is served chilled, as opposed to traditional cask-conditioned ale served at cellar temperature). But this advert is part of a campaign mainly shown on TV using the slogan ' . . . stays sharp to the bottom of the glass' in which the Harp *drinker* shows he is sharp. So Harp signifies sharpness. The Harp drinker is quick-witted, cool-headed in sticky situations. Drinking Harp becomes part of being smart and clever.

Fig. 8.27 Three Towns   *Det Bästa, Nov. 1968*
Translation of caption

Three towns is beautiful.
A little milder. Rounder.

Notes
The words are almost superfluous to this advert and, indeed, they are assigned to an unimportant position. The 'beauty' of Three Towns has its symbolic referents in the beauty of nature and the beauty of the people (and their beautiful relationship?). The 'mildness' and 'roundness' of this beer finds its correlation in the natural. Real consumption is not actually shown, as in the other Swedish adverts, but is imminent. Our anticipation is shared with the girl who will surely turn her head from her lover and consume the beer. Time is momentarily arrested; she has raised her glass; we anticipate the next act and are thus drawn into the world of the advert.

Fig. 8.28 Federation Best Scotch   *Newcastle upon Tyne, Jan. 1984*

Notes
Here are the lads down at the local club (the Federation Brewery produces beers for Working Men's Clubs)
having a good singalong, perhaps joining in with the night's entertainer (Clubs provide stage entertainment).
These are just ordinary blokes (a mirror image of what we would want to be?), the sort of people who enjoy a
good time with a pint of Federation Best Scotch. It's what clubs are all about – getting together with your
mates and drinking Federation Best Scotch (and are they in fact not toasting Best Scotch? – all the glasses are
full and they're singing a song in praise of the beer). It's clearly a Geordie club – the pint is 'bonny' and
'canny'. It's also the lads who are drinking Best Scotch (wives wouldn't, it's a man's drink); the only woman
is the barmaid in the centre, friendly and warmly glowing in the bright lights of the bar, mirroring the warm
welcome glow of the pint in the corner. The advert associates the beer with the warm social atmosphere of the
men in the local North East of England club. A Best Scotch design reminds you what to look for at the club
and in the off-licence.

Fig. 8.29 Dart   *Det Bästa, Feb. 1984*
Translation of caption

You're not really afraid of the dark?

Dark beer has more taste.
Dart has a rich colour which
means a rich taste.
Rounded and a full-bodied feeling.
Better for a good lunch.
More exciting as a social drink.

Dark beer is more exciting.

Notes
No one is afraid of the dark, it's irrational, so why be afraid of dark beer? The bowler hat is dark, but an everyday object, hardly frightening. And against the dark background the beer appears light, reaffirming that the colour of Dart should not be a cause of concern (dark beers are unusual in Sweden; most are light-coloured 'lager' type). Dart is rich, and British: the bowler hat signifies Britishness as does the name (darts is a game associated with British pubs). Indeed on old Dart beer labels from the 1960s a dart board was portrayed. On the contemporary (1983) packaging this is replaced by a British flag as in this advert. The text tells us that it is exciting to drink Dart, that it makes a good social drink. The sociability of British pubs is transferred to Dart, dark like British beers. Masculinity is also indicated; a woman's hat would be out of place. The advert makes play on the difference between British and Swedish drinking; by drinking Dart you can achieve the British freedom from alcohol restrictions.

Fig. 8.30 Newcastle Exhibition   *Newcastle upon Tyne, Jan. 1984*

Notes
This is one of a series of adverts which depend on puns on 'exhibition' (extrovert, exile, expert, etc.). In decoding the simple pun on 'sex' and 'ex' (the popular name for Newcastle Exhibition), helped if necessary by the picture of the drink, we are drawn into the system of meanings created by the advert. Exhibition, the beer, is associated with and becomes itself a part of everyday vocabulary and reality. The beer is thus given meaning (a function of adverts generally). There is also an implication that sex and Exhibition are actually interchangeable – 'I went out for a pint of Ex instead – it's more satisfying'. Such valuation of drinking accords with the popular mythology of the dedicated Northern drinker, and indeed the product is *Newcastle* Exhibition, a local brew.

Har man ett jobb där det gäller att vara skärp
passar Lyckholms fint på lunchen.
Det innehåller bara lite alkohol.
Men smakar som öl ska smaka.

Fig. 8.31 Lyckholms   *Det Bästa, April 1970*
Translation of caption

If you have a job in which it is necessary to be sharp,
Lyckholms makes a fine accompaniment to lunch.
It contains only a little alcohol.
But tastes as beer should taste.

Notes

The advert stresses the connection between alcohol and food and a concern with the strength of beer: this beer contains so little alcohol it is possible to work in forestry, with all its attendant dangers, after drinking it. However this does not mean the taste is sacrificed, nor does the drinker forfeit his masculinity – these men are forestry workers, lumberjacks. You can drink and impose bodily discipline at the same time; this product enables you to mitigate the contradiction. However, as Lyckholms is perfect for lunch on the job, it is implied that when not on the job another (stronger?) beer would be more suitable. The greenness of the forest and the workers' clothes blend into each other, as does the Lyckholms bottle, all making a harmonious whole. This beer is definitely not out of place or unusual in this situation. Just as the workers are in the natural forest, so it's natural to drink Lyckholms. Naturally in this situation (dangerous work) you'd be sensible to drink Lyckholms. The people are selected to look ordinary and masculine. The use-value of the beer is stressed but also the exchange-value: in such a situation Lyckholms can be substituted for a stronger beer without sacrificing taste or identity as a male. The advert thus addresses and 'solves' two problems: how to be masculine and drink weak beer, and how to drink and work, especially in a dangerous industry. There is a strong contrast with the British adverts; this problem would not occur in a British advert.

Porter och äggula!

Förr köpte man porter t.o.m. på apotek. På läkarrecept. Nu kan den beska
medicinen köpas överallt. Men det är en beska som man kommer över. Första pilsnern smakade inte heller gott.
Och inte första malörtsdroppen. Det finns folk som snobbar med att beställa porter. Säger att
det kräver en mera avancerad smak. Precis som sniglar och ostron. Skitsnack.
Porter är bra. Lättsmält. Näringsrikt. Smaken vänjer man sig vid. Ugh! Ursäkta.
Recept: Häll upp ett glas porter. Häll i en äggula. Rör om. Drick!

Fig. 8.32 Porter   *Det Bästa, May 1968*
Translation of caption

Porter and Egg yolk!

In the past you used to buy porter only from the chemist. On doctor's prescription. Now the bitter medicine can be bought everywhere. But it is a bitterness you get used to. The first glass doesn't taste at all good. Nor do the first drops of wormwood. There are people who show off by ordering porter. It is said that it requires a more advanced taste. Just like snails and oysters. Crap. Porter is good. Easily digested. Nutritious. You get used to the taste. Ugh! Sorry.
Recipe: Pour out a glass of porter. Pour in an egg yolk. Stir. Drink!

Notes

This black and white advert occurs in a publication in which all the adverts are in colour and so creates an immediate impact. The darkness of the advert matches the darkness of the porter. The black and white photography also signifies the past and it is the past and the traditional element which porter is made to signify. The reference to a time when porter could only be bought from the chemist refers to the history of alcohol control in Sweden when strong Class III beer could only be bought in this way. The medicinal and health angle is stressed: porter as medicine and medicine as bitter like porter. The nutritious qualities of porter are correlated with the richness and nutrition of an egg yolk. The text is in staccato style. The qualities of the porter are affirmed then denied: porter requires an 'advanced taste'. This is then ridiculed but reaffirmed at the end of the text when presumably a novice who has not cultivated the taste for porter is repelled by the drink. In this manner the status of porter as a drink for the connoisseur is reaffirmed. Unlike other beers, porter is not to be simply drunk but 'digested', thus asserting the nutritious qualities, that porter is more akin to food than to drink. Drinks don't usually require a recipe (unless a sophisticated cocktail) but porter does and one is provided at the end of the text. Porter is a snobbish drink, not for the ordinary person, but for those who would appreciate snails and oysters. The repelling qualities of snails and oysters, requiring an advanced taste, are correlated with the taste of porter. It is to be drunk in small quantities and savoured – note the size of the glass and there is only one foregrounded bottle. Porter is a drink you could order without embarrassment in an expensive restaurant: a drink for the cultivated. Clearly porter doesn't even require company; it is company in itself, hence the single male, an individual, apart from the crowd. He clearly knows what he is doing when drinking porter. The photo is in black and white, but porter is not a simple drink, a case of black or white; it can both repel and be cultivated, a unity of opposites.

234

Fig. 8.33 Vaux Double Maxim   *Sunderland, Jan. 1984*

Notes
The roast lamb of the Sunday dinner has been transformed into Double Maxim. The beer thus comes to represent all that Sunday dinner and the roasted joint of meat represents – homely English tradition, no fancy continental trimmings (the bottle label is consciously anachronistic (personal communication, M. Berriman, Marketing Manager, Vaux Breweries)). Lean meat, the stuff of life, wholesome, full of goodness, flavoursome, bringing strength: all these qualities are transferred to the beer.

TOWARDS AN UNDERSTANDING OF THE DESIGN OF BEER CANS

We noted a major contradiction between principles structuring drinking in the capitalist state, a contradiction between drinking as promoted consumer activity or as an act of self-definement connecting with life-styles, and drinking as being contrary to the requirements of bodily discipline in the production process and consumers' control over and conceptions of their bodies. In an advanced capitalist society such a contradiction is increasingly antagonistic, and more so in Sweden than in Britain, given the greater degree and nature of state intervention in defining alcohol as a dangerous substance with its contemporary concomitant in the increasing medicalization of drinking practices. The development of monopoly capitalism has involved an increasingly interventionist state imposing control through the norm, and measuring and defining deviation from that norm, rather than imposing direct disciplinary control as in the past.

As an institutional complex, the state guards the general interest of *all* classes with respect to capitalist exchange relations. In this manner the economic is politicized to an increased degree. However, 'although the circuit of state monopoly capital requires specific forms of political intervention, the institutional separation of the state casts doubt on its functionality' (Jessop 1982, p. 237). Through the politicization of the economic, the state mediates the consumerist compensation for asymmetry of control within the productive process and the ability of the productive process to maintain capital accumulation and deliver the goods. The state must reconcile the maintenance of expanded production and capital accumulation with the demands of the electorate and pressure groups. The separation of the state has entailed that the effects of its intervention have, as often as not, had the reverse effect to that intended, hence despite the massive degree of state intervention to control drinking throughout the twentieth century consumption has risen rather than declined.

The differences between British and Swedish can design may be understood as different ideological 'resolutions' of the consumption/discipline contradiction. In Britain due to the social position and development of public drinking as a mediation between work and leisure, the public house being a 'colonized' institution, the continued social importance of the public house as a focus of sociability which is nevertheless being supplemented by private consumption, and the pub as a focus of the symbolic expression of the 'ideals' of consumerism, discipline becomes subordinate to consumption with regard to the material forms of drinking. In Sweden consumption is subordinate to the requirements of discipline. Forced into the home, and largely hidden, private consumption for the purposes of intoxication opposes massive concern, state and independent, with the attendant restrictions and the proliferation of discourses concerned with alcohol consumption.

The presentation of alcohol in both countries is mediated by a particular logic of signification. In one respect the elaboration of can design is connected with the need of companies to create difference and, therefore, meaning for a consumer market. If this were not so we might expect the cans to be completely plain and state little more than 'beer' and the name of the company producing it. As a Swedish can designer puts it 'people drink with their eyes' (Ericson 1980). Beer may be good to drink but, in the market of images created, it is also good to think. The maintenance of differences allows possibilities for self-definement and this should not be considered in a purely negative light. Consumerism is not simply to be considered as a total and hermetic culture of mass ideological repression. We have concentrated in this chapter on the products of the brewing industry and images in advertising and the media and not so much on the reception and cultural use of beer. Clearly the disjunction between private consumption habits and temperance discourses in Sweden draws attention to the thoroughly mediated form of the consumption of commodities not simply reducible to a consumer ethic (Douglas and Isherwood 1978; Kellner 1983). Some, especially members of the Centre for Contemporary Cultural Studies have stressed the autonomous use of material culture in sub-cultural style and artifacts as contributing to non-ideological discourses and practices (e.g., Hall and Jefferson (eds.) 1976; Clarke 1976; Willis 1971; Hebidge 1979). In Sweden, the introduction of beer cans opened out a new way to drink appealing to the counter culture of youth groups in which the beer can could literally be ripped open with the forefinger, the contents drunk, and the can subsequently crushed and discarded – a style of drinking which took place on the streets and was heavily loaded with a deliberate flaunting of governmental restrictions and control of alcohol.

In Britain can designs create difference and establish meaning for particular beers and lagers; they are a part of a process of creation of exchange-values. Beer cans draw on and reproduce a set of meanings associated with beer: they emphasize tradition, place of origin (most beers until recently were local brews), and inherent differences – types of beer. Breweries are fully conscious of these possibilities for creating difference (personal communication, M. Berriman, Marketing Manager, Vaux Breweries): the efforts of the breweries in the early seventies to create 'national' new brews have been superseded by an awareness that beer with a local connection (real or invented) sells better (*cf.* Sharman 1983); old brewery names have been revived, local origin stressed, 'traditional', 'real' ales made more available.

The creation of exchange-values is particularly marked in relation to the distinction between beer and lager. Whether you're a lager drinker or a beer drinker clearly extends beyond the product itself and is associated with social categories. Lager cans, part of a marketing operation initiated by breweries to capture a new section of the market – young, seeking a distinctive social image – are designed to appeal to a classless consumer. There is considerably less use of traditional representational designs associated with beer – depictions of raw ingredients, oast houses, drays, etc. A different colour set is employed, abstract designs are more frequent than for beer and representational designs less common. There is less emphasis on the character of the beer or its place of origin, and more emphasis on strength and predominant use of foreign names. Thus a different, more abstract and less traditional image is stressed, a different style of drinking. The logic of competition with beer leads to the marketing of lager as a distinctive product fulfilling a different role and opening out further possibilities for defining social relationships.

Swedish cans make a similar reference to a symbol set which signifies masculinity and tradition and in addition quality and naturalness, and connection with foreign beers (with already-defined and accepted meanings), in creating significance for the marketed product. But this functional 'need' of brewing companies to manufacture difference and distinction, whatever their subsequent cultural use or transformation, cannot of itself provide a satisfactory account of the differences in the degree and type of elaboration of the British and Swedish can designs. The greater complexity of the Swedish cans is, however, in part explicable in terms of mechanisms of ideological control and legitimation emanating from the economic logic of capitalism when contradicted and mediated by structures of consumerism, health and bodily discipline.

Alcoholic drinks may be held to constitute an internally related symbolic field. As Bourdieu points out, the consumption of goods 'always presupposes a labour of appropriation, to different degrees depending on the goods and the consumers; or, more precisely, that the consumer helps to produce the product he consumes, by a labour of identification and decoding which . . . requires time and dispositions acquired over time' (Bourdieu 1984, p. 100). The symbolic field of alcoholic drinks may be represented as in Fig. 8.34, in which the three major forms of alcohol – beer, wine and spirits – are related to and yet at the same time opposed to each other. This is clearly apparent in the similarities and differences revealed by the statistical analysis of the adverts. At a secondary level, drinks are sub-divided according to quasi-objective features of taste and appearance and finally according to brands sold on the consumer market, at each point the distinctions proliferating. The choice of such and such a drink for one occasion or another is dependent on cultural conceptions of its social usage. In terms of general cultural connotations the relationship between classes of drinks, based on the newspaper and advertisement surveys in Britain and Sweden, may be presented as:

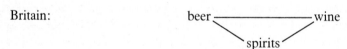

Britain:

distinctive differences in terms of cultural connotation and strength

Sweden: spirits → beer → wine
(*brännvin*)

increasing cultural connotation of refinement and style.

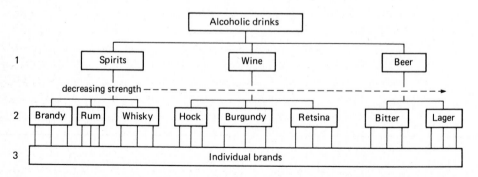

Fig. 8.34 Simplified representation of the structural relationship between various alcoholic drinks.

In Sweden, beer does not fit readily into established cultural connotations of alcohol. The history of alcohol control in Sweden has, by and large, been a history of attempts to reduce the consumption of spirits of *brännvin*, in terms of volume of pure alcohol the dominant drink (Fig. 8.18B). Spirits have always been associated in Sweden with drunkenness, crime, alcoholics, persons of low morality or, more recently, as constituting medical/psychiatric deviants. Wine, on the other hand, has been regarded as the drink of culture, of refined taste. Spirits and wine thus mark opposite extremes of a polarized scale: spirits relate to wine as the vulgar to the refined. Beer, however, does not fit readily in terms of such a categorization. On the one hand, it is the principal table drink in Sweden (at least for lunch, for dinner in less 'refined' social circles) and therefore culturally acceptable. On the other hand, beer has also been traditionally associated with drunkenness and a lack of bodily discipline in much the same way as *brännvin* (teenagers getting drunk on *mellanöl*, a fourth beer class sold between 1965 and 1977, was a principal cause of its removal). Brewers have always been able to claim that their products stimulate sobriety because of their low alcohol content yet, at the same time during the period of alcohol rationing it was strong beer (despite its strength still weak in alcohol content in relation to wine or spirits) and not drinks higher in alcohol content – wine and spirits – that was removed from the market. This is especially surprising in view of the particularly high level of spirits consumption (Fig. 8.18B).

Beer has an ambiguous status, a lack of fit into the established scheme of things. As such, it automatically becomes more dangerous, a substance requiring a finer degree of control. Because of this lack of fit it has become hedged around with boundaries and classes. These classes, unique to beer (there are no classes for wine or spirits), and by no means natural, enable consumers to measure and regulate alcoholic intake and to maintain self-surveillance over their bodies (see the Lyckholms advertisement, Fig. 8.31). Beer, then, is the type of alcoholic drink most subject to a contradictory nexus of meanings in Swedish society, symbolized through the development of a class system. By contrast in Britain beer much more clearly fits into an established scheme as a working-class drink in a symbolic field in which alcohol is not constituted as dangerous. The comparative lack of distinction between the Swedish beer classes, as compared with the beer/lager distinction, is explicable because beer classes, unlike beer brands or beer types, do not open out the same possibilities for the manipulation and construction of meanings. The meanings cross-cut the classes in terms of product brands. The differentiation that does exist between the classes can be related to social meanings connected with alcohol strength. Physiologically, it is very difficult to get drunk on Class I or II beer unless it is consumed very rapidly on an empty stomach and in vast quantities. As beer must be, and is presented by the breweries as alcohol rather than water, this has the concomitant that the strong beer cans usually have simpler designs because since this beer is only sold in the alcohol monopoly shops its qualities as beer rather than water lend it a self-legitimating force. The Class I cans with their emphasis on male imagery clearly reduce the potential threat to masculine prowess that drinking very weak beer might produce. The most complex designs occur on the medium strength Class II beer which because of its greater availability in supermarkets and increased strength when compared to Class I beer, has the largest market share. The proliferation of the designs on these cans creates a dense web of meanings and images drawing attention away from its strength and towards its exchange-value as alcohol, as a product to be consumed in leisure time.

Most of the differences noted in the discussion of British and Swedish beer can design can be considered in terms of a difference of complexity and elaboration. The Swedish can designs are far more elaborately designed in terms of colours, wording, styles, or orientation of lettering, numbers of representational or abstract designs. We suggest that this is because there is a greater need to mediate the consumption/discipline contradiction through the design in Sweden than in Britain especially given the ambiguous status of beer in Sweden in relation to other alcoholic drinks. However, the form of the mediation of the contradiction is effected in a similar way in both countries, but given the ambiguous nexus of meanings surrounding beer is more developed in Sweden. The creation of life-styles in relation to brand distinctions mediates the contradiction by obscuring it, by encouraging the focus of attention towards the product's exchange rather than use-value.

As part of everyday culture beer cans form systems of communication, expression and representation, creating a symbolic order of meaning. The power of the symbolism on the cans in the structuring of social attitudes towards alcohol in general and beer in particular is its seeming naturalness. As we have seen the representational designs are restricted in content and legitimate the product in terms of purity and naturalness, masculinity, as alcohol, and via the medium of the past or tradition. Beer cans with space age or high-tech designs simply do not exist. The very repetitiveness of the use of the same types of designs, endlessly connected and re-connected in various combinations, lends them a false obviousness or a naturalizing quality which they would not otherwise possess. The symbolism on the cans creates an *imaginary* set of relationships to the present and the consumption of the product in the present – by invoking a mythical past. The symbols used have little to do with present-day sociopolitical reality or the manner in which beer is actually produced or distributed. The designs on the cans, if looked at in a detached manner, are patently ridiculous: what *real* connection is there between lions or eagles, coats of arms or sailing ships and beer? Precisely, none. What is surprising is that these designs appear natural to all of us. The obviousness of the designs is an obviousness effected through the power of ideology. The more alcohol is considered dangerous, as in Sweden, the greater the number of codes employed to mediate the contradictions involved in consumption and effect an artificial view of reality – a reality in which the freedom of the consumer is to symbolically define him or herself and participate in the reproduction of capital.

PART IV

Conclusions

9

Archaeological theory and practice today

At the present archaeology is pervaded by two conflicting attitudes: a radical scepticism opposes a crude scientism seeking objectivity and reducing the archaeological record to the effect of mechanical adaptive process. The sceptical and empirically minded 'dirt' archaeologist digs and 'rescues' the past, describes and lodges the finds in a museum or archive. These sceptics, at heart, believe that all statements about the past (with possible exceptions when dealing in the realms of economy and technology) are little more than subjective whim enlivened by empathy. Those advocating scientism believe it possible to read off the past from its traces in the present without too much trouble providing a suitable technical apparatus can be developed. We replace scepticism with an optimism based on an intervention which denies the polarization of objectivity and subjectivity. For the subjective idealism of scientistic archaeology we substitute a view of the discipline as an hermeneutically informed dialectical science of past and present unremittingly embracing and attempting to understand the polyvalent qualities of the socially constructed world of the past and the world in which we live. We sustain throughout a rejection of the past as presented in archaeological texts as objective, or alternatively, as subjective. There is no question of choosing one or the other. Archaeological theory and practice as labour in the present completely transcend this artificial division, labour which draws past and present into a fresh perspective, a perspective which serves to rearticulate their interrelationship. The study presented in Chapter 7 does not pretend to be an account of what the past was really like, nor does Chapter 8 claim to be a pure and unsullied account of present social processes. Neither are the analytical narratives or 'stories' presented a pure figment of our imagination. They tie together past and present through a political interpretation of the materials, an interpretation which ultimately aims to write our lived present into a past. Archaeology is a particular and active relation between past and present.

In expressing a strong dissatisfaction with the project of modelling archaeology on the natural sciences, we have no intention of erecting the old division between the natural and social sciences. By stressing the need to move beyond the opposed terms subjectivity and objectivity, to hermeneutic interpretative processes, dialectics, praxis, and archaeology as critique, we are not proposing that archaeology as a social science provides a weak and in some way inferior kind of knowledge. Our rejection of empiricism is not simply a rejection in terms of its suitability or otherwise for archaeology. It also involves a rejection of assertions that natural science relies on empiricist procedures and knowledge claims. Recent post-empiricist philosophy of science is engaged in putting forth, in a large number of different expositions, some version or other of realism (e.g.,

Hesse 1974; Bhaskar 1978) which has led to a curious convergence with what might be termed analytical Marxist philosophy (Ruben 1977; Collier 1978; Callinicos 1983) and we adopted some essential realist tenets in Chapter 5. However, realism in an unrevised form(s) provides no panacea and there are a number of central flaws in the approach, such as the embodiment in one form or another of a correspondence theory of truth, i.e., the notion that propositions are either true or false by virtue of the state of the world rather than of human knowledge, with the concomitant that thought is, in some sense, a reflection or mirror of the world rather than at least in part constitutive of what that world is. In this book we have stressed a subject-object dialectic which questions both these realist assumptions and reveals truth and knowledge as essentially mediatory. Meaning is considered to be neither given to the world to be passively revealed by the operations of science nor as solely constituted by a 'knowing' subject. Knowledge instead is acquired through practice, through a subject-object dialectic, in which primacy is granted to neither. The essential question is not whether science is applicable to the study of human individuals and societies but what sort of science this should be. In so far as archaeology *is* concerned to study past social systems as the product of sentient social beings it becomes irrevocably a social science and should contribute towards social science as a whole.

This raises the question: what difference is there between sociology or geography or history or psychology and archaeology? Archaeology is archaeology is archaeology as Clarke (1968, p. 13) asserted only if archaeologists are to do no more than measure or describe artifacts while making no reference whatsoever to their meaning and significance, worth and value. Archaeologists have never been content to restrict their activities to this level and Clarke certainly was not. Attempting to reduce archaeology to the science of the artifact would entail silence. The attributes ascribed to artifacts are a product of social relations existing both in the past and the present, amongst dead social actors and the living archaeological community. They are always produced and the natural sciences can provide no exact guidelines on the basis of which the ascriptions of meanings might be made. Chemical reactions may be granted significance but they can never have any meaning in the sense that there is any purpose to them. It is above all the notion of purpose or intentional agency that distinguishes human beings and requires a framework which is not isomorphic with those of the natural sciences, although many features may well be shared. To underline the fact that human agency is intentional agency does not mean, of course, that explanation should be left at that level, as was discussed in Chapter 6. In terms of principles and procedures, we would argue that there is no difference between archaeology and sociology and geography or any other social science. In claiming this we are, of course, arguing that the fundamental characteristics of forms of knowledge are not based upon the empirical materials with which they may deal but instead on the problems that are posed and tackled and the kinds of concepts employed. The essential concern of all the social sciences is the manner in which people construct and deconstruct their own social worlds in various ways. Understanding the nature of this process crucially requires conceptualizations of the nature of social action, of the unintended and intended consequences of this action, of structure, power, ideology, symbolism and the creation and recreation of meaningful frameworks in which to live and work. Seen in this light archaeology can have no unique problems, concepts, or disciplinary structure, and in human geography a similar realization has developed with the widespread abandonment of the notion that geography might constitute an independent disciplinary structure, a 'science of space'.

There are no essentially archaeological ramifications of geographical, psychological or sociological conceptual structures. These should be commonly shared by all the social sciences and worked through in various ways in relation to different bodies of evidence. In archaeology this will involve a view of material culture-patterning as a *resource* employed in social strategies. The corollary is that the work of Freud or Foucault, Douglas or Derrida, Barthes or Bourdieu, Weber or Wittgenstein, or any other 'non-archaeological' writer, should be of essential concern to all archaeologists in all their practical work and not considered as totally or partially irrelevant distractions from the business of the discipline.

A mathematical archaeology which would explain material culture as an aspect of a logical relation, which would attempt to explain the complex data we investigate using statistical tests and procedures externally applied to the data is incompatible with archaeology being an active mediation of past and present. However, as we indicate in Chapters 7 and 8, statistical procedures, especially those which are computer-based, are a valuable heuristic device, manipulating large bodies of data, summarizing variability, redescribing, but in no way explaining anything or providing the basis for contentions.

We criticized many varieties of archaeology as ideology, as a passive function of the present, producing pasts relevant to and/or in support of particular interest groups. We are not passing judgement by claiming that we have established a viewpoint which is objective and value-free (no archaeology can be value-free and stand outside history). Nor are we claiming ours to be a framework simply based on another set of values. The criticisms made of cultural resource management were not directed at whether or not it is important to safeguard the past. They were criticisms levelled at the practice of archaeology (as were those of museum displays in Chapter 4) in the present.

In the arguments we presented for archaeology as an active mediation of past and present, we suggested that the discipline should rest on understanding, critique and commitment. Understanding: archaeology should consider the manner in which material culture forms a component of the social construction of reality, and the social reality it studies and within which it is located. Critique: archaeology should subject itself and that which it seeks to understand to criticism, self-reflection into the contemporary meanings and significance of the archaeological project. This negative moment implies a denial of finality, a denial of there being a final orthodoxy to grope towards, an unalterable past. Archaeology is primarily a critical contemporary discussion on the past (or the present) which has no logical end. Archaeology is historical and history has no end. A unitary and monolithic past is an illusion. What is required is a radical pluralism, a pluralism which recognizes that there are multiple pasts produced actively in accordance with ethnic, cultural, social and political views, orientations and beliefs. Asserting a crude scientism in the discipline merely fragments concerns and will never be productive.

We do not mean to suggest that all pasts are equal. Clearly, some pasts are inferior to others, especially those which are a non-reflective mirror of the present. A feminist archaeology, to mention one area, is likely to be substantially different in orientation from current archaeological practice. It remains the case that archaeology has been and is written substantially by men. Homo Artifex (Chapter 4) is not Femina Artifex; such concepts are male and do refer to a *mankind*. To obscure this may be to perform an ideological service for *mankind*. Archaeology, significantly, although eminently well placed to do so, has not paid much attention to the origins, nature and development of sexual repression and exploitation.

We can also mention in this context the conflicts of interests between American Indian groups and archaeologists. This conflict of concerns has its roots not only in the issue of whether or not archaeologists have the right to uncover Indian remains but also in the images created of the constructors of those remains (Trigger 1980). The white American having dispossessed the indigenous inhabitants of their land and possessions and virtually destroyed their culture now requires that the Indians respect his or her 'right' to reconstruct their past and if this involves the violation of sacred remains the type of empiricist science subscribed to ensures that this action is eminently justifiable (*cf.* Cheek and Keel 1984). Archaeological discourse may or may not have truth value. It certainly can have power effects operating to reproduce the relationship between the dominant and the dominated in contemporary society. It is this which must be opened to critique.

A radical pluralism involves discussion and critique according to an assessment of commitment. Subjecting particular archaeologies to ideology critique is in part to assess their commitment to the present, to assess the present and future worlds contained within any archaeological project. To repeat, propositional truth hinges on the intention of a true society.

We cannot stand outside history and arrest the past and present. What is important is that archaeology recognizes its temporality and fragility, recognizes itself as a contemporary practice in which men and women engage in discussions and debates and establish positions which *need* to be criticized and transcended.

September 1985

REFERENCES

Place of publication is London unless otherwise stated.

Adams, M. J. (1973). 'Structural aspects of a village age', *American Anthropologist* **75**: 265–79

Adorno, T. W. (1964). 'Nachtmusik' in T. Adorno *Moments Musicaux: Neugedruckte Aufsatze 1928 bis 1962*, Suhrkamp, Frankfurt

    (1967). 'Cultural criticism and society' in T. Adorno *Prisms*, Neville Spearman

    (1973a). *Negative Dialectics*, Routledge and Kegan Paul

    (1973b). 'Die Aktualitat der Philosophie' in T. Adorno *Gesammelte Schriften 1*, ed. R. Tiedemann, Suhrkamp, Frankfurt

    (1976a). 'Sociology and empirical research' in *Critical Sociology*, ed. P. Connerton, Penguin, Harmondsworth

    (1976b). 'Introduction' in T. Adorno *et al. The Positivist Dispute in German Sociology*, Heinemann

    (1978). *Minima Moralia*, Verso

Adorno, T. W. and Horkheimer, M. (1979). *Dialectic of Enlightenment*, Verso

Alt, J. (1976). 'Beyond class: the decline of industrial labour and leisure', *Telos* **28**: 55–80

Althusser, L. (1976). *Essays in Self-Criticism*, New Left Books

    (1977). 'On the materialist dialectic' in L. Althusser *For Marx*, Verso

Althusser, L. and Balibar, E. (1977). *Reading Capital*, New Left Books,

Andrén, G., Ericsson, L., Ohlsson, R. and Tännsjö, T. (1978). *Rhetoric and Ideology in Advertising*, Liber, Stockholm

Anell, B. and Persson, B. (1984). *Bryggerinäringen och pilsnerpolitiken*, Linköping

Bachelard, G. (1975). *La Philosophie du non: Essai d'une philosophie du nouvel esprit scientifique.* Presses Universitaires de France (7th edn.), Paris

    (1978). *Le Nouvel Esprit Scientifique*, Presses Universitaires de France, Paris

Bagge, A. and Kaelas, L. (1950). *Die Funde aus Dolmen und Ganggräbern in Schonen, Schweden I.*, Wahlström and Widstrand, Stockholm

Bakker, J. (1979). *The TRB West Group*, University of Amsterdam Press, Amsterdam

Balibar, E. and Macherey, P. (1981). 'On literature as an ideological form' in *Untying the Text*, ed. R. Young, Routledge and Kegan Paul

Bann, S. (1978). 'Historical text and historical object: the poetics of the Musée de Cluny', *History and Theory* **17**: 251–66

Barker, P. (1982). *Techniques of Archaeological Excavation*, Batsford

Barthes, R. (1973a). 'The Blue-Guide' in R. Barthes *Mythologies*, Granada, St Albans

    (1973b). 'Myth today' in R. Barthes *Mythologies*, Granada, St Albans

    (1973c). 'Wine and milk' in R. Barthes *Mythologies*, Granada, St Albans

    (1975). *S/Z*, Jonathan Cape

    (1977a). 'Writers, intellectuals, teachers' in R. Barthes *Image-Music-Text*, translated and edited by S. Heath, Hill and Wang, New York

    (1977b). 'The death of the author' in R. Barthes *Image-Music-Text*, Hill and Wang, New York

(1982). 'The plates of the encyclopedia' in *Selected Writings*, ed. S. Sontag, Fontana

(1985). *The Fashion System*, Jonathan Cape

Bath, J. (1981). 'The raw and the cooked: the material culture of a modern supermarket' in R. Gould and M. Schiffer (eds.)

Bauman, Z. (1978). *Hermeneutics and Social Science*, Hutchinson

(1983). 'Industrialism, consumerism and power', *Theory, Culture and Society* **1** (3): 32–43

Bayard, D. (1969). 'Science, theory and reality in the "new archaeology" ', *American Antiquity* **34** (4): 376–84

Bender, B. (19787). 'Gatherer-hunter to farmer', *World Archaeology* **10**: 203–22

Benjamin, W. (1955). *Schriften*, ed. T. Adorno (2 vols.), Suhrkamp, Frankfurt

(1973a). 'The task of the translator: an introduction to the translation of Baudelaire's Tableaux Parisiens' in W. Benjamin *Illuminations*, Fontana

(1973b). *Charles Baudelaire: A lyric Poet in the Era of High Capitalism*, Verso

(1973c). 'The storyteller: reflections on the work of Nikolai Leskov' in W. Benjamin *Illuminations*, Fontana

(1973d). 'The work of art in the age of mechanical reproduction' in W. Benjamin *Illuminations*, Fontana

(1973e). 'Theses on the philosophy of history' in W. Benjamin *Illuminations*, Fontana

(1979). 'Eduard Fuchs, collector and historian' in W. Benjamin *One Way Street*, New Left Books

Bennett, T. (1979). *Formalism and Marxism*, Methuen

Benton, T. (1977). *Philosophical Foundations of the Three Sociologies*, Routledge and Kegan Paul

Berger, J. (1969). *Art and Revolution: Ernst Niezvestny and the Role of the Artist in the USSR*, Weidenfeld and Nicolson

(1984). *And Our Faces, My Heart, Brief as Photos*, Writers and Readers

Berger, J. and Mohr, J. (1982). *Another Way of Telling*, Writers and Readers

Berger, J. *et al.* (1972). *Ways of Seeing*, Penguin, Harmondsworth

Bernstein, R. (1983). *Beyond Objectivism and Relativism*, Blackwell, Oxford

Bhaskar, R. (1978). *A Realist Theory of Science*, Harvester, Hassocks

(1979). *The Possibility of Naturalism*, Harvester, Hassocks

Binford, L. (1962). 'Archaeology as anthropology', *American Antiquity* **28** (2): 217–25

(1963). ' "Red ochre" caches from the Michigan area: a possible case of cultural drift', *Southwestern Journal of Anthropology* **19**: 89–108

(1964). 'A consideration of archaeological research design', *American Antiquity* **29**: 425–51

(1965). 'Archaeological systematics and the study of culture process', *American Antiquity* **31**: 203–10

(1972). *An Archaeological Perspective*, Seminar Press

(1977). 'General introduction' in *For Theory Building in Archaeology*, ed. L. Binford, Academic Press

(1978). *Nunamiut Ethnoarchaeology*, Academic Press

(1981). *Bones: Ancient Men and Modern Myths*, Academic Press

(1982). 'Objectivity – explanation – archaeology 1981' in *Theory and Explanation in Archaeology: The Southampton Conference*, ed. C. Renfrew, M. Rowlands and B. Segraves, Academic Press

(1983a). *Working at Archaeology*, Academic Press

(1983b). *In Pursuit of the Past*, Thames and Hudson

Binford, L. and Sabloff, J. (1983). 'Paradigms, systematics and archaeology' in L. Binford *Working at Archaeology*, Academic Press

Bloch, M. (1977a). 'The past and the present in the past', *Man* (N.S.) **12**: 278–92

(1977b). 'The disconnection between rank and power as a process' in J. Friedman and M. Rowlands (eds.)

Bologh, R. (1981). 'Grounding the alienation of self and body: a critical phenomenological analysis of the patient in western medicine', *Sociology of Health and Illness* **3** (2): 188–206

Bommes, M. and Wright, P. (1982). 'Charms of residence: the public and the past' in Centre for Contemporary Cultural Studies *Making Histories: Studies in History Writing and Politics*, Hutchinson

Borges, J. (1970). 'Pierre Menard, author of the Quixote' in J. Borges, *Labyrinths*, Penguin

Boston, R. (1977). *Beer and Skittles*, Fontana

Bourdieu, P. (1977). *Outline of a Theory of Practice*, Cambridge University Press
   (1979). 'Symbolic power', *Critique of Anthropology* **4**: 77–86
   (1984). *Distinction: A Social Critique of the Judgement of Taste*, Routledge and Kegan Paul

Bradley, M. and Fenwick, D. (1974). *Public Attitudes to Liquor Licensing Laws in Great Britain*, HMSO

Braithwaite, M. (1982). 'Decoration as ritual symbol: a theoretical proposal and an ethnographic study in southern Sudan' in I. Hodder (ed.)

Braithwaite, R. (1968). *Scientific Explanation*, Cambridge University Press

Braun, D. and Plog, S. (1982). 'The evolution of "tribal" social networks: theory and prehistoric north American evidence', *American Antiquity* **47**: 504–25

Braverman, H. (1974). *Labour and Monopoly Capital: The Degradation of Work in the Twentieth Century*, Monthly Review Press

Breed, W. and DeFoe, J. (1979). 'Themes in magazine alcohol advertisements; a critique', *Journal of Drug Issues* **9**: 511–22

Bremberg, L. (1973). *Treatment of Alcoholics and Drug Addicts in Stockholm*, Stockholm

Brodbeck, M. (1966). 'Methodological individualisms: definitions and reduction' in *Philosophical Analysis and History*, ed. W. Dray, Harper Row

Bromme, R. (1971). 'Status i alkoholreklamen' in *Alkoholreklamen – en motskrift*, ed. B. Arenader and K. Johanson, Sober, Vänersborg

Brown, P. (1934). 'The Friday Book of North Country Sketches', Beales, Newcastle upon Tyne

Bruun, K. (1984). 'Nya perspektiv på Brattsystemets tillkomsthistoria', *Alkoholpolitik*: 13–23

Bruun, K., Edwards, G., Lumio, M., Mäkelä, K., Pan, L., Popham, R., Room, R., Schmidt, W., Skog, O.-J., Sulkunen, P. and Österberg, E. (1975). *Alcohol Control Policies in Public Health Perspective*, Finnish Foundation for Alcohol Studies, Vol. 25

Buck-Morss, S. (1977). *The Origin of Negative Dialectics*, Harvester Press, Hassocks

Callinicos, A. (1983). *Marxism and Philosophy*, Oxford University Press

Carnegie, D. (1873). *The Licensing Laws of Sweden*, Alex MacDougall, Glasgow

Centre for Contemporary Cultural Studies, Popular Memory Group. (1982). 'Popular memory: theory, politics, method' in Centre for Contemporary Cultural Studies *Making Histories: Studies in History Writing and Politics*, Hutchinson

Chagnon, N. and Irons, W. (eds.) (1979). *Evolutionary Biology and Human Social Behaviour*, Duxbury Press, North Scituate, Mass.

Chapman, S. and Egger, G. (1983). 'Myth in cigarette advertising and health promotion' in *Language, Image, Media*, ed. H. Davis and P. Walton, Basil Blackwell, Oxford

Cheek, A. and Keel, B. (1984). 'Value conflicts in osteo-archaeology' in Green (ed.)

Childe, V. G. (1956). *Piecing Together the Past. The Interpretation of Archaeological Data*, Routledge and Kegan Paul

Chorley, R. and Haggett, P. (1967). *Models in Geography*, Methuen

Christenson, A. (1980). 'Change in the human niche in response to population growth' in *Modelling Change in Prehistoric Subsistence Economies*, ed. T. Earle and A. Christenson, Academic Press

Christie, N. and Bruun, K. (1968). 'Alcohol problems: the conceptual framework' in *28th*

International Congress on Alcohol and Alcoholism, ed. M. Keller and T. Coffey, Hillhouse Press, Highland Park, N.J.

Clark, J. G. D. (1970). *Aspects of Prehistory*, University of California Press, Berkeley
   (1972). *Archaeology and Society*, Methuen
   (1979). 'Archaeology and human diversity', *Annual Review of Anthropology* **8**: 1–20
   (1983). *The Identity of Man*, Methuen

Clark, R. M. (1975). 'A calibration curve for radiocarbon dates', *Antiquity* XLIX: 251–66

Clarke, D. (1968). *Analytical Archaeology*, Methuen
   (1972). 'Models and paradigms in contemporary archaeology' in *Models in Archaeology*, ed. D. Clarke, Methuen
   (1973). 'Archaeology: the loss of innocence', *Antiquity* XLVII: 6–18

Clarke, J. (1976). 'Style' in *Resistance Through Rituals*, ed. S. Hall and T. Jefferson, Hutchinson
   (1979). 'Capital and culture: the post-war working class revisited' in *Working Class Culture*, ed. J. Clarke, C. Critcher and R. Johnson, Hutchinson

Clarke, J., Hall, S., Jefferson, T. and Roberts, B. (1976). 'Subcultures, cultures and class: a theoretical overview' in *Resistance Through Rituals*, ed. S. Hall and T. Jefferson, Hutchinson

Cleere, H. (ed.) (1984). *Archaeological Approaches to our Heritage*, Cambridge University Press

Cleere, H. (1984). 'World cultural resource management: problems and perspectives' in H. Cleere (ed.)

Cohen, M. (1977). *The Food Crisis in Prehistory*, Yale University Press, New Haven

Coles, J. (1973). *Archaeology by Experiment*, Hutchinson
   (1979). *Experimental Archaeology*, Academic Press

Collier, A. (1978). 'In defence of epistemology' in *Issues in Marxist Philosophy Vol. 3: Epistemology, Science, Ideology*, ed. J. Mepham and D.-H. Ruben, Harvester, Hassocks

Collingwood, R. (1946). *The Idea of History*, Oxford University Press

Conkey, M. (1978). 'Style and information in cultural evolution: towards a predictive model for the Palaeolithic' in C. Redman *et al.* (eds.)

Conkey, M. and Spector, J. (1984). 'Archaeology and the study of gender' in *Advances in Archaeological Method and Theory*, ed. M. Schiffer, Vol. 7, Academic Press

Cooke, K. and Renfrew, C. (1979). 'An experiment on the simulation of culture changes' in C. Renfrew and K. Cooke (eds.)

Cornforth, M. (1968). *The Open Philosophy and the Open Society*, Lawrence and Wishart

Coward, R. and Ellis, J. (1977). *Language and Materialism*, Routledge and Kegan Paul

CPRS (Central Policy Review Staff) (1982). *Alcohol Policies in United Kingdom*, confidential document suppressed by the British government, published by Kettil Bruun in *Studier i Svensk Alkoholpolitik*, Stockholm

Cunningham, R. (1979). 'Why and how to improve archaeology's business work', *American Antiquity* **44**: 573–4

Cutler, A., Hindess, B., Hirst, P. and Hussain, A. (1977–8). *Marx's Capital and Capitalism Today* (2 vols.), Routledge and Kegan Paul

Dahlberg, G. (1939). *Alcoholism from a Social Point of View: A Survey of Conditions in Stockholm*, Stockholm
   (1951). 'A note on drinking and drunkards in Sweden', *Acta Genetica et Statistica Medica*: 6–41

Daniel, G. (1962). *The Idea of Prehistory*, Penguin, Harmondsworth
   (1981). *A Short History of Archaeology*, Thames and Hudson

Davidsen, K. (1978). *The Final TRB Culture in Denmark*, Akademisk Forlag, Copenhagen

Davis, H. (1982). 'Professionalism in archaeology', *American Antiquity* **47**: 158–63

Debord, G. (1983). *The Society of the Spectacle*, Black and Red, Detroit

Deetz, J. (1965). *The Dynamics of Stylistic Change in Arikara Ceramics*, Illinois Studies in Anthropology 4, University of Illinois Press, Urbana
   (1968). 'The inference of residence and descent rules from archaeological data' in *New*

Perspectives in Archaeology, ed. S. Binford and L. Binford, Aldine, Chicago

Derrida, J. (1974). *Of Grammatology* (trans G. Spivak), Johns Hopkins University Press, Baltimore

Dorfman, A. and Mattelart, A. (1975). *How to Read Donald Duck: Imperialist Ideology in the Disney Comic*, International General, New York

Douglas, M. and Isherwood, B. (1978). *The World of Goods*, Penguin, Harmondsworth

Doyal, L. (1979). *The Political Economy of Health*, Pluto Press

DsI, (1978: 34) (Industri- Departementet) *Bryggeriindustri - förslag till framtida struktur*, Liber, Stockholm,

Dunnell, R. (1978a). 'Style and function: a fundamental dichotomy', *American Antiquity* **43** (2): 197–202

(1978b). 'Archaeological potential of anthropological and scientific models of function' in *Archaeological Essays in Honour of I. B. Rouse*, ed. R. Dunnell and E. Hall, Mouton, The Hague

(1980). 'Evolutionary theory and archaeology' in *Advances in Archaeological Method and Theory*, ed. M. Schiffer, Vol. 3

(1984). 'The ethics of archaeological significance decisions' in *Ethics and Values in Archaeology*, ed. E. Green, Free Press, New York

Durkheim, E. (1915). *The Elementary Forms of the Religious Life*, Allen and Unwin

Dyer, G. (1982). *Advertising as Communication*, Methuen

Eagleton, T. (1976). *Criticism and Ideology*, Verso

(1981). *Walter Benjamin: Or Towards a Revolutionary Criticism*, Verso

(1983). *Literary Theory: An Introduction*, Blackwell, Oxford

Earle, T. (1980). 'A model of subsistence change' in *Modelling Change in Prehistoric Subsistence Economies*, ed. T. Earle and A. Christenson, Academic Press

Elshtain, J. (1976). 'The social relations of the classroom: a moral and political perspective', *Telos* **27**: 97–110

Engelbrecht, W. (1978). 'Ceramic patterning between New York Iroquois sites' in *The Spatial Organisation of Culture*, ed. I. Hodder, Duckworth

Englund, A., Solberg, J. and Svensson, P.-G. (1974). *Information om eller med anknytning till alkohol i dags-, populär och fackpress under 1970*, Rapport från alkoholpolitiska utredningar, Stockholm

Entwistle, H. (1979). *Antonio Gramsci: Conservative Schooling for Radical Politics*, Routledge and Kegan Paul

Ericson, H. (1980). 'Folk dricker öl med ögonen' in *Boken om burken*, PLM Pac, Malmö

Ewen, S. (1976). *Captains of Consciousness: Advertising and the Social Roots of the Consumer Culture*, McGraw-Hill, New York

Ewen, S. and Ewen, E. (1982). *Channels of Desire: Mass Images and the Shaping of American Consciousness*, McGraw-Hill, New York

Fabian, J. (1983). *Time and the Other: How Anthropology Makes its Object*, Columbia University Press, New York

Fagan, B. (1984). 'Archaeology and the wider audience' in *Ethics and Values in Archaeology*, ed. E. Green, Free Press, New York

Fagg, W. (1973). 'In search of meaning in African art' in *Primitive Art and Society*, ed. A. Forge, Oxford University Press

Fakta (1978). (*Fakta från svenska bryggareföreningen*) '10 starka argument för ölreklam', *Fakta*: 12–13

Faris, J. (1972). *Nuba Personal Art*, Duckworth

(1983). 'From form to content in the structural study of aesthetic systems' in *Structure and Cognition in Art*, ed. D. Washburn, Cambridge University Press

Featherstone, M. (1982). 'The body in consumer culture', *Theory, Culture and Society* **1** (2): 18–33

Feigl, H. (1970). 'The "orthodox" view of theories: some remarks in defence as well as critique' in *Minnesota Studies in the Philosophy of Science*, ed. M. Radner and S. Winokur, Vol. 4, Minneapolis

Fernandez, J. (1966). 'Principles of opposition and vitality in Fang aesthetics', *Journal of Aesthetics and Art Criticism*: 53–64

Flannery, K. (1968). 'Archaeological systems theory and early Mesoamerica' in *Anthropological Archaeology in the Americas*, ed. B. Meggers, Washington

   (1972). 'The cultural evolution of civilisations', *Annual Review of Ecology and Systematics* **3**: 399–426

   (ed.) (1976). *The Early Mesoamerican Village*, Academic Press

   (1982). 'The golden Marshalltown, a parable for the archaeology of the 1980s', *American Anthropologist* **84**: 265–78

Flannery, K. and Marcus, J. (1976). 'Formative Oaxaca and the Zapotec cosmos', *American Scientist* **64** (4): 374–83

Ford, R. (1973). 'Archaeology serving humanity' in *Research and Theory in Current Archaeology*, ed. C. Redman, Wiley, New York

Forge, A. (1973). 'Style and meaning in Sepik art' in *Primitive Art and Society*, ed. A. Forge, Oxford University Press

Foucault, M. (1974). *The Order of Things*, Tavistock

   (1979). *Discipline and Punish: The Birth of the Prison*, Penguin, Harmondsworth and Vintage Books, New York

   (1980). *Power/Knowledge: Selected Interviews and Other Writings 1972–1977* (ed. C. Gordon), Harvester, Hassocks

   (1981). *The History of Sexuality Volume 1: An Introduction*, Penguin, Harmondsworth

Fowler, P. (1977). *Approaches to Archaeology*, Adam and Charles Black

   (1981). 'Archaeology, the public and the sense of the past' in *Our Past Before Us: Why Do We Save It?*, ed. D. Lowenthal and M. Binney, Temple Smith

Frankel, D. (1978). 'Pottery decoration as an indicator of social relationships: a prehistoric example' in *Art in Society*, ed. M. Greenhalgh and V. Megaw, Duckworth

Frankenstein, S. and Rowlands, M. (1978). 'The internal structure and regional context of Early Iron Age society in south-western Germany', *Bulletin of the Institute of Archaeology, London* **15**: 73–112

Frere, S. (1975). *Principles of Publication in Rescue Archaeology*, Report for the Ancient Monuments Board for England, Committee for Rescue Archaeology, HMSO

Friedman, J. and Rowlands, K. (1978). 'Notes towards an epigenetic model of the evolution of "civilisation"' in *The Evolution of Social Systems*, ed. J. Friedman and M. Rowlands, Duckworth

Frisch, M. (1981). 'The memory of history', *Radical History Review* **25**: 9–23

Fritz, J. (1973). 'Relevance, archaeology and subsistence theory' in *Research and Theory in Current Archaeology*, ed. C. Redman, Wiley, New York

Fritz, J. and Plog, F. (1970). 'The nature of archaeological explanation', *American Antiquity* **35**: 405–12

Gabrielsson, A. (1970). *Koncentration och skalekonomi inom malt- och läskedrycks-industrin under 1950 och 1960- talen*, Forskningsrapporter från Kulturgeografiska institutionen, Uppsala Universitet

Gadamer, H-G. (1975). *Truth and Method*, Sheed and Ward

   (1979). 'The problem of historical consciousness' in *Interpretative Social Sciences: A Reader*, ed. P. Rabinow and W. Sullivan, University of California Press, Berkeley

Gardin, J-C. (1980). *Archaeological Constructs: An Aspect of Theoretical Archaeology*, Cambridge University Press

Garfinkel, H. (1967). *Studies in Ethnomethodology*, Prentice Hall, Englewood Cliffs
Gebhardt, E. (1978). 'A critique of methodology' in *The Essential Frankfurt School Reader*, ed. A. Arato and G. Gebhardt, Blackwell, Oxford
Gellner, E. (1982). 'What is structuralisme' in Renfrew, Rowlands and Segraves (eds.)
Giddens, A. (1976). *New Rules of Sociological Method*, Hutchinson
   (1977). 'Positivism and its critics' in A. Giddens *Studies in Social and Political Theory*, Hutchinson
   (1979). *Central Problems in Social Theory: Action, Structure and Contradiction in Social Analysis*, Macmillan
   (1981). *A Contemporary Critique of Historical Materialism*, Macmillan
   (1982). *Profiles and Critiques in Social Theory*, Macmillan
   (1984). *The Constitution of Society: Outline of the Theory of Structuration*, Polity Press, Cambridge
Gilman, A. (1984). 'Explaining the upper palaeolithic record' in *Marxist Perspectives in Archaeology*, ed. M. Spriggs, Cambridge University Press
Girouard, M. (1975). *Victorian Pubs*, Studio Vista
Gledhill, J. (1981). 'Time's arrow: anthropology, history, social evolution and Marxist theory', *Critique of Anthropology* **16**: 3–30
Gledhill, J. and Rowlands, M. (1982). 'Materialism and socio-economic processes in multilinear evolution' in *Ranking, Resource and Exchange*, ed. C. Renfrew and S. Shennan, Cambridge University Press
Gombrich, E. (1960). *Art and Illusion*, Phaidon
   (1979). *The Sense of Order*, Phaidon
Gould, R. and Schiffer, M. (eds.) (1981). *Modern Material Culture: The Archaeology of Us*, Academic Press
Gouldner, A. (1973). 'Anti-minotaur: The myth of a value-free sociology' in A. Gouldner *For Sociology*, Allen Lane
   (1976). *The Dialectic of Ideology and Technology*, Macmillan
Green, E. (ed.) (1984). *Ethics and Values in Archaeology*, The Free Press, New York
Gregory, D. (1982a). *Regional Transformations and Industrial Revolution*, Macmillan
   (1982b). 'Solid geometry: notes on the recovery of spatial structure' in *A Search for Common Ground*, ed. P. Gould and G. Olsson, Pion
Griffiths, D., Irvine, J. and Miles, I. (1979). 'Social statistics: towards a radical science' in *Demystifying Social Statistics*, ed. J. Irvine, I. Miles and J. Evans, Pluto Press
Grinsell, L., Rahtz, P. and Williams, D. (1974). *The Preparation of Archaeological Reports*, John Baker

Habermas, J. (1972). *Knowledge and Human Interests*, Heinemann
Hall, M. (1984). 'The burden of tribalism: the social context of southern African Iron Age studies', *American Antiquity* **49** (3): 455–67
Hall, S. and Jefferson, T. (eds.) (1976). *Resistance Through Rituals: Youth Subcultures in Post-War Britain*, Hutchinson
Hamberg, O. (1978). 'Ölkultur är bättre än supkultur', *Fakta från Svenska Bryggareföreningen* **1**: 1–2
Hammond, F. (1981). 'The colonisation of Europe: the analysis of settlement processes in *Pattern of the Past: Studies in Honour of David Clarke*, ed. I. Hodder, G. Isaac and N. Hammond, Cambridge University Press
Hansen, F. (1927). 'Undersökning af gånggrift i Fjälkinge', unpublished excavation report, Antikvarisk-Topografiska Arkivet, Stockholm
   (1938). *Stenåldersproblem*, Gleerups, Lund
Hanson, N. (1958). *Patterns of Discovery*, Cambridge University Press

Hantman, J. and Plog, S. (1982). 'The relationship of stylistic similarity to patterns of material exchange' in *Contexts for Prehistoric Exchange*, ed. J. Ericson and T. Earle, Academic Press

Harré, R. (1979). *Social Being*, Blackwell, Oxford

Harré, R. and Madden, P. (1975). *Causal Powers*, Blackwell, Oxford

Harrison, B. (1971). *Drink and the Victorians: The Temperance Question in England 1815–1872*, Faber and Faber

   (1973). 'Pubs' in *The Victorian City: Images and Realities*, ed. H. Dyos and M. Wolff, Routledge and Kegan Paul

Hawkes, C. (1954). 'Archaeological theory and method: some suggestions from the old world', *American Anthropologist* **56**: 155–68

Hawkes, J. (1968). 'The proper study of mankind', *Antiquity* **42**: 255–62

Hebdige, D. (1979). *Subculture: The Meaning of Style*, Methuen

   (1983). 'Travelling light: one route into material culture', *Royal Anthropological Institute News*: 11–13

Heidegger, M. (1962). *Being and Time* (trans. J. MacQuarrie and E. Robinson), Basil Blackwell

   (1972). 'Time and being' in *On Time and Being* (trans. J. Stambaugh), Harper and Row, New York

   (1978). 'The origin of the work of art' in *Basic Writings* (trans. D. F. Krell), Routledge and Kegan Paul

Held, D. (1980). *Introduction to Critical Theory: Horkheimer to Habermas*, Hutchinson

Hempel, C. (1959). 'The function of general laws in history' in *Theories of History*, ed. P. Gardiner, Free Press, New York

   (1965). *Aspects of Scientific Explanation*, Free Press, New York

Herner, T. (1972). 'The frequency of patients with disorders associated with alcoholism in mental hospitals and psychiatric departments in general hospitals in Sweden during the period 1954–1962', *Acta Psychiatrica Scandinavica Suppl.* **234**: 7–88

Hesse, M. (1974). *The Structure of Scientific Inference*, Macmillan

   (1978). 'Theory and value in the social sciences' in *Action and Interpretation*, ed. C. Hookway and P. Pettit, Cambridge University Press

Hill, J. (1970). *Broken K Pueblo: Prehistoric Social Organization in the American South-West*, Anthropological Papers of the University of Arizona **18**, Tucson, Arizona

   (1972). 'The methodological debate in contemporary archaeology: a model' in *Models in Archaeology*, ed. D. Clarke, Methuen

   (ed.) (1977). *The Explanation of Prehistoric Change*, New Mexico, Albuquerque

   (1977). 'Individual variability in ceramics and the study of prehistoric social organization' in Hill and Gunn (eds.)

   (1978). 'Individuals and their artifacts: an experimental study in archaeology', *American Antiquity* **43**, 245–57

Hill, J. and Gunn, J. (eds.) (1977). *The Individual in Prehistory*, Academic Press

Hindess, B. (1977). *Philosophy and Methodology in the Social Sciences*, Harvester, Hassocks

Hindess, B. and Hirst, P. (1977). *Mode of Production and Social Formation: An Auto-Critique of Precapitalist Modes of Production*, Macmillan

Hobsbawm, E. (1962). *The Age of Revolution*, Weidenfeld and Nicolson

Hodder, I. (1977). 'The distribution of material culture items in the Baringo district, western Kenya', *Man* **12**: 239–69

   (ed.) (1978). *Simulation Studies in Archaeology*, Cambridge University Press

   (1981). 'An ethnographic study amongst the Lozi, western Zambia' in *Pattern of the Past: Studies in Honour of David Clarke*, ed. I. Hodder, G. Isaac and N. Hammond, Cambridge University Press

   (1982a). 'Theoretical archaeology: a reactionary view' in I. Hodder (ed.)

   (1982b). *Symbols in Action*, Cambridge University Press

   (ed.) (1982). *Symbolic and Structural Archaeology*, Cambridge University Press

   (1984). 'Archaeology in 1984', *Antiquity* **58**: 25–32

Hollis, M. (1977). *Models of Man*, Cambridge University Press

Horkheimer, M. (1968). 'Zum Problem der Voraussage in den Sozialwissenschaften' in *Kritische Theorie*, ed. A. Schmidt, S. Fischer Verlag, Frankfurt

  (1976). 'Traditional and Critical theory' in *Critical Sociology*, ed. P. Connerton, Penguin, Harmondsworth

Horne, D. (1984). *The Great Museum: The Re-Presentation of History*, Pluto Press

Huff, D. (1973). *How to Lie with Statistics*, Penguin, Harmondsworth

Humphrey, C. (1971). 'Some ideas of Saussure applied to Buryat magical drawings', *ASA monograph* **10**, London

Hutt, C. (1973). *The Death of the English Pub*, Hutchinson

Inglis, F. (1972). *The Imagery of Power: A Critique of Advertising*, Heinemann

Jameson, F. (1977). 'Reflections in conclusion' in E. Bloch, G. Lukács, B. Brecht, W. Benjamin and T. Adorno *Aesthetics and Politics*, New Left Books

  (1984). 'Postmodernism, or the cultural logic of Late capitalism', *New Left Review* **146**: 53–92

Järbe, B. (1971). *Krogarnas Stockholm*, Tidens Förlag, Stockholm

Jarman, M., Bailey, G. and Jarman, H. (eds.) (1982). *Early European Agriculture*, Cambridge University Press

Jay, M. (1984). *Marxism and Totality: The Adventures of a Concept*, Polity Press, Cambridge

Jelinek, A. (1976). 'Form, function, and style in lithic analysis' in *Cultural Change and Continuity: Essays in Honour of James Griffin*, ed. C. Cleland, Academic Press

Jessop, B. (1982). *The Capitalist State*, Martin Robertson, Oxford

Jochim, M. (1976). *Hunter-Gatherer Subsistence and Settlement: A Predictive Model*, Academic Press

  (1983a). 'Optimization and models in context' in *Archaeological Hammers and Theories*, ed. J. Moore and A. Keene, Academic Press

  (1983b). 'Palaeolithic cave art in ecological perspective' in *Hunter-Gatherer Economy in Prehistory*, ed. G. Bailey, Cambridge University Press

Johnson, T., Dandeker, C. and Ashworth, C. (1984). *The Structure of Social Theory*, Macmillan

Jönsson, E. (1946). 'Socialdemokratien och nykterhetsrörelsen på 1800- talet'. *Tirfing* **40**: 141–72

Keene, A. (1979). 'Economic optimisation models and the study of hunter-gatherer subsistence-settlement systems' in C. Renfrew and K. Cooke (eds.)

  (1981). *Prehistoric Foraging in a Temperate Forest: A Linear Programming Model*, Academic Press

Kellner, D. (1983). 'Critical theory, commodities and the consumer society', *Theory, Culture and Society* **1** (3): 66–83

Kenny, A. (1973). *Wittgenstein*, Penguin, Harmondsworth

Kermode, F. (1967). *The Sense of an Ending: Studies in the Theory of Fiction*, Oxford University Press

King, T. (1983). 'Professional responsibility in public archaeology', *Annual Review of Anthropology* **12**: 143–64

Kohl, P. (1981). 'Materialist approaches in prehistory', *Annual Review of Anthropology* **10**: 89–118

Korn, S. (1978). 'The formal analysis of visual systems as exemplified by a study of Abelam (Papua New Guinea) paintings' in *Art in Society*, ed. M. Greenhalgh and V. Megaw, Duckworth

Krieger, A. (1944). 'The typological concept', *American Antiquity* **9**: 271–88

Kristiansen, K. (1984). 'Ideology and material culture: an archaeological perspective' in *Marxist Perspectives in Archaeology*, ed. M. Spriggs, Cambridge University Press

Kuhn, T. (1970). *The Structure of Scientific Revolutions* (2nd edition), University of Chicago Press

Laclau, E. and Mouffe, C. (1985). *Hegemony and Socialist Strategy*, Verso

Layton, R. (1981). *The Anthropology of Art*, Paul Elek

Leach, E. (1973). 'Concluding address' in *The Explanation of Culture Change*, ed. C. Renfrew, Duckworth

Leitch, V. (1983). *Deconstructive Criticism: An Advanced Introduction*, Hutchinson

Leone, M. (1972). 'Issues in anthropological archaeology' in *Contemporary Archaeology*, ed. M. Leone, Southern Illinois Press, Carbondale

  (1973). 'Archaeology as the science of technology: Mormon town plans and fences' in *Research and Theory in Current Archaeology*, ed. C. Redman, Wiley, New York

  (1978). 'Time in American archaeology' in C. Redman *et al.* (eds.)

  (1980). 'The presence of the present in St. Mary's City, Maryland', Paper for Cultural Separations and the Anthropology of Premodern and Modern America, American Anthropological Association Meetings, Washington

  (1981a). 'Archaeology's relationship to the present and the past' in *Modern Material Culture: The Archaeology of Us*, ed. R. Gould and M. Schiffer, Academic Press

  (1981b). 'The relationship between artefacts and the public in outdoor history museums', *Annals of the New York Academy of Sciences* **376**: 301–14

  (1982). 'Some opinions about recovering mind', *American Antiquity* **47**: 742–59

  (1984). 'Interpreting ideology in historical archaeology: the William Paca garden in Annapolis, Maryland' in D. Miller and C. Tilley (eds.)

Lévi-Strauss, C. (1968). 'Split representation in the art of Asia and America' in C. Lévi-Strauss *Structural Anthropology*, Allen Lane

  (1973). *Tristes Tropiques*, Penguin, Harmondsworth

Lipe, W. (1977). 'A conservation model for American archaeology' in *Conservation Archaeology: A Guide for Cultural Resource Management Studies*, ed. M. Schiffer and G. Gummerman, Academic Press

  (1984). 'Value and meaning in cultural resources' in *Archaeological Approaches to our Heritage*, ed. H. Cleere, Cambridge University Press

Longacre, W. (1970). *Archaeology as Anthropology: A Case Study*, Anthropological Papers of the University of Arizona, **17**, University of Arizona Press

Lowe, D. (1982). *History of Bourgeois Perception*, University of Chicago Press

Lowenthal, D. (1981). 'Introduction' in D. Lowenthal and M. Binney (eds.)

Lowenthal, D. and Binney, M. (eds.) (1981). *Our Past Before Us: Why Do We Save It?*, Temple Smith

Lukács, G. (1963). *The Meaning of Contemporary Realism*, Merlin

  (1971). *History and Class Consciousness*, Merlin

  (1980a). *Essays on Realism*, Lawrence and Wishart

  (1980b). *The Ontology of Social Being: Labour*, Merlin

Macherey, P. (1978). *A Theory of Literary Production*, Routledge and Kegan Paul

Mackie, J. (1974). *The Cement of the Universe*, Clarendon Press, Oxford

Magnusson, L. (1985). 'Orsaker till det förindustriella drickandet-supandet: hantverkets Eskilstuna', *Alkoholpolitik* **1**: 23–9

Mäkelä, K. and Viikari, M. (1977). 'Notes on alcohol and the state', *Acta Sociologica* **20** (2): 155–79

Mäkelä, K., Room, R., Single, E., Sulkunen, P. and Walsh, B. (1981). *Alcohol, Society and the State: A Comparative Study of Alcohol Control* (2 vols.), Addiction Research Foundation, Toronto

Malmén, G. (1966). *Människovård och samhällsskydd*, Stockholm

Malmer, M. (1962). 'Jungneolithische Studien', *Acta Archaeologica Lundensia*, series in 8°: 2

Marcuse, H. (1964). *One Dimensional Man: Studies in the Ideology of Advanced Industrial Society*, Routledge and Kegan Paul

(1978). 'On science and phenomenology' in *The Essential Frankfurt School Reader*, ed. A. Arato and E. Gebhardt, Blackwell, Oxford

Marglin, S. (1976). 'What do the bosses do? The origins and functions of hierarchy in capitalist production' in *The Division of Labour*, ed. A. Gorz, Harvester, Hassocks

Mårtensson, S. (1961). *Bryggerinäringen i Göteborg: Tiden från bryggaregillets tillkomst år 1661 intill 1800-talets början* (2 vols.), Göteborg

Martin, P. and Plog, F. (1973). *The Archaeology of Arizona*, American Museum of Natural History, New York

Marx, K. (1970). 'Theses on Feuerbach' in K. Marx and F. Engels *The German Ideology*, Lawrence and Wishart

Mathias, P. (1959). *The Brewing Industry in England*, Cambridge University Press

McGimsey, C. (1972). *Public Archaeology*, Seminar Press

McGimsey, C. and Davis, H. (1984). 'United States of America' in H. Cleere (ed.)

McLuhan, M., Parker H. and Harzun, J. (1969). *Exploration of the Ways, Means and Values of Museum Communication with the Viewing Public: A Seminar*, Museum of the City of New York

Meltzer, D. (1979). 'Paradigms and the nature of change in American archaeology', *American Antiquity* **44**: 644–57

(1981). 'Ideology and material culture' in R. Gould and M. Schiffer (eds.)

Miller, D. (1982a). 'Explanation and social theory in archaeological practice' in C. Renfrew, M. Rowlands and B. Segraves (eds.)

(1982b). 'Structures and strategies: an aspect of the relationship between social hierarchy and cultural change' in I. Hodder (ed.)

(1984). 'Modernism and suburbia as material ideology' in D. Miller and C. Tilley (eds.)

Miller, D. and Tilley, C. (1984a). 'Ideology, power and prehistory: an introduction' in D. Miller and C. Tilley (eds.)

(1984b). 'Ideology, power and long-term social change' in D. Miller and C. Tilley (eds.)

(eds.) (1984). *Ideology, Power and Prehistory*, Cambridge University Press

Millum, T. (1975). *Images of Women: Advertising in Women's Magazines*, Chatto and Windus

Monckton, H. (1966). *A History of English Ale and Beer*, Bodley Head

(1969). *A History of the English Public House*, Bodley Head

Morgan, C. (1973). 'Archaeology and explanation', *World Archaeology* **4**: 259–76

Muller, J. (1979). 'Structural studies of art styles' in *The Visual Arts Plastic and Graphic*, ed. J. Cordwell, Mouton, The Hague

Munn, N. (1966). 'Visual categories: an approach to the study of representational systems', *American Anthropologist* **68**: 936–50

(1973). 'The spatial presentation of cosmic order in Walbiri iconography' in *Primitive Art and Society*, ed. A. Forge, Oxford University Press

Nielsen, P. (1977). 'De tyknakkede flintøksers kronologi', *Aarbøger for Nordisk Oldkyndighed og Historie*: 5–66

Nietzsche, F. (1956). *The Birth of Tragedy and the Genealogy of Morals*, Anchor Doubleday, Garden City

(1981). *The Portable Nietzsche*, Penguin, Harmondsworth

Nycander, S. (1967). *Svenskarna och Spriten*, Prisma, Oskarshamn

Ollman, B. (1971). *Alienation: Marx's Conception of Man in Capitalist Society*, Cambridge University Press

Orton, C. (1980). *Mathematics in Archaeology*, Collins

Packard, V. (1981). *The Hidden Persuaders*, Penguin, Harmondsworth

Papineau, D. (1979). *Theory and Meaning*, Blackwell, Oxford

Park, P. (1983). 'Sketches toward a political economy of drink and drinking problems: the case of 18th and 19th century England', *Journal of Drug Issues* 13

Passmore, J. (1962). 'Explanation in everyday life, in science and history', *History and Theory* II (2)

Phillipson, M. (1972). 'Phenomenology, philosophy and sociology' in P. Filmer, M. Phillipson, D. Silverman and D. Walsh *New Directions in Sociological Theory*, Collier-Macmillan

Piggott, S. (1954). *The Neolithic Cultures of the British Isles*, Cambridge University Press

PLM. (1983). 'Marknadsandelar, burk, Sverige 1983', unpublished manuscript

Plog, F. (1974). *The Study of Prehistoric Change*, Academic Press
   (1975). 'Systems theory in archaeological research', *Annual Review of Anthropology* **4**: 207–24
   (1977). 'Archaeology and the individual' in J. Hill and J. Gunn (eds.)

Plog, S. (1976). 'Measurement of prehistoric interaction between communities' in *The Early Mesoamerican Village*, ed. K. Flannery, Academic Press
   (1978). 'Social interaction and stylistic similarity: a reanalysis' in *Advances in Archaeological Method and Theory I*, ed. M. Schiffer, Academic Press
   (1980). *Stylistic Variation in Prehistoric Ceramics*, Cambridge University Press
   (1983). 'Analysis of style in artifacts', *Annual Review of Anthropology* **12**: 125–43

Popper, K. (1959). *The Logic of Scientific Discovery*, Hutchinson
   (1963). *Conjectures and Refutations*, Routledge and Kegan Paul
   (1966). *The Open Society and its Enemies. Vol. 2. The High Tide of Prophecy: Hegel, Marx and the Aftermath*, Routledge and Kegan Paul
   (1974). 'Intellectual autobiography' in *The Philosophy of Karl Popper*, ed. P. Schilpp, Open Court, La Salle
   (1976). 'The logic of the social sciences' in *The Positivist Dispute in German Sociology*, ed. T. Adorno, Heinemann

Poster, M. (1984). *Foucault, Marxism and History: Mode of Production versus Mode of Information*, Polity Press, Cambridge

Price, B. (1982). 'Cultural materialism: a theoretical review', *American Antiquity* **47** (4): 709–41

Proposition (1976/77: 108). *Om alkoholpolitiken* (Swedish government white paper)

Protz, R. (1978). *Pulling a Fast One: What the Brewers Have Done to Your Beer*, Pluto Press

Putnam, H. (1978). *Meaning and the Moral Sciences*, Henley

Quine, W. V. O. (1960). *Word and Object*, Cambridge, Mass.
   (1961). 'Two dogmas of empiricism' in W. V. O. Quine *From a Logical Point of View*, Harvard University Press, Cambridge, Mass.

Raab, L. and Goodyear, A. (1984). 'Middle-range theory in archaeology: a critical review of origins and applications', *American Antiquity* **49** (2): 255–8

Rahtz, P. (ed.) (1973). *Rescue Archaeology*, Penguin, Harmondsworth

Rappaport, R. (1967). *Pigs for the Ancestors*, Yale University Press, New Haven
   (1971a). 'The sacred in human evolution', *Annual Review of Ecology and Systematics* **2**: 23–44
   (1971b). 'Ritual, sanctity and cybernetics', *American Anthropologist* **73**: 59–76

Rathje, W. (1981). 'A manifesto for modern material culture studies' in *Modern Material Culture: The Archaeology of Us*, ed. R. Gould, Academic Press

Redman, C. (1978a). 'Multivariate artifact analysis: a basis for multidimensional interpretations' in C. Redman *et al.* (eds.)
   (1978b). 'Mesopotamian urban ecology: the systemic context of the emergence of urbanism' in C. Redman *et al.* (eds.)

Redman, C., Berman, J., Curtin, E., Langhorne, W., Versaggi, N. and Wanser, J. (eds.) (1978). *Social Archaeology: Beyond Dating and Subsistence*, Academic Press

Renfrew, C. (1972). *The Emergence of Civilisation: The Cyclades and the Aegean in the Third Millennium B.C.*, Methuen

(1978a). 'Trajectory discontinuity and morphogenesis: the implications of catastrophe theory for archaeology', *American Antiquity* **43**: 202–22

(1978b). 'Space, time and polity' in *The Evolution of Social Systems*, ed. J. Friedman and M. Rowlands, Duckworth

(1979a). 'Transformations' in C. Renfrew and K. Cooke (eds.)

(1979b). 'Systems collapse as social transformation: catastrophe and anastrophe in early state societies' in C. Renfrew and K. Cooke (eds.)

(1982a). 'Explanation revisited' in C. Renfrew, M. Rowlands and B. Segraves (eds.)

(1982b). 'Discussion: contrasting paradigms' in *Ranking, Resource and Exchange in Early European Prehistory*, ed. C. Renfrew and S. Shennan, Cambridge University Press

(1982c). *Towards an Archaeology of Mind*, Cambridge University Press

(1983). 'Divided we stand: aspects of archaeology and information', *American Antiquity* **48**: 3–16

Renfrew, C. and Cooke, K. (eds.) (1979). *Transformations: Mathematical Approaches to Culture Change*, Academic Press

Renfrew, C. and Wagstaff, M. (eds.) (1982). *An Island Polity*, Cambridge University Press

Renfrew, C., Rowlands, M. and Segraves, B. (eds.) (1982). *Theory and Explanation in Archaeology: The Southampton Conference*, Academic Press

Ricoeur, P. (1981a). 'The hermeneutical function of distanciation' in P. Ricoeur *Hermeneutics and the Human Sciences* (ed. and trans. J. Thompson), Cambridge University Press

(1981b). 'Metaphor and the central problem of hermeneutics' in P. Ricoeur *Hermeneutics and the Social Sciences* (ed. and trans. J. Thompson), Cambridge University Press

(1981c). 'The narrative function' in P. Ricoeur *Hermeneutics and the Social Sciences* (ed. and trans. J. Thompson), Cambridge University Press

Romer, J. (1984). *Ancient Lives: The Story of the Pharoah's Tombmakers*, Weidenfeld and Nicolson

Rorty, R. (1980). *Philosophy and the Mirror of Nature*, Blackwell, Oxford

Rose, G. (1984). *Dialectic of Nihilism: Post Structuralism and Law*, Blackwell, Oxford

Rowlands, M. (1982). 'Processual archaeology as historical social science' in C. Renfrew, M. Rowlands and B. Segraves (eds.)

(1984). 'Objectivity and subjectivity in archaeology' in *Marxist Perspectives in Archaeology*, ed. M. Spriggs, Cambridge University Press

Royal College of Psychiatrists, Special Committee (1979). *Alcohol and Alcoholism*, Tavistock

Ruben, D.-H. (1977). *Marxism and Materialism*, Harvester, Hassocks

Sabloff, J. (ed.) (1981). *Simulations in Archaeology*, New Mexico, Albuquerque

Sackett, J. (1982). 'Approaches to style in lithic archaeology', *Journal of Anthropological Archaeology* **1**: 59–112

(1985). 'Style and ethnicity in the Kalahari: a reply to Wiessner', *American Antiquity* **50**: 154–60

Sahlins, M. (1976). *The Use and Abuse of Biology*, Tavistock

Sahlins, M. and Service, E. (eds.) (1960). *Evolution and Culture*, University of Michigan Press, Ann Arbor

Salmon, M. (1975). 'Confirmation and explanation in archaeology', *American Antiquity* **40**: 459–65

(1982). *Philosophy and Archaeology*, Academic Press

SAMO (1981: 21) (Samordningsorganet för alkoholfrågor) *Data om alkoholkonsumtionen och dess skadeverkningar*, Social-departementet, Stockholm

Samuel, R. (1983). 'Soft focus nostalgia', *New Statesman* 27/5/83 (Victorian Values Supplement ii–iv)

Sanders, W. and Webster, D. (1978). 'Unilinealism, multilinealism and the evolution of complex societies' in C. Redman *et al.* (eds.)

Sartre, J-P. (1958). *Being and Nothingness: An Essay on Phenomenological Ontology*, Methuen
   (1982). *Critique of Dialectical Reason*, Verso
Saxe, A. and Gall, P. (1977). 'The ecological evolution of culture: the state as predator in
   succession theory' in *Exchange Systems in Prehistory*, ed. T. Earle and J. Ericson, Academic
   Press
Sayre, K. (1976). *Cybernetics and the Philosophy of Mind*, Routledge and Kegan Paul
Scase, R. (1977). *Social Democracy in Capitalist Society*, Croom Helm
Schapiro, J. (1977). 'The slime of history: embeddedness in nature and critical theory' in *On
   Critical Theory*, ed. J. O'Neill, Heinemann
Schiffer, M. (1976). *Behavioural Archaeology*, Academic Press
   (1979). 'A preliminary consideration of behavioural change' in C. Renfrew and K. Cooke
   (eds.)
   (1981). 'Some issues in the philosophy of archaeology', *American Antiquity* **46**: 899–908
   (1983). 'Toward the identification of formation processes', *American Antiquity* **48**: 675–706
Schiffer, M. and Gummerman, G. (eds.) (1977). *Conservation Archaeology: A Guide for Cultural
   Resource Management Studies*, Academic Press
Schiffer, M., Downing, T. and McCarthy, M. (1981). 'Waste not, want not: an ethnoarchaeo-
   logical study of refuse in Tucson, Arizona' in R. Gould and M. Schiffer (eds.)
Schlereth, T. (1978). 'It wasn't that simple', *Museum News* **56** (3): 36–44
Schneider, J. (1978). 'Deviant drinking as disease: alcoholism as a social accomplishment', *Social
   Problems* **25**: 361–72
Schutz, A. (1972). *The Phenomenology of the Social World*, Heinemann
Sellars, W. (1963). *Science, Perception and Reality*, Humanities Press, New York
Service, E. (1975). *Origins of the State and Civilisation*, Norton, New York
Shanks, M. and Tilley, C. (1982). 'Ideology, symbolic power and ritual communication: a
   reinterpretation of neolithic mortuary practices' in I. Hodder (ed.)
   (n.d.). *Social Theory and Archaeology*, Polity Press, Cambridge (in press)
Sharman, H. (1983). 'Canny moves: brewers draw on bitter heritage', *Marketing Week*: 27 May
Shennan, S. (1978). 'Archaeological "cultures": an empirical investigation' in *The Spatial Organ-
   isation of Culture*, ed. I. Hodder, Duckworth
Sherratt, A. (1981). 'Plough and pastoralism: aspects of the secondary products revolution' in
   Pattern of the Past: Studies in Honour of David Clarke, ed. I. Hodder, G. Isaac and
   N. Hammond, Cambridge University Press
Sjöhagen, A. (1953). 'How a Swedish temperance board works', *Quarterly Journal of Studies on
   Alcohol* **14**: 69–77
   (1954). 'Measures between inpatient and outpatient care for alcoholics', *Quarterly Journal of
   Studies on Alcohol* **15**: 111–15
Smart, B. (1983). *Foucault, Marxism and Critique*, Routledge and Kegan Paul
Smith, M. (1983). 'Social uses of the public drinking house: changing aspects of class and
   leisure', *British Journal of Sociology* XXIV: 367–85
Socialstyrelsen (1952). *Social Sweden*, Stockholm
   (1983). *Bakgrunden: Fakta om Sveriges Alkoholpolitik*, Stockholm
Society of Professional Archaeologists (1984a). 'Code of Ethics' in E. Green (ed.)
   (1984b). 'Standards of research performance' in E. Green (ed.)
Sontag, S. (1979). *On Photography*, Penguin
SOU (1951: 43) (Statens offentlige utredningar) *Statistika undersökningar kring alkoholfrågan*,
   Stockholm
   (1952: 52). *Nykterhetsförhållanden i vissa främmande länder mm.*, Stockholm
   (1952: 53). *1944 års nykterhetskommitté V. Principbetänkande*, Stockholm
   (1974: 90). *Alkoholpolitik 1 Bakgrund*, Stockholm
   (1974: 91). *Alkoholpolitik 2 Åtgärder*, Stockholm
   (1974: 92). *Alkoholpolitik 3 Bilagor*, Stockholm

(1976). *Reklamen för alkohol och tobak*, Stockholm

Spanos, W. (1977). 'Breaking the circle: hermeneutics ad dis-closure', *Boundary* **2** 5: 421–57

Spivak, G. (1974). 'Introduction' in J. Derrida *Of Grammatology*, Johns Hopkins University Press, Baltimore

Sterud, E. (1978). 'Changing aims of Americanist archaeology: a citations analysis of "American Antiquity", 1964–75', *American Antiquity* **43**: 294–302

Steward, J. (1955). *Theory of Culture Change*, University of Illinois Press, Urbana

Storch, R. (1977). 'The problem of working class leisure. Some roots of middle-class moral reform in the industrial north 1825–1850' in *Social Control in Nineteenth Century Britain*, ed. A. Donajgrodzji, Croom Helm

Strickland, D., Finn, T. and Lambert, M. (1982). 'A content analysis of beverage alcohol advertising I. Magazine advertising', *Journal of Studies on Alcohol* **43** (7): 655–82

Strömberg, M. (1971). 'Die Megalithgräber von Hagestad', *Acta Archaeologica Lundensia*, series in 8° No. 9

Svensson, A. (1973). *Svensk alkoholpolitik*, Sober, Vänersborg

Swingewood, A. (1977). *The Myth of Mass Culture*, Macmillan

Systembolaget (1965). *10 år utan motbok*, Stockholm

Szasz, T. (1975). *Ceremonial Chemistry: The Ritual Persecution of Drugs, Addicts, and Pushers*, Routledge and Kegan Paul

Thomas, D. (1972). 'Western Shoshone ecology: settlement patterns and beyond' in *Great Basin Cultural Ecology: A Symposium*, ed. D. Fowler, Desert Research Publications in the Social Sciences 8

Thompson, E. P. (1963). *The Making of the English Working Class*, Penguin, Harmondsworth
  (1967). 'Time, work-discipline, and industrial capitalism', *Past and Present* **38**

Thompson, W. (1935). *The Control of Liquor in Sweden*, Columbia University Press, New York

Tilden, F. (1957). *Interpreting Our Heritage*, University of North Carolina Press

Tilley, C. (1981a). 'Conceptual frameworks for the explanation of sociocultural change' in *Pattern of the Past: Studies in Honour of David Clarke*, ed. I. Hodder, G. Isaac and N. Hammond, Cambridge University Press
  (1981b). 'Economy and society: what relationship?' in *Economic Archaeology*, ed. A. Sheridan and G. Bailey, British Archaeological Reports, Oxford
  (1982a). 'Social formation, social structures and social change' in I. Hodder (ed.)
  (1982b). 'An assessment of the Scanian Battle-Axe tradition: towards a social perspective', *Scripta Minora*: 1–72
  (1983). *Prehistoric Change: A Dialectical-Structuralist Perspective*, unpublished doctoral dissertation, Cambridge University
  (1984). 'Ideology and the legitimation of power in the middle neolithic of southern Sweden' in D. Miller and C. Tilley (eds.)
  (1985). 'Archaeology as sociopolitical action in the present' in *Critical Traditions in Contemporary Archaeology*, ed. V. Pinsky and A. Wylie, Cambridge University Press

Torrence, R. (1983). 'Time budgeting and hunter-gatherer technology' in *Hunter-Gatherer Economy in Prehistory*, ed. G. Bailey, Cambridge University Press

Trigger, B. (1968). *Beyond History: The Methods of Prehistory*, Holt, Rinehart and Winston, New York
  (1970). 'Aims in prehistoric archaeology', *Antiquity* **44**: 26–37
  (1978). *Time and Traditions: Essays in Archaeological Interpretation*, Edinburgh University Press
  (1980). 'Archaeology and the image of the American Indian', *American Antiquity* **45**: 662–76
  (1981). 'Anglo-American archaeology', *World Archaeology* **13**: 138–55
  (1984). 'Archaeology at the crossroads: what's new?', *Annual Review of Anthropology* **13**: 275–300

Tringham, R. (1978). 'Experimentation, ethnoarchaeology and the leapfrogs in archaeological methodology' in *Explorations in Ethnoarchaeology*, ed. R. Gould, University of New Mexico Press, Albuquerque

Ucko, P. (1983). 'Australian academic archaeology: Aboriginal transformation of its aims and practices', *Australian Archaeology* **16**: 11–26

Vastokas, J. (1978). 'Cognitive aspects of Northwest Coast art' in *Art in Society*, ed. M. Greenhalgh and V. Megaw, Duckworth
Vatanen, O. and Tengvall, G. (1983). 'Krogarnas krångliga labyrint', *Dagens Nyheter*, 14 July
Von Wright, G. (1971). *Explanation and Understanding*, Routledge and Kegan Paul

Walka, J. (1979). 'Management methods and opportunities in archaeology', *American Antiquity* **44**: 575–82
Wallace, M. (1981). 'Visiting the past: history museums in the United States', *Radical History Review* **25**: 63–96
Watkins, J. (1970). 'Methodological individualisms and social tendencies' in *Readings in the Philosophy of the Social Sciences*, ed. M. Brodbeck, London
Watson, P., LeBlanc, S. and Redman, C. (1971). *Explanation in Archaeology: An Explicitly Scientific Approach*, Columbia University Press, New York
Weber, M. (1964). *The Theory of Social and Economic Organisation*, Free Press, New York
Webster, G. (1974). *Practical Archaeology: An Introduction to Archaeological Fieldwork and Excavation*, Adam and Charles Black
Weissner, P. (1983). 'Style and social information in Kalahari San projectile points', *American Antiquity* **48**: 253–76
   (1985). 'Style or isochrestic variation? A reply to Sackett', *American Antiquity* **50**: 160–5
Welbourn, A. (1984). 'Endo ceramics and power strategies' in D. Miller and C. Tilley (eds.)
Wenke, R. (1981). 'Explaining the evolution of cultural complexity: a review' in *Advances in Archaeological Theory and Method Vol. 5*, ed. M. Schiffer, Academic Press
Whallon, R. (1968). 'Investigations of late prehistoric social organisation in New York state' in *New Perspectives in Archaeology*, ed. L. and S. Binford, Aldine, Chicago
   (1982). 'Comments on "explanation" ' in *Ranking, Resource and Exchange*, ed. C. Renfrew and S. Shennan, Cambridge University Press
Wheeler, M. (1954). *Archaeology from the Earth*, Penguin, Harmondsworth
White, L. (1959). *The Evolution of Culture*, McGraw-Hill, New York
Wiatr, J. (1969). 'Sociology-Marxism-Reality' in *Marxism and Sociology – Views from Eastern Europe*, ed. P. Berger, Appleton Century Crofts, New York
Wiklund, D. (1948). 'Proposal of the Swedish government committee for reform of the care of inebriates', *Quarterly Journal of Studies on Alcohol* **9**: 37–87
Willey and Sabloff, J. (1980). *A History of American Archaeology* (2nd edn), Freeman, New York
Williams, R. (1979). 'The growth and role of the mass media' in *Media, Politics and Culture*, ed. C. Gardner, Macmillan
   (1980). 'Advertising: the magic system' in R. Williams *Problems in Materialism and Culture*, Verso
Williamson, J. (1978). *Decoding Advertisements: Ideology and Meaning in Advertising*, Marion Boyars
Willis, P. (1977). *Learning to Labour: How Working Class Kids Get Working Class Jobs*, Saxon House
Wilson, E. O. (1975). *Sociobiology: A New Synthesis*, Harvard University Press
   (1978). *On Human Nature*, Harvard University Press, Cambridge, Mass.
Wilson, G. (1940). *Alcohol and the Nation*, London
Winship, J. (1981). 'Handling sex', *Media, Culture and Society* **3**: 25–42

Wishart, T. (1984). 'Sights and sounds of 10th century Coppergate', *Popular Archaeology*

Winter, J. (1984). 'The way to somewhere: ethics in American archaeology' in E. Green (ed.)

Wittgenstein, L. (1953). *Philosophical Investigations*, Blackwell, Oxford

(1969). *The Blue and Brown Books*, Blackwell, Oxford

Wobst, M. (1977). 'Stylistic behaviour and information exchange', *Anthropological Papers of the University of Michigan* **61**: 317–42

Wolff, J. (1981). *The Social Production of Art*, Macmillan

(1984). *Aesthetics and the Sociology of Art*, George Allen and Unwin

Wolin, R. (1982). *Walter Benjamin: An Aesthetic of Redemption*, Columbia University Press, New York

Wood, M. (1985). *In Search of the Trojan War*, BBC

Zubrow, E. (1972). 'Environment, subsistence and society: the changing archaeological perspective', *Annual Review of Anthropology* **1**: 179–206

(1980). 'International trends in theoretical archaeology', *Norwegian Archaeological Review* **13** (1): 14–23